Canonization and Alterity

Perspectives on Jewish Texts and Contexts

Edited by
Vivian Liska

Editorial Board
Robert Alter, Steven E. Aschheim, Richard I. Cohen, Mark H. Gelber,
Moshe Halbertal, Christine Hayes, Moshe Idel, Samuel Moyn,
Ada Rapoport-Albert, Alvin Rosenfeld, David Ruderman, Bernd Witte

Volume 14

Canonization and Alterity

Heresy in Jewish History, Thought, and Literature

Edited by
Gilad Sharvit and Willi Goetschel

DE GRUYTER

ISBN 978-3-11-099240-3
e-ISBN (PDF) 978-3-11-067158-2
e-ISBN (EPUB) 978-3-11-066817-9
ISSN 2199-6962

Library of Congress Control Number: 2020935452

Bibliographic information published by the Deutsche Nationalbibliothek
The Deutsche Nationalbibliothek lists this publication in the Deutsche Nationalbibliografie;
detailed bibliographic data are available on the Internet at http://dnb.dnb.de.

© 2022 Walter de Gruyter GmbH, Berlin/Boston
This volume is text- and page-identical with the hardback published in 2020.
Cover image: Detail from the floor mosaic of the synagogue in Hammat Tiberias, depicting
the sun God Helios. Copyright of photograph: Zev Radovan.
Typesetting: Integra Software Services Pvt. Ltd.
Printing and binding: CPI books GmbH, Leck

www.degruyter.com

Acknowledgments

This volume is the result of the valuable contribution of many people. First and foremost, we would like to thank Vivian Liska for her kind support and the generous invitation to publish this volume in her book series "Perspectives on Jewish Texts and Contexts." Some of the chapters in the volume originated in a conference on Jewish heresy that took place in Tel Aviv in May 2019. We thank the Minerva Institute for German History, the School of Philosophy, Linguistics, and Social Sciences, and the Stephen Roth Institute for the Study of Contemporary Antisemitism and Racism at Tel Aviv University for co-sponsoring the event. We also thank the Stephen Roth Institute for the Study of Contemporary Antisemitism and Racism at Tel Aviv University and the Social Sciences and Humanities Research Council of Canada for their support with the preparation of the manuscript for publication. We also would like to thank Andrew Melvin and Marlo Burks for their outstanding copyediting. Lastly, we are grateful to Katja Lehming and Ulrike Krauss of De Gruyter Press for their help and guidance throughout the production of this volume.

Contents

Acknowledgments —— V

Willi Goetschel and Gilad Sharvit
Introduction —— 1

Part 1: Jewish Antiquity

Erich S. Gruen
Was Hellenism a Jewish Heterodoxy? —— 17

Adiel Schremer
Negotiating Heresy: Belief and Identity in Early Rabbinic Literature —— 30

Shraga Bar-On and Eugene D. Matanky
Revelation as Heresy: Mysticism and Elisha ben Abuyah's Apostasy in Classic Rabbinic Literature —— 50

Part 2: Jewish Mysticism from the Middle Ages to Modernity

Ruth Kara-Ivanov Kaniel
King David as the Fourth Leg of the Chariot – Gender, Identity, and Heresy —— 87

Moshe Idel
Abraham Abulafia: The Apotheosis of a Medieval Heretic in Modern *Me'ah She'arim* —— 125

Part 3: Literature in Jewish Modernity

Robert Alter
The Authentic Paganism of Saul Tchernikhovsky —— 161

David Suchoff
Heretical Canines: Kafka's "*Forschungen eines Hundes*" (Investigations of a Dog) —— 175

Noam Gil
Isaac Bashevis Singer and the Poetics of Negativity —— 194

Part 4: Modern Jewish Thought

Willi Goetschel
Spinoza, Heresy, and the Discourse of Modernity —— 209

Gilad Sharvit
The Dialectics of Heresy: Trauma and History in Freud —— 228

Agata Bielik-Robson
Liquid Theology and the Messianism of Life: Marrano Heresy in Benjamin and Derrida —— 244

Shaul Magid
Is the Academic Study of Judaism Heresy? —— 266

List of Contributors —— 291

Index —— 293

Willi Goetschel and Gilad Sharvit
Introduction

This volume explores the way various aspects of heresy – as difference, variation, and deviation – have come to function in Jewish history and tradition. The main argument of this volume is that heresy not only distinguishes, demarcates, and separates groups, but creates a social, political and religious dynamics that has proved to sustain rather than disrupt tradition. The contributions collected here examine various aspects of canonization and its discontents as a result of a rich, complex, and often conflicted process in which alterity plays a formative role. Exploring this phenomenon in various historical, cultural, social, and political contexts, the authors of this volume offer studies of a rich panoply of creative responses to the challenge that the interplay of canonization and alterity poses in Jewish tradition, its history, thought, and literature.

1 Terms of Heresy

In Greek antiquity, the term αἵρεσις (hairesis) initially denotes taking and receiving, a choice, or inclination. From the second century BCE, the term mostly refers to groups, which oftentimes had creedal or philosophical organizing principles, and comes later to represent a school of thought.[1] In Patristic writings, the term receives new meaning and describes the alienation of different sects from the Christian teaching. Josephus uses the term to denote religious Jewish sects like the Essenes, Sadducees, or Pharisees, and a Christian sect then called the Nazarenes.[2]

The Talmud uses several different terms to designate heretics. There are references to "min," "ḥiẓonim" (outsiders), "apiḳoros," "kofer ba-Torah" (R. H. 17a), and "kofer ba-'ikkar" (he who denies the fundamentals of faith; Pes. xxiv. 168b). There are references also to "poresh mi-darke ẓibbur" (he who deviates from the customs of the community), and "mumar le-hak'is" (one who transgresses the Law, not for personal advantage, but out of defiance and spite). The Hebrew word *harisah* appears only late in a Kabbalist work in 1558 in Mantua. Remarkably, the anonymous author musters a biblical alliteration in Exodus 19:24 to motivate

---

[1] Religious party or sect, of the Essenes, Josephus, *Bellum Judaicum*, 2.8.1; the Sadducees and Pharisees, Acts, 5.17, 15.5, 26.5; the Christians, ibid.24.5,14, 28.22, generally, faction, party, Appianus, *Bella Civilia*, C5.2. (Liddell and Scott 1966, 41).
[2] Kohler and Greenstone (1906, 6: 353–354).

https://doi.org/10.1515/9783110671582-001

the use of the loanword by making a linguistic connection to Hebrew: "But let not the priests or the people break through [yeharesu] to come up unto the Lord." The word "yeharesu" here literally means "to break through a boundary or framework" (Gries 1987, 338f).[3]

However, Jewish tradition never produced a unified generalized term for, or concept of heresy.[4] The term may be stabilized in common speech, and yet in Judaism the concept of heresy is multifaceted by its very function. Indeed, the sheer variety of terms for various forms of internal differences and deviation highlights the impossibility of reducing the diversity of Jewish tradition to one unified principle or another, be it purely doctrinal, halachic, communal, creedal, spiritual, or intellectual. Rather, the different terms address disparate aspects that defy unification. This resistance to the reduction to a purely doctrinal or halachic structure reflects the various strands of narratives that inform the dynamics of Jewish tradition. The local minhag (custom) trumps that of another community and there is no higher order that supersedes the particular to control and police it.

2 Multiple Sources

Hermann Cohen famously suggested that Jewish tradition rests on multiple sources that mutually complement and enrich each other. Moses and the prophets, written and oral law, Torah and Talmud, Palestinian and Babylonian, Halacha and Haggadah, Ashkenazi and Sephardi strands combine to form a continuous exchange that gives life to its various traditions (Cohen 1995 [1919], 20–28).[5] The

---

[3] The title of the book is Ma'arekhet ha-Elohut (The Order of God) and the chapter is called "Shaar ha-harisah bo yitbaer inyan kizzuz ha-netiot she-hu ha-minut ve ha-epkorsut" (Chapter on heresy in which the matter of the 'cutting of the plants,' which refers to minut and epikorsut will be explained.)

[4] It is always problematic to introduce a term from another context to account for phenomena in a particular tradition. The muddling however seems justified in the case of a history that is so saturated if not even in part constituted by narratives of mutual appropriations of distinctions of the other tradition that it can be fairly considered a formative part. However, it remains important to differentiate the genealogical interferences in order to grasp the particularity of the specific valences that come to bear on terms such as heresy when we apply them to Jewish history, tradition, and cultural production. For an exhaustive study of the history and application of the term hairesis, see Staden (1982) and Glucker (1978, 159–92).

[5] Cohen speaks of the doubled sources of Jewish tradition, but even in Cohen's writings we see them proliferate into a multiplicity: Moses and the prophets, oral and written with its subdivisions of Talmud and Midrash, etc. Jewish tradition thus cannot even be contained within a simple doubling of its sources.

narratives of figures like Abraham, Moses, and the later sages and rabbis reflect such rich and varied trajectories, which often stand in tension with each other. Arguably these tensions inscribe the heretical as a formative moment present even in the foundational narratives themselves.

Abraham, the founder of the dynasty of biblical patriarchs, typifies this formulation. He becomes who he is (Abraham from Abram) through what could be called an act of heresy. Destroying the idols of his native city, he breaks camp and leaves for a life of his own. Abraham, put differently, becomes the founding father by moving out of his native community and creating a tradition of his own. At the beginning of Jewish communal existence there stands a pointedly singular figure reminding us that tradition does not arise from some kind of an already meaningful, clear and well-demarcated point of origin, but through a move of difference and self-differentiation.

The narrative of Moses reflects similar aspects of embracing internal difference as the foundational moment in the formation of tradition. However, the accent in his story shifts. The differences are reflected not only in Moses' blurred Jewish-Egyptian origins but in the tensions and conflicts erupting in the years in the desert and later during the settlement of the new land. In its later development, the Mosaic narrative presents a story fraught with dissent, disobedience, conflict, and heresy. Yet here, the story presents a series of tensions not just between Moses and his people, but also between Moses and God, and ultimately a tension that defines Moses himself. Freud will explore the meaning of this drama in psychoanalytic terms in his *Moses and Monotheism* (1939).

To these aspects are also to be added the Prophetic and other biblical traditions, the Rabbinic traditions, and the later mystic and Messianic traditions. Layer upon layer, the various strands add complexity to a historical process that defies any claims to dogmatic or creedal unity. Rather, Jewish tradition is – as Gershom Scholem suggested in a letter in 1936 – more like the sum total of all its different manifestations, no more or no less:

> The Torah is the essence and integral of all religious tradition, from Moishe Rabbenu to Israel Hildesheimer, and if you are a Jew, Herr Lehmann, to you yourself [...].
> (Scholem 2002, 37)

Half a century later, Scholem reiterated this point with emphatic resolve:

> [Judaism] cannot be defined according to its essence, since it has no essence. Judaism cannot therefore be regarded as a closed historical phenomenon whose development and essence came into focus by a finite sequence of historical, philosophical, doctrinal, or dogmatic judgments and statements. Judaism is rather a living entity...
> (Scholem 1987, 505)

This passage echoed the resolute admonition that Scholem had issued in his magnum opus, *Sabbatai Sevi: The Mystical Messiah* (1973). There he notes:

> There is no way of telling a priori what beliefs are possible or impossible within the framework of Judaism. Certainly, no Jewish historian would accept the specious argument that the criteria of 'Jewish' belief were clear and evident until the kabbalah beclouded and confused the minds. The 'Jewishness' in the religiosity of any particular period is not measured by dogmatic criteria that are unrelated to actual historical circumstances, but solely by what sincere Jews do, in fact, believe, or – at least – consider to be legitimate possibilities. [...] Extreme caution should, therefore, be exercised before pronouncing on the 'Jewish' (namely, 'un-Jewish') character of spiritual phenomena in Jewish history.
> (283–84)

Similarly, Heinrich Graetz, one of the founding fathers of modern Jewish historiography and exponent of the "Science of Judaism," which Scholem so fiercely challenged, had noted that,

> the totality of Judaism is discernible only in its history. Its complete nature the sum of its powers, becomes clear only in the light of history. (Graetz 1975 [1846], 65)

And if there is, throughout the ages, an occasionally obsessive fascination with the heretical, the reason might be precisely that Jewish tradition does not know any hard and fast rules of how exactly to "fix" the borders. Historically, there was never a particular urgency to demarcate and institutionalize fixed distinctions to determine in- and exclusion in theologically unequivocal terms. If heresy is normally understood as the border crossing that questions the distinction between inside and outside, the narratives of Jewish tradition point to such border crossing as a formative feature. Rather than inverting the distinction, these narratives suggest that crossing the border and moving out is the condition for arriving at home and being at one with oneself. The move from Abram to Abraham inscribes this insight into the biblical narrative as a move that embraces change and transition rather than closure and the fixing of borders. This defining feature of what is normally considered heretic – the recognition of the other as what belongs to the innermost of one's tradition – demands that we attend to the heretic in Jewish tradition from its beginnings as its constitutive element. Rather than a mere reversal, the heretic impulse is to be understood as what empowers and drives the dynamics of tradition. Tradition and heresy interweave in such a way that to speak of heresy as distinguished from tradition proper is to misconceive the very dynamics that defines its life. Or to put it otherwise, in Jewish tradition, the heretical represents that aspect of tradition that makes tradition possible in the first place.

3 Discourses of Heresy

Over the last few decades, various discourses of heresy have found new inspiration and provocation. In the study of Jewish and Christian antiquity, for example, scholars built on new modulations of heresy to cast doubt on traditional configurations of the relationship between Judaism and Christianity. Specifically, some called into question the idea that Judaism existed prior to Christianity, as a mother religion from which Christianity developed as daughter religion. Instead, heresy is seen as the site of the construction of both. Daniel Boyarin, for example, argued in *Dying for God* (1999) that "we need to speak of a twin birth of Christianity and rabbinic Judaism as two forms of Judaism, and not of a genealogy in which one – Judaism – is parent to the other – Christianity" (2). Similarly, Alan Segal had claimed in *Rebecca's Children* (1986) that "the time of Jesus marks the beginning not of one but of two great religions of the west, Judaism and Christianity [...] So great is the contrast between previous Jewish religious systems and rabbinism that Judaism and Christianity can essentially claim a twin birth" (1).[6] This line of argumentation follows Walter Bauer, who famously challenged the widespread notion of heresy as a by-product of Christian orthodoxy in *Orthodoxy and Heresy in Earliest Christianity* (1971). Rather, in this study published first in German in 1934, Bauer argued that heretics were simply Early Christians whose views had become inopportune in the process of the church's attempts at codifying orthodox doctrine.

The discourse of heresy in Judaism, the argument continues, was critical in this historical context as it produced the required conditions for the transition from Second-Temple heterogeneous Jewish religious reality to a supposedly unified vision of rabbinic Judaism. That is, heresy is seen not as an act of rebellion in which one turns against a preexisting orthodoxy (Judaism) to form a new sect or group (Christianity), but rather as foundational to the formation of rabbinical Judaism itself: Jewish norms, values, and beliefs were shaped in the ongoing negotiations between different Jewish and Christian sects that came to exist in and through this discourse.[7] Heresy – as scholarship has come to focus in the last decades more on "heresiology" as the "science" of heresies – is now understood to have served a crucial function in structuring the basic Jewish tenets out of a multitude of liturgical practices and systems of beliefs that existed prior to the

---

[6] See also Boyarin (2004), Cohen (1980), Goodman (2007), Reiner (1998), Schäfer (2012), and Yuval (2006).

[7] "[...] the talk of *minim* and *minut* comes to do some work that was 'necessitated' – in the eyes of the Rabbis, of course – by the challenge, or identity question, raised by Justin Martyr and company," writes Boyarin (2004, 55).

destruction of the Temple in Jerusalem in 70AD. In this new formulation of the heretic, largely informed also by Alain Le Boulluec's Foucauldian intuitions in *La notion d'hérésie dans la littérature grecque, IIe-IIIe siècles* (1985), the heretic is seen to be crucial for the construction of imaginary borders between Judaism and Christianity. By recognizing and defining the heretic and his or her religious and social values and ideals, the Jews were able to self-identify their own ideals, to form their own values, to mark a border. In other words, if heresy is an act of transgression against coherent and previously formed dogmas, the recent focus on "heresiology" emphasizes the constructive and constitutive function of heresy: it is a discourse that draws the border lines of religion rather than presenting an act that subverts them. The other, in this reading, mediated rabbinic Judaism's self-conception,[8] or, put otherwise, heresy is better understood as the discourse through which post-second Temple Judaism as a product of late antiquity came into existence. Adiel Schremer, on the other hand, argues in *Brothers Estranged: Heresy, Christianity and Jewish Identity in Late Antiquity* (2010) against the notion that Christianity was important to Judaism in general, and to the development of rabbinic Judaism in particular. Instead, he advocates a return to understanding the Jewish term *minut* as an *inner* Jewish "social-communal issue [rather] than a doctrinal one" (16). More below and in Schremer's contribution to this volume.

As Christianity evolved from a Jewish sect of early Christians into the official state religion of the Roman Empire, heresiology emerged as the discourse that regulated the policing of internal differences. But more decisively, it became the means by which theological discourse constructed its borders: "Heresiology was an argument about religious assimilation and authority in the larger Roman context as well as an internal argument concerning theological formulae" (Lyman 2008, 299). While the consolidation of the Roman church was a function of a political unification that facilitated the rule by state decrees, heresiology became the discourse that negotiated theological unification: "Heresiology as an aggressive language of conflict was used deliberately for calculated effect, and for constructing borders to give meaning to compromised and often still volatile centres of definition" (Lyman 2008, 299). Judaism thus became one of the foils of the dominant theological disputes and remained thus until modernity. This situation had direct impact on the way Jewish tradition addressed the challenge of its own internal differences. Lacking state-backed power and authority, and increasingly seen as the heretic but foundational foil and guarantor of Christianity, Jewish tradition found itself in an environment that made its own negotiation of internal differences a difficult affair.

---

8 See also, the recent work of Ophir and Rosen-Zvi (2018) for a discussion of the use of the term goy.

Heresy, however, did not just have a foundational function in antiquity. Throughout Jewish history, thought, and literature the life of tradition reflects the dynamics of continuity and discontinuity. The discourse of heresy informs our understanding of the Karaite community and mystical thought in the Middle Ages, the Sabbatian movement in the seventeenth, and the Frankist movement in the eighteenth century, and even Jewish Haskalah well into the nineteenth century, to just give the most prominent examples.

With this volume, we suggest thinking beyond the discourse of heresiology. Heresy, we argue, is the construction site of canonization that serves as the scene of canonization's continuous re-examination. Jewish tradition's inner tension between the desire for a canon and its hermeneutic openness, which reframes and reimagines canonical constructions as it renegotiates them, highlights the notion of a canon as anything but conducive to fixed, hard, and fast dogmatic commitments. Difference and alterity that canonization seems to control and domesticate if not to mute return as vital necessities without which the canon becomes illegible and unintelligible. This distinctively open feature of Jewish tradition allowed it not only to survive after the destruction of the Temple, it also gave the tradition a new form of spiritual life that had become possible precisely thanks to this new creative and forward-moving, diasporic openness that signaled the transition to its post-biblical phase.

A marker of borders, the heretic in Jewish history, literature, and thought is, in this context, the double agent who represents both the border and its transgression as he or she draws the border by his or her transgression. The insight in this double-dealing marks the heretic as pivotal for the canonical construction of tradition. The border-drawing function of the heretic marks exclusion by way of (albeit conflicted) canonical inclusion. Rather than an outcast to be purged from memory, the heretic remains pivotal for a tradition whose identity rests on the internal difference required for tradition to exist. This function is so profoundly embedded that it continues to inform Jewish modernity even in its most secular and post-secular variations.

The contributions collected in this volume demonstrate the enduring significance of this spiritual force from antiquity to the present. They demonstrate a rich and vibrant interest in exploring questions of difference and alterity as intrinsic and foundational rather than external and contingent concerns that would confront tradition merely from the outside. In varying degree and with changing temperament, vision, and outlook, the contributions of this volume highlight the critical significance of heresy in the formation and working of tradition. These contributions demonstrate a rich, vibrant, and sustained engagement of Jewish tradition throughout its history in exploring questions of difference and alterity as fundamental, central, and formative rather than contingent to the Jewish experience from antiquity to the present.

4 From Antiquity to the Present

The first part of the book, on heresy in Jewish Antiquity, examines the role of heresy from the Hellenic period to the late rabbinic period. The opening paper by Erich Gruen, "Was Hellenism a Jewish Heterodoxy?" offers an illuminating critique of the common notion that Judaism and Hellenism represent historically separate and antagonistically opposed social, political and theological modes of existence, which Christianity, as is often argued, blended into a unified, coherent whole. Judaism, the traditional argument goes, focused on moral conduct, on sin and social justice, while Hellenism offered a new critical-rational way of thinking as well as scientific and cultural achievements. However, rather than arguing against the differences between Hellenism and Judaism, Gruen aims to question their differentiation. For Gruen, Judaism and Hellenism were never isolated as modern scholarship presents them to be. In terms of this volume, the introduction of Hellenism to Judaism did not suggest a form of heterodoxy. Addressing a wealth of historical materials – from Josephus and Eupolemos – and literary works by Artapanos, Gruen portrays a fluid cultural world of Second Temple Judaism in which the introduction of Hellenism "injected no alien element" and the term heterodoxy, which presupposes distinct and pre-established normative dogmas, is "simply inapplicable."

In his paper "Negotiating Heresy: Belief and Identity in Early Rabbinic Literature," Adiel Schremer, offers another layer to our understanding of heresy in antiquity. Here as well, recent scholarship of heresy in Judaism is being questioned. Schremer critically examines arguments that focus on Jewish heresy in terms of deviation from certain creedal matters, that is, from a specific set of theological "thoughts" or "views." This allows Schremer to ask about the nature of early rabbinic Judaism: is it organized around or built on theological dogmas, or, put otherwise, do beliefs inform Jewish identity, like they do in early Christianity? According to Schremer, rabbis in the first century did not seem to be interested in addressing the topic of heresy; they did not define it, nor did they see any necessity to refute heresy. And when they did consider the category of belonging, this was not in terms of the question of "correct belief," but rather in terms of social and ethical concerns. Schremer grounds his argument on a famous passage from the early rabbinic midrash on Leviticus, the *Sifra*, one of the few passages that address the term "the children of Israel," to argue that the rabbis considered adherence to the covenant as true marker of belonging; thus demonstrating that they were interested much more in ritual practice and ethical behavior than in questions of beliefs.

With the paper "Revelation as Heresy: Mysticism and Elisha ben Abuyah's Apostasy in Classic Rabbinic Literature," Shraga Bar-On and Eugene D. Matanky add to the conversation by addressing the dynamics of formulations of heresy in rabbinic Judaism. Their work explores the changing perception of revelation, a "cornerstone" of biblical Judaism, into a hallmark of heresy in rabbinic literature. In order to track this formative shift, Bar-On and Matanky focus on the interpretation and evaluation of the story of the archetypal rabbinic heretical figure Elisha ben Abuyah and his revelatory experience in three rabbinic circles: the hyper-mystical circle of Rabbi Yoḥanan ben Zakkai, the anti-mystical circle of Rabbi Judah ha-Nasi, and the moderate mystical circle of Rabbi Akiva. The chapter delineates an important dialectics of interpretation: while we would expect the rabbis to completely denounce and reject Ben Abuyah and exclude him from their midst, as was the case in the Mishna, Bar-On and Matanky portray a fascinating attempt in the Talmud to reintegrate Ben Abuyah back into the rabbinic community, an effort led by the circle of Yoḥanan ben Zakkai. This attempt demonstrates for the authors the liminal space of the heretic in rabbinic literature: Acher is outside, as he was alien to rabbinic norms, but he also remains to be considered inside, as the rabbinic sage he was recognized to be. Abuyah assumes mythical stature and interestingly returns as an important figure in modernity in the writing of a young Martin Buber, who identified at an early stage of his literary career with Ben Abuya (Friedman 1982, 42–43), as well as in Kafka, as David Suchoff's paper will discuss.

Turning to heresy in Jewish mysticism, the second part of the book examines the trajectories of heresy in Jewish antiquity and rabbinic literature by exploring two incidences of heresy in the Kabbalah: the role of femininity in Sabbatian heresy, and the readmission of the thirteenth-century Kabbalist Abraham ben Samuel Abulafia to the Jewish community in modern *Me'ah She'arim*.

In her essay, "King David as the Fourth Leg of the Chariot: Gender, Identity, and Heresy," Ruth Kara-Ivanov Kaniel explores the under-researched interrelations of femininity and heresy in the Sabbatian movement. Customarily, women in the Sabbatian movement supposedly enjoyed an elevated status – they participated in rituals previously forbidden to women and were granted relative sexual liberation – in a way that would centuries later be interpreted as a "feminine revolution." Yet, Kara-Ivanov Kaniel's chapter focuses not on the aspects of the social and political revolution of Sabbatai Zevi and his followers, but on the particular function that the "feminine" came to play in the movement. She does so by examining the function of attributing particular forms of masculinity and femininity to the mythical heroes of the movement, Sabbatai Zevi and King David. By delineating the function of femininity in the portrayal of King David as the fourth leg of the divine Chariot from the Zohar to the Sabbatian literature, Kara-Ivanov Kaniel demonstrates the heretic nature of the feminine in Sabbatianism. In descriptions of both Sabbatai Zevi and Kind David, femininity serves as a marker of imperfection which releases the two heroes from their responsibility for their inherently heretical transgressions. The feminine-as-heretic produces multiplicity and variability in a previously unified conceptual field: whereas the feminine messiah is regarded as weak or sick, his portrayal still allows the messiah to be seen as a male figure.

In the chapter "Abraham Abulafia: The Apotheosis of a Medieval Heretic in Modern *Me'ah She'arim*," Moshe Idel adds to the debate on the historical dynamics between heresy and orthodoxy with his discussion of the afterlife of Abulafia's thought. A self-proclaimed messiah and prophet, and undoubtedly one of the most radical Kabbalists in thirteen-century Spain and Italy, Abulafia was ostracized for centuries by Kabbalists and rabbinic authorities alike. Abulafia purported an inclusive approach to non-Jewish speculative thought and considered Judaism as predominantly a matter of spiritual activity, and he saw in prophecy actual possibility in the present. He was consequently marginalized by his contemporaries and was accused of heresy later in history. Yet, as Idel carefully shows, the accusations turned into adoration in the long history of his reception. While his books were rarely printed or studied, his writings on prophecy received much attention by fifteenth-century Kabbalists and later by Haim Vital, who took great interest in the topic. But it is only much later, indeed in recent decades, that Abulafia would emerge as a mythical figure for ultra-orthodox groups in *Me'ah She'arim*. Now, "a perfect and comprehensive sage," Abulafia came to represent an opportunity to learn of ecstatic mystical experiences. In this context he is no heretic, but a "luminary, and a great genius," who teaches of secrets of experiential religious dimensions so rare in modern experience. For Idel, the case of Abulafia is so important exactly because it highlights the significance of the historical interplay between heresy and tradition, rejection and reception, but also because it sheds light on the conceptual shifts and turns this mode of reception produces. As Idel shows, while Abulafia is idolized in the present, this is not what he himself had intended: his important contribution to the study of spiritual experiences and his practical advice are well-accepted but his theological vision is still considered harmful and problematic.

Robert Alter's "The Authentic Paganism of Saul Tchernikhovsky" opens the third part of the volume that examines the role of heresy in Jewish Literature. Tchernikhovsky, an important leader of the so-called "Canaanite poets" famously aimed to introduce pagan themes and images into Hebrew literature. This attempt, as Alter suggests, signaled a "rebellion against Judeo-Christian values," and presented "an affirmation of the life of the body in nature." In his poems – Tchernikhovsky wrote pagan poems like "A Song for Ashtoreth and for Bel" and "The Death of Tammuz" already quite early in his career – he explicitly rejected not only Jewish tradition, but also, and perhaps more radically, "Judaism's fundamental orientation toward reality." Alter's chapter focuses on Tchernikhovsky's monumental poem "To the Sun," and the peculiar place of the biblical language in Tchernikhovsky's evidently pagan world view. For Alter, the poet writes in Hebrew because it is through this linguistic act that his pagan poem "consummates" the

Hebrew language. Indeed, it is in his writing in Hebrew that we find the core of Tchernikhovsky's heresy as the actualization of Hebrew; this allows the poet to finally assert a "pagan trajectory almost as if the Bible had never existed." Tchernikhovsky, the heretic, accepts the border, only to move beyond it.

In "Heretical Canines: Kafka's "Forschungen eines Hundes" (Investigations of a Dog)," David Suchoff examines the rich and profound way Kafka explores the nexus of tradition and heresy as foundational for the Jewish experience, and not just in modernity. Suchoff's reading renders Kafka's writing legible as a subtle yet pointed commentary on the decisive function of heretical thought and behavior in keeping tradition's dynamic power alive, to feed it, so to speak, and to reclaim its decisive significance. Acher – the Other – as the tradition calls Elisha Ben Abuya, is a figure that looms large in Kafka's thinking about Judaism, just as it did for others of his generation (like Buber). In Kafka, the figure of Acher presents a "critical constellation," as Suchoff argues, that delineates the vital dynamics of Jewish tradition. Kafka's "Investigations of a Dog" brings home "this notion of internalized heresy with a quiet humor" that highlights the open hiddenness that gives Jewish tradition its enduringly liberating thrust.

Noam Gil's "Isaac Bashevis Singer and the Poetics of Negativity" examines the strands of heretical thinking that inform Singer's writings and his work's diverse but mostly heretically inclined roll call of characters. Remarkably, the heresy that populates Singer's stories does not indicate any decline or demise of Jewish life in modernity but suggests the opposite: the enduring vitality of Jewish tradition even under the sign of its apparent dissolution. As Gil notes: "Singer's stories are not narratives of despair." Instead, they celebrate a "negativity of life" where grotesque forms of happy-endings have their characters go on to a better world where all pressures of this-earthly forms of identities are transcended and replaced with an otherworldly universe where heretics are embraced as the most genuine modern forms of Jewish tradition.

Part four examines the formative relation between modern Jewish thought and heresy by way of a discussion of the thought of Spinoza, Freud, Benjamin and Derrida. It concludes with a general reflection on the status of Jewish Studies as an academic field straddling the borders between heresy and tradition. In "Spinoza, Heresy, and the Discourse of Modernity," Willi Goetschel follows the trajectory of Spinoza's reception as a narrative whose heresiological features suggest a story of modernity that is more conflicted than might appear at first glance. First rejected, excommunicated and condemned as renegade and traitor of his people, Spinoza returns in the age of secularism and at the current postsecular juncture as a paradigm of the modern discourse on the heretic, that curiously enough remains committed to the stereotypical notions of religion and spirituality, which he in fact – among the first of an emerging tradition of modern Jewish thought – so resolutely fought to challenge. In modernity, Spinoza serves as a Shibboleth for Jewish tradition and thought that indicates the fault lines of the internal conflicts of a dynamic tradition that resists easy assimilation, not only in traditional contexts, but also in a society that considers itself enlightened and secular. Remarkably, it is precisely at the current juncture of late modernity that the critical edge of Spinoza's thought asserts a particularly potent challenge to revisit the hidden assumptions of today's life that exposes it as unexamined in its most fundamental aspects.

Gilad Sharvit's "The Dialectics of Heresy: Trauma and History in Freud," investigates the complicated place of heresy in Freud's momentous *Moses and Monotheism* (1939). Sharvit argues that heresy gives structure to Freud's last book, since, as Freud notoriously speculates, the first act of the Israelites in the Sinai Peninsula was heretical – they killed Moses, their prophet and leader, who took them out of Egypt. Then, in order to fight with their guilt, they joined a different, pagan religion of a second, Midian Moses. This act of heresy, had, however, unexpected results. The Israelites did not simply forget the first Moses and his monotheistic religion: after a period of latency the trauma of the murder returned to the surface of their social reality and compelled them to return to the religion they previously rejected. This series of events, Sharvit argues, first suggests a psychoanalytic theory of heresy, one that sheds light on the hidden, traumatic implications of heresy. Second, Freud's story uncovers the dialectics of heresy since in Freud's story the heretical act promised the hold of Moses' monotheism on the Israelites. In Sharvit's reading, the trauma of heresy is thus crucial for the survival of Judaism.

In "Liquid Theology and The Messianism of Life: Marrano Heresy in Benjamin and Derrida," Agata Bielik-Robson shows how Benjamin's and Derrida's interventions as Marrano – i.e. crypto-(anti)theological – moves can be understood to recapture the hidden but fundamentally vital force at the heart of Jewish tradition. Charged with a healthy dose of an antinomian impulse that Benjamin, Scholem, and Derrida – each in their own particular way – seek to recover, she argues, their projects are both upping the ante of the terms of heresy and profoundly committed to bring, through their heretical turn, Jewish tradition to life anew. Bielik-Robson highlights the notion that informs Jewish tradition from its earliest beginnings: that to regain its "essence," "substance," and vital, life-giving power, the hardened shells or vessels need ever again to be broken up to – as she formulates it – set them free by liquefying them and returning them to life. Embracing Jewish tradition and its emancipatory impulse this way, both Benjamin and Derrida continue the Jewish rejection of a Pauline dichotomizing of spirit and law by undermining the distinction as a false one. For Bielik-Robson, the antinomian move of heresy is what ultimately keeps Jewish tradition alive and paradigmatic for modernity.

In the essay that concludes the volume, "Is the Academic Study of Judaism Heresy?" Shaul Magid returns the issue closer to home and to the scene of the volume's project itself: is what we do when we study Jewish tradition, history, and culture academically itself a form of heresy? Looking at the current American landscape of the discourse on Jewish thought in academe, he argues that the work of Jacob Neusner, Susannah Heschel, and Martin Kavka in particular respond to this question differently. However, together their work illustrates how Jewish Studies as an academic discipline has yet to openly and critically address its predicament: the uneasy oscillating between commitment to academic work on the one hand and the engagement for the cause of an identity politics in search of its representation on the other; a situation often exacerbated by the appropriation of theological trappings, it highlights a conflict that seems to be precariously oblivious of the distinction between method and the object of its study. In other words, Jewish Studies finds itself still trapped in a situation defined by a confusion of first and second order observation, where the study of a living tradition is by different parties harnessed for their various normative claims that call for critical examination in the first place.

Highlighting the epistemological minefield of this conundrum concerning the field of Jewish Studies, and Jewish thought in particular, Magid exposes a problem we can no longer afford to ignore. And in an illuminating way, this problem once recognized as such puts us right back where we began, but now maybe with the understanding that heresy is no longer what separates the Jewish heretic from Jewish tradition, but what makes the heretic a decisive, crucial, and vital part of that tradition: just as the so-called "Acher" or Other, Elisha Ben Abuya, always remained a part of a tradition whose dynamic development he helped to enable through his questioning thereby capturing Judaism's most vital impulse – the one that guarantees its existence.

Bibliography

Bauer, Walter. *Orthodoxy and Heresy in Earliest Christianity*. Eds. Robert A. Kraft and Gerhard Krodel. Trans. Philadelphia Seminar on Christian Origins. Philadelphia: Fortress Press, 1971.

Boyarin, Daniel. *Dying for God: Martyrdom and the Making of Christianity and Judaism*. Stanford: Stanford University Press, 1999.

Boyarin, Daniel. *Border Lines: The Partition of Judaeo-Christianity*. Philadelphia: University of Pennsylvania Press, 2004.

Goodman, Martin. "The Function of Minim in Early Rabbinic Judaism." *Judaism in the Roman World: Collected Essays*. Leiden: Brill, 2007. 163–173

Cohen, Hermann. *Religion of Reason Out of the Sources of Judaism*. Trans. Simon Kaplan. Atlanta: Scholars Press, 1995.

Cohen, Shaye J. D. "A Virgin Defiled: Some Rabbinic and Christian Views on the Origins of Heresy." *Union Seminary Quarterly Review* 36.1 (1980): 1–11.
Friedman, Maurice. *Martin Buber's Life and Work: The Early Years 1878–1923*. London and Tunbridge Wells: Search Press, 1982.
Glucker, John. *Antiochus and the Late Academy*. Göttingen: Vandenhoeck and Ruprecht, 1978.
Graetz, Heinrich. "The Structure of Jewish History." *The Structure of Jewish History, and Other Essays*. Trans. and intro. Ismar Schorsch. New York: Jewish Theological Seminary of America, 1975, 63–124.
Gries, Ze'ev. "Heresy." *Contemporary Jewish Religious Thought: Original Essays on Critical Concepts, Movement, and Beliefs*. Ed. Arthur A. Cohen and Paul Mendes-Flohr. New York: Scribner, 1987. 338–352.
Kohler, Kaufmann and Julius H. Greenstone. "Heresy and Heretics." *Jewish Encyclopedia*, 12 vols. Eds. Cyrus Adler, Isidore Singer, et al. New York: Funk and Wagnalls, 1906, vol. 6, 353–4.
Le Boulluec, Alain. *La notion d'hérésie dans la litterature grecque, IIe-IIIe siècles*. Paris: Etudes Augustiniennes, 1985.
Liddell, Henry George and Robert Scott (Eds.). *A Greek-English Lexicon*. Oxford: Calderon Press, 1966.
Lyman, J. Rebecca. "Heresiology: The Invention of 'Heresy' and 'Schism'." *The Cambridge History of Christianity*, vol. 2: *Constantine to c. 600*. Ed. Augustine Casiday and Frederick W. Norris. Cambridge: Cambridge University Press, 2007. 296–316.
Reiner, Elchanan. "From Joshua to Jesus: The Transformation of a Biblical Story to a Local Myth (A Chapter in the Religious Life of the Galilean Jew)." *Sharing the Sacred: Religious Contacts and Conflicts in the Holy Land*. Eds. Arieh Kofsky and Guy G. Stroumsa. Jerusalem: Yad Izhak Ben Zvi, 1998. 223–27.
Schäfer, Peter. *The Jewish Jesus: How Judaism and Christianity Shaped Each Other*. Princeton, N.J.: Princeton University Press, 2012.
Scholem, Gershom. *A Life in Letters, 1914–1982*. Trans. Anthony David Skinner. Cambridge, Mass. and London: Harvard University Press, 2002.
Scholem, Gershom. *Sabbatai Sevi: The Mythical Messiah 1626–1676*. Trans. R. J. Zwi Werblowsky. Princeton: Princeton University Press, 1973.
Scholem, Gershom. "Judaism." *Contemporary Religious Jewish Thought: Original Essays on Critical Concepts, Movements, and Beliefs*. New York: Scribner, 1987, 505–508.
Schremer, Adiel. *Brothers Estranged: Heresy, Christianity, and Jewish identity in Late Antiquity*. Oxford: Oxford University Press, 2010.
Segal, Alan F. *Rebecca's Children: Judaism and Christianity in the Roman World*. Cambridge: Harvard University Press, 1986.
Staden, Heinrich von. "Hairesis and Heresy: The Case of the haireseis iatrikai." *Jewish and Christian Self-definition*. Vol. 3. Self-definition in the Greco-Roman World. Ed. Ben F. Meyer and E.P. Sanders. Philadelphia: Fortress Press, 1982. 76–100.
Ophir, Adi and Ishay Rosen-Zvi. *Goy: Israel's Multiple Others and the Birth of the Gentile*. Oxford: Oxford University Press, 2018.
Yuval, Israel Jacob. *Two Nations in Your Womb: Perceptions of Jews and Christians in Late Antiquity and the Middle Ages*. Trans. Barbara Harshav and Jonathan Chipman. Berkeley: University of California Press, 2006.

Part 1: **Jewish Antiquity**

Erich S. Gruen
Was Hellenism a Jewish Heterodoxy?

"What has Athens to do with Jerusalem?" That famous statement, memorably uttered by Tertullian in the late third century CE, remains emblematic of the long-standing conception that Hellenism and Judaism represented two independent strands in tension or in conflict with one another (Tertullian, *De Praescriptione Haereticorum*, 7). Friction and confrontation marked the encounter in antiquity, it was assumed, until Christianity entered the scene to blend the two strands into an amalgam long overdue and long foreordained. Such is the comfortable teleology that underpinned conceptualization in the nineteenth century and much of the twentieth.[1] In the formulation of Matthew Arnold, Judaism, or "Hebraism" as he termed it, entailed a focus on moral conduct, a rigid straitjacket that dwelled on sin and righteousness, evidently a reflection cast back from his own contemporary Puritanism, whereas "Hellenism" epitomized critical thinking, rationality, and intellectual and artistic achievement (Arnold, 1869/1965).[2] The contrast echoed a similar one fashioned by Heinrich Heine somewhat earlier, between those who seek a joyless religion (the Jews) and those who take pleasure in life: everybody else (Heine 1961–1964, xi.14–16; Rajak 2000, 542–544).

However, scholarship in the past generation or so has shifted away from that simplistic dualism, softened those contours, complicated the contrasts, and challenged the idea of a "*Kulturkampf*." The prevailing notion now is that of the infiltration of Hellenism into Jewish heritage, an overlapping or interpenetration, indeed a blending, an alloy, a fusion (e.g. Hengel 1974; Goldstein 1981, 64–87; Will and Orrieux 1986; Gruen 1998; Levine 1998; Collins 2000; Collins 2005, 1–20). But that leaves the fundamental concept intact. A *Verschmelzung* is hardly a more productive image than a *Kulturkampf*. In either perspective, Hellenism and Judaism constituted two separate and distinct entities, either in contention with one another or brought together as a merged amalgam. In other analyses, emphasis rests on Hellenism as a cultural phenomenon and Judaism as a religion, a distant echo of Matthew Arnold's old distinction. What possible meaning could one attach to such formulation? That Jews had no culture and that Greeks had no religion? A *reductio ad absurdum*. We obviously need a different conceptualization.

Was there in fact ever a collision of Hellenism and Judaism that required resolution through some composite mixture? Or, to put it in the terms of this volume,

---

1 The classic and most influential presentation of this view stems from Droysen (1843/1980).
2 See Rajak (2000, 548–553).

did the entrance of Hellenism into Jewish life and tradition introduce a heterodox element into a normative world?

The presumptive confrontation itself may be a modern fabrication. Given the enormous ink spilled over "Hellenism" and "Judaism," it is remarkable how rarely those terms ever surface in ancient texts. The classic site for the framing of this issue comes in the Second Book of Maccabees, with reference to the background and circumstances of the Maccabean rebellion. The terms appear there for the first time in our evidence. The author five times makes reference to "*Hellenismos*," and three times to "*Ioudaismos*."[3] But nowhere does he pit them against one another as rival or competing concepts. What resonance would "Hellenism" carry anyway to readers of the text? It is noteworthy that the meaning varies in each of the passages that conveys the term. The "Hellenism" that Jews encountered in second-century BCE Palestine was itself an amalgam of Greek, Phoenician, and Syrian elements, not some pure strain of Attic high culture. And how should one understand the essence, if there be any such thing, of second-century Judaism, with its diverse strands, sects, and practices? Hybridity inhered on both sides. And if there was no orthodoxy, could there be a heterodoxy?

Where did the idea of a cultural confrontation arise? The *locus classicus* for the insertion of Hellenism into the society of the Judeans is the introduction of a gymnasium into Jerusalem. The quintessential Hellenic institution entered the very heart of Jewish life and tradition. The fact is bitterly bemoaned by the author of 2 Maccabees, who reckons the gymnasium to be the "peak of Hellenism and the accession of foreignness" (2 Macc. 4:13). That is the core testimony for most modern reconstructions of a compromise of Jewish integrity. Worse still, the impetus for the gymnasium came not from the wicked Hellenic king Antiochus IV, but from the Jewish High Priest Jason himself. And its installation gained a warm welcome from the other priests who joined enthusiastically in the sporting events of the palaestra (2 Macc. 4:8–14). The author of 2 Maccabees a half century or more later found the development abhorrent. For him the embrace of this emblem of Hellenism by the priestly leaders of the nation constituted an odious injection of heterodoxy (2 Macc. 4:15). Yet it is noteworthy that Jason's contemporaries expressed no displeasure. Judah Maccabee took up arms against the abominations of Antiochus IV, not against the Hellenic way of life. Even more striking is the fact that nothing in our evidence, not even in 2 Maccabees, suggests that the gymnasium was ever torn down. If Judah Maccabee's success in the Jewish uprising and in the rededication of the Temple was accompanied by

---

[3] Hellenism: 2 Macc. 4:10, 4:13, 4:15, 6:9, 11:24; Judaism: 2 Macc. 2:21, 8:1, 14:38.

destruction of the gymnasium, the author of 2 Maccabees would hardly have missed the opportunity to gloat over it. But he says not a word.

There is no need here to go into the history of Judah Maccabee and the Hasmoneans who followed him. Their adoption of various Hellenic features and elements are well known. The Hasmoneans engaged regularly in diplomatic dealings with Greek kings, adopted Greek names, donned garb and paraded emblems redolent with Hellenic significance, erected monuments, displayed stelae, and minted coinage inspired by Greek models, and even took on royal titulature.[4] One of them indeed designated himself as "philhellene" (Jos. *BJ*, 1.70; *AJ*, 13.301). None was charged with betraying the legacy of the revolt. Embrace of a range of Hellenic customs and institutions was perfectly compatible with maintaining adherence to the traditions of the forefathers.

One can argue, of course, that none of this is relevant to the core of Judaism. Greek coinage, Greek monuments, Greek names, even participation in Greek gymnasial games are merely marginal to what constitutes the central institutions of the people. They simply nibble around the periphery. But where is the center? The essential norms in the period of the Second Temple are not easy to isolate. But one element surely belongs there: embrace of the Torah as the foundational document of the nation, transmission of the word of God. Now, the Torah itself, in some version at least, experienced a monumental shift in this period: its translation into Greek. Exactly how and when this happened is unknown to us, unless one wishes to believe the fanciful tale in the *Letter of Aristeas* that it was all done in one fell swoop by the 72 sages from Jerusalem at the behest of Ptolemy II in Alexandria in the mid-third century BCE.[5] Whatever one thinks of that legend, a Greek version or versions at least of the Pentateuch was/were available by the end of the third century, for we have texts that drew on what later took shape as the Septuagint already in the second century BCE. The process occurred surely not because Ptolemy wanted a readable copy of the Hebrew Bible to add to the shelves of the Alexandrian library, but because many Jews in the Diaspora had lost the use of Hebrew. Scriptures in Greek were not only valuable for liturgical purposes but also allowed Jews to maintain a more meaningful connection to their origins.

Did this inject an element of heterodoxy? A rendering into Greek as such would not do so. But might it not encourage tampering with the text, tinkering with traditions, altering the central narrative of the nation's history? This is

---

4 Recent work on the Hasmoneans is abundant. See Eshel (2008); Regev (2013); Seeman (2013); Atkinson (2016); Bernhardt (2017); Berthelot (2018).
5 See the magisterial commentary on the *Letter of Aristeas* by Wright (2015).

no mere idle speculation. Sacred scriptures had powerful impact. One did not meddle with them lightly. For this we have forthright and unequivocal testimony from Josephus. At the outset of his 20-volume work on Jewish antiquities, he asserts that he will set forth the entire ancient history of his people and the constitution of the state translated directly from the Hebrew writings themselves (Jos. *AJ*, 1.5). He reiterates the commitment a few lines later, affirming quite explicitly that he promised neither to add nor to omit anything (Jos. *AJ*, 1.17).[6] Later in his text, Josephus underscores the point that he has inserted nothing for the sake of embellishment that was not already there in Moses' own composition (Jos. *AJ*, 4.196). The historian, in his last work, the *Contra Apionem*, still insists that he, like all faithful Jews, approaches their writings in such a way that no one would be so bold as to add, remove, or change a thing; every Jew from the day of his birth, says Josephus, inherently considers them as the decrees of God (Jos. *CAp*. 1.42).

All this seems quite consistent and categorical. Josephus declares unremitting faithfulness to the text, lest there be the slightest hint of heterodoxy. Yet, as is well known, Josephus himself glaringly ignored his own precepts. Not only did he depart considerably from a mere reproduction of the biblical text, offering in general a paraphrase rather than a literal translation of the Hebrew Bible or the Septuagint. He also omitted numerous portions of the received text, dropping a number of somewhat embarrassing stories, such as that of Jacob's deception of Isaac in Genesis or the construction of the Golden Calf in Exodus. He also inserted several episodes not found in the Bible, like Moses' wedding to an Ethiopian princess, and he often reduced the role of God and of miracles in the biblical narrative, perhaps to put greater stress on human agency. The discrepancy between Josephus' pronouncements of absolute adherence to the sacred text and the fact of his frequent straying from it is quite striking.[7]

Scholars have gone to great lengths to reconcile this ostensible inconsistency, suggesting that Josephus employed loose phraseology or commonplace rhetoric, or that he referred only to Halakhah rather than Haggadah, or that he hoped to get away with his sweeping statements since readers, in the absence of bound manuscripts, indexes, or research assistants, let alone search engines, would be unable to challenge his claims of exactitude.[8] But it is not easy to get around Josephus' unequivocal and repeated statements. The historian (and his readers) evidently understood this notion of exactitude rather differently from our conventional

---

[6] See also 10.218; cf. 2.347, 9.208, 14.1, 20.261; *CAp*. 1.42.
[7] See the examples collected by Feldman (1998), 37–39; *idem* (2000), 7.
[8] A valuable summary of opinions, with their principal proponents, may be found in Feldman (1998), 39–44; *idem* (2000), 7–8. See also Sterling (1992), 252–256; Barclay (2007), 31; Inowlocki (2005), 50–51.

usage. Yes, the sacred scriptures were inviolable. But those who reproduced them in other languages or other genres were not thereby precluded from altering, adapting, or departing from the original whose sacrosanctity was, in their view, uncompromised by alternative versions. Such versions neither substituted for nor supplanted their model. The latter remained untouched and intact. Josephus did not here engage in a tortured attempt to disguise exegesis as faithful rendering. For him and his readers this *was* faithful rendering. And it was certainly not heterodoxy.

What I want to stress here is that Josephus stood in a long tradition in which Jewish authors, composing in Greek for audiences steeped in Hellenic literature and learning, recast biblical traditions in novel forms. The practice, one could argue, has its origins in the Bible itself. One needs think only of the Book of Deuteronomy, which substantially revised the Book of the Covenant in Exodus, or the two books of Chronicles, which offered their own retelling of material to be found in the books of Samuel and Kings. Subsequent retellings in Hebrew or Aramaic can readily be illustrated by the Book of Jubilees, the Genesis Apocryphon, or the extensive *Biblical Antiquities* of Pseudo-Philo, originally a Hebrew composition, though preserved now only in Latin translation.

A whole industry preceded Josephus. It has given rise to a description denoting a presumed genre, that of the "rewritten Bible." The very concept, however, is problematic. Was there such a genre at all? The idea is a strictly modern concoction. The ancients possessed no such classification. And indeed, a still more fundamental complication lurks behind it. Can there be such a thing as a "rewritten Bible," however loosely defined, at a time when the canonical Bible did not yet exist? This is, of course, not the place to discuss the interminable problem of the canon, its form, and the date (if there was one) when it came into being. On any reckoning, the so-called canon was in flux during the Second Temple period, as the Dead Sea Scrolls clearly indicate. But some body of sacred writings was certainly acknowledged in this era, as is demonstrated by the rendering of the Pentateuch into Greek. The author of *Jubilees* had some texts of Genesis and Exodus in front of him, the Genesis Apocryphon certainly relied on a text that went at least through part of the Abraham story which it then freely revised, and Pseudo-Philo drew heavily, though erratically, on the Book of Judges, among others.

Studies of what constituted "rewritten Bibles," or "rewritten scriptures" as is now the preferred phrase, have proliferated in the past generation or so.[9] But

---

9 The term was evidently coined by Vermes (1961), 95. Numerous efforts have been made to define a genre or to identify the texts that would fit into that concocted category. It goes without saying that no such pigeon-hole ever receives mention in antiquity. Among attempts to provide a frame and to assemble works that can be set within it, see, in general, the survey of Nickelsburg

their focus has been almost exclusively on texts in Hebrew or Aramaic, most of them to be found in Qumran. What I want to emphasize here is that Jewish intellectuals, whether in the Diaspora or in Palestine, who composed in Greek for a Greek-speaking Jewish readership engaged regularly in this same sort of liberal refashioning of biblical narratives, without concern that this might be reckoned as deviation from any putatively normative Judaism.

A few notable examples can make the point. Several Hellenistic Jewish historians operated with tales familiar to us from the Scriptures, and then manipulated them at will. Unfortunately, we have them mostly in fragments, their works collected by an assiduous polymath named Alexander Polyhistor, a Greek intellectual from Miletos whose own compilation is available only in fragments.[10] But we owe him a lot. Many Jewish writers and indeed Polyhistor himself would have disappeared into the void were it not for the Church Father Eusebius and, to a lesser degree, Clement of Alexandria. As so often, we are in the debt of Christian theologians, with their own special motives, for this slender link to important Jewish writers who were ignored or scorned by the rabbis.

Take, as an illustration, the historian Eupolemos, who composed a work entitled "On the Kings in Judaea."[11] Eupolemos plainly felt no restrictions that obliged him to stick to any received text of the Septuagint. He depicts Moses, interestingly enough, as the first wise man and the first to give the alphabet to the Jews. The latter then passed it on to the Phoenicians, and from them it came to the Greeks. He mentions Moses as lawgiver only as an afterthought. For Eupolemos, Moses is the font of cultural evolution of both the Near East and Hellas (Clem. Alex. *Strom*.1.23.153.4; Euseb. *PE*, 9.25.4–9.26.1). And the author takes even greater liberties. He boasts of David's victories that go well beyond any biblical warrant, having him subjugate Assyrians, push into Asia Minor, rout the Phoenicians, clash with the Nabataeans, and conduct international relations with Egypt (Euseb. *PE*, 9.30.3–4). It is noteworthy that amidst all the peoples and lands with whom Eupolemos has David clash, the one missing is precisely the one which

---

(1984), 89–156; further, Harrington (1986), 239–247; Alexander (1988), 99–121; Halpern-Amaru (1994), 4–5; Najman (2003), 7–8; Crawford (2008), 2–15; Kugel (2012), 3–23; Bernstein (2005), 169–196, ostensibly questions the value of the category but struggles at length to define criteria, more narrow than loose, that would include some texts and exclude others. This seems to be a singularly fruitless endeavor. See also Zahn (2012), 271–288. She does reckon "rewritten Bibles" as a genre, but with a flexible and nuanced understanding. Most recently, Mroczek rightly and cogently questions the whole concept (2016), *passim*, especially 118–123.

10 The fullest study of Polyhistor remains Freudenthal (1874/1875).

11 See the text and translation of Eupolemos' fragments, with commentary, in Holladay (1983), 93–156.

is the centerpiece of the biblical story: the Philistines. The historian is clearly calling attention to his own originality.

Eupolemos is equally idiosyncratic in recounting the deeds of Solomon. After the building of the Temple, organized and dictated by the king with the assistance of craftsmen and laborers from Phoenicia and Egypt, Solomon sent a handsome gift to the Phoenician monarch: nothing less than a golden column to be set up at Tyre in the temple of Zeus (Euseb. *PE*, 9.34.18). No scriptural basis, of course, exists for this. Modern readers have found the passage puzzling and unacceptable. How could a Jewish historian credit Solomon, whose piety and magnanimity had been responsible for the First Temple in Jerusalem, with setting up a gold pillar in Tyre to honor the chief god of the Phoenicians (e.g. Wacholder 1974, 217–223; Mendels 1987, 131–143)? But Eupolemos saw no inconsistency or contradiction here. Solomon emerges as both a dedicated devotee of Yahweh and as patron of foreign princes and benefactor of their cults. Nor is there reason to believe that such a portrait would be marginalized as heterodox opinion.

Another fashioner of out-of-the norm biblical narrative, Artapanos, took still greater, even stunning, liberties. Artapanos is a most enigmatic figure – but also a most fascinating one. He had a Persian name, composed his work in Greek, and wrote about characters in the Torah. The surviving fragments are also preserved by Polyhistor via Eusebius. Of Artapanos the man no external evidence exists. But his free-wheeling representation of biblical figures casts a revealing light on the attitudes of Hellenistic Jews toward sacred texts.[12] Artapanos is not content with the image of Moses as rescuer of the Hebrews from Egypt, leader of the flock, and lawgiver of the nation. Instead, his Moses takes on an international stature, hailed by the Greeks as Mousaios, their legendary father of poetry and music, and given credit for inaugurating the Egyptian system of nomes as administrative districts, for allocating land and sacred writings to the priests, and even for assigning the deities to be worshipped in each location – including cats, dogs, and ibises (Euseb. *PE*, 9.27.3–4). Artapanos, unrestrained by text or tradition, turns Moses into a military hero as well as a purveyor of culture. Moses, in Artapanos' presentation, conducts a ten-year campaign, on the model of the Trojan War, against the Ethiopians, whom he conquers while at the same time obtaining their approbation, even introducing them to the practice of circumcision – which they eagerly embrace (Euseb. *PE*, 9.27.7–10). That piece of gratuitous whimsy gives some insight into the playful character of Artapanos' composition, which has Moses bring hieroglyphics and animal worship to the Egyptians but never mentions his role as lawgiver for the Hebrews. And there is much more in this inventive text than I have space

---

[12] See the discussion of Artapanos and his whimsicality by Gruen (2015), 31–44.

to recount (Euseb. *PE*, 9.27.11–22). The Scriptures, as we know them, supplied little more than a springboard for inventive imagination.

Artapanos' work was no theological tract aimed at harmonizing the religions or promoting tolerance, as it is sometimes adjudged. It was an entertaining rendition of the Exodus story that fits into the tradition of Jewish writers who regarded the historical craft as a creative enterprise that could reinvigorate biblical narratives for a Hellenistic readership.

Nor was this true of historians alone. Tragic drama could also serve this function. We have a substantial portion of a remarkable work of this genre, the *Exagoge* or *Exodus*, composed in Greek by a certain Ezekiel some time between the late third and early first centuries BCE. Of the author we know little more than his name. But the *Exagoge* was only one of several tragedies that Ezekiel wrote, although the others have sadly disappeared. That information, however, is enough to show that tragic drama in Greek mode had a following of some significance among Hellenistic Jews.[13]

Ezekiel hewed closely to the narrative line contained in the Book of Exodus. But his drama was more than just an adaptation for the stage of the familiar story. Among other things, Ezekiel added a remarkable scene which has no biblical analogue. He has Moses report a dream in which he had a vision of a great throne high upon a summit extending to the cleft of heaven. Upon it sat a noble figure wearing a diadem and wielding a scepter. That imposing figure then handed the diadem and scepter to Moses, descended from the throne, and departed. Moses now had a panoramic view of earth and sky, with the stars falling on their knees before him. The dream then received an interpretation by Moses' father-in-law, who reassured him that this dream was a sign from God that Moses will lift up a great throne, will issue judgments, and will serve as a guide to mortals (Euseb. *PE*, 9.29.4–6).[14] This stunning image corresponds to nothing in the Book of Exodus. Indeed, no other tale anywhere in literature ascribes a dream vision to Moses. And certainly nowhere else does God relinquish his seat in the heavens to anyone. Ezekiel obviously wanted to capture his readers' attention here. The playwright had an arresting and powerful scene in mind: the forecast of Moses' future through a dramatic dream that gave him access to divinity. Moses will be executor of God's will on earth, with absolute authority, on the model of Hellenistic kings.

Ezekiel thus applied the standard conventions of Greek drama to a Jewish theme presented in an altogether unique scenario. Is this heresy? Ezekiel nowhere

---

13 See the excellent study of the *Exagoge* by Jacobson (1983).
14 Jacobson (1983), 89–97, provides valuable parallels for the several parts of the scene, but leaves little room for Ezekiel's originality.

disputes or denies the biblical account. Moses as prophet has scriptural roots in his final forecasts before death at the conclusion of Deuteronomy. But Ezekiel raised this to a new level, dramatized by the vast sweep of Moses' vista when set upon God's throne. He draped Moses in the emblems of royal power that would resonate with those who lived in the era of the great Hellenistic monarchies. The Israelite hero thus becomes a beacon for humankind, a representative of the divinity on earth, described in phraseology that struck responsive chords among Ezekiel's Hellenic or Hellenized compatriots. There is little reason to think, however, that his Jewish readership would have found this offensive or heretical. The tragic poet held scriptural authority in awe. But that did not prevent him from occasionally improving upon it.

One final illustration is particularly noteworthy. As everyone knows, the Scroll of Esther in its Hebrew version conspicuously leaves out God. Esther and Mordecai are on their own against the wicked Haman and the buffoonish Ahasuerus. The text makes no allusion to religious tenets, beliefs, or practices. Divine authority is starkly and startlingly absent. As is also well known, the Book of Esther is the one canonical text that fails to appear at Qumran – very possibly because God is absent. Maybe so. But the denizens of Qumran were not the only ones to notice this yawning gap. When the work surfaced in a Greek translation in the late Hellenistic period, it contained some quite fascinating and surprising additions. Two of them supplied a dream of Mordecai and its interpretation (Esther Add. A, F). Two others purported to be documents issued by the Persian king, the first authorizing extermination of the Jews, the second rescinding the order (Esther Add. B, E). And there were still two other insertions, one of which records the prayers of Mordecai and Esther prior to Esther's audience before the king, and the second records the audience itself (Esther Add. C, D).

The additions accord a very different flavor to the story. The Hebrew version conveyed a straightforward tale of intrigue at the Persian court in which the virtuous Jew and Jewess triumphed over their villainous antagonist, and the God of the Hebrews had no hand in the proceedings. The additions, however, reinstate Yahweh, and infuse spirituality into Mordecai and Esther with undeviating devoutness. While the Hebrew text furnishes the setting for the festival of Purim, a lively and largely secular celebration, the supplements in the Greek Esther leave Purim out of the account and bring spiritual considerations to the forefront. The additions stress the religiosity of the hero and heroine and have the Lord intervene to assure the victory of Jewish piety over its enemies.[15] The most arresting

---

[15] On the character of the work, see Moore (1977), 153–168; Wills (1995), 116–131; Koller (2014), 113–123.

feature here surely is that the insertions into the text come from the thoroughly Hellenized Jewish community, who felt that the scriptural text failed to transmit the essential sanctity of the nation. So, what constitutes the norm and what the heterodoxy here? The Greek Esther and its additions turn the whole construct on its head.

These fascinating insertions convey more than just pious pronouncements. The additions exhibit considerable creativity. The directives of Ahasuerus, first to eradicate, then to spare, the Jews, are presented as official documents, but in fact are filled with overblown rhetoric and bombast. Among other things, the king, after the scales fell from his eyes, proceeds to lavish praise upon the Jews, calling them children of the highest and greatest living god, and sanctioning the new festival of Purim as the order of God – the very festival that has virtually no religious overtones (Esther Add. E:15–24). The author here not only restores religion, but renders the monarch ridiculous. Further, the dream of Mordecai, also an addition to the original, conveys a titanic battle between two dragons, with natural and supernatural signs of cosmic clash between the nations, contributing an element of apocalyptic fantasy, quite out of tune with the rest of the text (Esther Add. A:4–10).

The author also has no hesitation in radical refashioning of Esther herself. The celebrated scene in which she finally approaches Ahasuerus in order to save her people is drastically revised. Her effort is preceded by a pleading prayer to God by Mordecai, who praises the Lord's power and authority and begs for his intervention to protect Esther and the nation itself, a prayer nowhere evident in the Hebrew version. As for Esther, the Bible accords her the famously courageous statement before confronting the king: "if I perish, I perish" (Esther 4:16). Nothing like that is in the additions. On the contrary, they have her petrified in the preliminaries to the visit, stripping herself of her splendid garments, covering herself with ashes and dung, and uttering an abject entreaty to God to forgive the sins of his people (Esther Add. C:12–22). She confesses sins of her own but tries, rather clumsily, to explain them away. Yes, she concedes, I slept with the uncircumcised king – but I hated every minute of it. Yes, I wear a crown, but only in public and only because I have to; in fact, I despise it, and never put it on when I am off duty (Esther Add. C:26–27). The author plainly exposes Esther's discomforting compromises and self-consciousness. And when she does finally enter into Ahasuerus' chamber, far from doing so boldly and confidently, she is racked with fear, and, once the king casts an angry glance at her, she passes out on the spot. She has to be revived – only to faint once again (Esther Add. D:1–15). This is not the stuff of which a heroine is made. The interpolator augmented the tale at both Mordecai's and Esther's expense. They are not in control. Only the Lord determines events. The two Jewish characters, who simply outwit Haman through their own resources in the canonical tale, become devotees of the divinity in the Greek additions and owe their success only to his intervention.

The Greek additions to the Book of Esther offer a quite intriguing instance of amending a scriptural narrative. Far from infecting it with a heretical element, they inoculate the tale with a heavy dose of traditional religion. The power of God is appealed to repeatedly in the prayers, given shape in the dream and its interpretation, and acknowledged even by the Persian king. Esther and Mordecai gain their ends through the intervention of the Lord, and the whole narrative takes on a pious, even hyper-pious, character.

To conclude: the tensions that we might feel about divergences from scriptural texts evidently did not disturb the consciences of Jewish Hellenistic writers. None of them claimed to replace or supplant a sacred original. Their works served as supplements, expansions, or revised reproductions, designed to accompany received texts or to offer novel ways of looking at them, but not to substitute for them or to supersede them. When Josephus declared his faithfulness to the Scriptures, he engaged in no deception, not even self-deception. His was a reproduction, not a replication. And those who had been familiar with "rewritten Bibles," in various languages, for many generations would have fully understood him. Their stories ran parallel with scriptural narratives, but possessed a life of their own. They did not engage in exegesis or midrash. Nor did they see their mission primarily as setting the record straight. They provided arresting twists on traditional tales, alternative versions, provocative variations, and, very frequently, engaging aberrations. The sacred nature of the Scriptures was never at issue. It remained unscathed.

In short, neither norm nor heterodoxy characterized the fluid cultural world of Second Temple Judaism. When texts multiplied and traditions took manifold forms and shapes, those terms are simply inapplicable. The introduction of Hellenism into the mix injected no alien element. It brought heterogeneity, not heterodoxy. Indeed, it enriched the tradition through diversification, expansion – and even entertainment.

Bibliography

Alexander, Philip. "Retelling the Old Testament." *It is Written: Scripture Citing Scripture*. Eds. D.A. Carson and H.G.M. Williamson. Cambridge: Cambridge University Press, 1988. 99–121.
Arnold, Matthew. *Culture and Anarchy*. 1869. Ann Arbor: University of Michigan Press, 1965.
Atkinson, Kenneth. *A History of the Hasmonean State: Josephus and Beyond*. London: Bloomsbury, 2016.

Barclay, John M.G. *Flavius Josephus, Translation and Commentary*. Vol. 10: *Against Apion*. Leiden: Brill, 2007.
Bernhardt, Johannes Christian. *Die jüdische Revolution: Untersuchungen zu Ursachen, Verlauf, und Folgen der hasmonäischen Erhebung*. Berlin: De Gruyter, 2017.
Bernstein, Moshe J. "'Rewritten Bible': A Generic Category Which Has Outlived its Usefulness?" *Textus* 22 (2005): 169–196.
Berthelot, Katell. *In Search of the Promised Land? The Hasmonean Dynasty Between Biblical Models and Hellenistic Diplomacy*. Göttingen: Vandenhoeck & Ruprecht, 2018.
Collins, John, J. *Between Athens and Jerusalem: Jewish Identity in the Hellenistic Diaspora*. 2nd ed. Grand Rapids: Dove, 2000.
Collins, John, J. *Jewish Cult and Hellenistic Culture: Essays on the Jewish Encounter with Hellenism and Roman Rule*. Leiden: Brill, 2005.
Crawford, Sidnie White. *Rewriting Scripture in Second Temple Times*. Grand Rapids: William B. Eerdmans, 2008.
Droysen, Johann Gustav. *Geschichte des Hellenismus*. 1843. Munich: Deutscher Taschenbuch, 1980.
Eshel, Ḥanan. *The Dead Sea Scrolls and the Hasmonean State*. Grand Rapids: William B. Eerdmans, 2008.
Feldman, Louis H. *Jew and Gentile in the Ancient World*. Princeton: Princeton University Press, 1998.
Feldman, Louis H. *Flavius Josephus, Translation and Commentary*. Vol. 3: *Judaean Antiquities, 1–4*. Leiden: Brill, 2000.
Freudenthal, Jacob. *Alexander Polyhistor*. Breslau: H. Skutsch, 1874/1875.
Goldstein, Jonathan. "Jewish Acceptance and Rejection of Hellenism." *Jewish and Christian Self-Definition*. Ed. E.P. Sanders. Philadelphia: Fortress Press, 1981. 64–87.
Gruen, Erich S. *Heritage and Hellenism: The Reinvention of Jewish Tradition*. Berkeley: University of California Press, 1998.
Gruen, Erich S. "The Twisted Tales of Artapanus: Biblical Rewritings as Novelistic Narrative." *Early Christian and Jewish Narrative: The Role of Religion in Shaping Narrative Forms*. Eds. Ilaria Ramelli and Judith Perkins. Tübingen: Mohr Siebeck, 2015. 31–44.
Halpern-Amaru, Betsy. *Rewriting the Bible: Land and Covenant in Postbiblical Literature*. Valley Forge: Trinity Press International, 1994.
Harrington, Daniel J. "Palestinian Adaptations of Biblical Narratives." *Early Judaism and its Modern Interpreters*. Eds. Robert A. Kraft and George W.E. Nickelsburg. Atlanta: Scholars Press, 1986. 239–247.
Heine, Heinrich. *Sämtliche Werke*. Munich: Kindler Verlag, 1961–1964.
Hengel, Martin. *Judaism and Hellenism*. Trans. John Bowden. London: SCM Press, 1974.
Holladay, Carl. *Fragments from Hellenistic Jewish Authors*. Vol. 1: *Historians*. Chico: Scholars Press, 1983.
Inowlocki, Sabrina. "Neither Adding nor Omitting Anything: Josephus' Promise not to Modify the Scriptures in Greek and Latin Context." *Journal of Jewish Studies* 56.1 (2005): 48–65.
Jacobson, Howard. *The Exagoge of Ezekiel*. Cambridge: Cambridge University Press, 1983.
Koller, Aaron J. *Esther in Ancient Jewish Thought*. Cambridge: Cambridge University Press, 2014.
Kugel, James L. "The Beginnings of Biblical Interpretation." *A Companion to Biblical Interpretation*. Ed. Matthias Henze. Grand Rapids: William B. Eerdmans, 2012. 3–23.
Levine, Lee. *Judaism and Hellenism in Antiquity: Conflict or Confluence*. Seattle: University of Washington Press, 1998.

Mendels, Doron. *The Land of Israel as a Political Concept in Hasmonean Literature*. Tübingen: Mohr Siebeck, 1987.
Moore, Carey A. *Daniel, Esther and Jeremiah: The Additions*. Garden City: Doubleday, 1977.
Mroczek, Eva. *The Literary Imagination in Jewish Antiquity*. Oxford: Oxford University Press, 2016.
Najman, Hindy. *Seconding Sinai: The Development of Mosaic Discourse in Second Temple Judaism*. Leiden: Brill, 2003.
Nickelsburg, George W.E. "The Bible Rewritten and Expanded." *Jewish Writings of the Second Temple Period*. Ed. Michael E. Stone. Philadelphia: Fortress Press, 1984. 89–156.
Rajak, Tessa. *The Jewish Dialogue with Greece and Rome: Studies in Cultural and Social Interaction*. Leiden: Brill, 2000.
Regev, Eyal. *The Hasmoneans: Ideology, Anthropology, Identity*. Göttingen: Vandenhoeck & Ruprecht, 2013.
Seeman, Chris. *Rome and Judea in Transition: Hasmonean Relations with the Roman Republic and the Evolution of the High Priesthood*. New York: Peter Lang, 2013.
Sterling, Gregory E. *Historiography and Self-Definition: Josephus, Luke-Acts, and Apologetic Historiography*. Leiden: Brill, 1992.
Vermes, Géza. *Scripture and Tradition in Judaism*. Leiden: Brill, 1961.
Wacholder, Ben Zion. *Eupolemus: A Study of Judaeo-Greek Literature*. Cincinnati: Hebrew Union College-Jewish Institute of Religion, 1974.
Will, Edouard, and Claude Orrieux. *Ioudaismos-Hellènismos: Essai sur judaisme judéen à l'époque hellénistique*. Nancy: Presses universitaires de Nancy, 1986.
Wills, Lawrence M. *The Jewish Novel in the Ancient World*. Ithaca: Cornell University Press, 1995.
Wright, Benjamin G. *The Letter of Aristeas: Aristeas to Philocrates or On the Translation of the Law of the Jews*. Berlin: De Gruyter, 2015.
Zahn, Molly M. "Genre and Rewritten Scripture: A Reassessment." *JBL* 131 (2012): 271–288.

Adiel Schremer
Negotiating Heresy: Belief and Identity in Early Rabbinic Literature

Heresy is a label. It is a pejorative term of opprobrium used by some members of a community to delegitimize and deny membership from other members of that community by attaching to them that tag, thus constructing them as deviants and "others".[1] As such, heresy is an important social category, for its very employment enables us to gaze at those issues which are considered determinative for belonging by those who use it in a given society. However, of the endless possible issues in relation to which one can be considered by others as deviating from the accepted social norms, heresy has to do specifically with creedal matters. The heretic is he or she who, according to the opinion of some members of society, espouses "thoughts", "views", and "beliefs" that are considered different (and therefore wrong and illegitimate) from those held by most members of that society.[2] Hence, the marking (in order to deny membership) of some members of a given group specifically by the employment of the category "heretics" indicates that for the speaker belief is the main constituent of the collective identity of his or her community.

---

[1] For a general discussion of social labeling and the labeling theory, see: Gove 1975, 3–20; Sumner 1994, 197–248.

[2] This is the foundation, to give but one example, of a statement such as Petri Luomanen and Antti Marjanen's, in the introduction to their co-edited *A Companion to Second-Century Christian 'Heretics'*: "Bardaisan's *thoughts* have to be gleaned from the Book of the Laws of the Countries ... Basilides', Marcion's, Valentinus', and the Montanists' ... *views* can be painted ... Cerinthus' *ideas* can also be reconstructed ... Although a scholar who aims at a historical-critical reconstruction of the original *ideas* and teachings of 'heretics' like these faces difficulties, the task is by no means impossible. The chapters in this book show that after a careful assessment of the source materials, some distinctive *ideas* of these alternative second-century Christian movements can be delineated." See: Marjanen and Luomanen 2005, ix–x (emphasis added). Indeed, as Maureen Tilley has written: "heresy has to do with creedal matters, with believing wrongly." See: Tilley 2007, 3. Cf. Cameron 2008, 106, n. 19.

Note: Parts of this paper appear (in a different and much lengthier form) in my paper, "Thinking about Belonging in Early Rabbinic Literature: Proselytes, Apostates, and 'Children of Israel,' or: Does Is Make Sense to Speak of Early Rabbinic Orthodoxy?", *Journal for the Study of Judaism* 43 (2012), pp. 249–275. The focus and the conceptual framework of the present study are different than those of its remote antecedent.

As Donald Lopez has written, "making belief the measure of what religion is understood to be" is a characteristically Christian outlook (1998, 33).³ It is not a coincidence, therefore, that in the history of Christianity "heresy" has been so central a category to the degree that, as David Christie-Murray has written, "To write the history of Christian heresy adequately would be to compile a complete Church history" (1976, vii). The discursive combat against theological deviants developed among the early Church Fathers from the very early centuries of the Christian Era, and it is now accepted wisdom that it was a central factor in the development of Christianity from its very early stages.⁴ This indicates that belief was understood by Christian writers as the main constituent of Christian identity.⁵

Was rabbinic Judaism a religious tradition that, like early Christianity, considered belief as the core of its identity? Because rabbinic Judaism developed in chronological and geographical proximity to early Christianity, it is probably not a coincidence that some modern scholars answer this question in the affirmative.⁶ As has been noted by Wayne Meeks, "Christian scholars tend to think of group identity in terms of theological systems or 'confessions', and in spite of our best intentions, we almost inevitably ask Christian theological questions of Jewish documents" (1985, 108–109). In this paper I wish to challenge this methodological and conceptual widespread approach. Focusing on the earliest documents of rabbinic Judaism – the Mishnah, the Tosefta, and the so-called Halakhic Midrashim – which were compiled and edited in the third century CE, I shall argue that the place of heresy in shaping Jewish identity was limited, and heresy occupied only a very modest place in the religious thought of the rabbis of the first, second, and early third centuries CE. This indicates that for the early rabbis belief was not the core of Jewish identity.

My point of departure is terminological: the Greek word "αιρεσίς" (heresy) does not appear in classical rabbinic literature in any form.⁷ True, it is frequently claimed that the Hebrew word "*minut*", which does occur in classical rabbinic

---

3 See also McCarthy 2009.
4 The literature on heresy and heresiology in early Christianity is immense. For a good summary see: Lyman 2007; Iricinschi and Zellentin 2008.
5 For this reason, the second-century-CE Church Father Irenaeus of Lyons (as quoted by Eusebius of Caesarea, *Church History*, 5.24.13) did not find disagreement between different Christians concerning the precise date of Lent as threatening Christian unity, for: "The disagreement in the fast confirms our agreement in the faith." Cf. Petersen 1992, 316–317; Alexander 2008, 46–49.
6 See Schremer 2012, 249–253.
7 Only in the late medieval period did heresy enter into Hebrew texts, in the form of *harissa* (הריסה), the literal meaning of which is "destruction". See: Gries 1987.

texts, should be understood as its rabbinic equivalent (and hence *minim* should be translated as "heretics").[8] The problem with this assumption is that the etymology of *minut* (and *minim*) is not truly known,[9] so its relation to "heresy" necessarily derives from an a priori assumption concerning the meaning of *minut* as "a flaw in the doctrine of God" (Boyarin 2004a, 131),[10] an assumption that in fact has never been established. Were we even to accept the view that *minut* is indeed the rabbinic equivalent of "heresy" (as used by early Church Fathers),[11] one could not deny that it is mentioned very rarely in early rabbinic literature: it is found only in five places in the entire Tannaitic corpus.[12] To be sure, *minim* (the plural form of *min*), which is the noun associated with *minut*, appears more frequently in Tannaitic literature;[13] however, as Shaye Cohen has recently emphasized, a

---

8 See, for example, the oft-cited Sperber 1971. Daniel Boyarin expressed this claim in the clearest possible manner when he wrote that: "the concept of *minut* [is] the rabbinic equivalent to heresy" (2004a, 74). (And already above, at page 45: "*minim* and *minut* [heretics and heresy]".) Similarly, Ruth Langer has written: "Rabbinic discussions of *minim* ... suggest that what was suspicious was the *min's* theology; the term thus would mean 'heretic', or 'sectarian'" (2012, 22). And so too wrote Shaye Cohen: "Here in translation is the text of all Mishnaic references to *min*, 'heretic', *minim*, 'heretics', and *minut*, 'heresy'" (2017, 318). This is a widely held view.
9 As correctly noted by Langer (2012), "The term itself tells us nothing, as the word simply means 'types', or 'kinds'" (22, echoing Simon 1996, 181). Saul Lieberman maintained that *min* is actually an ellipsis and should be understood as: "other type" (ואף 'מינא', 'מיניי', פירושו מין אחר, שהולך בדרך אחרת) (Rosenthal and Lieberman 1983, 206, n. 1). Lieberman may have had in mind *Sifre Deuteronomy* 218 (Finkelstein 1969, 251): "*min* is he who rules for himself a different way (מין שמורה לעצמו דרך אחרת)" (he mentions this text in his discussion of *t. Berakhot* 6:6 – "this is a different way" – in Lieberman 1955–1988b, 1.111). However, such a reading in the *Sifre* is unattested by any text-witness. See Finkelstein's comment, ad loc., and Epstein 1988, 2.897. Recently, Robert Brody suggested that: "The traditional understanding of *minim* as heretics finds support in etymological data ... the root *m-y-n* means, in Arabic and Ethiopic, 'to lie', or 'to falsify'" (2017, 283). Surprisingly, Brody did not cite, as a support of his suggested etymology, the passage in *Mekhilta de-Rabbi Ishmael, Kaspa*, 20 (Horovitz and Rabin 1970, 327), in which Rabbi Nathan comments on Ex. 23:7, "Keep yourself far from a false matter" (מדבר שקר תרחק), and sees this as "a warning to separate from *minut*". However, Brody's following proposal, "that *minim* are those who, in the opinion of the rabbis misrepresent the true nature of God by denying the principle of monotheism" (2017, 283–284), seems to rest on a partial treatment of the early rabbinic material and it does not represent it adequately. See: Schremer 2013.
10 = Boyarin 2004b, 335.
11 An attempt to problematize this assumption can be found in Schremer 2013.
12 See: *m. Megillah* 4:8–9; *t. Hullin* 2:24; *Mekhilta de-Rabbi Ishmael, Kaspa*, 20; and *Sifre Numbers* 115. It is mentioned also in a well-known passage in *m. Sottah*. 9:15, but that passage is a later gloss, not a genuine part of the Mishnah. See Epstein 1964, 976. See also: *Avot de-Rabbi Nathan*, Version B, chapter 3 (ed. Schechter, 13).
13 For a survey of this material see Schremer 2013.

collection of all references to *minim* in the Mishnah and the Tosefta yields a very modest corpus, "barely equal in length one typical Mishna chapter" (2017, 320).[14]

From the available evidence it appears, then, that in contrast to their Christian counterparts, the rabbis of the first, second and early third centuries did not seem to have been engaged in any systematic attempt to define and refute heresy.[15] No rabbinic work "against heretics" has ever been composed, and no "Irenaeus", "Tertullian", or an "Epiphanius" – some of the Church Fathers whose works "against heretics" have survived and came down to us – is known to have ever existed among the early rabbis.

1 Belief and Belonging

"Heresy" was a major category used by the Fathers of the Church to establish boundaries within and thus to decide matters of belonging, that is to declare who is in and who is out (King 2003, 24). In sharp contrast, when Palestinian rabbis of the second and early third centuries CE discussed the question of belonging they did not raise belief as a category relevant to the discussion at all. The only two options they considered were either that of belonging through lineage and belonging by means of adherence to the covenant; that is, the Torah and the commandments. Correct belief, as a category determining belonging, was not even raised in these contexts.

A passage from the early rabbinic midrash on the biblical book of Leviticus, the *Sifra*, is instructive in this context and it therefore deserves a close reading. On the words of Lev. 1:2, "Speak to the people of Israel and say to them, When any man of you brings an offering to the Lord", we find in the *Sifra* the following interpretive discussion:

[A] "Speak to the children of Israel ... he shall lay his hand" (Lev. 1:2–4) – the children of Israel lay their hands [upon the head of the burnt offering], the gentiles do not lay their hands ...

---

[14] The addition of the references to *minim* and *minut* found in all other rabbinic works of roughly the same period (that is, the Tannaitic midrashic compilations) does not change the picture in any significant manner.

[15] Cf. Martin Goodman's correct observation that Palestinian rabbis of the Tannaitic period (that is, late first to early third century CE) "do not seem to have been concerned much of the time either to analyse [sic] the precise constituents of *minuth* [sic], or to define their own views in contrast to heresies ... Despite their general interest in the classification of phenomena in the world about them the rabbis do not seem from the extant evidence to have been concerned to define *minim* or *minuth*; it was enough that the general category existed" (1996, 506–507).

[B] "Children of Israel" – [sons of Israel] lay their hands [upon the head of the burnt offering], daughters of Israel do not lay their hands …
[C] "Any man" (Lev. 1:2) – this incorporates the proselytes.
[D] "Of you" (Lev. 1:2) – this excludes the apostates.
[E] What brings you to say so, "Any man" incorporates the proselytes; "Of you" excludes the apostates? After Scripture used a broad term it used a narrow term!
[F] Scripture teaches: "Sons of Israel."
[G] What characterizes "Israel" is that they accept the yoke of the covenant, this includes the proselytes, who accept the yoke of the covenant, and excludes the apostates, for they do not accept the yoke of the covenant.
[H] Perhaps [you should say]: What characterizes "Israel" is that they are the descendants of those who accepted the yoke of the covenant, and this includes the apostates, for they are the descendants of those who accepted the yoke of the covenant, but excludes the proselytes, for they are not the descendants of those who accepted the yoke of the covenant?
[I] Scripture teaches: "Of you." Therefore do not conclude so, but [as we said first]: What characterizes "Israel" is that they accept the yoke of the covenant, this includes the proselytes, who accept the yoke of the covenant, and excludes the apostates, for they do not accept the yoke of the covenant.
[J] And so does Scripture say: "The sacrifice of the wicked is an abomination, how much more when he brings it with evil intent" (Prov. 21:27).[16]

The interpretive question guiding this passage's treatment of the biblical verse is: what is the relation between the different group designations mentioned therein, "The children of Israel"; "a man"; "of you"? The midrash begins with emphasizing, in [A], that the group designation "children of Israel" indicates that Scripture excluded non-Jews, as a gentile is not part of "Israel". This leads the midrash, in [B], to assert that likewise a female Israelite is not included in the commandment under discussion, because females are not included in the term "children of Israel".[17]

While a reading of the biblical phrase "children of Israel" as excluding female Israelites is quite rare in Tannaitic literature,[18] the *Sifra's* understanding of that

---

[16] *Sifra, Nedava*, 2 (Finkelstein 1983–1990, 2.20–21). Compare *y. Sheqalim*, 1:5, 46b; *b. Eruvin* 69b; *b. Hullin* 5a.
[17] Underlying this interpretation is a strict literal reading of the construct form בני ישראל, according to which its meaning is specifically "sons of Israel". For this reason, the homilist concludes that the phrase excludes "daughters of Israel"; that is, female Israelites.
[18] The only other place in *Tannaitic* works known to me, where the biblical phrase "children of Israel" is taken to imply an exclusion of female Israelites, is *Sifra, Tzav* 11:11: בני ישראל מניפים אין בנות ישראל מניפות ("[Male] Children of Israel wave, daughters of Israel do not wave").

phrase as excluding non-Jews is very common. In numerous cases Scripture's use of the phrase "children of Israel" is read by early, Tannaitic works as intending to exclude non-Israelites from the realm of the commandment under discussion. As the phrase is read by these midrashic works in a strict, literal manner, it is frequently understood in a narrow, genealogical sense. As a result, the group designated by the phrase "children of Israel" is understood to refer specifically to those who bear a status of Israelites on account of their birth, to the exclusion of other members in the Jewish community, who joined the Jewish people in other ways (whether by choice, or by force); that is, proselytes.[19]

The widespread understanding, shared by Tannaitic biblical interpretation, that proselytes are not included in the biblical category "children of Israel" (though they belong in the community) operates in our case as well. Having stated that gentiles and women are excluded, the *Sifra* maintains, in [C], that the phrase "any man" (אדם) in Lev. 1:2 indicates that Scripture refers to *any* (male) member of the Jewish community; that is, not only to native-born Israelites, but to proselytes as well.

What, then, is the legal function of the following phrase in the biblical verse, "of you" (מכם)? As Scripture's use of the plural personal pronoun, "you", in legal contexts is frequently understood by Tannaitic midrash as an address to the Jewish community as a group,[20] the *Sifra* suggests, in [D], that this phrase

---

19 See, for example, *Sifra, Hova*, 1:1 (Finkelstein 1983–1990, 118); ibid., *Tzav*, 10:1; ibid., *Zavim (Metzora)*, 1:1; ibid., *Aharei Mot*, 6:6; ibid., *Emor*, 11:11; *Sifre Zutta on Numbers* 5:6; 5:12; 6:2; 9:10 (Horovitz 1966, 230; 232; 239; 259). Cf. Finkelstein 1983–1990, 4.21. Tannaitic interpretation, in these cases, does not attempt to exempt proselytes from the duty to fulfill the commandments; rather it argues that the phrase "children of Israel" cannot carry the burden of indicating that proselytes are included in those to whom Scripture refers. For this reason Tannaitic interpretation seeks, in these cases, another verse, or another phrase, that would enable and justify (in the interpreter's view) an inclusionary approach, so as to arrive at the conclusion that the commandment under discussion applies to proselytes as well. Thus, for example, the *Sifre Zutta* on Numbers 5:12 (Horovitz 1966, 232) reads the biblical phrase "children of Israel" in that verse as excluding non-Jews. This, however, gives rise to the possibility that proselytes too are excluded, because proselytes are not understood by the midrash as belonging in the biblical category of "children of Israel." For this reason, the midrash finds a different phrase that enables the inclusion of the proselyte.

20 See, for example, *Mekhilta de-Rabbi Ishmael, Pisha*, 1 (Horovitz and Rabin 1970, 7); ibid., 7 (Horovitz and Rabin, 24); ibid., 9 (Horovitz and Rabin, 32); *Mekhilta de-Rabbi Shimon bar Yochai* on Ex. 12:16 (Epstein and Melamed 1979, 21); *Sifra, Ahrei Mot*, 5:7; ibid., 8:8; ibid., 10:10; *Sifra, Behar*, 1:1. See also *t. Bikkurim* 1:2 (Lieberman 1955–1988a, 2.286), in which the precise wording of Num. 10:32 ("and if you go *with us*" [עמנו]) is used as a basis for the halakhic stance that includes Kenites within the Jewish community (compare, however, Lieberman 1955–1988b, 2.825–827]). See also *m. Sheqalim* 1:5.

should be understood in a restrictive manner, and accordingly be interpreted as indicating that in fact not "any man" is included, for some are excluded. There are some Jews, claims the *Sifra*, who belong in the category of "children of Israel" but nevertheless are excluded here by Scripture. These are the apostates (משומדים).[21]

Although possible, this reading is not conclusive. It is true that the phrase "any man" may indeed be understood as having an inclusionary function, and the phrase "of you" as having an exclusionary meaning; however, nothing in these phrases themselves forces us to assume that the former refers to proselytes while the latter refers to apostates. The entire opposite could well have been suggested! This is, indeed, the homilist's question, in [E]: "What brings you to say so, 'Any man' incorporates the proselytes; 'Of you' excludes the apostates?" Scripture, claims the homilist, merely used a broad, inclusionary phrase ("any man") and a narrowing, exclusionary one ("of you"), without attaching any specific meaning to either one of them. Why, then, should we accept the reading that includes proselytes and excludes apostates? Perhaps the Torah should be understood in the opposite way?

The *Sifra* answers this question, in [F], by reference to the category of "children of Israel", mentioned in the interpreted verse (Lev. 1:2). This phrase, the *Sifra* now claims, in [G], refers specifically to those who "accept the yoke of the covenant", because *what characterizes "Israel"*, more than anything else, is the adherence to the Law.[22] For this reason, it is to be assumed that the Torah meant to include the proselytes, as they adhere to the covenant, and not the apostates, who do not accept its yoke upon themselves. The homilist's interpretation ("'Any man' incorporates the proselytes; 'Of you' excludes the apostates") is thus maintained.

---

[21] To the best of my knowledge there exists in Tannaitic literature no clear definition of the apostate. The closest that we have is *t. Horayot* 1:5 (Zuckermandel 1970, 474): "He who eats abominations, lo, this one is an apostate. [If] he ate carrion and *treifah*, abominations and creeping things [...?] he who eats pig-meat and he who drinks libation-wine, he who desecrates the Sabbath, and he who draws up the foreskin, Rabbi Yossi ben Rabbi Yehuda says, also he who is clothed in mixed species." The text seems corrupt, but its main message is clear enough. On the etymology of the term see Lieberman 1965, 531–532; Lieberman 1955–1988b, 3.402, n. 45. See also Milikowsky 1986, 332–333, and recently Brody 2017, 284–285.

[22] "The Covenant means nothing but the Torah, as it is said: 'These are the words of the covenant which the lord commanded Moses' (Deut. 28:69). He [Moses] said to them [to the Israelites]: withdraw your hands from idolatry, and adhere to the commandments" (*Mekhilta de-Rabbi Ishmael, Pisha*, 5 [Horovitz and Rabin 1970, 15]). On the concept of the covenant in rabbinic literature see also: Nitzan 2014, 186–188 (this section does not appear in the earlier English version of that article: Nitzan 2001).

The homily could have ended here; however, it does not. The *Sifra* proceeds, in [H], to challenge its own assumption, expressed in the previous section, [G], that what characterizes "Israel" is the acceptance of the yoke of the covenant: "Perhaps what characterizes 'Israel' is that they are the *descendants* of those who accepted the yoke of the covenant?". The implication of such an alternative reading would obviously be that the Torah "includes the apostates, for they are the descendants of those who accepted the yoke of the covenant, but excludes the proselytes, for they are not the descendants of those who accepted the yoke of the covenant". This alternative suggestion, which lays emphasis on *descent* as the pivotal, determinative issue for belonging, is, in fact, in line with the *Sifra's* own interpretive assumption, operating, as we have seen, throughout the midrash, namely that the biblical phrase "children of Israel" should be understood as a genealogical term. The *Sifra*, however, refuses to follow this path. Instead, it insists, in [I], that the phrase "of you" (מכם) is the decisive linguistic point in the biblical verse, which creates the preference for the former line of interpretation.[23]

Two competing answers to the question of belonging in the Jewish people are present in this homily. The first lays emphasis on descent and genealogy, and it characterizes the group called "the Jewish people" as the group of those who are of Jewish ancestry. Regardless of one's manners and way of life, one is considered a Jew if one was born to Jewish parents. In contrast, the other answer characterizes the "Jewish people" as those who adhere to the covenant; that is, the Torah and its legal demands.[24] One might cease to be regarded a member of that group if

---

[23] The logic is that, since we work under the assumption that "children of Israel" is a genealogical term, which, by its standard midrashic meaning, does not include proselytes, one cannot exclude the proselytes without, first, providing a reason to include them. Put differently: if, as the alternative reading [H] suggests, "any man" should not be understood as including the proselytes, but rather as including the apostates, what else in the biblical verse would make us assume, in the first place, that proselytes are "in", so that Scripture needs to say "of you" in order to make clear that they are "out"? Apostates, in contrast, are Jews by birth, and therefore they are intuitively included in "children of Israel." To claim that "of you" is meant to exclude them poses, therefore, no interpretive difficulty, and it is for this reason that the first interpretive suggestion [C–D] should be preferred over the latter [H]. As a final support for this conclusion the homilist quotes, in [J], Prov. 21:27, which states explicitly, as it were, that sacrifices brought by apostates are not wanted, as it says that a sacrifice brought by an "evil person" is considered abomination. This verse supports, then, the homilist's hermeneutical procedure, in which he attempted to establish that apostates are excluded from the realm of the biblical commandment under discussion. Compare: Finkelstein 1950, 226–227, n. 4.
[24] Cf. Schwartz 1992, 5–15; Schwartz 1990a; Cohen 1999, 109–139.

one does not follow the Law and does not fulfill the commandments, even if that person is of an Israelite lineage.[25]

The *Sifra* clearly follows the view that the most important identity marker of the Jewish people is their adherence to the covenant, in agreement with the central line of rabbinic thought,[26] at least with respect to the status of proselytes.[27] It says nothing, however, about belief! When the *Sifra* "reflects" upon the question of belonging in the people of Israel, beliefs are simply not being considered. It is not that beliefs have no value; it is simply that *beliefs are out of the orbit of the midrash*. Heretics are simply not brought up. What might cause one to be

---

[25] This same logic underlies the *Mekhilta de-Rabbi Ishmael's* interpretation of the biblical phrase, "foreigner" (בן נכר), in Ex. 12:43, as referring to an apostate Jew: " 'No foreigner shall eat it' (Ex. 12:43) – both an apostate Jew and a Gentile are meant. For it is said: 'Thus said the Lord God: No alien, uncircumcised in heart and uncircumcised in flesh, shall enter into My sanctuary, even any alien that is among the children of Israel' (Ezek. 44:9)." See: *Mekhilta de-Rabbi Ishmael, Pisha*, 15 (Horovitz and Rabin 1970, 53). What is striking about this midrashic passage is not merely the fact that it considers the apostate as a "foreigner", but far beyond: the form of the Hebrew term for "foreigner" (בן נכר) was read by Tannaitic rabbis, as we have seen in the *Sifra*, as implying a genealogical frame of thought. And yet the *Mekhilta* ignores this point and treats the Jewish apostate as if he or she is not of Jewish *descent*! The homilist answers this difficulty by quoting Ezek. 44:9, which is understood to suggest the possible existence of a non-Jew among those who are at the same time considered "children of Israel" (בן נכר אשר בתוך בני ישראל).

[26] In a recently published paper Yedidah Koren maintained that Palestinian rabbis of the Tannaitic period constructed Jewish identity primarily as a matter of birth; that is, they viewed belonging in the Jewish people as dependent solely on genealogy. Focusing on the early rabbinic treatment of the case of a native-born Jew who is not circumcised, Koren has suggested that: "The status of the 'foreskinned Jew' offers an interpretive key to the Tannaitic reconstruction of Judaism. By neutralizing the significance that was previously ascribed to the physical foreskin, and waiving the necessity of circumcision in defining one as Jewish, the rabbis based Jewish identity on birth alone, and established a Judaism dependent solely on genealogy." See: Koren 2017 (the above citation is taken from the English summary). The passage in the *Sifra*, discussed above, complicates the issue, as it seems to be directing our thinking about belonging in the Jewish community in a different way.

[27] As we are told in many Tannaitic texts, "The proselyte is equal to the native-born Jew with respect to all the commandments of the Torah." See: *Mekhilta de-Rabbi Ishmael, Pisha*, 15 (Horovitz and Rabin 1970, 57); *Sifre Numbers* 71 (Horovitz 1966, 67); *Sifre Numbers* 109 (Horovitz 1966, 113). See also *t. Nedarim* 2:4 (Lieberman 1955–1988a, 104). Cf. Schwartz 1990b, 127; Cohen 1998 (= Cohen 2010, 361–371). Cohen concludes his study by stating that: "the rabbis consider proselytes to be equal to the native born. No ancient rabbinic text known to me contradicts this conclusion". However, in his discussion of the "Inequality of the Convert" (Cohen 1999, 324–327), he is careful to notice that proselytes were not considered entirely equal to the native-born Jew. See also Hayes 2002, 164–192. It is against this background that homilies striving to uplift the image and status of the proselyte, such as the one found in *Mekhilta de-Rabbi Ishmael, Neziqin*, 18 (Horovitz and Rabin 1970, 311–312), should be read as social polemic.

treated as having left the confines of the Jewish people is one's lack of adherence to the covenant;[28] the beliefs one entertains, even if unacceptable, are not even considered in such a context.

2 Those Who Do Not Have a Share in the World to Come

Despite the marginal role assigned in classical rabbinic thought to belief, as determining belonging to the Jewish community, and despite the relatively minor place heresy and the combat against heretics occupy in early rabbinic texts, correct belief was not an entirely alien concern to the rabbinic enterprise. Although the rabbis of the first and second centuries CE did not enter into intensive attempts to define orthodoxy and to combat heretics, they did designate from time to time certain theological opinions as illegitimate.

Many would probably agree with Lawrence Schiffman that "[t]he starting point for any discussion of heresy in tannaitic Judaism must be the *locus classicus* of *m. Sanhedrin* 10:1" (Schiffman 1985, 41). Not only does this fairly well-known and frequently discussed text deal with issues of belief, but it is also frequently interpreted as implying a claim about belonging. It reads as follows:

---

[28] The logic of the *Sifra* necessitates that just as one can join the Jewish people one can also leave, and the *meshumad* occupies the structural place of such a person. In contrast, in *b. Avoda Zara* 26a we read: "Rabbi Abbahu recited [the following Tannaitic source] before Rabbi Johannan: 'The gentiles and the shepherds of small cattle neither brought out nor thrown in; the apostates, the *minim* and the informers are thrown in and not brought out'. He [Rabbi Johannan] said to him: I recite [a Tannaitic source, saying], 'To any of your brother's lost property, this includes the apostate', and you say 'the apostates are thrown in and not brought out?!' Omit from here 'the apostate!'" Rabbi Johannan rejected the Tannaitic tradition cited by Rabbi Abbahu because he was familiar with a Tannaitic tradition that emphatically treats the apostate as "your brother", and therefore he demanded that Rabbi Abbahu amend the text of his tradition by deleting the apostates from the list of those who are "thrown in and not brought out" (compare *t. Bava Metzia* 2:33 [Lieberman 1955–1988a, 72]). These contradicting traditions indicate that the status of the apostate was disputed by Palestinian rabbis of the second and early third century (cf. Milikowsky's brief comments in Milikowsky 1986, 332–333). It is therefore important to note that the oft-cited Talmudic aphorism, "*Israelite, even though he had sinned he is nevertheless still an Israelite*" (ישראל אף על פי שחטא ישראל הוא), from which one might get the impression that in Judaism "you can check in any time you like but you can never leave", has been interpreted as applying to the Jewish apostate only in medieval times. Cf. Katz 1958 (= Katz 1984, 255–269).

And these [people] do not have a share in the world to come: he who says there is no resurrection of the dead; and there is no Torah from heaven; and an epicurean. Rabbi Akiva says: also he who reads in external books, and whispers over a wound and says 'All the diseases which I put upon the Egyptians I will not put upon you, for I am the Lord, your healer' (Ex. 15:26). Abba Shaul says: even he who pronounces the Name by its letters.[29]

In discussing this text Christine Hayes asserted that: "The mishnah's formulation makes it clear that those who doubt resurrection are those outside the community of Israel" (1998, 276).[30] While Hayes did not furnish any explanation for this assertion, Daniel Boyarin has provided the rationale behind it:

> According to the version preserved in the *textus receptus* of the Sanhedrin Mishna, it would be the case there too that the deviants are excluded from the name 'Israel', for in the Talmudic version and in the prints we read: 'All Israel have a place in the next world, and these are they who have no place, etc.' The most straightforward interpretation of the Mishnaic passage on this reading seems to be that the three who are denied a place in the next world are indeed not Israel. Otherwise the text logically contradicts itself. (2001, 443, n. 55)[31]

Because the mishnah, as it is presented in the vulgar printed editions, is prefixed by the declarative statement "All Israel have a share in the world to come", it seems necessary to understand it as implying that one who espouses one of the beliefs mentioned immediately after, and therefore has no share in the world to come, is not considered as "Israel". As Boyarin himself noted, however, "this exegetical point is only strictly valid with respect to the later reworking of the Mishna as we find it in the Talmuds and the prints of the Mishna" (2004a, 252). In MS Kaufman of the Mishnah, as well as in other reliable medieval manuscripts, the opening, declaratory statement – "All Israel have a share in the world to come", etc. – does not appear at all![32] One cannot base an interpretive argument

---

29 *M. Sanhedrin* 10:1, according to the reading of MS Kaufmann, Budapest A50, which is considered the most important text-witness of the Mishnah. See: Kutscher 1977, 73–107; Bar-Asher 1986, 184; Strack and Stemberger 1996, 141. I shall shortly relate to the absence of the famous opening sentence – "All Israel have a share in the world to come, as it said 'and your people are all righteous they will inherit the land forever'" – from the text of the mishnah in this and other reliable text-witnesses.

30 Cf. Finkelstein 1950, xxxviii (and in more detail in the Hebrew section, 222–223, n. 2); Sanders 1977, 149.

31 = Boyarin 2004a, 252, n. 128.

32 This textual fact, which was noted already by Urbach 1987, 999, n. 11, has not been sufficiently internalized in scholarly literature. See, for example, Grossberg 2010, 520, n. 7, who noted the absence of the opening declaratory statement from MS Kaufman, and still, when presenting the text of the mishnah, included the opening statement as it appears in the vulgar printed editions (2010, 555).

concerning this Mishnaic passage on this statement, for it is a post-Mishnaic gloss, not a genuine part of the text.³³

Nor does the phrase "do not have a share in the world to come", as such, hint at a possibility of understanding the mishnah as implying a claim about belonging. This same phrase appears in the following passages in the Mishnah and in parallel Tannaitic texts, related to this mishnah, where it applies to various ancient non-Jewish groups of people, and this indicates that a "share in the world to come" is not limited to Jews. Thus, we are told by *m. Sanhedrin* 10:3 and *t. Sanhedrin* 13:6–8 that:

> The people of the generation of the Flood do not have a share in the world to come … The people of the generation of the Tower [of Babylon] do not have a share in the world to come … The people of Sodom do not have a share in the world to come.

The Tosefta also records a dispute between Rabbi Eliezer and Rabbi Joshua over whether or not gentiles have a share in the world to come.³⁴ Be the precise function of these statements as it may,³⁵ their very application to groups who have never been considered "Israel" indicates that a denial of a portion in the world to come cannot be understood as implying a claim regarding belonging in the Jewish people.

As Shaye Cohen has correctly emphasized, those who espouse the theological errors mentioned in *m. Sanhedrin* 10:1 are claimed to have no share in the world to come, but they are not punished by any human agency in one of the punishments normally used toward criminals, which are mentioned in tractate Sanhedrin (or elsewhere in the Mishnah). Nor are they cursed or threatened with excommunication or any other form of communal discipline. To say of someone that he or she (or they) has no share in the world to come is the rabbis' way of expressing their disapproval, but it does not imply a claim about belonging in the community. As

---

33 Epstein conjectured that the opening statement in the vulgar printed editions is actually a *baraita* (that is, tannaitic text). See Epstein 1957, 418, n. 8. It stands to reason that its insertion into the mishnah emanated from the desire to furnish the mishnah with an opening sentence, which, in its original form (as preserved by the Kaufman manuscript), seems lacking. As Epstein himself noted, however, *m. Sanhedrin* 10:1 is a continuation of *m. Sanhedrin* 6:2, which states that: "[everyone] who confesses [his sins before his death] has a share in the world to come" (1957, 418).
34 *T. Sanhedrin* 13:2 (Zuckermandel 1970, 434).
35 They have no practical or legal implication (as opposed to the first mishnah in the chapter, which may be read at least as a threat), as they relate to past generations. Declaring that these people "do not have a share in the world to come" cannot, obviously, be understood as a "threat", and it must therefore be understood differently. This question, however, is beyond the scope of the present paper and I shall therefore not deal with it here.

Cohen concluded: "the Mishna does not establish strong boundaries around its community; it is not interested in defining orthodoxy, suppressing deviance, or establishing the limits of dissent" (2017, 322).

3 Heresy and Sectarianism

Despite its image as "[t]he starting point for any discussion of heresy in tannaitic Judaism", *m. Sanhedrin* 10:1, in fact, does not address all the views considered "heretical" by early rabbinic texts. Thus, for example, the Mishnah, in tractate Sanhedrin itself, knows of *minim* who maintain that there are "many Powers in heaven" (*m. Sanhedrin* 4:5),[36] yet *m. Sanhedrin* 10:1 does not include "he who maintains that there are many Powers in heaven" in its list of those who do not have a share in the world to come. Nor does it include in its list atheists, "who maintain that there is no Power in heaven", or those who maintain that God has "no power to revive nor to kill".[37] Similarly, the Tosefta (in tractate Sanhedrin itself) explains that "Adam was created at the end [of the creation] so that the *minim* would not claim that he was God's co-partner in His deed."[38] Yet, *m. Sanhedrin* 10:1 does not include such a claim in its list of errors that cause one to lose his or her share in the world to come. The Mishnah also knows of *minim* who deny the idea of two worlds and maintain instead that "there is but one world" (*m. Berakhot* 9:9), but *m. Sanhedrin* 10:1 does not mention them and does not denounce their theological error.

The fact that the mishnah does not mention and does not denounce all the theological views considered erroneous and problematic by Palestinian sages of its day indicates that rather than being a text addressing heresy, as such, it

---

[36] This theological claim is probably related to the claim that there are "two Powers in heaven", which is mentioned in other places in Tannaitic literature. See: *Mekhilta de-Rabbi Ishmael*, *Shirta*, 4 (Horovitz and Rabin 1970, 129–130), and its parallel in *Mekhilta de-Rashbi* on Ex. 15:3 (Epstein and Melamed 1979, 81); *Mekhilta de-Rabbi Ishmael*, *Ba-Hodesh*, 5 (Horovitz and Rabin 1970, 219–220); *Sifre Zutta* on Numbers 15:30 (Horovitz 1966, 286); *Sifre Deuteronomy* 329 (Finkelstein 1969, 379), and its parallel in *Mekhilta* on Deuteronomy, 32:39 (Kahana 1988, 190; Kahana 2005, 355). Segal 1977, devoted to that theological stance, suffers from the methodological flaw of not distinguishing between early (that is, Tannaitic) and late (that is, Amoraic and especially post-Amoraic) rabbinic sources, a flaw that characterizes also some of the later contributions to this theme, to which I hope to return in the future.
[37] *Sifre Deuteronomy* 329 (Finkelstein 1969, 379); *Mekhilta* on Deuteronomy 32:39 (Kahana 2005, 355).
[38] *T. Sanhedrin* 8:7 (Zuckermandel 1970, 428).

may be understood as having a specific target in mind. Indeed, it has been frequently suggested that the issues denounced by *m. Sanhedrin* 10:1 indicate that the Mishnah rejected specifically views known to be held by the Sadducees.[39]

The question of the exactitude of this identification notwithstanding,[40] it is important to note that the Sadducees are never referred to in the Mishnah with respect to their beliefs, and their disagreements with the sages are always pre-

---

39 See, for example: Schiffman 1985, 42–45; Boyarin 2001, 440–442; Boyarin 2004a, 58–59.

40 The identification is not as simple as it is sometimes thought, and it is not a coincidence that Urbach, when discussing this mishnah, was careful not to speak explicitly of the Sadducees; rather he suggested that: "the entire Mishna – including R. Akiba's supplement – is directed against sectarians who held certain views" (1987, 653). The suggestion that the mishnah had specifically the Sadducees in mind rests on Josephus's claim that the Sadducees deny "the persistence of the soul after death" (*Jewish War* 2.165; *Jewish Antiquities*, 18.4). However, how precisely is this "inextricably connected with the doctrine of resurrection as mentioned in our mishnah" (Schiffman 1985, 42), requires more clarification. See also: Klawans 2012, 106–111. The same holds true with respect to the denial of the concept of Torah from heaven. "It is tempting", as Schiffman (1985, 42) writes, "to view the Torah here as a reference to *torah she-be-'al peh*, the oral Law" (as Boyarin 2001, 440, indeed took it for granted), and to note that: "Resurrection and the revealed Oral Torah are precisely the major doctrinal points at issue between the Pharisees and the Sadducees" (2001, 441). Nothing forces us, however, to accept this assumption, and, as Schiffman correctly concluded, "It is most likely that our mishnah is directed against those who ... had come to deny the divine origin of the Torah" (1985, 43). It is possible, moreover, that a deeper consideration of a variant reading with respect to the other error the mishnah denounces (the denial of the resurrection of the dead), may affect also our understanding of the denial of "Torah from heaven". According to the reading of the vulgar printed editions the mishnah denounces "he who says there is no *biblical foundation* for the resurrection of the dead" (האומר אין תחיית המתים מן התורה). Although this reading may be an old one (as it seems to have been the basis on which the Talmudic sugya at *b. Sanhedrin* 90b rests), as has been occasionally noticed in MS Kaufman and other reliable manuscripts the words "from the Torah" are lacking. See, for example: Finkelstein 1950, 229, n. 5; Urbach 1987, 991, n. 11; Sanders 1992, 528, n. 28; Hayes 1998, 276, n. 58; Grossberg 2010, 520, n. 7. According to this latter reading, the mishnah is troubled by one who denies the *very concept* of the resurrection, not with one who denies a specific detail concerning it, that is, its biblical roots (*pace* Boyarin, 2001). And it seems that along similar lines we should understand the claim of he or she who says that "there is no Torah from heaven". That person denies the very concept, that is, the very possibility of a Torah given by God to human beings. The mishnah, in other words, does not condemn one who denies the divine origins of a *specific* Torah (whether the Written Torah of Moses, or the Oral Torah), but rather it polemicizes against one who denies the very idea of God communicating with humans and giving them a law. I dare to offer this interpretation because it may better account for the relation between the first two "crimes" mentioned by the mishnah and the Epicurean that follows them. The mishnah, on this reading, refers to people who reject, in different ways, God's relation with the world, and it views all of them as "epicureans" (compare Finkelstein, ibid., n. 6). The *vav* of והאפיקורס should not of itself be considered as obstructing such a reading; it may be treated as *vav explicativum*. See: Epstein 1964, 1076–1087.

sented as relating to halakhic, rather than creedal, matters.[41] This is so even in *m. Nidda* 4:2, which has been interpreted by some scholars as contrasting Sadducees to "Israel", and thus implying a claim about belongings to the Jewish people:

> Sadducean women, when they are accustomed to walk in the ways of their ancestors, they are [considered] as Samaritan women. If they separated to walk in the ways of Israel they are [considered] as Israel. Rabbi Yossi says: They are always [considered] as Israel until they separate to walk in the ways of their ancestors. (*m. Niddah* 4:2)[42]

On this mishnah Daniel Boyarin has commented:

> The ways of their [the Saducean daughters'] fathers' are contrasted with the 'ways of Israel', ergo, those fathers' traditional ways (very likely ancient norms), and indeed those very fathers themselves, are excommunicated from Israel [...] In other words, this text projects a situation in which there are historical and genealogical Israelites who are not 'Israel' [...] the 'Sadducees' are heretics who are beyond the pale and outside the name Israel.
> (2001, 443–444)

According to Boyarin's interpretation, the mishnah contrasts "the ways" of Sadducean women with "the ways of Israel", and therefore its rhetoric implies that it views Sadducees as not belonging to the Jewish people (2001, 443).

Even if we were to accept this interpretive claim,[43] it cannot be denied that the mishnah depicts the Sadducees with respect to their halakhic norms, not with respect to their beliefs. This indicates that even in cases where the rabbis criticized certain Jewish groups (and, in an interpretation such as Boyarin's, viewed them as not-Israel) the main prism through which they looked at these groups was not that of belief, and they did not consider them as heretics. Heresy, it appears, is simply not the best category to think with when attempting to discuss the issues that had troubled the rabbis.

Summary

In a well-known and oft-cited passage in his *Dialogue with Trypho the Jew* the second-century Church Father Justin Martyr refers to people who are called Christians, but who, in his opinion, cannot be really considered so:

---

[41] See: Cohen 1987, 155–156. Cf. Sussman 1990, 53, n. 175.
[42] Compare the parallel text in *t. Niddah* 5:3 (Zuckermandel 1970, 645).
[43] Elsewhere I attempted to explain why such a conclusion is not really necessary. See: Schremer 2012, 272.

> For even if you yourselves have ever met with some so-called Christians ... who say too that there is no resurrection of the dead, but that their souls ascend to heaven at the very moment of their death – do not suppose that they are Christians, any more than if one examined the matter rightly he would acknowledge as Jews those who are Sadducees, or similar sects ...[44]

Justin denies that people who reject the idea of the resurrection of the dead really are Christians, even if they consider themselves as such and call themselves Christians. To be considered a Christian one is required to espouse certain beliefs (such as the belief in the resurrection), so that if a person who is so-called Christian does not accept those beliefs that Justin thinks characterize Christianity that person is not really a Christian.

Along the same line, Justin claims, there are some people (like the Sadducees) who consider themselves Jews, but "if one examined the matter rightly" he would realize that they really are not. According to Shaye Cohen, Justin reflects here the rabbinic ideology of the early second century: there are Jews, and there are sectarians "who scarcely deserve the name Jew".[45] In this paper I argued that this is a Christianizing interpretation, which lacks firm basis in early rabbinic texts. The rabbis of the second and early third centuries hardly thought with categories such as "the name Jew", and Justin's insistence on matters of belief as determinative for eligibility for the title "Christian" does not find parallel in early rabbinic discourse.

I do not wish to be understood as claiming that the rabbis were indifferent to matters of belief, and that these matters were of no importance for them. However, as David Aune has written: "The crux of the problem lies in the necessity of making a balanced assessment of the relative structural significance and function of the belief system vis-à-vis ritual practice and ethical behavior within the Judaism of the Graeco-Roman period" (1976, 3). For second- and early-third-century-CE rabbis the latter seem to have been of much greater weight than the former. For this reason, heresy, as a category, never occupied a central place in their thought.

Just as these rabbis did not have a developed discourse concerning heresy, they did not develop an idea of orthodoxy. There is admittedly a Tannaitic expression which is, indeed, an exact literal equivalent of "orthodoxy"; that is: "straight way" (דרך ישרה). However, that expression is found in a single Tannaitic text, and reading that text in its entirety is revealing:

---

[44] See: Justin, *Dialogue with Trypho*, 80:4, (Williams 1930, 170). I hope to return to this much-discussed passage in the future.
[45] See: Cohen 1984, 49 (and already at 35). See also Boyarin 2004a, 42.

> Rabbi says: Which is the straight way that one should choose? That which is an honor to him gets him honor from men. And be heedful of a light precept as of a weighty one, for you do not know the recompense of reward of each precept. And reckon the loss through the fulfilling of a precept against its reward, and the reward that come from transgression against its loss.[46]

To follow the "straight way" (that is, literally speaking, to be "orthodox") is to be meticulous in the *observance of the commandments*. Belief, important though it may be, was not considered by the early rabbis as constitutive for Judaism and for Jewish identity. In complete contrast to the second-century-CE Church Father Irenaeus of Lyons, for whom "agreement in faith" was the determinative issue for Christian identity, so that it allowed for "disagreement in the fast",[47] for the early rabbis faithfulness to the commandments was the key aspect of Jewish identity. For this reason, defining heresy and the combat against heretics were not central to the rabbinic project, and unlike Irenaeus (and other Church Fathers) they never composed a treatise "Against *Minim*."

Bibliography

Alexander, Loveday. "Community and Canon: Reflections of the Ecclesiology of Acts." *Einheit der Kirche im Neuen Testament*. Ed. Anatoly Alexeev et al. Tübingen: Mohr-Siebeck, 2008. 45–78.
Aune, David E. "Orthodoxy in First Century Judaism? A Response to N.J. McEleney." *Journal for the Study of Judaism* 7 (1976): 1–10.
Bar-Asher, Moshe. "Linguistic Studies in the Manuscripts of the Mishnah: Language Types and Salient Features." *Proceedings of the Israeli Academy of Sciences and Humanities* 7 (1986): 183–210 (Hebrew).
Boyarin, Daniel. "Justin Martyr Invents Judaism." *Church History* 70 (2001): 427–461.
Boyarin, Daniel. *Border Lines: The Partition of Judaeo-Christianity*. Philadelphia: University of Pennsylvania Press, 2004a.
Boyarin, Daniel. "Two Powers in Heaven; Or, The Making of a Heresy." *The Idea of Biblical Interpretation: Essays in Honor of James L. Kugel*. Ed. Hindy Najman and Judith H. Newman. Leiden-Boston: Brill, 2004b. 331–370.
Brody, Robert. "'Rabbinic' and 'Nonrabbinic' Jews in Mishnah and Tosefta." *The Faces of Torah: Studies in the Texts and Contexts of Ancient Judaism in Honor of Steven Fraade*. Ed. Michal

---

46 *M. Avot* 2:1. The expression "straight way" is found also in *m. Avot* 2:9, but the reading of the most reliable manuscripts of that mishnah is rather "good way" (דרך טובה). See: Sharvit 2004, 98. This reading is confirmed by the negation in the following passage, which refers to "bad way" (דרך רעה).
47 See above, n. 6.

Bar-Asher Siegal, Tzvi Novick, and Christine Hayes. Göttingen: Vandenhoeck & Ruprecht, 2017. 275–291.
Cameron, Averil. "The Violence of Orthodoxy." *Heresy and Identity in Late Antiquity*. Ed. Eduard Iricinschi and Holger M. Zellentin. Tübingen: Mohr-Siebeck, 2008. 102–114.
Christie-Murray, David. *A History of Heresy*. Oxford and New York: Oxford University Press, 1976.
Cohen, Shaye J.D. *From the Maccabees to the Mishnah*. Philadelphia: Westminster Press, 1987.
Cohen, Shaye J.D. "The Significance of Yavneh: Pharisees, Rabbis, and the End of Jewish Sectarianism." *Hebrew Union College Annual* 55 (1984): 27–53.
Cohen, Shaye J.D. "On Murdering or Injuring a Proselyte." *Hesed Ve-Emet: Studies in Honor of Ernest S. Freriches*. Ed. Jodi Magness and Seymour Gitin. Atlanta: Scholars Press, 1998. 95–108.
Cohen, Shaye J.D. *The Beginnings of Jewishness: Boundaries, Varieties, Uncertainties*. Berkeley: University of California Press, 1999.
Cohen, Shaye J.D. *The Significance of Yavneh and Other Essays in Jewish Hellenism*. Tübingen: Mohr-Siebeck, 2010.
Cohen, Shaye J.D. "The Ways That Parted: Jews, Christians, and Jewish-Christians, ca. 100–150 CE." *Jews and Christians in the First and Second Centuries: The Interbellum 70–132 CE*. Ed. Joshua J. Schwartz and Peter J. Tomson. Leiden-Boston: Brill, 2017. 307–339.
Epstein, Jacob N. *Introduction to Tannaitic Literature*. Jerusalem: Magnes, and Tel-Aviv: Dvir, 1957 (Hebrew).
Epstein, Jacob N. *Introduction to the Text of the Mishnah*. (2nd ed). Jerusalem: Magnes, and Tel-Aviv: Dvir, 1964 (Hebrew).
Epstein, Jacob N. *Studies in Talmudic Literature and Semitic Languages*. Ed. Ezra Z. Melamed. Jerusalem: The Hebrew University Magnes Press, 1988 (Hebrew).
Epstein, Jacob N., and Ezra Z. Melamed. *Mekhilta D'Rabbi Šim'on b. Jochai*. Jerusalem: Hillel, 1979² (Hebrew).
Finkelstein, Louis. *Mabo le-Massektot Abot ve-Abot d'Rabbi Natan*. New York: Jewish Theological Seminary of America, 1950 (Hebrew).
Finkelstein, Louis. *Sifre on Deuteronomy*. New York: Jewish Theological Seminary of America, 1969 (Hebrew).
Finkelstein, Louis. *Sifra on Leviticus*. New York: Jewish Theological Seminary of America, 1983–1990 (Hebrew).
Goodman, Martin. "The Function of *Minim* in Early Rabbinic Judaism." *Geschichte–Tradition–Reflexion: Festschrift für Martin Hengel zum 70. Geburtstag*. Ed. H. Cancik, H. Lichtenberger, and P. Schäfer. Tübingen: Mohr-Siebeck, 1996. 501–510.
Gove, Walter R. "The Labeling Perspective: An Overview." *The Labeling of Deviance*. Ed. Walter R. Gove. New York: Sage, 1975. 3–20.
Gries, Zeev. "Heresy." *Contemporary Jewish Religious Thought*. Ed. Arthur A. Cohen and Paul Mendes-Flohr. New York: Free Press, 1987. 339–352.
Grossberg, David M. "Orthopraxy in Tannaitic Literature." *Journal for the Study of Judaism* 41 (2010): 517–561.
Hayes, Christine E. "Displaced Self-Perception: The Deployment of Minim and Romans in B. Sanhedrin 90b–91a." *Religious and Ethnic Communities in Later Roman Palestine*. Ed. Hayim Lapin. Bethesda: University Press of Maryland, 1998. 249–289.
Hayes, Christine E. *Gentile Impurities and Jewish Identity: Intermarriage and Conversion from the Bible to the Talmud*. Oxford: Oxford University Press, 2002.
Horovitz, Haym S. *Sifre and Sifre Zutta on Numbers*. Jerusalem: Wahrmann Books, 1966 (Hebrew).

Horovitz, Haym S., and I.A. Rabin. *Mechilta D'Rabbi Ismael*. Jerusalem: Wahrmann Books, 1970 (Hebrew).
Iricinschi, Eduard, and Holger M. Zellentin. "Making Selves and Marking Others: Identity and Late Antique Heresiologies." *Heresy and Identity in Late Antiquity*. Ed. Eduard Iricinschi and Holger M. Zellentin. Tübingen: Mohr-Siebeck, 2008. 1–27.
Kahana, Menahem. "Pages of the Deuteronomy Mekhilta on *Ha'azinu* and *Wezot Ha-berakha*." *Tarbiz* 57 (1988): 165–201 (Hebrew).
Kahana, Menahem. *The Genizah Fragments of the Halakhic Midrashim, Part I*. Jerusalem: Magnes, 2005 (Hebrew).
Katz, Jacob. "Though He Sinned He Remains an Israelite." *Tarbiz* 27 (1958): 203–217 (Hebrew).
Katz, Jacob. *Halakah and Kabbalah: Studies in the History of Jewish Religion, its Various Faces and Social Relevance*. Jerusalem: Magnes, 1984 (Hebrew).
King, Karen L. *What is Gnosticism?* Cambridge, MA, and London: Harvard University Press, 2003.
Klawans, Jonathan. *Josephus and the Theologies of Ancient Judaism*. Oxford and New York: Oxford University Press, 2012.
Koren, Yedidah. "The 'Foreskinned Jew' in Tannaitic Literature: Another Aspect of the Rabbinic (Re)Construction of Judaism." *Zion* 82 (2017): 397–437 (Hebrew).
Kutscher, Eduard Y. "Mishnaic Hebrew." *Hebrew and Aramaic Studies*. Ed. Zeev Ben-Hayyim et al. Jerusalem: Magnes Press, 1977. 73–107 (Hebrew).
Langer, Ruth. *Cursing the Christians? A History of the Birkat Haminim*. New York and Oxford: Oxford University Press, 2012.
Lieberman, Saul. "Some Aspects of After Life in Rabbinic Literature." *Harry Austryn Wolfson Jubilee Volume*. Ed. Saul Lieberman. Jerusalem: American Academy for Jewish Research, 1965. 2: 495–532.
Lieberman, Saul. *The Tosefta*. New York: Jewish Theological Seminary of America, 1955–1983 (Hebrew).
Lieberman, Saul. *Tosefta Ki-fshutah*. New York: Jewish Theological Seminary of America, 1955–1988 (Hebrew).
Lopez, Donald S., Jr. "Belief." *Critical Terms for Religious Studies*. Ed. Mark C. Taylor. Chicago: University of Chicago Press, 1998. 21–35.
Lyman, J. Rebecca. "Heresiology: The Invention of 'Heresy' and 'Schism'." *The Cambridge History of Christianity, 2: Constantine to c. 600*. Ed. Augustine Casiday and Frederick W. Norris. Cambridge: Cambridge University Press, 2007. 296–316.
Marjanen, Antti, and Petri Luomanen. *A Companion to Second-Century Christian 'Heretics'*. Leiden-Boston: Brill, 2005.
McCarthy, Michael C.S.J. "Modalities of Belief in Ancient Christian Debate." *Journal of Early Christian Studies* 17 (2009): 605–634.
Meeks, Wayne A. "Breaking Away: Three New Testament Pictures of Christianity's Separation from the Jewish Communities." *"To See Ourselves as Others See Us": Christians, Jews, "Others" in Late Antiquity*. Ed. Jacob Neusner and Ernest S. Frerichs. Chico: Scholars Press, 1985. 93–115.
Milikowsky, Chaim. "Gehenna and 'Sinners of Israel' in the Light of *Seder 'Olam*." *Tarbiz* 55 (1986): 311–343 (Hebrew).
Nitzan, Bilha. "The Concept of the Covenant in Qumran Literature." *Historical Perspectives: From the Hasmoneans to Bar Kokhba in Light of the Dead Sea Scrolls*. Ed. David Goodblatt, Avital Pinnick, and Daniel R. Schwartz. Leiden: Brill, 2001. 85–104.

Nitzan, Bilha. *Philosophy and Practice in the Dead Sea Scrolls: Theology, Wisdom, Law, and Biblical Exegesis*. Jerusalem: Yad Izhak Ben-Zvi, 2014 (Hebrew).

Petersen, William L. "Eusebius and the Paschal Controversy." *Eusebius, Christianity, and Judaism*. Ed. Harold W. Attridge and Gohei Hata. Detroit: Wayne State University Press, 1992. 311–325.

Rosenthal, Eliezer S., and Saul Lieberman. *Yerushalmi Nezikin: Edited from the Escorial Manuscript with an Introduction*. Jerusalem: Israel Academy of Sciences and Humanities, 1983 (Hebrew).

Sanders, Ed P. *Paul and Palestinian Judaism*. Minneapolis: Fortress Press, 1977.

Sanders, Ed P. *Judaism: Practice & Belief 63 BCE–66 CE*. London: SCM Press and Philadelphia: Trinity Press, 1992.

Schiffman, Lawrence H. *Who Was a Jew? Rabbinic and Halakhic Perspectives on the Jewish-Christian Schism*. Hoboken: Ktav, 1985.

Schremer, Adiel. "Thinking about Belonging in Early Rabbinic Literature: Proselytes, Apostates, and 'Children of Israel', or: Does It Make Sense to Speak of Early Rabbinic Orthodoxy?" *Journal for the Study of Judaism* 43 (2012): 249–275.

Schremer, Adiel. "Wayward Jews: *Minim* in Early Rabbinic Literature." *Journal of Jewish Studies* 64 (2013): 242–263.

Schwartz, Daniel R. *Agrippa I: The Last King of Judaea*. Tübingen: Mohr Siebeck, 1990a.

Schwartz, Daniel R. "On Two Aspects of a Priestly View of Descent at Qumran." *Archaeolog and History in the Dead Sea Scrolls*. Ed. Lawrence H. Schiffman. Sheffield: Sheffield University Press, 1990b. 157–179.

Schwartz, Daniel R. *Studies in the Jewish Background of Christianity*. Tübingen: Mohr Siebeck, 1992.

Segal, Alan. *Two Powers in Heaven*. Leiden: Brill, 1977.

Sharvit, Shimon. *Tractate Avoth through the Ages: A Critical Edition, Prolegomena and Appendices*. Jerusalem: Bialik Institute and Ben-Yehuda Research Center for the History of Hebrew, Hebrew University of Jerusalem, 2004 (Hebrew).

Simon, Marcel. *Verus Israel: A Study of the Relations between Christians and Jews in the Roman Empire AD 135–425*. London: Littman Library of Jewish Civilization, 1996.

Sperber, Daniel. "Min." *Encyclopedia Judaica*. Jerusalem: Keter, 1971. 12.1–3.

Strack, H.L., and Günter Stemberger. *Introduction to the Talmud and Midrash*. Trans. Markus Bockmuehl. Minneapolis: Fortress Press, 1996.

Sumner, Colin. *The Sociology of Deviance: An Obituary*. New York: Continuum, 1994.

Sussman, Yaaqov. "The History of *Halakha* and the Dead Sea Scrolls - Preliminary Observations on Miqsat Ma'ase Ha-Torah (4QMMT)." *Tarbiz* 59 (1990): 11–76 (Hebrew).

Tilley, Maureen A. "When Schism Becomes Heresy in Late Antiquity: Developing Doctrinal Deviance in the Wounded Body of Christ." *Journal of Early Christian Studies* 15 (2007): 1–21.

Urbach, Ephraim E. *The Sages: Their Concepts and Beliefs*. Cambridge, MA, and London: Harvard University Press, 1987.

Williams, Lukyn A. *Justin Martyr: The Dialogue with Trypho*. London, New York, and Toronto: Macmillan 1930.

Zuckermandel, M.S. *Tosephta*. Jerusalem: Wahrmann Books, 1970 (Hebrew).

Shraga Bar-On and Eugene D. Matanky
Revelation as Heresy: Mysticism and Elisha ben Abuyah's Apostasy in Classic Rabbinic Literature

1 The Root of Faith is the Root of Heresy

Judaism is the oldest of what are commonly referred to as Abrahamic or revealed religions. Its revealed status is of paramount importance within its self-understanding. The recorded revelation experienced by the patriarchs, prophets, and the people of Israel, as a collective, cemented the foundations of the Jewish faith, its relation to ethics, and its conception of law. The Jewish monotheistic revolution was not satisfied with the minimalist claim of believing in only one God and worshipping him alone, but rather identified this God with being the creator of the cosmos, directing the course of history, and giving the Torah through unmediated revelation to the people of Israel and Moses.[1]

Yet, surprisingly in classic rabbinic literature, revelation – the cornerstone of biblical Judaism – is transformed from "the root of faith into the root of heresy."[2] Many have discussed the dramatic differences that characterize the passage from biblical to rabbinic Judaism (Brettler, 1999, 429–447; Cohen, 2006; Schwartz and Weiss, 2011; Talmon, 1991, 23; Zevit, 2008, 164–190), especially the cessation of prophecy (Cook, 2012; Greenspahn, 1989; Polen, 2015, 83–85; Sommer, 1996, 31–47; Urbach, 1988b, 9–49).[3] However, although it has been noted that revelation in the rabbinic period was suspended, scholars have failed to conceptualize the intriguing paradox that not only did revelation cease to occur, but those who continued to claim to have experienced revelation are deemed heretics.[4] In other

---

[1] Concerning God as divine-lawgiver and Moses as royal-lawgiver, see Watts (1998, 415–426). Concerning Moses role as the royal-lawgiver, see Römer (2013, 81–94).
[2] For a survey of this phrase, see Pachter (2004, 13–130).
[3] Concerning the prophet/sage dichotomy, see Goshen-Gottstein (2006, 37–77); Neusner (2014, 1–26); Walzer et al. (2000, 257–264); Wolfson (2009, 186–205). Other key differences include communal boundaries and places of worship; see respectively, Cohen (1999a; 1999b, 298–325).
[4] For example, David Weiss Halivni (1991, 136) wrote: "Only when prophecy 'dried up' and disappeared as a ready, available source of enlightenment and instruction did the reliance on text become a religious necessity ... Canonization and midrash were the natural and efficacious byproducts of the expiration of prophetic revelation ... Midrash replaced, or substituted for, prophecy as the prime carrier of God's revelation." However, he does not discuss the innate danger of allowing revelatory prophecy a place within rabbinic Judaism. Furthermore, the sages themselves never

words, revelation – a defining characteristic of biblical Jewish religion – transforms into its exact opposite – a defining characteristic of apostasy from rabbinic Judaism.

This chapter tracks this religious shift through several stages. First, we will set out the stark difference between revelation and heresy as it appears in the Bible and as it appears in classic rabbinic literature. We will then present the rabbinic argument concerning contact with the divine through a characterization of three rabbinic circles: the hyper-mystical circle of R. Yoḥanan ben Zakkai, the anti-mystical circle of R. Judah ha-Nasi, and the moderate mystical circle of R. Akiva, which may be discerned through the various editorial layers found in rabbinic literature. Lastly, we will present the archetypical heretical figure Elisha ben Abuyah and this figure's engagement with the revelatory mystical arts.[5]

Before we delve into the evolution of Elisha's heresy it is important to note a few items concerning the classic rabbinic portrayal of Elisha and heresy. The manner in which the Babylonian Talmud, based on Tannaitic sources, portrayed Elisha's "going out to evil ways" (*tarbut ra'a*) is an exceptional example of rabbinic heresiology. Until the medieval period, rabbinic culture did not systematically define principles of faith in such a manner as to cast out those who did not accept them (Kellner 1986, 1–9; 2006, 26–43; Shapiro 2004, 3–5). We find inklings of this type of theological development in the famous *m. Sanhedrin* 10 (*b. Sanhedrin* 90a–113b), known as *Pereq Ḥeleq*, in which we find explicit discussion of heretical beliefs that disqualify one from the world-to-come. The passages designate some of these people as *minim* and *apiqorsim*, and while we may be tempted to translate these terms as *heretics*, a number of scholars have discussed the problems involved in such a translation (Cohen, 2006, 120–122; Grossberg, 2017, 24; Schremer, 2008, 14–16).[6]

While rabbinic literature, from the earliest strata until the latest strata, created a clearer differentiation between the rabbinic community and those outside of it,[7] Elisha b. Abuyah presents an interesting case study, as he is never

---

explicitly discussed this transformation. Perhaps the closest discussion of true and false revelation is that of rabbinic framing of the distinction between true and false prophecy; see Stroumsa (2015, 82). Concerning false prophecy in classic rabbinic literature, see Shemesh (2001). Also, see the interesting discussion of false prophecy offered by Suzanne Last Stone (2009).

5 In the forthcoming footnotes we will reference the works that have dealt with this figure in rabbinic literature. Concerning this figure's medieval reception in Maimonides's thought, see Diamond (2002); Schwartz (2018, 49–51); Stroumsa (1992–93); for his modern reception, see Be'eri (2007, 7–32); Dubler (1991).

6 Cf. Boyarin (2004a, 54–58); Goodman (2007); Siegal (2019, 7–17).

7 Concerning the construction of rabbinic identity, see Boyarin (2000); Cohen (1999a; 2006); Hayes (2018); Lavee (2017); Ophir and Rosen-Zvi (2018, 68); Stern (1994).

referred to as a *min*, *apiqorses*, or *meshumad*, and therefore was never entirely ostracized from the rabbinic community. As we will argue, his heresy lies in the mere fact that he went on a mystical journey and, according to the final configuration of his story in the Babylonian Talmud, his primary sin lies in the conclusions that he deduced from said journey. While ascending to and penetrating the orchard his fate was sealed by a *bat qol* (divine voice), which proclaimed him as an "other" (*aḥer*). In m. Ḥagigah 1:7, it is stated that the biblical verse "What is crooked cannot be made straight" (Eccl. 1:15), may refer to "a sage who separates from Torah." We will demonstrate that ultimately Elisha's sin is that he separated from the Torah taught in the rabbinic study hall (*beit midrash*) out of the desire to achieve direct revelation – as depicted within the Torah itself – which he erroneously interpreted. The consequence of his mystical journey is his turning into Aḥer, the ultimate other. To this extent the term "heretic," although borrowed from Christian theology and studies (Dulk, 2018, 13–37; Goodman, 2007, 165; Iricinschi and Zellentin, 2008; Royalty Jr., 2013, 3–29), is very useful. For, it does not denote a contra to a strict theological dogma, but rather "it names a person or a position as other ... [it] comments on the inside and outside of human communities" (Lazier, 2012, 3–4). Thus, the heretic acts within a liminal space; being both within and without. It is with this lens of heresy in mind that we should approach the rabbinic discourse concerning Elisha.

2 Revelation, Faith, and Heresy: Between Biblical and Rabbinic Literature

The heresy of yesterday is the innocent faith of today. The monotheistic faith that gradually took shape throughout the pages of the Bible constitutes a drastic reform of the religious beliefs prevalent in the ancient Near East (Kaufmann, 1937–57; Knohl, 2007; Weinfeld, 1972). In this light, the Bible can be understood as a heretical work; calling for the disbelief in the numerous gods of the polytheistic faiths found in that geographic location and instead for belief in only the one God of the Israelites.[8] While within the biblical portrayal of God we may still find mythic and anthropomorphic elements, the biblical God is distanced from the more egotistical, immoral, and sexual behavior associated with the numerous gods of the various pantheons. Furthermore, the God of the Bible is not subservient to fate,

---

[8] A similar characterization has been made concerning the "heretical" monotheism of the Egyptian king Akhenaten; see Redford (1984).

nor to other celestial beings (Rofé, 2012). Through this iconoclastic process, the Bible not only depletes the ancient beliefs, but also denounces them as heresies. The Bible assumes a self-evident belief in monotheism. It does not combat paganistic and polytheistic beliefs, but rather denies them outright. Thus, loyalty to or worship of other gods is presented as a great betrayal of the relationship between God and Israel – a heretical choice. Even in specific places in which belief in other gods is discussed, this belief is portrayed not only as wrong, but spurious.[9]

Nevertheless, despite this debilitating attack on idolatry and non-Israelite faith, the rabbinic reader of the Bible is still fascinated by the magical rites and the draw of the dominant belief systems of the ancient Near East. The biblical portrayal of the polytheistic faiths as mere idol worship leaves the reader with a need to reconstruct a more complex conception of these systems of beliefs.[10] The heretical turn of the Bible against polytheism was executed through an *argumentum ad absurdum*, in which the gods of other nations are conceived as idols and statues; not as mythical beings with rich inner lives and cosmic powers. The biblical faith is a mirror image of its representation of idolatry. In place of gods who can be seen, but cannot communicate with their people, the God of the Bible – the true God – cannot be seen, but he can communicate with his prophets. For this reason, the

---

[9] For example: "Let the nations not say, 'Where, now, is their God?' when our God is in heaven and all that He wills He accomplishes. Their idols are silver and gold, the work of men's hands. They have mouths, but cannot speak, eyes, but cannot see; they have ears, but cannot hear, noses, but cannot smell; they have hands, but cannot touch, feet, but cannot walk; they can make no sound in their throats" (Ps. 115:2–7). All biblical translations are either from or based on the NRSV Bible.

[10] This is wonderfully illustrated by a Talmudic narrative concerning Manasseh and his idolatrous practice found in *b. Sanhedrin* 102a–b: "Rabbi Abbahu regularly expounded about the three kings [Jeroboam, Ahab, and Manasseh, who have no share in the World-to-Come]. He fell ill, and he accepted upon himself that he would not expound [about them]. Once he recovered, he then expounded [about them]. They said to him, 'Did you not accept upon yourself that you will not expound about them? He said, 'Did they repent, so that I should reconsider?' Rav Ashi ended [his exposition before] the three kings. He said, 'Tomorrow we will begin with our colleagues. He [Manasseh] came and appeared to him in his dream. He said, 'You referred to us as "your colleague and the colleagues of your father?"' [Manasseh said] 'From which [part of the bread] are you obligated to do *ha-moṣi* [blessing over bread] on?' [Rav Ashi] said to him, 'I do not know,' [Manasseh] said to him, 'You did not learn from which [part of the bread] are you obligated to do *ha-moṣi* [blessing over bread] on, and you refer to us as your colleagues?' … [Rav Ashi] said to him, 'Teach it to me and tomorrow I will expound about it in your name.' … [Rav Ashi] said to him, 'Since you are so wise, what is the reason that you engaged in the worship of the stars (*avodat kokhavim*)?' [Manasseh] said to him, 'Had you been there, you would have grabbed the hem of your garment and ran after me.'" Concerning the figure of Manasseh in late-biblical, post-biblical, rabbinic, and Christian literature, see Graham (2002, 51–114); Handy (2013, 221–235); Henze (2016, 183–228).

dominating characteristic of the biblical belief is the direct and unmediated revelation of the divine. The words "God spoke," and variations, are without doubt the most central locution in the Bible, both quantitatively and more importantly theologically.[11] God has disappeared, but his words are heard for all eternity.

Considering this analysis, the theological turn during the Second Temple period cannot be overstated. Second Temple Jewish literature presents an almost opposite picture from that presented by the Bible. On the one hand, there are almost no references to the temptation of foreign worship (*avodah zarah*), which throughout the Bible plagued the Jewish people.[12] On the other hand, this literature is full of lengthy descriptions of angelic beings and the many entities that inhabit the heavens alongside God (Reeves and Reed, 2018, 170–209; Reiterer et al., 2007). In other words, the most significant heresy from the Bible's perspective has disappeared, but the visionary realm that the Bible sought to neutralize was reopened.[13]

Indeed, the stark contrast between biblical literature and Second Temple and classic rabbinic literature is the atrophy of prophecy. Prophecy can be found spanning the entirety of the Bible, including post-exilic prophets of the Persian era (Haggai, Zechariah, and Malakhi) and early Hellenistic era (Daniel). However, with Promethean daring the sages sealed off prophecy. In the world of the sages no room remained for unmediated divine correspondence or prophetic authority. The central locution, "God spoke," lost its hold; already in apocalyptic literature of the Second Temple era God rarely speaks directly, even when there are those who claim prophecy (Kister, 2004, 21–22).[14] In the wake of the destruction of the Second Temple, the sages go even further – not only do they present themselves as not having access to the direct divine word, they became "merely" the interpreters of the recorded divine word found in the Bible. Furthermore, they transformed the claim of revelation from a sign of religious piety and excellence into a fallacious claim.[15] As a result, Judaism was transformed from a revelatory into a

---

[11] See, for example, Abraham J. Heschel's discussion of this idiom and its theological importance (1955, 181–183).

[12] For example, we find in *b. Sanhedrin* 63b–64a a remarkable story in which the sages retell how in the days of Nehemiah the desire for idolatry was completely obliterated. Concerning this passage in the thought of later Jewish thinkers, see Reiser (2018, 200–208).

[13] Concerning the realm of visionary experience in classic rabbinic literature and Jewish mysticism, see Boyarin (1990, 532–550); Halbertal (2007, 13–17); Kaniel (2017, 146–172); Lieberman (1965); Pedaya (1995); Reiser (2018, 219–226); Wolfson (1994, esp. 33–51).

[14] See Fraade (1991) and Fraade (2011), which demonstrates the emphasis on exegesis and the almost complete absence of verbal communication.

[15] For example, the sages developed phrases such as, "These are nothing other than words of prophecy" (*b. Bava Batra* 12a; *b. Eruvin* 60b), which means that the preceding statement has no logic; similarly, "They rendered their statements in this case like statements of prophecy" (*b. Bekhorot* 45a),

hermeneutical religion. To borrow Weberian terminology, it shifted from being a charismatic to a legalistic religion (Weber, 1947, 324–362).

3 The Debate Concerning Mysticism in Second Temple Literature and Tannaitic Sources

Esoteric knowledge circulated widely in Second Temple non-canonical Jewish literature. Second Temple revelatory literature (Collins, 1974), such as apocalyptic, Enochic, Qumranic, Early Christian, Gnostic, and other types, contains diverse and variegated descriptions of revelation (Himmelfarb, 1993). These texts encourage engagement with mysteries related to the laws of creation, the nature of the supernal realms, communicating with angels, and especially the liturgical activity in their communities (Alexander, 2006). The authors of mystical literature from the Second Temple era claimed to know the secrets of creation, which enabled them to understand the secrets of the past, events occurring in the present, and often offer insight into the unfolding of the future, especially the eschatological future.

Although prophecy was sealed off within rabbinic circles, the religious aspiration for prophecy did not dissipate. An expression of this aspiration can be found within the foundation of ancient Jewish mysticism. Within this framework, direct divine revelation was substituted with mediated revelation – the spoken divine word with that of the biblical text (Dimant, 2013, 41; Fishbane, 2007, 11; Idel, 2002, 164–181; Schäfer, 2009, 175–213; Wolfson, 2006, 63–64).[16] God was distanced from humans and therefore communication between God and humans was to be mediated. We also find other forms of indirect revelation, such as angelophany, demonophany, and the appearance of classic biblical characters, such as Elijah the prophet (Deutsch, 1999, 27–47; Fossum, 1985; Grabbe, 2000, 219–225; Orlov, 2017, 9–60; Wolfson, 1994, 13–51). Nonetheless, these inferior forms of revelation did not satisfy the religious urge and desire to encounter God himself, which was viewed as the apex of mystical experience.

An in-depth analysis of classic rabbinic sources reveals a fierce struggle concerning mysticism. This ideological clash is reflected throughout classic rabbinic

---

which has an identical meaning. However, it should be noted that medieval Jewish sages disagreed concerning the meaning of these phrases; for example, see Tosafot, ad loc., b. Eruvin 60b s.v. "ein elu ela divrei nevi'ut."

16 The conception of the Torah as a medium for revelation can be found throughout Jewish literature from the Second Temple era until our own times. The above list is a mere sampling of various studies that have discussed this phenomenon in Second Temple Jewish literature.

literature. However, it is especially evident in the "mystical collection" found at the beginning of the second chapter of the tractate Ḥagigah, as it appears in the Mishnah, Tosefta, and Talmud. At the center of this collection is the famous story of "the four who entered the orchard (*pardes*)." These four enthralling figures represent archetypes of those who yearn for revelation, while being cognizant of the reward and risks entailed therein.[17] Two of these figures deeply influenced Jewish culture for generations: the model for believers and the model for heretics – R. Akiva and Elisha b. Abuyah, commonly known as Aḥer (*other*). What follows is the great debate concerning mystical endeavors in the world of the rabbinic sages as expressed through three different circles: the hyper-mystical circle of R. Yoḥanan b. Zakkai, the anti-mystical circle of R. Judah ha-Nasi, and the moderate mystical circle of R. Akiva.

4 M. Ḥagigah 2:1 – Mystical or Anti-Mystical Mishnah

The most mystical mishnah found in Judah ha-Nasi's compilation is often considered to be *Ḥagigah* 2:1, which states:

> One may not explicate (*dorshin*) the laws of forbidden sexual relations (*arayot*) before three people, nor the Account of Creation before two, nor the Divine Chariot before one, unless he is wise and understood (*hevin*) from his own knowledge.[18] Anyone who looks (*ha-mistaqel*) into four things is worthy of not having come into the world: what is above, what is below, what is in front, and what is behind. And anyone who has no consideration for the honor of his Maker (*qono*) would be better off if he had not come into the world.[19]

This mishnah is the core of the "mystical collection" of rabbinic literature (Halperin, 1980). The beginning of the mishnah places a limitation upon certain biblical sections when being read or explained aloud in public. The mishnah creates a level of reserve appropriate for each subject. Engaging with the issue of forbidden sexual relations (Lev. 18) is restricted to a teacher and two pupils, while engagement with the Account of Creation (Gen. 1) is constrained to a teacher and one

---

[17] On the tension and dialectic between yearning for revelation, while fearing the inherent risks, see Pedaya (1995, 237–277; 2002, 20–23, 81); Reiser (2018, 219–226); Wolfson (1994, 91, 95, 122; 2005, 288–289).
[18] According to MS Kaufmann.
[19] The majority of this text is according to the standard printed edition. In the various manuscripts we find material that collaborates the following argument. However, we are unable to expand upon them here.

pupil.[20] However, it should be noted that these two subjects were permitted, even if severely limited, whereas the explication of the Account of the Chariot (Ez. 1; 10) was forbidden from being taught to any mere individual. Rather, the individual must be "wise and understood (*hevin*) from his own knowledge."[21]

The ending of the mishnah formulates a similar prohibition in a more abstract and general fashion. It is not concerned with specific biblical sections, but rather with forbidden *content*. This prohibition is not formulated as a prohibition against a type of learning or exposition, but rather a type of speculation or visualization. The four prohibited domains are: "what is above" – the supernal divine realm; "what is below" – the underworld; "what is in front" – that which will happen in the future; and "what is behind" – that which preceded the creation of the world. The last line of the mishnah creates an additional prohibition, which should also be connected to the general theme of the restriction of learning, "And anyone who has no consideration for the honor of his Maker (*qono*) would be better off if he had not come into the world." Ostensibly, it should be understood in connection with the prohibitions listed in the first part of the mishnah, especially the prohibition to expound upon the Account of the Chariot. A person who expounds upon the Accounts of Creation and the Chariot and peers into the forbidden fields of knowledge is likely to cause damage as a result of his conclusions, either from the mere engagement with these matters or through the desecration of God's honor.

Several scholars have noted that there is a tension, even a possible contradiction, between the three parts of this mishnah. The beginning of the mishnah allows for the teaching of the Chariot to one student under restrictive conditions, while the end of the mishnah prohibits engaging in mystical speculation completely. Yet, the juxtaposition of the different elements leads us to naturally read

---

[20] From the Palestinian Talmud it emerges that there was a disagreement between two rabbinic schools concerning the permission to expound upon the biblical verses concerning illicit sexual relations and the account of creation. While the school of Akiva, whose opinion is found in the mishnah, profoundly limited the study of these verses, the school of Yishmael permitted it (and the law is actually in accordance with their opinion in *y. Ḥagigah* 2:1; Sussmann (2001, 782). Regarding the exposition of the account of creation as a characteristic of this school, see Kahana (2006, 347–376).

[21] The difference between these biblical sections and other biblical sections has been exquisitely formulated by Leopold Zunz (19th cen.), who wrote: "The laws of Israel and its history and the providence of God revealed in them are the content of the holy books. However, two episodes rise to the source of these matters: to God and creation; the episode of creation recounted in the first chapter of the Book of Genesis, and the glory of God depicted by Ezekiel, and both of them were already utilized in ancient times as important and unique aspects of *midrash* as a foundation of faith and wisdom" (1947, 71). For more on this scholar, see Schorsch (2016).

them together and in a connected manner (Halperin, 1980, 21–22n12; Lifshitz, 1983, 514; Rowland and Morray-Jones, 2009, 226–277; Urbach, 1974, 193).

However, this contradiction may be solved if we assume that the closing statement of the beginning of the mishnah, "unless he is wise and understood (*hevin*) from his own knowledge," was added to the mishnah from an independent source. This type of source may be found in Tosefta *Ḥagigah*, which we will discuss in detail later, which states:

> They do not expound upon the laws of prohibited relationships (*arayot*) before three persons, but they do expound them before two; or about the Account of Creation before two, but they do expound them before one; or about the Chariot before one, unless he was a sage [who] understands (*ḥakham mevin*) of his own knowledge.

This Baraita is seemingly superfluous, as obviously what cannot be taught to three can be taught to two.[22] However, if we presume that the mishnah's beginning section concluded with the statement "nor the Divine Chariot before one," thereby closing-off mystical engagement, then we may understand the precise wording of the Tosefta, which builds on the composition of our mishnah and reopens the possibility of teaching the Account of the Chariot to a wise and understanding individual. Thus, the concluding line of the Toseftan Baraita was added to the mishnah to soften the strict restriction of mystical engagement.

This is the only mishnah that explicitly engages with esoteric wisdom and its mystical content. It is especially instructive to compare the ending of the mishnah with a section of *Raz Nihyeh* of Qumranic wisdom literature:

Raz Nihyeh	m. Ḥagigah 2:1
You, under[stan]ding one, [...] 2 [...] ... consider the wonder[ful] mysteries [of the God of awe. Pay attention to the principle of ...] 3 [...] ... [...] ... consider [... of old (?), why something exists, and what exists (4Q417:1:I:1–3; *DSSSE*, 859).[23]	Anyone who looks (*ha-mistaqel*) into four things is worthy of not having come into the world: what is above, what is below, what is in front, and what is behind.

---

22 See Lieberman (1993–1996, 1286–1287) concerning the redundant nature of this Baraita and its possible interpretations.
23 Also, see Goff (2013, 137–172). Cf. 1QS:XI:3–6 (DSSSE, 122), "For from the source of his knowledge he has disclosed his light, and my eyes have observed his wonders, and the light of my heart the mystery of existence. What always is, is support for my right hand ... from the wonderful mystery is the light in my heart. My eyes have observed what always is, wisdom that has been hidden from mankind, knowledge and prudent understanding (hidden) from the sons of man." For further discussion of these passages in connection to mysticism in Qumranic and rabbinic literature, see Furstenberg (2013, 48–53); Goff (2013); Kister (2009, 299–320).

This demonstrates a serious disagreement between the ethos characterizing the Qumran sect and their contemporary Second Temple peers, Ben Sira and the Mishnah.[24] While the Qumranic literature encourages mystical speculation, the Mishnah deplores it. As Gershom Scholem (1941, 42–43) wrote, "it is a well-known fact that the editor of the Mishnah, the patriarch Jehudah 'the Saint,' a pronounced rationalist, did all he could to exclude references to the Merkabah, the angelology, etc." Even if Scholem's remarks are slightly exaggerated and based on an argument of absence and not a negation or denigration of mysticism, this mishnah in *Ḥagigah* is not merely non-mystical, but even anti-mystical.

Scholarship concerning Mishnaic literature has demonstrated the importance of the editing decisions made by the redactors of this corpus; the elements that they have included and those they have excluded, as well as where topics have been positioned. An analysis of the context of this mishnah produces surprising results. First, this mishnah is placed within a tractate that is concerned with the festival offering (*qorban ḥagigah*). Second, it is weaved within a set of Mishnaic passages that are concerned with the biblical verse "A twisted thing that cannot be made straight, a lack that cannot be made good" (Eccl. 1:15), which concluded the previous chapter in the tractate.[25]

The other Mishnaic passages ask, "Who is 'a twisted thing that cannot be made straight'?" One answer is a sacrificial offering that was not brought on time; a second answer is that of a person who engaged in illicit relations and brought forth into this world a *mamzer* (bastard); a third answer is, "A sage who separates from Torah" (*m. Ḥagigah* 1:7).[26] Following these teachings is an exposition of laws that are not biblically rooted, such as the festival offering, and then our mishnah.

---

[24] Cf. Boyarin (2018, 545–548), who likewise connects this passage with the mishnah for a similar purpose, specifically, "I would offer that the Mishnah's primary objection to such kinds of knowledge was the implicit claim of authority that they made independent of and perhaps in competition with the Rabbi's Oral Torah, the exclusive possession of the rabbinic community and authority structure."

[25] Jacob N. Epstein (1957, 46–47) argued that there is continuity between the end of the first chapter of this Tosefta and the beginning of the second chapter, and that the mishnahs 1:8–2:1 are a kind of introduction to the mishnahs 2:2–4. Halperin (1980, 20), on the other hand, has demonstrated the fragmentariness of this Mishnaic collection. This disagreement is also related to the dating of the mishnah in question. Epstein claimed that the mishnah is a very early stratum in the Tannaitic compositions (due to its contextualization with *m. Ḥagigah* 1:8, which in his opinion is of very early origin), whereas Halperin rejected this claim. Also, see the discussion of Goshen-Gottstein (1995, 77–79).

[26] According to Epstein (1957, 48) mishnah 1:7 and the expositions of the verse "What is crooked that cannot be made straight?" is a later addition to the mishnah.

Hanoch Albeck (1952, 393) wrote in his commentary on this mishnah a short, but insightful, remark:

> The juxtaposition of this mishnah ... here, whose primary purpose is not the laws of festivals adjacently referenced, but rather the hint in these mishnahs of the reasons that led the sages to separate from the Oral Torah ... Some people entered the orchard and engaged with the Accounts of Creation and Chariot and were injured or gone astray.[27]

This demonstrates how the editor of the Mishnah denounced mystical practice by juxtaposing it with the Mishnaic passages that appear in this set. However, as we will shorty demonstrate, this was not the only position among the rabbinic sages.

5 Between the Mishnah and Tosefta

Alongside the Mishnah appears another collection of Tannaitic sources referred to as Tosefta. The Tosefta was arranged in accordance with the layout of the Mishnah; however, it contains a great deal of material that did not find its way into the Mishnah. Therefore, one may analyze competing positions and ideologies to those expressed in the circle of Judah ha-Nasi.[28] At the beginning of the second chapter of Tosefta Ḥagigah appears an expanded "mystical collection."[29] It consists of seven different units, which are centered around the story of "four who entered the orchard." The first unit correlates to the first half of our mishnah and is followed by a story of R. Eleazar ben Arakh, who successfully expounded upon the Account of the Chariot in front of his teacher R. Yoḥanan b. Zakkai. The second unit depicts a chain of master–disciples expounding upon the Account of the Chariot. The third and fourth units are the central passage, which depict the four sages who entered the orchard. The fifth unit contains two enigmatic parables, which we will discuss below. The sixth unit relays a parallel story to that of

---

27 Cf. Knohl (2000, 60–66) concerning Menahem the Essene.
28 The Tosefta, to an extent, serves as a complementary composition to that of the Mishnah. It is a matter of scholarly debate concerning its precise dating: while some scholars, such as Yaakov Elman (1991) and Abraham Goldberg (1987), place it within the early Amoraic period, others, such as Shamma Friedman (1991; 1999, 99–121; 2000a, 196–198; 2000b, 39–43; 2002) and Judith Hauptman (1999; 2000; 2005a; 2005b) have claimed that parts or even most of the Tosefta predates the Mishnah. Other scholars, such as Avraham Walfish (2005–2006, 78–79), have sidestepped this debate and instead focused on how both the Mishnah's and Tosefta's redactors utilize different techniques for different goals.
29 Specifically, Tosefta Ḥagigah 2:1–7. The translations of this Tosefta in this chapter are based on Neusner (2002, 668–670).

R. Eleazer and R. Yoḥanan, in which Ben Zoma expounds upon the Account of Creation in the presence of R. Joshua. However, dissimilar to the former story, here there are disastrous results. Finally, the seventh unit begins with an altered version of the second half of our mishnah.

Scholars who have discussed this Tosefta have assumed that it was vigorously edited. The various disagreements mainly concern its meaning.[30] While its editorial stages are important (Bar-On, forthcoming), we would like to discuss the various voices that are interwoven in the passage. An analysis of the literary unit in this way will put the emphasis on internal tensions in the main part of the chapter and will demonstrate that different layers of the text relate differently to mystical practice – its revelatory rewards and its heretical hazards.

Two Sages, Two Stories: The Death of Ben Zoma and Blessing of Eleazer b. Arakh

This tension is exquisitely demonstrated when comparing the second and sixth unit.[31] The two stories betray a reciprocal connection: both describe an encounter between two *tannaim*, the first between Yoḥanan b. Zakkai and Eleazar b. Arakh and the second between Joshua and Ben Zoma; both engage with some form of esoteric knowledge, the first with the weightier Account of the Chariot and the second with the lighter Account of Creation; the first *tanna* mentioned (Yoḥanan b. Zakkai and Joshua) is senior, while the second *tanna* mentioned (Eleazar b. Arakh and Ben Zoma) is a pupil; lastly, in both stories the first *tanna* does not offer the mystical knowledge – rather, it is the pupil who expounds upon the esoteric doctrine. Thus, these stories follow the Mishnaic ruling that one does not teach mystical knowledge, but it may be disclosed through a dialogue between student and teacher.[32]

---

30 A thorough summary of the different suggestions concerning this *aggadah* can be found in Rowland and Morray-Jones (2009, 341–378). Also, see Fraenkel (2001, 317–345).
31 As Halperin (1980, 69) remarked, the rest of the Tosefta does not have clear linguistic connections to the mishnah in question.
32 As the mishnah states: "One may not explicate (*dorshin*) … the Divine Chariot before one, unless he is wise and understanding from his own knowledge." This raises the question, "If one is wise and understanding from his own knowledge, then why do they need to be taught?" The Babylonian Talmud answers with a Baraita, "R. Ḥiyya taught, 'But we do tell him the 'heads of chapters' (*rashei peraqim*)." This process is detailed in the Palestinian Talmud: "At the start his teacher indicates the topics of the verses and summarizes" (*y. Ḥagigah* 2:1; trans. Guggenheimer, 2015, 419).

This last aspect of a pupil expounding upon these mysteries is how we should understand the second Toseftan unit, which depicts how the Account of the Chariot was passed down from teacher to student, or better yet how it was conveyed from student to teacher:

> R. Yose b. Judah says, "R. Joshua laid matters out before Rabban Yoḥanan b. Zakkai. R. Akiva laid matters out before R. Joshua. Ḥananiah b. Kinai laid matters out before R. Akiva."[33]

To return to the units at hand, despite the similarities between these stories, the difference between them is clear: the moral. While the first story ends with praises and blessings, which Yoḥanan b. Zakkai confers upon Eleazar b. Arakh, who masterfully presents his understanding of the Account of the Chariot, the second story ends with the dark prophecy of Joshua concerning the death of Ben Zoma, who speculated concerning the Account of Creation. Since these stories appear in the same textual collection, scholars have attempted to explain how they are only seemingly contradictory, and have offered reconciliatory readings.[34] However, if we consider that they may represent two different schools of thought, then the question itself is not sustained. One seeks to expand mystical practices, viewing them as important channels of religiosity, while the other seeks to limit them, viewing them as heretical dangers.

---

[33] Especially prominent in this list is Yoḥanan b. Zakkai, who is attributed with heading the major institutions of the Patriarchate and Sanhedrin after the destruction of the Temple; see Goodblatt (1994, 224–240), Lapin (2012, 46), Levine (1989, 23–42). However, noticeably absent is the patriarchal line of Hillel the Elder, from whom the anti-mystical Judah ha-Nasi descends. The presentation of learning the Account of the Chariot as the presentation of a student to their teacher further reinforces the MS Kaufmann version of the mishnah, "Nor the Divine Chariot before one, unless he is wise and understood (*hevin*) from his own knowledge." This student may present his knowledge to his teacher and receive approval. Our claim is that this approach is highly indicative of Akiva's circle, for esoteric knowledge is not being taught, yet it is not occluded.

[34] Alon Goshen-Gottstein (1995, 83–84), suggested that while the first story presents a model of a teacher and his disciple, Ben Zoma engages with mystical topics without a teacher. Thus, the message that emerges from both stories is the prohibition on engaging with mysticism without an intermediary teacher. According to Fraenkel (2001, 331–333), the problem with Ben Zoma's exposition is not the lack of the mediating teacher, incompetence, or heresy, but rather the fact that he *publicly* expounded upon the Account of Creation and Divine Chariot. Another possibility is that while the first story deals with the exposition, a permitted and legitimate mystical activity, the second story deals with gazing, which is a forbidden activity. However, it is difficult to confirm these hypotheses, which are seemingly born out of the textual tensions, since they could have been formulated explicitly. These matters are reinforced through the continuation of the tradition by Yoḥanan b. Zakkai's students, which appears in both the Palestinian and Babylonian Talmud, to be discussed below.

Yoḥanan b. Zakkai's and his circle's mystical tendencies are amplified and referenced in both the Palestinian and Babylonian Talmuds. We find an expanded version of the Eleazar b. Arakh story, which includes an angelophanic pronouncement concerning Eleazar b. Arakh's exposition in the presence of his master, that it "is the very Account of the Chariot." For which:

> Yoḥanan b. Zakkai stood and kissed [Rabbi Eleazar b. Arakh] on his head, and said: Blessed be God, Lord of Israel, who gave our father Abraham a son, who knows how to understand, investigate, and expound the Account of the Chariot. There are some who expound well but do not fulfill well, who fulfill well but do not expound well, you expound well and fulfill well. Happy are you, our father Abraham, that Eleazar b. Arakh came from your loins.
> (b. Ḥagigah 14b; cf. y. Ḥagigah 2:1)

This episode was recounted to other students of Yoḥanan b. Zakkai – R. Joshua and R. Yosi the Priest. They too began to expound the Account of the Chariot, *not in the presence of their teacher*, causing meteorological disturbances and a celestial gathering of angels. Yosi relayed this to Yoḥanan b. Zakkai, who said:

> Happy are you, and happy are those who gave birth to you; happy are my eyes that saw this. As for you and I, in my dream we were seated at Mount Sinai, and a Divine Voice (*bat qol*) came to us from heaven: Ascend here, ascend here, large halls (*teraqelin*) and pleasant couches are made up for you. You, your students, and the students of your students are invited to the third group (*le-kat shelishit*). (b. Ḥagigah 14b; cf. y. Ḥagigah 2:1)

This cluster of stories develops and augments the pro-mystical message that arises from the Tosefta concerning R. Yoḥanan's school. While the first story follows the Mishnaic guidelines of a student expounding in the presence of his teacher, the second story, concerning R. Joshua and R. Yosi, transgresses these guidelines. They expounded upon the Account of the Chariot on their own. For their actions they are not reprimanded; rather, they receive an angelic audience, the approval of their teacher, and divine approval, even an invitation to the "third group."[35] In sum, within Mishnaic and Toseftan traditions we find evidence of a mystical circle connected to Yoḥanan b. Zakkai, which viewed mystical engagement in a positive light.

In contrast to these stories, which neutralize the fear and amplify the divine benefit associated with mystical engagement, Ben Zoma's story compounds them. For even though he is more stringent than the mishnah, as the Account of Creation may be expounded upon in the presence of one and Ben Zoma expounds upon it by himself, he still loses his world. The meaning of this story is very clear: even the Account of Creation which one is permitted to teach is too dangerous and

---

[35] For additional references to the third group, see *b. Sanhedrin* 38b.

should not be taught; one should not speculate concerning the supernal realms and esoteric knowledge. This trend is apposite of the path of Judah ha-Nasi mentioned above, which may be further exemplified in the following story: "Rebbi (Judah ha-Nasi) had a competent student who explained one Chapter in the Work of the Chariot to which Rebbi did not concur; he was stricken with scabies" (y. Ḥagigah 2:1; Guggenheimer, 2015, 419). This story is of one student, whom the Palestinian Talmud emphasizes as competent; however, Judah ha-Nasi's reservations caused disaster. It is possible that Judah ha-Nasi disapproved of the content, but it is quite reasonable that he was opposed to engagement with the Account of Creation and the Chariot, even according to the Mishnaic guidelines.

Two Mystical Parables

The next layer in the Tosefta is the fifth unit, which incorporates a pair of parables (*meshalim*). They state the following:

> 2:5a To what is the matter (*mashal*) to be compared? To a royal orchard, with an upper room built over it. What should a person do? Only to peer, but not feast his eyes upon it.
>
> 2:5b And they further compared the matter (*mashal*) to what? To a main throughway (*isterata*) passing between two paths, one of light (*or*) and one of snow. [If] he turns to this side, he will be smitten by light, [and if] he turns to that, he will be smitten by snow. Now what should a person do? He should go right down the middle, and not turn either to this side or to that.

In the present sequence of the Tosefta the meaning of the *meshalim* are not clear. The opening phrase, "To what is the matter to be compared," implies that the text immediately preceding is the *nimshal* (meaning of the parable), which the parable is interpreting. Yet, the text immediately preceding it is the story of four who entered the orchard, which we will discuss below. How do the parables of the royal orchard or the main throughway passing between two paths, one of light and one of snow, elucidate the story of the orchard? The relationship between the *mashal* and *nimshal* is quite unclear.[36]

However, if we approach the text in question as one that has been formed across different stages, incorporating multiple and contradicting trends, then we are not required to find a solution to the above issues; rather, we may suggest a different type of question: why was this passage inserted into this textual

---

[36] Indeed, see the exasperating attempts to connect the story of the four who entered the orchard to the parable of the orchard, Halperin (1980); Urbach (1988a).

continuity? Clearly, these parables were inserted at a later point and their original intent is not to clarify the story of the orchard. However, by being injected in this text they ultimately shape the Tosefta to be in line with a certain trend. Following this line of thought, we would like to propose that the story of the orchard was not even part of this textual composition when these parables were inserted. These parables were introduced to demonstrate a mitigated path for mystical practices, situated between the overly permissive position set by Yoḥanan b. Zakkai's school and the sweeping prohibition discerned from the story of Joshua and Ben Zoma.[37]

André Neher suggested that the origin of these parables is to be found in *m. Middot* 4:5 (MS Kaufmann 4:6–7) (Neher, 1951, 59–82). This mishnah depicts the winding walkway and the roof of the upper chamber of the Temple:

> Then [he would] traverse until he reached the opening of the upper chamber ... In the opening of the upper chamber were two columns of cedar by which they used to climb up to the roof of the upper chamber, and at the top of them was a row of stones showing the division in the upper chamber between the holy part and the Holy of Holies. Trap doors (*u-velulim*)[38] would be opened in the upper chamber between the Holy of Holies in which the artisans were descended in baskets so that they should not feast their eyes on the Holy of Holies.

The parables that we have discussed are a type of "Tosefta" (addition) to this Mishnah, for which, as far as is known, no Tosefta exists. The cautious traversing, done according to protocol, correlates to the guardian of the king's orchard and the row of stones separating the upper chamber correlates to the main throughway that is between the paths of light and snow. Thus, these parables were originally intended to instruct the priests, the guards, and the artisans in the Temple about how they should deal with the numinous elements of the Temple and, specifically, the Holy of Holies.[39] The Temple is the intended meaning of the royal orchard and each person who enters the royal inner sanctuary must avert their eyes from feasting; rather, they must only glance (*le-ḥeṣiṣ*)![40]

---

[37] Possible evidence for this may be culled from MS Erfurt, f. 206–207, which places these parables after the story of Joshua and Ben Zoma and not the story of "four who entered"; see Ḥagigah 2:6, Zuckermandel (1970); Ḥagigah 2:5, Lieberman (1993–1996).

[38] This is as it appears in MS Kaufmann, Florence, and Munich. However, in *b. Pesaḥim* 26a, MS Parma, it appears as *lulin*, cf. *b. Menaḥot* 34a. The terms originated in I Kings 6:8: "The entrance for the middle story was on the south side of the house: one went up by winding stairs to the middle story, and from the middle story to the third." Seemingly, the *lul* is an empty space or chimney; see Rabbi Nathan of Rome (1928, 5:26).

[39] Also, in the various parables concerning orchards in classic rabbinic literature, which Goshen-Gottstein (1995, 97) discussed, we find parallels between the orchard and temple.

[40] If this reading is correct then the utilization of the same parable in *Avot de-Rabbi Natan* A, 28:10, is inconsequential, unlike Goshen-Gottstein's opinion (1995, 119). Therefore, it is easy to

The placement of this parable within the mystical composition of Tosefta *Ḥagigah* means it is no longer in its original context and is now read as referring to the supernal orchard. It should be noted that although the original context is the priestly and temple ethos, this new context should be understood as an expansion of this ethos. As is well known, the orchard is already found in Second Temple-era literature and is identified with the third firmament found in the Aramaic Enoch, Qumranic literature, and in Corinthians II (Bremmer, 1999, 13; Rowland and Morray-Jones, 2009, 374–377; Scholem, 1965, 14–19). Thus, as Rowland and Murray-Jones (2009, 377) demonstrate, instructions concerning the proper conduct within the sanctified spaces of the Temple were expanded to be understood as instructions concerning proper conduct in the heavens.

Four Who Entered the Orchard

The most famous units in this Tosefta chapter are obviously the third and fourth units, which depict the four sages who entered the orchard:

> 2:3 Four entered the orchard [Paradise]: Ben Azzai, Ben Zoma, the Other (*aḥer*) [Elisha], and R. Akiva. One peered (*heṣiṣ*) and perished, one peered and was smitten (*nifgah*), one peered and cut down (*qiṣeṣ*) shoots, and one went up whole and came down whole. Ben Azzai peered and perished. Concerning him Scripture says, "Precious in the sight of the Lord is the death of his saints" (Ps. 116:15). Ben Zoma peered and was smitten. Concerning him Scripture says, "If you have found honey, eat only enough for you, lest you be sated with it and vomit it" (Prov. 25:16). Elisha peered and cut down shoots. Concerning him Scripture says, "Let not your mouth lead you into sin" (Eccl. 5:5).
>
> 2:4 R. Akiva went up whole and came down whole. Concerning him Scripture says, "Draw me after you, let us make haste. [The king has brought me into his chambers]" (Song of Songs 1:4)

Interestingly, this story also presents two opposing positions concerning mystical engagement. These positions are demonstrated through the fate of the three sages smitten by the encounter and in contrast, Akiva's successful ascension to and descension from the supernal realm.

First, three textual problems, which create internal gaps and attest to its different stages of composition, should be noted in this unit. Let us begin with the gap between the parable of the orchard and the story of the four who entered the orchard. The parable demonstrates that a person may glance from the upper

---

ascertain that the parable there does not match the intended meaning, which discusses the preference for words of Torah above that of *derekh ereṣ* (way of the world) in the world-to-come.

chamber upon the orchard, but he is not allowed to enter. Yet, the story is of the four who *entered* the orchard, and no type of upper chamber or balcony is depicted.[41] A second gap exists between the figure of Elisha b. Abuyah and the figures of Ben Zoma and Ben Azzai. Concerning Ben Zoma and Ben Azzai it is not at all clear what caused one to be smitten and the other to perish. The reader must fill in the gap between the glance of the orchard and the results. In the story, as it appears in the Tosefta, there is no explanation for the inherent dangers of the orchard. Moreover, it is only in the case of Elisha that the parable of the royal orchard is understandable. Elisha entered the orchard and cut down the shoots. While the gazing of the guard in the parable is appropriate for Ben Zoma and Ben Azzai, the orchard itself is more suitable for Elisha. In light of this, it can be hypothesized that the nucleus of the story of the four who entered the orchard dealt only with one person who entered the orchard and cut down the shoots.[42]

An even more conspicuous gap may be seen between Akiva's "ascent and descent" and the other three sages' "entrance and exit" to and from the orchard.[43] It should also be noted that the biblical verse ascribed to Akiva's ascent and descent is easily understood and is appropriate for the mystical context. Likewise, the biblical verse ascribed to Elisha's apostasy is also clearly understandable. However, the biblical verses ascribed to Ben Azzai's and Ben Zoma's fates are entirely obscured.

In light of this, we would like to argue that after the nucleus of the story was initially expanded there were three sages who entered the orchard. This formulation continues the parables mentioned in the fifth unit, which instructed the mystic to only "peer" or "glance" into the orchard. The story indeed discusses the sages who "peered" into the "orchard." However, it was recast as to be vehemently opposed to peering into the orchard, which the parable implies, by describing the tragic fate of the three sages who did thusly. Two of them were injured: "Ben Azzai

---

41 However, if the temple structure is taken into account then this gap between the parable and the intended meaning may be overcome to an extent, for one could be lowered into the Holy of Holies; nevertheless, one would expect the legend to be closer to the parable.

42 Scholars of this legend have discussed the appearance of these four in *Avot de-Rabbi Natan*. Goshen-Gottstein and Rowland and Murray-Jones have hypothesized that the names for our legend are from there. Goshen-Gottstein insisted that this tradition is earlier, and accordingly one who sees Elisha should expect disaster. One should take into account that originally we only have a tradition concerning one sage: Elisha, who "cut down the shoots." The other sages are added at later stages. This original tradition correlates better with the parable of the royal orchard, which appears later in the pericope in the Palestinian Talmud, "A king's orchard and an observation deck built on it, to look at it but not to touch" (*y. Ḥagigah* 2:1; Guggenheimer, 2015, 431).

43 An exception to this phrasing can be found in MS Erfurt, in which the copyist (either intentionally or accidentally) unified the formulations.

gazed and perished ... Ben Zoma gazed and was smitten." While the third was not damaged, but rather damaged the royal orchard, "Elisha gazed and cut down the shoots."[44] It seems, therefore, that the conception of this passage is found within the circle of those who opposed mysticism, who employed the same tactic that we observed beforehand. They conjoined another element into the Tosefta, thereby reshaping it. Contrary to the implication of the parables we discussed, and without overtly opposing them, these sages wholly rejected even peering into the royal orchard.

In contrast to this anti-mystical trend, Akiva's story was placed here from a different location – representing another editing stage of this particular story and the mystical collection in general. This source did not discuss peering into the orchard, but rather ascending to heaven, as part of a homily (*midrash*) on the verse in Song of Songs, "Draw me after you, let us make haste. The king has brought me into his chambers (Song. 1:4)." The mystical potential of the verse is self-explanatory and its meaning – which reopens the possibility for rabbinical mystical engagement – is also quite clear.[45]

As Alon Goshen-Gottstein (1995, 84–85) demonstrated, presumably the original Baraita concerning glimpsing into the orchard was anonymous and did not mention the names of the three sages, as is found in typological Baraitot. In addition, it seems that the verses attributed to each sage belong to a later stage in the development of the Baraita, since they do not match the situation and are closely linked to the narrative. It can certainly be assumed that the names of the sages and the verses appeared only when the source added Akiva to the original typological Baraita. After he appears as the "successful" hero together with a biblical verse describing his success, then the names of the three sages were added together with their biblical verses.[46]

---

[44] Thus, the literary opposition in this typology is between those who were damaged and those who caused damage. This contrasts with Goshen-Gottstein's position (1995, 103). Also, see his other suggestion (1995, 104). Fraenkel (2001, 329) interprets it differently and claims that the cutting of the shoots is an action that not only damages the orchard but exposes it, allowing anyone to see the orchard's nakedness without having to enter or glance.

[45] It is reasonable to presume that "his chambers" are related to "the rooms of the chariot." Concerning this phrase, see Halperin (1980, 25–26). In contrast, see Goshen-Gottstein (1995, 84–85), who claimed that the focus of the verse is its beginning, "Draw me after you," for which "after you" is referring to following one's teacher.

[46] This is apposite to Alon Goshen-Gottstein's reading (1995, 107–108), according to which the names of the sages were chosen for the story of "Four who entered the orchard." Considering earlier traditions found in *Avot de-Rabbi Natan*. In other words, at a later stage, Akiva's name was added to the story, and the editor added three more names. He used the three last names appearing in this list: Ben Azzai, Ben Zoma, and Elisha b. Abuyah. This explains the opening sentence

The addition of Akiva to the original, typological, and anonymous Baraita was, of course, another attempt to restructure the original Baraita so as to present a possible case of success and to reopen the path of mystical practice through the image of Akiva, one of the greatest *tannaim*.[47] Now any person, or at least a veteran sage, is able to engage in the exposition of the Account of the Chariot in a limited framework.

In this context we would like to suggest, despite the current absence of solid textual evidence, the possibility that the Baraita, which had Akiva as its hero, was also built according to a tripartite typology. This may have been a possible structure:

> Three ascended to heaven:
>
> Enoch ascended and did not descend as it is written, "Enoch walked with God; then he was no more, for God took him." (Gen. 5:24)
>
> Elijah ascended and did not descend, as it is written, "Elijah went up to heaven in a whirlwind." (II Kin. 2:11)
>
> R. Akiva went up whole and came down whole. Concerning him Scripture says, "Draw me after you... The king has brought me into his chambers." (Song. 1:4)[48]

The story of the four who entered the orchard crystallized, we therefore argue, in several stages. First, there was a heretic who entered the orchard and damaged it. The story was then expanded to include three sages, two of whom only peered and were nevertheless injured; thus, mystical endeavors were sealed off. However, another writer with the opposite view added the figure of Akiva and reopened the possibility of mystical engagement as a worthy endeavor. As a result, the Baraita of three who peered into the orchard turned into a Baraita about four who entered the orchard. In order to balance the Baraita, the anonymous characters

---

that appears in the versions of the Tosefta and Palestinian Talmud: "One gazed and perished, one gazed and was smitten, one gazed and cut the shoots, and one ascended whole and descended whole" (*y. Ḥagigah* 2:3). Ostensibly this sentence was superfluous, for immediately following it is written: "Ben-Azzai gazed and perished ... Ben Zoma gazed and was smitten" (*y. Ḥagigah* 2:3). Indeed, in the Babylonian version of the story this sentence was omitted (as well as in Tosefta MS Erfurt). According to our suggestion, this anonymous sentence was at the heart of the typological Baraita (even before the fourth sage, who had "ascended whole and descended whole," was identified), and at a later stage, when the names of the sages and verses below were added to the story, it was expunged.

47 Akiva is cast perfectly for this role. As Goshen-Gottstein (1995, 105) noted, different groups competed for the (re)forming of his personality and figure; among these different configurations was Akiva the mystic, as exemplified in the Hekhalot literature.

48 In Second Temple literature, many candidates can be identified as those who ascended to heaven and descended again to teach Torah to the people; see Himmelfarb (1993).

who peered into the orchard were identified with the names of particular sages, and then the homiletical explanations of the verses were added to connect what happened to them to hints found in the Torah. If this reconstruction is correct, then Alon Goshen-Gottstein, who claimed that the identification of the heretic with Elisha b. Abuyah is a relatively late innovation and secondary to the story itself, is correct.

6 The Talmudic Traditions Concerning the Heresy of Elisha b. Abuyah

Both the Palestinian and Babylonian Talmud discuss Elisha b. Abuyah's apostasy. However, it is only within the Babylonian Talmud that his heretical turn is contextualized within his quest for mystical revelation (Rubenstein, 1998, 206). The Palestinian Talmud, which chronologically precedes its Babylonian counterpart, contains no less than four different traditions concerning the reason for his heresy. One reason proffered is that Elisha was always destined for heretical activities, since his father wanted him to become a respected Torah scholar for ulterior, power-hungry motives; another possible reason is that his mother, while he was *in utero*, received pleasure from the odor of forbidden food; the other two reasons offered may be classified as theodically motivated. Many scholars have discussed how these Talmudic stories are unconnected to the story of the orchard that appeared in the Tosefta and that they do not concern themselves with the issue of revelation (Rovner, 2012, 199–206). Considering this, we would like to suggest that these traditions were originally unrelated to our mishnah – a misplaced Talmudic pericope.[49] These stories originally belonged to *m. Ḥagigah* 1:7:

> R. Shimon ben Menasya says: Who is 'a twisted thing that cannot be made straight?' ... Rabbi Shimon ben Yohai says: They only call something 'twisted' if it was straight at first and then became twisted. And who is this? A disciple of the sages who forsakes the Torah.

There is no doubt that the stories concerning Elisha are of this nature – a disciple of the sages (*talmid ḥakham*) who has forsaken the Torah and even caused others

---

[49] Indeed, a basic examination of the Palestinian Talmudic pericope's structure reveals that the discussion centered around Elisha's apostasy is disconnected from the context of the mishnah. The Palestinian Talmud interprets the cutting of the shoots in a unique manner as Elisha's killing of young Torah students (medieval commentators related this action to his sons). Afterward the Tosefta is quoted concerning Akiva, who "entered whole and exited whole," and only then begins the stories of Meir and Elisha.

to as well. Indeed, if our hypothesis is correct then the relation between the Talmudic pericope and mishnah is surprisingly powerful. While the mishnah claims that there is no rectification for the sage who forsakes the Torah, the Palestinian Talmudic pericope – as well as the Babylonian one in its wake – disagree with the mishnah and attempt to rectify this very sage who abandoned the Torah (Rubenstein, 1998; 1999, 64–104). The Talmudic pericopes depict how collegial activities can save their irredeemable friend, especially those of Elisha's disciple R. Meir, whose loyalty knows no bounds. Indeed, instead of being punished by angelic entities and God, Meir is given recognition by them.[50]

The Babylonian Talmud offers an explanation for Elisha's heresy which continues and deepens the controversy concerning revelation found in the Tosefta's version of "four who entered the orchard." According to the Babylonian Talmud, Elisha apostatized due to revelation:

> Aḥer cut the shoots. Concerning him Scripture states, "Do not let your mouth bring you into sin (laḥṭi)" [Eccl. 5:5]. What was it? He saw Metatron, who was given permission (rishuta) to sit and write the merits of Israel. He said, "It has been taught that above there is no sitting, no rivalry, no back, and no weariness. Perhaps, heaven forfend, there are two divine powers." Immediately they brought out Metatron and struck him with sixty lashes of fire. Why did you not stand up in front of him?[51] He was given permission to erase the merits of Aḥer. A heavenly voice (bat qol) went out and said to him, "Return, rebellious children" (Jer. 3:22) – except Aḥer. (b. Ḥagigah 15a)

Through this miniature story the Babylonian Talmud recontextualizes the pericope within its new environment, thereby granting new significance not only to Elisha's heresy, but also concerning the very possibility of a sage abandoning the Torah. According to the Babylonian Talmud, Elisha's heresy is a result of his mystical vision. Elisha ascended to the heavenly heights and saw the angel Metatron

---

50 Concerning the ambivalent attitude toward Meir due to his loyalty to Elisha, see the discussion in b. Ḥagigah 15b: "Rabbah b. Shila met Elijah. He said to him, 'What is the Holy One, blessed be He, doing?' He answered, 'He utters traditions in the name of all the rabbis, but in the name of R. Meir he does not utter.' Rabbah asked him, 'Why?' – Because he learnt traditions at the mouth of Aḥer. Said [Rabbah] to him: 'But why? R. Meir found a pomegranate; he ate the inside, and the husk he threw away!' He answered, 'Now He [God] says: "Meir my son says: When a man suffers, to what expression does the Shekhinah give utterance? 'My head is heavy; my arm is heavy.'" If the Holy One, blessed be He, is thus grieved over the blood of the wicked, how much more so over the blood of the righteous that is shed." Seemingly, this story is based on the literary phenomenon that anonymous mishnayot are attributed to Meir, although he is not mentioned. For more concerning the divine ambivalence, see Rovner (2012, 241–242).
51 This sentence is only found in the printed version and MS Vatican; see Rubenstein (1998, 174n70).

seated. In Isaiah 6:1–2 we witness the following vision: "I beheld my Lord seated on a high and lofty throne; and the skirts of His robe filled the Temple. Seraphs stood in attendance on Him." While the fact that God is visualized as sitting and that the Seraphs are standing may seem inconsequential, these different positions were understood in a hierarchical fashion – only God sits (Boyarin, 2010, 2013, 2019).[52] Seeing an additional divine entity sitting in the heavenly realm threw Elisha into a theological crisis; perhaps there *are* two powers in heaven.[53] In this context we should pay special attention to the introductory biblical verses that accompany Elisha's act: "Don't let your mouth bring you into sin, and don't plead before the angel (*ha-malakh*) that it was an error, else God may be angered by your talk and destroy your possessions" (Eccl. 5:5). In the Septuagint, we find that instead of "before the angel," it is written, "before God."[54]

This heretical stance is also reminiscent of Gnostic doctrines (Bar-On and Paz, 2017). However, it should be noted that many extant Gnostic texts have explicitly anti-Judaic elements. Some of them even include scathing critiques of the biblical God and the system of commandments that are attributed to the "wicked" creator of the world. Yet this perspective is not referenced at all in our story and the significance of believing in two authorities remains quite enigmatic. Can there be a different solution?

The Babylonian Talmud stresses that the entity that Elisha saw is the angel Metatron and not God. It also emphasizes that Metatron does not sit on high regularly, but rather has been given special permission (*reshut*) to act as a scribe and record the merits of Israel. The significance of this action – the writing of Israel's merits – is difficult to understand. It may be suggested that from an apologetic motive, the pericope incorporated an ancient tradition, which states that there is an angel who serves as a scribe in heaven. In later Babylonian sources, this angel

---

[52] However, see Kister (2013), who claims that contradicting traditions may be found concerning this matter.
[53] Some scholars, such as Rubenstein (1998, 184), Goshen-Gottstein (1995, 107–108), Goldberg (1987, 182–183), and Grossberg (2017, 182–183), have noted that the additional words "perhaps, God forbid" are meant to convey Elisha's doubt concerning this heretical stance, while other scholars, such as Segal (1977, 61), Alexander (1987, 57), Kister (2013, 66), Morray-Jones (1991, 30), and Deutsch (1999, 55), with whom we agree, assume that the editor of the pericope added these words as to not restate Elisha's heresy in such absolute terms, or do not pay much attention to these words; see Boyarin (2004a, 142–143). This strong editing hand demonstrates and emphasizes how Elisha's speculation was so disturbing. Also, see Rovner (2012, 198n12).
[54] Menahem Kister (2013, 64n107) has suggested that this Greek translation may act as a textual witness to an original Hebrew that becomes clearer in light of Elisha's binitarianistic view, reading, "Don't let your mouth bring you into sin, and don't say before (*lifnei*) the angel – in front of me (*lefanai*) is God"; thereby Elisha places the angel on par with God.

was identified with Enoch and Metatron.⁵⁵ In order to fulfill his duty, he must sit down, thus explaining how Elisha erred.

However, it seems that the Talmud introduces into the mystical system another important variable – the historical situation. It should be remembered that the generation of Elisha b. Abuyah and his peers is one of upheavals. The catastrophes of the destruction of the Temple in 70 CE and the failure of the Bar Kokhba revolt of 132–135 CE were quite traumatic. In the Apocrypha and Talmud there are hints and testaments about the severe crises of faith that many Jews experienced in the wake of the destruction and which, to an extent, have guided Jewish culture since. The transcribing of Israel's merits can be conceived as a celestial occupation concerning the fate of the Jewish people. If Metatron records the people's merits, then he is engaged in the defense of the Jewish people, in order to shield them in times of trouble. Elisha's interruption of Metatron's scribal session may be construed as a violation of a process meant to defend the Jewish people, for which the consequences are disastrous. Elisha's "cutting of the shoots" may therefore be understood as interrupting Metatron's salvific efforts, thus causing a national tragedy. An even more radical interpretation may understand the phrase "writing the merits" as a euphemism. In classic rabbinic sources it is the norm to avoid direct criticism of the Jewish people. Accordingly, Metatron is not sitting to record the merits, but rather the faults of Israel in order to condemn them. This interpretation thereby places the onus of Israel's misfortune on an angel, while God himself remains exempt.⁵⁶

In this context it should be noted that belief in two powers was one way to deal with the problem of evil in the world and the historical suffering of the Jewish people, and especially with the sorrow of the Temple's destruction and its theological implications.⁵⁷ While the Babylonian Talmud did not have Elisha explicitly state this, it is reasonable to assume that through his mystical vision, Elisha was perceived as a kind of binitarian, albeit in unique Jewish garb that differs from Gnostic teachings. Elisha ascended to heaven with the expectation of seeing the God of Israel, who chose his people, loved them, and continued to protect them despite this terrible historical situation. However, instead of seeing this God, he

---

55 Concerning Metatron, see Boyarin (2010; 2013; 2019); Idel (2007, 1–193); Orlov (2017); Paz (2019).
56 Compare this pericope to *b. Yoma* 77a and the discussion of Yehuda Liebes (1990, 29–50). Much of our discussion here relies on Liebes's study, but we come to different conclusions. Liebes states that the difference between Akiva's success and Elisha's failure lies in Akiva's humility and Elisha's hubris.
57 Concerning this belief, see Boyarin (2004a, 126–147; 2004b; 2012); Orlov (2018); Schremer (2008); Segal (1977).

sees a divine entity sitting and recording the sins of Israel. The assumption that there are two authorities, a good authority and an evil authority, theoretically solves the problem of evil and the historical subservience of the Jewish people, but it makes believing in a single God, who is the guardian of Israel, difficult, and therefore leads one of the great sages to abandon his faith.

The Talmudic story continues and adds the surprising scene quoted above from *b. Hagigah* 15a, in which Metatron is struck with lashes of fire, for according to the Talmud, Metatron is also responsible for Elisha's heresy. It was expected of him to stand when Elisha entered the orchard, as not to mislead him. The rabbinic conception of the celestial realm is dynamic and complicated, in which angels are also capable of sin, and consequently may be punished.[58] Metatron's punishment informs the reader that he is only a servant; beholden to divine law and rule.[59] However, in light of our interpretation, it is possible to see Metatron's punishment as a rekindling of the special relationship between the people of Israel and their God. Metatron is punished, for it is because of him that the people of Israel have suffered. It is possible that following his punishment, and perhaps unrelated to it, Metatron was given permission to sit down again and erase Elisha's merits.

Following his erring interpretation, Elisha still received a divine revelation through the heavenly voice. The tragedy, however, is that the heavenly voice condemned him to eternal disgrace. The voice came out and announced the magnitude of the sin and of Elisha's personal tragedy. Had the sages not been able to rescue Elisha by virtue of his Torah (Goshen-Gottstein, 2000, 154–157; Rovner, 2012, 229; Rubenstein, 1999), then his sin would have been so grave that he would have been lost and unable to repent. In contrast to the Palestinian Talmud, the Babylonian squarely situated Elisha's heresy in his visual revelatory experience, which is then followed by his monumental sins: the desecration of the Sabbath, solicitation of prostitution, and even murder of children. Thus, Elisha became an archetype of the sinning mystic, whose mystical vision drove him astray and caused a national disaster.[60]

---

[58] The most famous example of angelic sin is of the Nephilim discussed in Gen 6:1–4, which are later expounded upon in Second Temple literature, both rabbinic and extra-rabbinic; for example, Adelman (2009, 109–137); Harkins (2014); Reed (2005); Reimer (2000). Also, see Stuckenbruck (2017, 1–57). Specifically concerning Metatron's fall, see Deutsch (1999, 48–77).

[59] Concerning angels beholden to divine law, see Rebiger (2007, 640). Also, connected to this subject, see the second characterization of angel–man comparison: Hayes (2017, 139–142).

[60] It should be noted that the Talmud does not cast doubt on the vision itself – Elisha saw Metatron sitting. The problem with Elisha's vision is with its interpretation. However, Elisha's interpretation appears to be quite reasonable from the Talmudic account. It stemmed from a lack of knowledge – Metatron is given permission to sit for a specific role rather than due to malicious intent.

The conclusion that emerges from these sources is not that the events of the supernatural realm should be interpreted differently, but that the attempt to ascend to the heavenly heights must be forsaken and the aspiration for direct visual revelation given up. Thus, the school of the sages who developed the story of Elisha's heresy turned the visionary journey into the celestial realm into an improper pursuit. The legend of the four who entered the orchard, and the tension between the characters of Ben Azzai, Ben Zoma, and Elisha on the one hand and the figure of Akiva on the other, demonstrates the ambivalent attitude found in different rabbinic circles concerning the engagement with mystical endeavors and the contemporary significance of immediate revelation. The compilation of variant sources and opinions demonstrates the dynamics of theological and ideological trends in rabbinic literature. The rabbinic community was not only defined by theological notions, but also hermeneutical practices concerning how Torah was to be studied and which methods were legitimate. These factors played a major role in the makeup of rabbinic identity as a significant circle viewed visual revelatory mystical activities in a negative light. Through the figure of Elisha, who aspired for Icarian heights and ultimately fell from grace, the anti-mystical rabbinic circle transformed revelation from a feature of religious excellence and piety into a rabbinic heresy par excellence.[61]

7 Conclusion: Heresy, Otherness, Friendship, Rehabilitation, and Historical Meaning

Both the Babylonian and Palestinian Talmuds portray Elisha as an outright sinner. The otherness that he internalized in his ascent to the heavenly realm caused him to sin gravely in this earthly realm. Yet, both Talmuds refused to accept the decision of the mishnah and even that of God to denounce Elisha as wholly other. Elisha remains a liminal and paradoxical figure. He is completely outside – now an alien to rabbinic norms – and he is completely inside – continuing his

---

[61] It is worth noting that the Babylonian Talmud is extremely terse concerning the alternative presented by Akiva regarding his mystical practice. In the Babylonian Talmud, Akiva is only mentioned in two passages that allow for the legitimization of revelatory mystical practice. The first is his warning to his colleagues, "When you come to the stones of pure marble, do not say water, water because it is stated: 'He who speaks falsehood shall not be established before My eyes' (Ps. 101:7)" (*b. Ḥagigah* 14b). The second passage explains how Akiva avoided Elisha's catastrophe through the explicating of biblical verses (*b. Ḥagigah* 16a). We hope to explore elsewhere the development of the legitimization of mystical revelatory activity in post-Talmudic sources.

relationship and Torah study with his disciple Meir. It is his revelatory fascination with the heavenly realm that places him in this position – at the absolute edge of the rabbinic community; standing with one foot inside and one foot outside. Ultimately, it is the courageous collegiality of Torah scholars that saves Elisha from complete otherness. However, while revelation is transformed from the arena of faith to the arena of heresy, the study of Torah, common to all the sages, rescues Elisha, even from God, and rehabilitates him and his student and confers upon them the recognition of being rabbinic sages. It seems that the moderate mystical school, which created a synthesis between the school of Yoḥanan b. Zakkai and the school of Judah ha-Nasi, also contributed to the re-admission of the heretical mystic. The leadership of this school was identified with the legacy of most prominent sage and Meir's other primary teacher: Akiva. Akiva demonstrated a third path that combined a total commitment to tradition, while fully immersed in mystical preoccupation (Yadin-Israel, 2014, 104). In any case, despite the historical irony that Elisha, who insisted on divine revelation in times of crisis, later became the archetype of the Zionistic heretical ideology (Dubler, 1991; Be'eri, 2007, 20–25), it is unsurprising that the revived Jewish culture shaped his character in order to favor the integrity of the community over the integrity of faith.

Bibliography

Adelman, Rachel. *The Return of the Repressed: Pirqe De-Rabbi Eliezer and the Pseudepigrapha.* Leiden: Brill, 2009.
Albeck, Hanoch. *The Mishna: Seder Moed.* Jerusalem: Bialik Institute, 1952. Hebrew.
Alexander, Philip S. "*3 Enoch* and the *Talmud.*" *Journal for the Study of Judaism* 18.1 (1987): 40–68.
Alexander, Philip S. *The Mystical Texts.* London: Bloomsbury Academic, 2006.
Bar-On, Shraga. "Three Entered the Orchard and Three Ascend to the Heights." Forthcoming. Hebrew.
Bar-On, Shraga, and Yakir Paz, "'The Lord of All' and 'The Creator of the World': Aleinu le-Shabeach as an Anti-Binitarian rayer." *Jewish Studies* 52 (2017): 19–46. Hebrew.
Be'eri, Nurit. *He Went Forth into Evil Course: Elisha ben Abuya – Aher.* Tel Aviv: Yediot Ahronoth Books, 2007. Hebrew.
Boyarin, Daniel. "The Eye in the Torah: Ocular Desire in Midrashic Hermeneutic." *Critical Inquiry* 16.3 (1990): 532–550.
Boyarin, Daniel. "A Tale of Two Synods: Nicaea, Yavneh, and Rabbinic Ecclesiology." *Exemplaria* 12.1 (2000): 21–62.
Boyarin, Daniel. *Border Lines: The Partition of Judaeo-Christianity.* Philadelphia: University of Pennsylvania Press, 2004a.
Boyarin, Daniel. "Two Powers in Heaven; or, The Making of a Heresy." *The Idea of Biblical Interpretation: Essays in Honor of James L. Kugel.* Ed. Hindy Najman and Judith H. Newman. Leiden: Brill, 2004b. 331–370.

Boyarin, Daniel. "Beyond Judaisms: Metatron and the Divine Polymorphy of Ancient Judaism." *Journal for the Study of Judaism* 41.3 (2010): 323–365.
Boyarin, Daniel. "Once Again: 'Two Dominions in Heaven' in the Mekhilta." *Tarbiz* 81 (2012): 87–101. Hebrew.
Boyarin, Daniel. "Is Metatron a Converted Christian?" *Judaïsme Ancien – Ancient Judaism* 1 (2013): 13–62.
Boyarin, Daniel. "The Talmudic Apocalypse: Ḥagigah, Chapter 2." *Wisdom Poured Out Like Water*. Ed. J. Harold Ellens, Isaac W. Oliver, Jason von Ehrenkrook, James Waddell, and Jason M. Zurawski. Berlin, Boston: De Gruyter, 2018. 541–555.
Boyarin, Daniel. "The Quest of the Historical Metatron: Enoch or Jesus." *A Question of Identity*. Ed. Dikla Rivlin Katz, Noah Hacham, Geoffrey Herman, and Lilach Sagiv. Berlin, Boston: De Gruyter, 2019. 153–162.
Bremmer, Jan N. "Paradise: From Persia, via Greece into the *Septuagint*." *Paradise Interpreted: Representations of Biblical Paradise in Judaism and Christianity*. Ed. Gerard P. Luttikhuizen. Leiden: Brill, 1999. 1–21.
Brettler, Marc Zvi. "Judaism in the Hebrew Bible? The Transition from Ancient Israelite Religion to Judaism." *Catholic Biblical Quarterly* 61.3 (1999): 429–447.
Cohen, Shaye J. D. *The Beginnings of Jewishness: Boundaries, Varieties, Uncertainties*. Berkeley: University of California Press, 1999a.
Cohen, Shaye J. D. "The Temple and the Synagogue." *The Cambridge History of Judaism*, Volume 3: *The Early Roman Period*. Ed. William Horbury, W. D. Davies, and John Sturdy. Cambridge: Cambridge University Press, 1999b. 298–325.
Cohen, Shaye J. D. *From the Maccabees to the Mishnah*. Louisville: Westminster John Knox Press, 2006.
Collins, John J. "Apocalypse, Morphology of a Genre." *Semeia* 14 (1974): 1–20.
Cook, L. Stephen. *On the Question of the Cessation of Prophecy in Ancient Judaism*. Tübingen: Mohr Siebeck, 2012.
Deutsch, Nathaniel. *Guardians of the Gate: Angelic Vice Regency in Late Antiquity*. Leiden: Brill, 1999.
Diamond, James A. "The Failed Theodicy of a Rabbinic Pariah: A Maimonidean Recasting of Elisha ben Abuyah." *Jewish Studies Quarterly* 9 (2002): 353–380.
Dimant, Devorah. "4Ezra and 2Baruch in Light of Qumran Literature." *Fourth Ezra and Second Baruch: Reconstruction after the Fall*. Ed. Matthias Henze, Gabriele Boccaccini, and Jason Zurawski. Leiden: Brill, 2013. 31–61.
Dubler, Ariela. "From Heretic to Hero: Moshe Leib Lilienblum's Transformation of Elisha ben Abuyah." *Mosaic: A Review of Jewish Thought and Culture* 11 (1991): 45–50.
Dulk, Matthijs den. *Between Jews and Heretics: Refiguring Justin Martyr's Dialogue with Trypho*. New York: Routledge, 2018.
Elior, Rachel. *The Three Temples: On the Emergence of Jewish Mysticism*. Oxford: Littman Library of Jewish Civilization, 2004.
Elman, Yaakov. "Babylonian Baraitot in the Tosefta and the "Dialectology" of Middle Hebrew." *AJS Review* 16.1–2 (1991): 1–30.
Epstein, Jacob N. *Introductions to Tannaitic Literature: Mishnah, Tosefta, and Halakhic Midrashim*. Jerusalem: Magnes Press, 1957. Hebrew.
Fishbane, Michael. "Spiritual Transformations of Torah in Biblical and Rabbinic Tradition." *Journal for the Study of Religions and Ideologies* 6.18 (2007): 6–15.
Fossum, Jarl E. *The Name of God and the Angel of the Lord: Samaritan and Jewish Concepts of Intermediation and the Origin of Gnosticism*. Tübingen: Mohr Siebeck, 1985.

Fraade, Steven D. *From Tradition to Commentary: Torah and Its Interpretation in the Midrash Sifre to Deuteronomy*. Albany: State University of New York Press, 1991.

Fraade, Steven D. *Legal Fictions: Studies of Law and Narrative in the Discursive Worlds of Ancient Jewish Sectarians and Sages*. Leiden: Brill, 2011.

Fraenkel, Jonah. *The Aggadic Narrative: Harmony of Form and Content*. Tel Aviv: Hakibbutz Hameuchad, 2001. Hebrew.

Friedman, Shamma. "On the Origin of Textual Variants in the Babylonian Talmud." *Sidra* 1 (1991): 67–102. Hebrew.

Friedman, Shamma. "The Primacy of Tosefta to Mishnah in Synoptic Parallels." *Introducing Tosefta: Textual, Intratextual and Intertextual Studies*. Ed. Harry Fox and Tirzah Meacham. Hoboken: KTAV, 1999. 99–121.

Friedman, Shamma. "The Baraitot in the Babylonian Talmud and their Parallels in the Tosefta." *Atara L'Haim: Studies in the Talmud and Medieval Rabbinic Literature in Honor of Professor Haim Zalman Dimitrovsky*. Ed. Daniel Boyarin, Shamma Friedman, Marc Hirshman, Menahem Schmelzer, and Israel M. Tashma. Jerusalem: Magnes Press, 2000a. 163–201. Hebrew.

Friedman, Shamma. "Uncovering Literary Dependencies in the Talmudic Corpus." *The Synoptic Problem in Rabbinic Literature*. Ed. Shaye J. D. Cohen. Providence: Brown Judaic Studies, 2000b. 35–57.

Friedman, Shamma. *Tosefta Atiqta, Pesah Rishon: Synoptic Parallels of Mishna and Tosefta Analyzed with a Methodological Introduction*. Ramat-Gan: Bar-Ilan University Press, 2002. Hebrew.

Furstenberg, Yair. "The Rabbinic Ban on *Ma'aseh Bereshit*: Sources, Contexts and Concerns." *Jewish and Christian Cosmogony in Late Antiquity*. Ed. Lance Jenott, and Sarit Kattan Gribetz. Tübingen: Mohr Siebeck, 2013. 39–63.

Goering, Greg Schmidt. "Creation, Torah, and Revealed Wisdom in Some Second Temple Sapiential Texts (Sirach, 4QInstruction, 4Q185, and 4Q525): A Response to John Kampen." *Canonicity, Setting, Wisdom in the Deuterocanonicals: Papers of the Jubilee Meeting of the International Conference on the Deuterocanonical Books*. Ed. Géza G. Xeravits, József Zsengellér, and Xavér Szabó. Berlin: De Gruyter, 2014. 121–144.

Goff, Matthew J. *4QInstruction*. Atlanta: Society of Biblical Literature, 2013.

Goldberg, Abraham. "The Tosefta: Companion to the Mishna." *The Literature of the Jewish People in the Period of the Second Temple and the Talmud*, Volume 3: *The Literature of the Sages – First Part: Oral Tora, Halakha, Mishna, Tosefta, Talmud, External Tractates*. Ed. Shmuel Safrai. Leiden: Brill, 1987. 283–302.

Goodblatt, David M. *The Monarchic Principle: Studies in Jewish Self-Government in Antiquity*. Tübingen: Mohr Siebeck, 1994.

Goodman, Martin. "The Function of *Minim* in Early Rabbinic Judaism." *Judaism in the Roman World: Collected Essays*. Leiden: Brill, 2007. 163–174.

Goshen-Gottstein, Alon. "Four Entered Paradise Revisited." *Harvard Theological Review* 88.1 (1995): 69–133.

Goshen-Gottstein, Alon. *The Sinner and the Amnesiac: The Rabbinic Invention of Elisha ben Abuya and Eleazar ben Arach*. Stanford: Stanford University Press, 2000.

Goshen-Gottstein, Alon. "'The Sage Is Superior to the Prophet': The Conception of Torah through the Prism of the History of Jewish Exegesis." *Study and Knowledge in Jewish Thought*. Ed. Howard Kreisel. Beer Sheva: Ben-Gurion University of the Negev, 2006. 37–77. Hebrew.

Grabbe, Lester L. *Judaic Religion in the Second Temple Period: Belief and Practice from the Exile to Yavneh*. London: Routledge, 2000.

Graham, Steven A. "Manasseh in Scripture and Tradition: An Analysis of Ancient Sources and the Development of the Manasseh Tradition." Master's thesis, George Fox University, 2002.

Greenspahn, Frederick E. "Why Prophecy Ceased." *Journal of Biblical Literature* 108 (1989): 37–49.

Grossberg, David M. *Heresy and the Formation of the Rabbinic Community*. Tübingen: Mohr Siebeck, 2017.

Guggenheimer, Heinrich W. *The Jerusalem Talmud: Second Order, Mo'ed: Tractates Ta'aniot, Megillah, Hagigah and Mo'ed Qata (Mašqin)*. Berlin: De Gruyter, 2015.

Halbertal, Moshe. *Concealment and Revelation: Esotericism in Jewish Thought and its Philosophical Implications*. Princeton: Princeton University Press, 2007.

Halperin, David J. *The Merkabah in Rabbinic Literature*. New Haven: American Oriental Society, 1980.

Handy, Lowell K. "Rehabilitating Manasseh: Remembering King Manasseh in the Persian and Hellenistic Periods." *Remembering Biblical Figures in the Late Persian and Early Hellenistic Periods: Social Memory and Imagination*. Ed. Diana Vikander Edelman and Ehud Ben Zvi. Oxford: Oxford University Press, 2013. 221–235.

Harkins, Angela Kim, ed. *The Fallen Angels Traditions: Second Temple Developments and Reception History*. Washington DC: Catholic Biblical Association, 2014.

Hauptman, Judith. "Women and Inheritance in Rabbinic Texts." *Introducing Tosefta: Textual, Intratextual and Intertextual Studies*. Ed. Harry Fox and Tirzah Meacham. Hoboken: KTAV, 1999. 221–240.

Hauptman, Judith. "Nashim be-Massekhet Pesaḥim." *Atara L'Haim: Studies in the Talmud and Medieval Rabbinic Literature in Honor of Professor Haim Zalman Dimitrovsky*. Ed. Daniel Boyarin, Shamma Friedman, Marc Hirshman, Menahem Schmelzer, and Israel M. Tashma. Jerusalem: Magnes Press, 2000. 63–78. Hebrew.

Hauptman, Judith. *Rereading the Mishnah: A New Approach to Ancient Jewish Texts*. Tübingen: Mohr Siebeck, 2005a.

Hauptman, Judith. "The Tosefta as a Commentary on an Early Mishnah." *Jewish Studies, an Internet Journal* 4 (2005b): 109–132.

Hayes, Christine. "'The Torah was not Given to Ministering Angels': Rabbinic Aspirationalism." *Talmudic Transgressions: Engaging the Work of Daniel Boyarin*. Ed. Charlotte Elisheva Fonrobert, Ishay Rosen-Zvi, Aharon Shemesh, Moulie Vidas, and Daniel Boyarin. Leiden: Brill, 2017. 123–160.

Hayes, Christine. "Inventing Rabbis." *Early Judaism: New Insights and Scholarship*. Ed. Frederick E. Greenspahn. New York: NYU Press, 2018. 199–226.

Henze, Matthias. "King Manasseh of Judah in Early Judaism and Christianity." *On Prophets, Warriors, and Kings: Former Prophets through the Eyes of Their Interpreters*. Ed. George J. Brooke and Ariel Feldman. Berlin: De Gruyter, 2016. 183–228.

Heschel, Abraham Joshua. *God in Search of Man: A Philosophy of Judaism*. New York: Farrar, Straus & Cudahy, 1955.

Himmelfarb, Martha. *Ascent to Heaven in Jewish and Christian Apocalypses*. Oxford: Oxford University Press, 1993.

Idel, Moshe. *Absorbing Perfections: Kabbalah and Interpretation*. New Haven: Yale University Press, 2002.

Idel, Moshe. *Ben: Sonship and Jewish Mysticism*. London: Continuum, 2007.
Iricinschi, Eduard, and Holger M. Zellentin, eds. *Heresy and Identity in Late Antiquity*. Tübingen: Mohr Siebeck, 2008.
Kahana, Menachem. "On the Order of the Bereshit Passage in Genesis Rabba." *Higayon L'Yona: New Aspects in the Study of Midrash, Aggadah and Piyyut in Honor of Professor Yona Fraenkel*. Ed. Joshua Levinson, Jacob Elbaum, and Galit Hasan-Rokem. Jerusalem: Magnes Press, 2006. 347–376. Hebrew.
Kaniel, Ruth Kara-Ivanov. *Holiness and Transgression: Mothers of the Messiah in the Jewish Myth*. Boston: Academic Studies Press, 2017.
Kaufmann, Yehezkel. *Toledot ha-Emunah ha-Yisre'elit*. Jerusalem, Tel Aviv: Bialik Institute; Dvir, 1937–57. Hebrew.
Kellner, Menachem. *Dogma in Medieval Jewish Thought: From Maimonides to Abravanel*. Oxford: Littman Library of Jewish Civilization, 1986.
Kellner, Menachem. *Must a Jew Believe Anything?* 2nd ed. Oxford: Littman Library of Jewish Civilization, 2006.
Kister, Menahem. "Wisdom Literature and its Relation to Other Genres: From Ben Sira to Mysteries." *Sapiential Perspectives: Wisdom Literature in Light of the Dead Sea Scrolls*. Ed. Collins, John J. Sterling, Gregory E. Clements, Ruth A. Leiden: Brill, 2004. 13–47.
Kister, Menahem. "Wisdom Literature at Qumran." *The Qumran Scrolls and Their World: Between Bible and Mishnah – The Ancient Literature of Eretz Israel and Its World*. Ed. Menahem Kister. Jerusalem: Yad Ben-Zvi Press, 2009. 299–320. Hebrew.
Kister, Menahem. "Metatron, God, and the 'Two Powers': The Dynamics of Tradition, Exegesis, and Polemic." *Tarbiz* 82 (2013): 43–88. Hebrew.
Knohl, Israel. *The Messiah before Jesus: The Suffering Servant of the Dead Sea Scrolls*. Berkeley: University of California Press, 2000.
Knohl, Israel. *Biblical Beliefs: The Borders of Biblical Revolution*. Jerusalem: Magnes Press, 2007. Hebrew.
Lapin, Hayim. *Rabbis as Romans: The Rabbinic Movement in Palestine, 100–400 CE*. Oxford: Oxford University Press, 2012.
Last Stone, Suzanne. "Between Truth and Trust: The False Prophet as Self-Deceiver?" *Hebraic Political Studies* 4.4 (2009): 337–366.
Lavee, Moshe. *The Rabbinic Conversion of Judaism: The Unique Perspective of the Bavli on Conversion and the Construction of Jewish Identity*. Leiden: Brill, 2017.
Lazier, Benjamin. *God Interrupted: Heresy and the European Imagination between the World Wars*. Princeton: Princeton University Press, 2012.
Levine, Lee I. *Rabbinic Class of Roman Palestine in Late Antiquity*. Jerusalem: Yad Izhak Ben-Zvi, 1989.
Lieberman, Saul. "Mishnat Shir ha-Shirim." *Jewish Gnosticism, Merkabah Mysticism, and Talmudic Tradition*. New York: Jewish Theological Seminary of America, 1965. 118–126. Hebrew.
Lieberman, Saul. *Tosefta ki-Feshuta*. New York: Jewish Theological Seminary of America, 1993–1996. Hebrew.
Liebes, Yehuda. *The Sin of Elisha: The Four that Entered the Orchard and the Nature of Talmudic Mysticism*. Jerusalem: Academon, 1990. Hebrew.
Lifshitz, Berachyahu. "Expounding the Work of Creation." *Jerusalem Studies in Jewish Thought* 3.4 (1983): 513–524. Hebrew.
Morray-Jones, Christopher R. A. "Hekhalot Literature and Talmudic Tradition: Alexander's Three Test Cases." *Journal for the Study of Judaism* 22.1 (1991): 1–39.

Neher, André. "Le voyage mystique des quatre." *Revue de l'histoire des religions* 140.1 (1951): 59–82.
Neusner, Jacob. "The Rabbis and Prophecy." *The Review of Rabbinic Judaism* 17.1 (2014): 1–26.
Neusner, Jacob. *The Tosefta*. Peabody: Hendrickson Publishers, 2002.
Ophir, Adi, and Ishay Rosen-Zvi. *Goy: Israel's Multiple Others and the Birth of the Gentile*. Oxford: Oxford University Press, 2018.
Origen. *The Song of Songs: Commentary and Homilies*. Ed. R. P. Lawson. Westminster: Newman Press, 1957.
Orlov, Andrei A. *Yahoel and Metatron: Aural Apocalypticism and the Origins of Early Jewish Mysticism*. Tübingen: Mohr Siebeck, 2017.
Orlov, Andrei A. "Two Powers in Heaven ... Manifested." *Wisdom Poured Out Like Water*. Ed. J. Harold Ellens, Isaac W. Oliver, Jason von Ehrenkrook, James Waddell, and Jason M. Zurawski. Berlin, Boston: De Gruyter, 2018. 351–364.
Pachter, Mordechai. *Roots of Faith and Devequt: Studies in the History of Kabbalistic Ideas*. Los Angeles: Cherub Press, 2004.
Passaro, Angelo. "The Secrets of God: Investigation into Sir. 3:21–24." *The Wisdom of Ben Sira: Studies in Tradition, Redaction and Theology*. Ed. Angelo Passaro and Giuseppe Bellia. Berlin: De Gruyter, 2008. 155–171.
Paz, Yakir. "Metatron is Not Enoch." *Journal for the Study of Judaism* 50.1 (2019): 52–100.
Pedaya, Haviva. "Seeing, Falling, Song and Longing: Seeing God and the Spiritual Element in Early Jewish Mysticism." *Asufot* 9 (1995): 237–277. Hebrew.
Pedaya, Haviva. *Vision and Speech: Models of Revelatory Experience in Jewish Mysticism*. Los Angeles: Cherub Press, 2002. Hebrew.
Polen, Nehemia. "The Spirit Among the Sages: Seder Olam, the End of Prophecy, and Sagely Illumination." *"It's Better to Hear the Rebuke of the Wise than the Song of Fools" (Qoh 7:5): Proceedings of the Midrash Section, Society of Biblical Literature*, Volume 6. Ed. W. David Nelson and Rivka Ulmer. Piscataway: Gorgias Press, 2015. 83–94.
Rabbi Nathan of Rome. *Aruch Completum*. Vienna: n.p., 1928.
Rebiger, Bill. "Angels in Rabbinic Literature." *Angels: The Concept of Celestial Beings Origins, Development and Reception*. Ed. Friedrich v. Reiterer, Tobias Nicklas, and Karin Schöpflin. Berlin, New York: Walter de Gruyter, 2007.
Redford, Donald B. *Akhenaten: The Heretic King*. Princeton: Princeton University Press, 1984.
Reed, Annette Yoshiko. *Fallen Angels and the History of Judaism and Christianity: The Reception of Enochic Literature*. Cambridge: Cambridge University Press, 2005.
Reeves, John C., and Annette Yoshiko Reed. *Enoch from Antiquity to the Middle Ages: Sources from Judaism, Christianity, and Islam*. Oxford: Oxford University Press, 2018.
Reimer, Andy. "Rescuing the Fallen Angels: The Case of the Disappearing Angels at Qumran." *Dead Sea Discoveries* 7.3 (2000): 334–353.
Reiser, Daniel. *Imagery Techniques in Modern Jewish Mysticism*. Berlin: De Gruyter, 2018.
Reiterer, Friedrich V., Tobias Nicklas, and Karin Schöpflin, eds. *Angels: The Concept of Celestial Beings: Origins, Development and Reception*. Berlin: De Gruyter, 2007.
Rofé, Alexander. *Angels in the Bible: Israelite Belief in Angels as Evidenced by Biblical Traditions*. Jerusalem: Carmel, 2012. Hebrew.
Römer, Thomas C. "Moses, the Royal Lawgiver." *Remembering Biblical Figures in the Late Persian and Early Hellenistic Periods: Social Memory and Imagination*. Ed. Diana V. Edelman and Ehud Ben Zvi. Oxford University Press, 2013. 81–94.

Rovner, Jay. "Structure and Ideology in the Aher Narrative (bHag 15a and b)." *Jewish Studies, an Internet Journal* 10 (2012): 183–255.

Rowland, Christopher, and Christopher R. A. Morray-Jones. *The Mystery of God: Early Jewish Mysticism and the New Testament*. Leiden: Brill, 2009.

Royalty, Robert M., Jr. *The Origin of Heresy: A History of Discourse in Second Temple Judaism and Early Christianity*. New York: Routledge, 2013.

Rubenstein, Jeffrey L. "Elisha ben Abuya: Torah and the Sinful Sage." *Journal of Jewish Thought and Philosophy* 7 (1998): 139–225.

Rubenstein, Jeffrey L. *Talmudic Stories: Narrative Art, Composition, and Culture*. Baltimore: Johns Hopkins University Press, 1999.

Schäfer, Peter. *The Origins of Jewish Mysticism*. Tübingen: Mohr Siebeck, 2009.

Schneider, Michael. *The Appearance of the High Priest – Theophany, Apotheosis and Binitarian Theology: From Priestly Tradition of the Second Temple Period through Ancient Jewish Mysticism*. Los Angeles: Cherub Press, 2012. Hebrew.

Scholem, Gershom. *Major Trends in Jewish Mysticism*. New York: Schocken Books, 1941.

Scholem, Gershom. *Jewish Gnosticism, Merkabah Mysticism, and Talmudic Tradition*. New York: Jewish Theological Seminary of America, 1965.

Schorsch, Ismar. *Leopold Zunz: Creativity in Adversity*. Philadelphia: University of Pennsylvania Press, 2016.

Schremer, Adiel. "Midrash, Theology, and History: Two Powers in Heaven Revisited." *Journal for the Study of Judaism* 39.2 (2008): 230–254.

Schwartz, Daniel R., and Zeev Weiss, eds. *Was 70 CE a Watershed in Jewish History? On Jews and Judaism before and after the Destruction of the Second Temple*. Leiden: Brill, 2011.

Schwartz, Dov. "The Passion for Metaphysics in Maimonides' Thought." *Scepticism and Anti-Scepticism in Medieval Jewish Philosophy and Thought*. Ed. Racheli Haliva. Berlin, Boston: De Gruyter, 2018. 41–66.

Segal, Alan F. *Two Powers in Heaven: Early Rabbinic Reports about Christianity and Gnosticism*. Leiden: Brill, 1977.

Shapiro, Marc B. *The Limits of Orthodox Theology: Maimonides' Thirteen Principles Reappraised*. Oxford: Littman Library of Jewish Civilization, 2004.

Shemesh, Aharon. "Halacha and Prophecy: The False Prophet and the Rebellious Elder." *Renewing Jewish Commitment: The Work and Thought of David Hartman*. Ed. Avi Sagi and Zvi Zohar. Tel Aviv: Hakibbutz Hameuhad, 2001. 923–941. Hebrew.

Siegal, Michal Bar-Asher. *Jewish-Christian Dialogues on Scripture in Late Antiquity*. New York: Cambridge University Press, 2019.

Sommer, Benjamin D. "Did Prophecy Cease? Evaluating a Reevaluation." *Journal of Biblical Literature* 115 (1996): 31–47.

Stern, Sacha. *Jewish Identity in Early Rabbinic Writings*. Leiden: Brill, 1994.

Stroumsa, Guy G. *The Making of the Abrahamic Religions in Late Antiquity*. Oxford: Oxford University Press, 2015.

Stroumsa, Sarah. "Elisha ben Abuyah and Muslim Heretics in Maimonides' Writings." *Maimonidean Studies* 3 (1992–93): 173–193.

Stuckenbruck, Loren T. *The Myth of Rebellious Angels: Studies in Second Temple Judaism and New Testament Texts*. Grand Rapids: William B. Eerdmans, 2017.

Sussmann, Yaacov, ed. *Talmud Yerushalmi*. Jerusalem: Academy of the Hebrew Language, 2001.

Talmon, Shemaryahu. "The Internal Diversification of Judaism in the Early Second Temple Period." *Jewish Civilization in the Hellenistic-Roman Period*. Ed. Shemaryahu Talmon. Sheffield: JSOT Press, 1991. 16–43.

Urbach, Ephraim E. *The Sages: Their Concepts and Beliefs*. Jerusalem: Magnes Press, 1974.

Urbach, Ephraim E. "The Traditions about Esoteric Lore in the Tannaitic Period." *The World of the Sages: Collected Studies*. Jerusalem: Magnes Press, 1988a. 486–513. Hebrew.

Urbach, Ephraim E. "When Did Prophecy Cease?" *The World of the Sages: Collected Studies*. Jerusalem: Magnes Press, 1988b. 9–20. Hebrew.

Walfish, Avraham. "Approaching the Text and Approaching God: The Redaction of Mishnah and Tosefta Berakhot." *Jewish Studies* 43 (2005–2006): 21–79.

Walzer, Michael, Menachem Lorberbaum, Noam J. Zohar, and Yair Lorberbaum. *The Jewish Political Tradition*, Volume 1: *Authority*. New Haven: Yale University Press, 2000.

Watts, James W. "The Legal Characterization of Moses in the Rhetoric of the Pentateuch." *Journal of Biblical Literature* 117.3 (1998): 415–426.

Weber, Max. *The Theory of Social and Economic Organization*. Glencoe: Free Press, 1947.

Weinfeld, Moshe. *Deuteronomy and the Deuteronomic School*. Oxford: Oxford University Press, 1972.

Weiss Halivni, David. *Peshat and Derash: Plain and Applied Meaning in Rabbinic Exegesis*. New York: Oxford University Press, 1991.

Wolfson, Elliot R. *Through a Speculum that Shines: Vision and Imagination in Medieval Jewish Mysticism*. Princeton: Princeton University Press, 1994.

Wolfson, Elliot R. *Language, Eros, Being: Kabbalistic Hermeneutics and Poetic Imagination*. New York: Fordham University Press, 2005.

Wolfson, Elliot R. *Alef, Mem, Tau: Kabbalistic Musings on Time, Truth, and Death*. Berkeley: University of California Press, 2006.

Wolfson, Elliot R. "'Sage is Preferable to Prophet': Revisioning Midrashic Imagination." *Scriptural Exegesis: The Shapes of Culture and the Religious Imagination: Essays in Honour of Michael Fishbane*. Ed. Deborah A. Green and Laura Suzanne Lieber. Oxford: Oxford University Press, 2009. 186–205.

Yadin-Israel, Azzan. "Bavli Menaḥot 29b and the Diminution of the Prophets." *Journal of Ancient Judaism* 5 (2014): 88–105.

Zevit, Ziony. "From Judaism to Biblical Religion and Back Again." *The Hebrew Bible: New Insights and Scholarship*. Ed. Frederick E. Greenspahn. New York: New York University Press, 2008. 164–190.

Zuckermandel, Moses Samuel, ed. *Tosefta*. Jerusalem: Sifrei Wahrman, 1970. Hebrew.

Zunz, Leopold. *Ha-Drashot be-Yisrael ve-Hishtalshelutan ha-Hisṭorit*. Ed. H. Albeck. Jerusalem: Bialik Institute, 1947. Hebrew.

Part 2: Jewish Mysticism from the Middle Ages to Modernity

Ruth Kara-Ivanov Kaniel
King David as the Fourth Leg of the Chariot – Gender, Identity, and Heresy

The Shabbatean movement included many revolutionary and subversive elements that are as intriguing to contemporary scholars as they were disturbing to the movement's opponents at the time. First among these ideas was the theological, messianic claim that Shabbatai Zevi was the redeemer, an idea that spread through both popular superstitions and doctrinal beliefs. In the realm of practical *Halakhah*, Shabbatai Zevi permitted forbidden foods and illicit sexual relations, in addition to canceling fasts and adding holidays. And in the realm of mysticism and interpretation, Nathan of Gaza and his followers put forward new readings of kabbalistic sources and situated the God of Israel and the *sefirah* of *Tiferet* at the center of the mystery of faith.

In light of these revolutions, one question arises: are the Shabbatean views of women similarly revolutionary and divergent? Do they deviate from the generations of tradition that marginalized women in religious and spiritual life, or are they merely a reiteration of traditional structures masked as rebellion and heresy?

In his monumental book on Shabbatai Zevi, Gershom Scholem posited that in Shabbateanism women enjoyed an elevated status, participating in rituals such as *Aliyah la-Torah* and communal prayer, which he viewed as a feminist revolution. Nevertheless, Scholem failed to recognize the ultimate significance of this phenomenon.[1] Ada Rapoport-Albert was the first to emphasize feminine centrality and leadership as a distinguishing characteristic of the movement:

> The Sabbatian movement emerged as a unique and remarkable anomaly, striving to transcend the intransigent polarity of the prevailing gender paradigm by overturning the halakhic norms that set the ritual, social and – most sensationally – the sexual boundaries dividing male from female [...] One of Sabbateanism's most distinctive and persistent

---

[1] Scholem 1973, vol. I, 127–129. Scholem argued that it was Shabbatai Zevi who instigated this revolution, having "envisaged a change in the status of women" (1973, I, 326–327).

Note: My gratitude to Moshe Idel, Ada Rapoport-Albert, Art Green, Yehuda Liebes, Iris Felix, Vivian Liska, Levi Morrow, Levana Chajes, Biti Roi, Gilad Sharvit, Daniel Price for their comments. Tzippi Kauffman Z"l helped me to crystalize the ideas in this paper but unfortunately she did not live to see its completion.

https://doi.org/10.1515/9783110671582-005

features was the high visibility of women within its ranks. They were among the movement's earliest and most ardent supporters – championing the messianic cause, proclaiming its gospel and from time to time emerging its chief protagonists [...] It pointed to what I now believe to have been the veritable gender revolution that the Sabbatian movement envisaged, and in no small measure put into effect. (Rapoport-Albert 2011b, 10–13)

Rapoport-Albert argues that the centrality of women in Shabbateanism testifies to its detachment from the rabbinic world – and led to its eventual denunciation. In contrast to Christianity and Islam, which have histories of female mystic leadership, no such feminine echelon appeared in rabbinic, kabbalistic, or hasidic Judaism. In those societies, prophecy, righteousness, and erudition among women were seen as an aberration of nature and a social deviation, since "religious ethics prescribed for women and confined them to the sphere of material existence."[2] In the concluding chapter of *Women and the Messianic Heresy of Sabbatai Zevi: 1666–1816*, Rapoport-Albert notes that one might have expected that within its framework of idealized sanctification and spiritualization of matter, the hasidic movement would have continued the gender equality revolution that emerged in Shabbateanism. Instead, this movement reverted to the former, oppressive paradigm.[3] With the benefit of historical perspective, we could suggest that the backlash against Shabbatean sexual deviance culminated in the dissolution of the budding feminist revolution.

Following Rapoport-Albert's groundbreaking research on the topic, I will explore questions of femininity/masculinity, leadership and heresy, in revolutionary movements, examining whether contemporary terms such as "gender liberation" and "sexual freedom" can be applied to events that transpired in the seventeenth and eighteenth centuries. Indeed, a glimpse at a later Frankist-era testimony illustrates this complexity:

> It is known that the Frankists sinned by violating the Sabbath, eating non-Kosher animals, and having forbidden sexual relations. However, the most unwavering proof for the abominations of the Frankists' secrets is that *most of their wives left them and fled for their lives, choosing a life of despair and fear rather than returning to their husbands who had relinquished them.* (Baer Gottlober 1976, vol. II, 41; emphasis mine)

These words were written by Avraham Baer Gottlober (1810–1899), an opponent of the hasidic movement, in reference to the "hateful act" in Lanzkron at 1756. Even though it constitutes a *maskilic*, tendentious, and historically non-credible essay, based on the words of Emden, Graetz, and others, we can determine from this

---

[2] Rapoport-Albert 2011b, 9. For her discussion of Scholem's claims, see 13, 321.
[3] Rapoport-Albert 2011b, 13–14, 258–295; Rapoport-Albert 2017, 318–367.

testimony that in Baer Gottlober's opinion – as well as others' – the abominations of the Frankists pertained to sexuality and the immoral treatment of women. If *halakhic* observance was not Baer Gottlober's chief concern and it is not the issue with which he wished to contend, then it may be that his testimony demonstrates the existence of a widespread phenomenon of women's suppression disguised as sexual liberation. Similarly, Emden quotes from a letter he received from his relative Baruch Yavan: "The women who fled from their husband confessed their sins and cry out against them and their despicable acts; it is within our power only to excommunicate them"[4] (Emden, *Sefer Shimush* 4a).

Indeed, the rabbinical institution was itself oppressive toward women. In a Polish report documented by Meir Balaban, a group of Shabbatean women testified that their husbands confessed their sins before a rabbinic court in Brody at 1752, and were received as repentants, while the women were instead deemed promiscuous and expelled from their communities and families. Then, having no means and no other choice, they turned to the Polish municipal authorities for financial support.[5] The women were caught between the two poles, condemned to ostracism by both communities, the Shabbatean and the rabbinic.

1 Gender, Heresy, and Prophecy

The connection between women and heresy has always been a central theme in the history of religion. So it was in the Greek and Roman worlds, in early Christianity, in Talmudic literature, and in Islam, and was exhibited in full throughout the witch hunts and burnings of the Inquisition in the Middle Ages and at the outset of the Early Modern Period.

Adam Ferziger has discussed the tendency to link heresy and religious deviation with female powers of seduction. Throughout the ages, female occupations such as healing and midwifery were accompanied by allegations of magic and demonic powers. Women were often suspected of having been manipulated by the Devil, and even in the contemporary Jewish world, female spiritualists and leaders are often accused of heresy.[6] It is in this context that the Shabbatean messianic

---

4 Amsterdam (Altona), 1758; Rapoport-Albert 2011b, 89 no. 9.
5 Rapoport-Albert 2011b, 96.
6 Ferziger 2009; Elliott 1999. As John Henderson notes, in the struggle against a new heretical movement, its opponents attempt to associate it with an "already defeated heresy," thus creating a "monstrous amalgam" synthesizing all the deviant teachings of the various heretical movements throughout history. Cited in Ferziger 2009, 498–499.

myth is so interesting to this volume, as it has its foundation in the tradition of the messianic mothers (such as Lot's daughters, Tamar and Ruth). Yet, whereas the transgressive deeds of these ancient figures were merely "imaginary" deviant behavior, that appeared only on the hermeneutical level,[7] in Shabbateanism, the revolution took place in real life and was performed by actual bodies, of men and women. As I will suggest, although female figures were protected usually from a definition of "heretics," in fact, it is precisely this exclusion that facilitated the possibility of them evading prosecution. Thus, we must explore not only the centrality of women leaders, but also feminine identities that are attributed to male heroes in Shabbatean thought.

In addition to the connection between heresiology and gender issues, I would like to add another association – between the psychoanalytical study of sexual perversion, and the role of harlotry in myths of redemption. Yet, in this case, instead of addressing the "already defeated heresy," Shabbateanism instead offers a glorified radicalization of the existing kabbalistic and talmudic messianic theme of "sin for its own sake (*aveirah lishmah*)," "a commandment (*mitzvah*) brought about through sin," and "redemption through sin" – all cases in which the sin is performed by women who are then elevated to an exalted position.[8]

Following this idea, Nathan of Gaza declared, "In the serpent of *kelippah* (shell), the feminine power is greater than the masculine" (*Derush ha-taninim*, 47). However, we must consider that this ideological constellation remains within the realm of biblical exegesis; it is the redemptive heroines whom the kabbalists depict as "saintly prostitutes," not actual women in their community. What happens when Shabbatean thinkers turn to their female contemporaries and grant them complete sexual freedom? How far can we take the interpretation of this phenomenon, and can we truly view it as a feminist revolution, an emancipation of women? Consider, for example, Rochus, Frank's son, who is described as having raped a virgin on Yom Kippur in the name of ideological antinomianism and mythical heresy – a traumatizing event that silenced the young woman's voice.[9] Moreover,

---

[7] I have discussed this topic on my book on the Davidic dynasty: see Kara-Kaniel 2017.
[8] See, for example, Scholem 1982. Moshe Hayyim Luzatto deals with this topic in an unusual manner when referring to the rape of his female contemporaries for the purpose of bringing about redemption. He indicates that these women were initiators who willingly sacrificed their bodies ("*gedolah averah lishmah*"), but he also depicts them as passive in their characterization as *karka 'olam* (inactive "soil"), and as having been ravished: "They ravished the women in Zion" (Lam. 5:11); see Kara- Ivanov Kaniel 2017, Ch. 4.
[9] This event evoked contradictory testimonies; the first one glorified Rochus and describes the maiden's happiness, the other emphasized her traumatic silence and crying. See Rapoport-Albert 2011b, 44–45. Elior 2001, II, 519–520.

the rumors of Shabbatai Zevi's seclusions with his ex-wives and the virgins he summoned for himself, alongside his advocacy for the breaking of the boundaries of *arayot* (forbidden sexual relationships) as a religious act of *tikkun* (rectification), also may be interpreted as behavior that ultimately led to exploitation – even if his acts have been romanticized as a progressive revolution.[10]

Consider Jacob Sasportas's well-known assertion that Sarah, Shabbatai Zevi's third wife, was the one who motivated him to declare himself Messiah and Redeemer.[11] Similar claims condemning Sarah's central role were made by R. Emmanuel Frances, whose poem "How a Donkey's Voice Brays" describes her as a "transgressive doe (*zevia*), charitable with any passer-by."[12] According to Avraham Elqayam, unlike the Shabbatean opponents who express only contempt for prostitution, the image of Sarah in the new discourse reflects a "change of values in relation to women, ... [which] presents her as a liberated woman whose deviation and struggle against the social order threaten to destroy its boundaries and bring about the redemption."[13] More recently, in his treatment of this enigmatic figure, Alexander van der Haven dubbed Sarah "the Queen of the Shabbateans."[14] Thus, Sarah had gained a reputation as both licentious and virginal, a dualism that bears an affinity to the Christian cult of the Virgin, as well as to the Jewish myth of the Mother of the Messiah.[15] Indeed, Sarah is not the only "Mariological" figure depicted as fluctuating between prostitution and virginity. Shabbatai's mother was also the victim of such slander: "His father would be content with shoes and his mother was a prostitute demanding *treifa* (non-kosher meat)."[16]

Female Shabbatean heroines were surrounded by an aura of promiscuity, and therefore the claim that sexual and gender repression occurred under the Shabbatean and Frankist movements is certainly reasonable.[17] Yet, it does seem

---

[10] This idea is alluded to by writers such as Sherman in the play *Messiah*, which was also the first to raise the issue of sisterhood in Shabbateanism; see also – albeit with less awareness of this question – Barnai 2017.
[11] Scholem 1973, I, 46.
[12] *The Divan of R. Emanuel ben David Francis*, Tel Aviv, 1932, 188.
[13] Elqayam 2016, 227. He also adds that prostitution "was considered to be destructive in the old world, becomes a symbol of Shabbatean Messianic renewal" (235).
[14] van der Haven 2018.
[15] Scholem 1973, I, 146–149, and more; Kara- Ivanov Kaniel 2017, esp. the Epilogue.
[16] Sasportas 1973, 94; see also Scholem 1973, I, 86.
[17] On the other hand, we cannot ignore the testimonies of women who, by their own initiative, abandoned their husbands and families to join the Frankist camp, and of groups of women who alone and of their own volition came to his court and remained faithful to their Shabbateanism despite the opposition of their husbands – which often led to divorce. See: Rapoport-Albert, 2011b; Maciejko, 2015.

that cases of female Jewish prophetesses indicate an exceptional departure from the norm. In his discussion of mass female prophecy that accompanied Shabbatai Zevi's appearance, Gershom Scholem noted the affinity of these instances to the parallel phenomenon in the Christian world, where we find numerous examples of women who documented their mystical experiences.[18]

The roots of female Jewish prophecy can actually be traced to the Iberian Peninsula in a number of exceptional testimonies, the main one being Inés from Herrara at the generation of the expulsion – an independent woman who merited a revelation of Elijah the Prophet.[19] As J. H. Chajes has shown, this phenomenon spread in sixteenth-century Safed's Vitalian school of Kabbalah, where one finds descriptions of female prophetesses as well as women possessed by *maggidim*.[20] There are testimonies as early as the medieval Ashkenazi Hasidim of female revelations that followed the massacres of 1096. Another unique example was found in the Cairo Geniza describing a young prophetess in Baghdad at the beginning of the twelfth century, who told of her visions at the synagogue at the time of *Torah reading*, an act that led to the Abas Caliph's intervention and the arrest of some Jews from the community.[21]

In most of these cases, from the Middle Ages up until to the mass Shabbatean female revelations, the heroines are virgins, an idea that supports Rapoport-Albert's claim that both Christian and Sufi women were required to deny their sexuality and femininity in order to serve as holy figures. In this way, the virgin Jewish prophetesses imitate the Christian model, rather than the Jewish traditional ideal.[22] The feminist thinker Bertha Pappenheim (Josef Breuer's patient *Anna O*, who is described in *Studies in Hysteria*) argued in 1907 that in contrast to other religions, the Jewish tradition fixated on a woman's sexual functions.[23] It thus may be argued that the characteristic of Jewish female leaders to be virgins or harlots, based on earlier messianic traditions, reflects a patriarchal unwillingness to tolerate normative women's leadership, which could destabilize Jewish communities and disturb gender power relations.

Still, while in rabbinic and halakhic sources women were identified with fertility and corporeality and thereby were exempted from time-bound ritual responsibility and barred from holding communal leadership, the Shabbatean move-

---

[18] Scholem 1973, I, 206–210; II, 505, and more.
[19] Melammed 2001, 348–352.
[20] Chajes 2002.
[21] I am grateful to Micha Perry, who brought these sources to my attention. For further discussion, see: Goitein 1952; on *Sefer Hasidim* and parallel testimonies: Dan 1971.
[22] Rapoport-Albert 2011b, 35–36. See there also for more on Inés from Herrara, 59–75.
[23] Pappenheim 1907.

ment stressed sexual antinomianism and focused on breaking the law through physical and demonstrative acts. It would seem that in Shabbateanism, Jewish women could finally express themselves through their bodies, in a communal framework that guaranteed them equality. Later, with the decline of Shabbateanism into an underground movement, the female mass prophecy that had characterized the messianic movement in its heyday ceased. Eventually the sectarian frameworks were emptied of their original content, including sexual antinomianism, and became assimilated either into Jewish communities in the process of modernization and secularization, or into gentile society. Nevertheless, the egalitarian participation of women in ritual practice (alongside the men), the teaching of Zohar to women, and the phenomenon of authoritative women and prophetesses, were sustained for the entirety of the eighteenth century in Frank's court, Shabbatai Prague's circle, and evidently also among the Dönmeh.[24]

2 Masculinities and Zoharic Influence

The longstanding identification of the feminine with the body and the perception of woman as a "vessel" in Jewish texts leads us to one reason why redemption is necessarily tied up with perversion and the breaking of sexual boundaries on the one hand, and virginity and abstinence on the other: since femininity is a category through which people conceived of messianism, the messianic was defined in terms that expressed either destruction and harm, or preservation and purification, of the feminine. The feminine was the underlying structure through which messianism was conceived – not merely as a metaphor but in practice as well.

Yet, in order to investigate the links between sexual promiscuity and messianic leadership, we must ask whether similar antinominian stereotypes are applied to male figures. In other words, are the men associated with messianic leadership accused of the similar licentious behavior? Are these figures also associated with sexual promiscuity and transgressive ideals? Putting the question in Raewyn Connell's terms, how is hegemonic masculinity defined in kabbalistic texts, and what are the relations between masculinity and femininity in the messianic-mystical order?[25]

Rapoport-Albert's research stresses the role of female leaders in the Shabbatean and Frankist world, yet the perception of femininity in the thoughts of

---

24 Rapoport-Albert 2017.
25 Connell 1995; Connell & Messerschmidt 2005.

Nathan of Gaza and in the writings of his disciples has yet to be examined.²⁶ How did the believers view the role of women in the doctrine of salvation? Which mythological heroines were compared to Shabbatai Zevi, and what was the impact of the Zoharic homilies on Nathan's writings? For example, *Derush ha-taninim* (*Treatise on the Dragons*) emphasizes the status of the concubines Bilhah and Zilpah in their representation of the *ahorayim* (the hidden sides) of Rachel and Leah, and discusses the figures of Judith and Reumah in connection with the mystery of the two birds. This reading draws on allusions to this theme in Zoharic and Lurianic literature, yet it has not received sufficient scholarly investigation. Research in this direction would likely shed light on ideological and textual influences and contribute to our understanding of the myriad forces at work in Shabbatean theology.

Moreover, if the sexual liberation heralded by Shabbatai Zevi, Frank, and their followers was neither a call for the debauching of women and their sexual exploitation nor the liberation of women, then we must reexamine the prevalent nexus between prostitution and messianism.

In this paper I shall therefore illustrate this issue through a discussion of the idea of David as the fourth leg of the Chariot (*Merkavah*). I will focus on themes of femininity and masculinity, subversion, heresy, transgression, and sexual ethics as a basis for understanding Shabbatean thought and its kabbalistic sources.

3 Shabbatai Zevi and King David in the Image of the Shekhinah

In the Shabbatean literature, Shabbatai Zevi's character was clearly based on King David, a messianic and androgynous hero whom the Zohar identifies with the *Shekhinah* and the *sefirah* of *Malkhut* (kingship/ kingdom). Below, we shall see how David was integrated into the *ilan* (divine tree) as a liminal figure mediating between heaven and earth. In Kabbalah we find a formulation stemming from the school of Nahmanides that pronounces the *Shekhinah* as connected with the *sefirot* "by Emanation (*atzilut*) and not in Unity," an idea that might bring us to a mistaken marginalization or *kitzutz* (cutting) of the divine feminine.²⁷ The Zohar

---

26 Rapoport-Albert 2011b, 143–327. As she states, within the Shabbatean movement women were equal to men regarding their accessibility to belief in the Messiah, in their power to transgress and violate negative commandments, and in their prophetic ability, through their chastity, which engendered them as masculine (Rapoport-Albert 2011b, 35–36).
27 *Nahmanides on the Torah*. Lev. 23:36. *Ma'arekhet ha-elohut* (Jerusalem, 2012), Ch. 13; as Idel claims, this statement emphasizes positive aspects of the *Shekhinah* and her unique ability to

responded to this danger by emphasizing *Shekhinah*'s importance and describing her elevation to the crown and upper *sefirot*.[28] Yet the *Shekhinah*, like King David – the male protagonist that is identified with her – represents the brokenhearted, the poor, the oppressed.

David says in Psalms, "I am a stranger to my brothers, a foreigner to my mother's sons" (Ps. 69:8), just as the *Shekhinah* is considered the "stone that the builders rejected [that] has become the cornerstone" (Ps. 118:22).[29] The two appear together in almost every Zoharic homily, and their biographies are woven into one. Together they represent an integration of sin and rectification, promiscuity and redemption. Later on, Shabbatai Zevi was also called "the fourth leg of the Chariot," and identified as a messianic and androgynous figure. Both King David and Shabbatai Zevi were integrated into the *ilan* as mythic figures symbolizing the feminine *sefirah* of *Malkhut*.

As Peter Schäfer and Art Green argue, the rise of the *Shekhinah* in kabbalistic sources from the end of the twelfth century was influenced by the veneration of Mary, a cult strongly represented in the public spheres of Provence and Christian Spain.[30] Both cultures used female figures to represent their collective religions, sub-consciousness, and aspirations. For example, we can see this representation in the prevalent sculptures of *Ecclesia* and *Synagoga* in art and architecture of the time. David, as a messianic figure and representative of the Jewish people (*Knesset Israel*), had to take on, as it were, a feminine image. Later in this paper I will address David's dual role in relation to anti-Christian polemic that adds another layer to the inner development of Kabbalah and its manifestation in the Shabbatean world, and from which both David and the *Shekhinah* benefit. On the one hand, the *Shekhinah* in David's image benefits from the embodiment of "masculine strength"; as the Zohar says, David knows how to "draw the world to come into this world" (Zohar III 21a). Thus, she never stands alone as a focal point of religious ritual, since the messianic figure of David supports her. On the other hand, through this identification David is enriched by the "multiple self" of the divine consort. Already in the Bible he symbolizes the "hero with a thousand faces"; now he is not only an earthly hero but is also colored by celestial attributes and attains supernatural features.

---

rule the lower worlds: Idel (forthcoming). See also Weiss 2015, 96–102.
28 Idel 2018.
29 On the *Shekhinah* as the "stone that the builders rejected" in *Tikunei ha-zohar*: Roi 2017, 405–407.
30 see Green, 2002; Schäfer, 2002: 147–172.

4 The Fourth Leg – From the 12th Century Book Bahir to the 13th Century Geronese Kabbalah

David's appearance in the divine chariot was not foregone; rather, it entailed the resolution of gender and messianic issues. David does not appear in the "first draft" of the chariot in the Book Bahir, nor does the supernal Anthropos in the image of man include King David. The granting of supernatural attributes and canonization of human figures as *sefirot* began with the Patriarchs, without any mention of David, and only later was he granted transcendent status and the position of the fourth leg of the Chariot. I suggest that this identification reflects a creative way of including David in the mystical shape of the godhead, imagined in such a way that it does not threaten the hegemonic masculinity of the Patriarchs who alone represent the sacred male trinity. David is female and is therefore not entirely included in the divine realm; rather, he is partially still associated with the lower, feminine, and corporeal world.

Indeed, the Book Bahir describes the bestowing of the attributes of *Hesed*, *Gevurah*, and *Tiferet* upon the Patriarchs Abraham, Isaac, and Jacob (§92–94). David does not appear by their side, and in other texts the Bahir only alludes to his relationship to the *Shekhinah*. However, the Patriarchs are again discussed at the end of §131, which suggests that David may have received the precious stone that the Patriarchs did not want:

> [God] constructed a beautiful precious stone. In it He included all the commandments. Abraham came, and He sought a power to give him. He gave him this precious stone, but he did not want it ... Isaac came, and he sought a power, and they gave him this attribute but he did not want it ... Jacob came and wanted it, but it was not given to him ... This is a complete inheritance, comprising *Hesed*, *Pahad*, *Emet* and *Shalom*. It is therefore written, 'The stone the builders rejected has become the chief cornerstone.' (Ps. 118:22) This is the stone that was rejected by Abraham and Isaac, the builders of the world, and became the chief cornerstone.[31]

According to this description, Jacob was granted the attribute of *Emet*, which balances *Hesed* and *Din* (justice), and perhaps suggests that David received the lowest stone, *Dar*, which is positioned before the supernal precious stone, the *Soharet*, which is connected to the "supernal righteous one (*tzaddik*)." According to §50, David was granted his attribute, entitled "*Yamim*" (days), and did

---

[31] The Book Bahir §131, 215–217 (Abrams edition). For Bahir §92–94 see 117–179. Translations of the Bahir are based also on: The Book of Bahir – Flavius Mithridates' Latin translation, the Hebrew text, and an English version. Translated and edited with a foreword by Giulio Busi and edited by Saverio Campanini. Torino: Nino Aragano Editore, 2005.

not receive the attributes of *Emet* and *Shalom* that represent Jacob.³² Regardless, it seems that David's messianic role is not a central theme in the Book Bahir.

David's superiority over the Patriarchs is already alluded to in the Talmud: "Chief of the captains, *rosh hashalishim* (Chr. I 11:11) you will be head of the three Patriarchs,"³³ as well as in the description of David in b. *Sanhedrin* 107. Here, David desires to be put to the test so that he might deserve the same blessing that is attributed to the Patriarchs, "God of Abraham, Isaac and Jacob."

The liturgical practice of joining David to the Patriarchs can be attributed to Isaac the Blind, whose custom it was to pray using the phrase, "the God of David and the Rebuilder of Jerusalem."³⁴ Later in the thirteenth century, R. Azriel of Gerona quotes the formula "the Patriarchs are themselves the Chariot." This ancient formula of Reish Lakish in Gen. Rabbah³⁵ is used in R. Azriel's *Commentary on the Talmudic Aggadoth*: "the Angels say *kadosh kadosh kadosh* and [in parallel] Israel say God of Abraham, Isaac, and Jacob ... and David is the fourth."³⁶ This statement references not David's representation in the Chariot, in this case, but the combination of the three recitations of the *Kedushah* prayer, which correspond to the Blessing of the Patriarchs recited in the prayer of *Amidah*.

It seems that in his *Sefer ha-emuna ve-habitahon* (*The Book of Faith and Trust*), R. Jacob bar Sheshet is the first to explicitly identify David as the fourth leg of the Chariot:

> The Patriarchs are only three, and there is no Chariot with less than four – *who is the fourth? David* ... Our rabbis did not mention him [in the daily prayer service], just as they only brought proof of Abraham and Jacob, but it is with the four of them where we find that the name of God is united through each one, as God is called their God and no one else's ... like the God of Abraham, Isaac, Jacob, *and David*.³⁷

---

32 The Book Bahir §50, 147. On *Dar* and *Soharet* in the *Or ha-ganuz*, see: Pedaya 2003, 364.
33 b. Moed Katan 16b.
34 Pedaya 2001, 166–169. For the discussion of whether R. Isaac the Blind was referring to the prayer of *Amidah* or to the Grace after Meals, see: Abramson 1974, 93–101; and A. Goldreich's discussion in which he debates with J. Katz: Goldreich 1981, 384–387, 44–47, 66, and more.
35 Genesis Rabbah 47:6 (28); 82:6 (13), 475, 793, 983.
36 Azriel of Gerona 1982, 56–57, and also 98. R. Azriel there calls the *sefirot* "gods" and "crowns," and thus the Patriarchs are their offspring based on the verse from Ps. 29:1, "Ascribe to the LORD, you heavenly beings [*Benei Elim*]." See also Ben David 1996, 54.
37 Bar Sheshet 1964, 353–448, 396; emphasis mine. It is important to note that Bar Sheshet does not mention his use of the Book Bahir, despite discussing the division of the attributes to the Patriarchs in Ch. 13–16. For more on this, see: Tishby 1989, 149, 416–417; Afterman 2011, 201,

David as a redeemer is included by the first kabbalists in the theosophical structure as well as in the liturgical praxis. However, it is only in the distinct Zoharic identification of him with the *Shekhinah* (based on Bar Sheshet's innovation) where we find a fusion of the mythical, gendered, and mystical spheres.

5 The Zohar and the Kabbalists of its Generation

The expansion of the Chariot to a framework of four legs is based on the idea found in the Bahir that the Patriarchs "merited their attributes," and every one of them transformed their unique trait into a divine power that operates in the world (§92–94).

According to the Zohar, the Patriarchs "inherit" and receive their divine portion, while David "conjoins with them," having "dressed" himself in the attribute of *Malkhut* and masquerading as her.[38] It is important to note the variety of terms that link the character to the *sefirah* as well as to the dual process in which not only the Patriarch is granted a certain *sefirah*, but the *sefirah* is granted the figure of the Patriarch, thus obtaining through it a human countenance, identity, sex, and gender.[39] The Zohar enriches the idea of the dual movement of ascent and descent, the apotheosis and theophany that originated in the Bahir, and thus expands the "divine persona."[40]

Almost every Zoharic homily describes King David as an image of the feminine divine presence, the *Shekhinah*, who has many names and symbols: the

---

270–279. Idel and Afterman both expound on Bar Sheshet as a Kabbalist who compiled traditions from the school of R. Isaac the Blind, the Bahir, Gerona, and more.

38 In contrast to Abraham and Jacob, Isaac usually "exits" from within *Hesed* in a passive way, thereby taking hold of his portion. See Zohar I 96a; Abraham inherits his attribute (as in Zohar I 96a); Jacob inherits *Tiferet* (Zohar I 1b); R. Simeon Bar Yohai and the sages inherit the earth according to Zohar I 216a–216b, III 213b, and more.

39 Schneider, Idel, Afterman, and others, discuss this movement and its roots in ancient mysticism. The idea that there are existing attributes in the supernal world which later are tailored to human figures that actualize and materialize them differs from the radical idea that the Patriarchs create the divine attributes, a matter alluded to in the writings of R. Jacob and R. Isaac Cohen which I will not be able to discuss here. On the enclothement of the righteous in the *Shekhinah* without revoking the body, see: Pedaya 2003, 333–349. And in her words: "If the Divine is "enclothed" in order to descend to man, then man must become "enclothed" in order to ascend ... in turning from the Divine towards human the garments are like a screen, camouflage, and in the turn from the human towards the Divine the garment resembles the act of becoming enwrapped in enlightenment."

40 Kara-Ivanov Kaniel 2019b.

sefirah of *Malkhut*, the moon, the gazel, the rose, the sea, and the wheel of souls. Particularly conspicuous are portrayals of David as the moon:

> When the moon is deprived of light and does not shine, She is impoverished on all sides and darkened, without any light at all. And when the sun turns back toward Her, illumining Her, She adorns Herself for Him, like a woman adorning herself for a man. Then She gains dominion throughout the world. So David adorned himself in the same manner.
> (Zohar II 232b–233a; vol. VI 338–340)

The moon, the *Shekhinah*, in kabbalistic terms, has "nothing of her own," and thus receives all of her light from the masculine. In other words, the *Shekhinah* who cannot be the focal point of religious ritual is represented by the messianic figure of David.[41] To use Judith Butler's terminology, this is a "performance" of fluid identities, only it operates in one direction.[42]

In another homily, David has double faces, feminine and masculine, while the Zohar designates "Another David" whose beauty is not found among humans:

> The blessed Holy One has Another David, who is appointed over many cohorts and camps. When the blessed Holy One wishes to be compassionate to the world, He gazes upon this one, shines His countenance upon him, and has mercy upon the world, and the beauty of this David illumines all worlds. (Zohar III 84a; vol. VIII 22–23)

Another example of the feminized David can be seen in the Zohar's description of his lifeless birth:

> David derives from the side of darkness. Whoever inhabits darkness has no light at all, no life, so David had no life at all. But these, containing light, illumined King David, who had to be illuminated and animated by them, since from the side of darkness he has no life at all.
> (Zohar I 168b; vol. III, 18)

The Zohar states that David comes from the feminine side of darkness, since he "has no life of his own," yet he gains masculine power and eventually "possesses" eternal life. Unlike the midrash, according to which Adam bequeathed to David seventy years of his own life,[43] the Zohar's innovative claim stresses that

---

41 I expounded on this in my article "King David and Jerusalem: From Psalms to the Zohar" (2019a).
42 Butler 1990, 619–633. Today, Butler's arguments represent a mode of thinking that is also implemented in American realia, and it is interesting to see how these ideas began appearing in the Zohar.
43 b. Sukka 52a. According to the midrash, David was born as a non-viable infant, and therefore was gifted seventy years of life by Adam. See *BT Sanhedrin*, 97a; Zohar I 168b; Zohar III 279a; for traditions on the lending of life to David, see: Liebes 2012, 460–461; Shinan 1995, 183. I hope

all the Patriarchs are involved in the process of "reviving the Messiah" and giving him life. Clearly this homily was influenced by a new concept of David as the fourth leg of the Chariot.

Haviva Pedaya suggests that an awareness of the *Shekhinah* led the Zoharic kabbalists to add the fourth leg to the Chariot, in contrast to Nahmanides, who notably spoke of "the three-legged throne." The Zoharic traditions were influenced, according to Pedaya's reading, by the writing of the Castile circle (especially R. Isaac ha-Kohen, the author of *On the Left Emanation*), and his notion of the potential impurity of *Shekhinah*'s camps.[44]

Following Pedaya as well as Adam Afterman's notion of apotheosis, I identify the innovation with R. Jacob bar Sheshet, who was – as we have seen – the first to highlight, in *Sefer ha-emuna ve-habitahon*, David's feminine nature as the fourth leg of the Chariot. It was a concept that the Zohar then developed into a profound structure: rooted in the school of R. Isaac the Blind, alluded to by R. Ezra and Azriel of Gerona, and then innovatively formulated by Bar Sheshet.

Tracking the development of this theme will help to determine the degree to which Shabbatean theology subverted the traditions that preceded it, but also how conservative it was and how much it relied on early kabbalistic conventions.

The Zoharic passages all exhibit a gender fluidity as well as the ascribing of "female" attributes to males and vice versa. This gives rise to a surprising – albeit anachronistic – correlation with the principles of queer theory and cross-dressing created in feminist studies by theoreticians such as Eve Kosofsky Sedgwick, Sandy Stone, Michael Warner, Judith Shapiro, and others who research cross-cultural transsexualism.[45] David, "the fourth," is represented as a kind of hybrid between the androgynous, transgender, and queer. In contrast to him, the other three Patriarchs –Abraham, Isaac, and Jacob – represent much more stable and masculine aspects of divinity. They are the sefirot *Hesed* (kindness), *Gevurah* (judgment), and *Tiferet*, or the "Three Knots of Faith."[46]

---

to expand elsewhere on the subject, using the psychoanalytic term of the "stillborn infant" of Ogden.

44 Pedaya 2013, 87–151. On early kabbalistic traditions, see: Pedaya 2001, Ch. 3. See n. 81 below for discussion of Adam Afterman's claims.

45 On theory of transgender identity, see, for example: Sedgwick 2010; Stone 1992; Warner 2000; Shapiro 1991.

46 The term was Nehemiah Hayyun's, who hinted at the Trinity and spurred such intense controversy that he was eventually expelled from the Jewish community of Amsterdam.

From another perspective, Erich Neumann suggested adding to the three dimensions of the soul developed by Jung (the reality field, the archetypal field, and the Self) a fourth, relating to mystical apprehension: *the participation mystique*. While the triad embodies stability, the fourth dimension represents a concealed addition, that of shadow and the unconscious.[47] Adapting this structure to our discussion, we could view David as the unstable leg of the Chariot. He is an inevitable but not entirely accepted addition which the kabbalists wove into the divine constellation, so as to establish a theosophy of female leadership that in practice was not actually led by women.

6 David as the Shekhinah in Theosophical-Theurgical Kabbalah in Thirteenth- and Fourteenth- Century Castile

Unlike the Zoharic literature, which presented rich narratives as the foundations for its expression of mystical theosophy, other kabbalists of its generation did not share this tendency for personalization.

The kabbalists employ a wealth of metaphors when describing David as the fourth leg. As per the prevalent model in the Zohar, the writings of R. Moses de Leon, *Ma'arekhet ha-elohut* (*Constellation of the Godhead*), *Avodat ha-kodesh* (*Sacred Service*), and additional theurgic compositions, – King David as *Malkhut* reflects the unstable position of the fourth leg.[48] Like the Zohar, de Leon states that "King David is conjoined with them, with the Patriarchs, without any separation. Therefore, because of the exile and evil, everything is separate. When the supernal structure is moved, the lower levels are moved from their place."[49] This image first appears in the writings of de Leon in MS Munich 47:

---

47 Neumann 2013, 28–33, 51–63 [Die Psyche und die Wandlung der Wirklichkeitsebenend (1952); Mensch und Sinn (1959); Die Psyche als Ort der Gestaltung (1960)]. See also Neumann 1973.
48 As in Zohar I 168b; Zohar I 248b; Zohar II 106a, and more; Idel 1998, 110–112.
49 Moses de Leon, *Shekel ha-kodesh*, 12 no. 114; and de Leon *Perush le-ma'aseh merkavat yehezkel*, 53; and in de Leon, *Sefer ha-rimon*, 239; de Leon, *Mishkan ha-Edut*, 116a, and more.

> Indeed, the Kingdom of the House of David, the Holy Land, which is illuminated by his glory, is a speculum that does not shine ... when King David is a Chariot with the Patriarchs, he then completes the whole, so that the unique name is in the mystery of oneness.[50]

Later on, books such as *Ma'arekhet ha-elohut* and *Avodat ha-kodesh* adopt a similar structure in their portrayal of David as the fourth leg: "The tenth is the Kingdom of Israel ... the attribute of David, the fourth leg of the Chariot" (Ch. 9), and "Indeed, the *Atarah* (crown) is the fourth leg of the Chariot, and she is the attribute of David" (Ch. 11).

An alternative kabbalistic and theurgic model views David as the fourth leg, but struggles *not* to identify him with a feminine *sefirah*, portraying him instead as masculine and identifying him with a masculine *sefirah* such as *Tiferet* in the spirit of *Sefer ha-pliah* (*The Book of Wonder*),[51] or as the *sefirah* of *Yesod* (foundation) as R. Joseph of Shushan (which I discussed elsewhere).[52] A similar idea can be found in R. Joseph Gikatilla's *Sha'arei orah* (*Gates of Light*):

> He would observe the Torah with the attribute of 'Good Sight,' *Tov Roi* [Sam. I 16:12] ... These three attributes – *Hesed, Din,* and *Rahamim* – were conjoined with the attribute of *El Hai*, and David grasped all three of them and thus became the fourth *regel* (leg) of the Throne (*kiseh*) which the other three bear ... What did Leah say? 'This time I will give thanks (*odeh*) to God, so she called his name Yehudah and stopped giving birth' (Gen. 29:35). 'This time' certainly [refers to] three, which is the mystery of the fourth time, the fourth leg; 'I will give thanks,' which is David, who was overflowing with thanks and praise for God; 'and she stopped giving birth,' until this point is the structure (*amidath*) of the *sefirot, from here on there is separation*. When *Zakhor* (remember) and *Shamor* (keep) are conjoined, *the Kingship of the House of David to David*, then 'A river flows from Eden to water the Garden, and from there it separates into four headstreams.'[53]

In *Sha'arei orah* David is represented by *Yesod* (foundation – *El Hai* and *Tov Roi*), which indicates the end of the world of *Yihud* (unity), while the *Shekhinah* represents the World of Division. It is particularly interesting to compare this

---

50 MS Munich 47, 374b. As I learned from Avishai Bar Asher, in his work *Or Zarua* (*Shining Light*) de Leon describes the Chariot in a cosmogenic context, without the accepted sefirotic structure that relates to the Patriarchs.
51 *Sefer ha-pliah*: "Know, my son, that King David is the *Tiferet* of Israel [...] that is to say, the *Tiferet* that is David is called brother, together with *Hesed*, since both of them were emanated from one place." (See the statement beginning with "See my son a great thing".)
52 See my article on mutual responsibility *Journal of Jewish Studies* (forthcoming); and in the words of Rabbi Joseph of Shushan: "*Hesed, Gevurah, Tiferet, Tzaddik* [=*Yesod*], corresponding to the four attributes of the Passover, Shavuot, Sukkot, and Hag ha-shmini." Joseph of Shushan.
53 Gikatilla 1981, 148–149, emphasis mine.

discussion to a similar reading in Zohar *Vayetze*, where there is a depiction of the birth of Judah and the idea that the fourth leg is *Malkhut*:

> 'This time I will praise God' (Gen. 29:45) 'Then she stopped giving birth,' (ibid.) for here four supports were established ... Why did she say 'I will praise God [=YHWH]' concerning this one and not all the others? From here we learn that *as long as the Assembly of Israel is in exile, the Holy Name is incomplete* ... Come and see: Although there were three sons, the throne was incomplete until she gave birth to Judah. Therefore, 'This time I will praise God,' not for all the others. So ותעמוד (*va-ta'amod*), 'she stopped, giving birth.' Why '*va-ta'amod* (she stood)'? Because the throne stood on its supports. '*Va-ta'amod* (She stood)' for until here She stands *in unity*; from here below is the World of Division.[54]

Both homilies refer to the same verse. However, it is evident that while Gikatilla emphasizes the birth of the son and his masculine and phallic quality, the Zohar, in light of the myth of the exile of the *Shekhinah*, establishes the affinity of Judah and David to *Malkhut* while alluding to their role in the redemption as the completers of the tetragrammaton. In contrast to Gikatilla, who calls the fourth leg *El Hai* and distinguishes it from *Malkhut*, the World of Division as discussed in the Zohar, indicates the liminality of the fourth leg that is stable but also represents the source of separation.

The Zohar focuses primarily on the idea of unity: the difficulty in separating the masculine from the feminine, the *Tiferet* from *Malkhut*, the three Patriarchs from David, and the letters *YHW* from the lower H. Gikatilla speaks of the completion of the constellation and describes this state as the flowing of the river from Eden to the material world that separates into four rivers, and then again separates between David (*Yesod, zahor*) and between *Malkhut* and the house of David (*Shekhinah, shamor*). A similar duality can be found in Gikatilla's words in Gate Nine, "Abraham is the right, and Isaac is the left, and David, who is the fourth leg, is the last of the *sefirot*, and he grasps the point of the lower *vav*, which is called *Yesod*."[55]

There are also ambiguous instances in which it is not entirely clear if the fourth leg is identified with *Malkhut* or *Yesod*, as in the words of R. Isaac of Acre in *Meirat 'Einayim* (Illumination of the Eyes):

> Our rabbis further said that David is the fourth leg of the Chariot ... This is why there are those who conclude the Blessing of Thanksgiving in the Grace After Meals with the phrase 'God of David and rebuilder of Jerusalem'; God drew David close to him and anointed him

---

54 Zohar II 154b, vol. II, 364–365, emphasis mine.
55 Gikatilla 1981, 9, vol. 2, 86.

with Holy Oil, and he became the fourth leg of the Chariot, but the Sages did not include him in the daily prayer service, so they included him in the Grace After Meals.[56]

More to the point of my argument, in the Zohar there is a pronounced tendency to portray David as a feminine character, in contrast to other kabbalists who are less comfortable with the duality of gender and sex and prefer not to emphasize the fluid symbolism of the *Shekhinah* and her identification with a masculine figure.[57] This process teaches us as much about the exegetists as it sheds light on theosophical Kabbalah. As Yehuda Liebes states: "Man and the Divine create each other and are created in the image of each other continuously throughout human culture."[58] As I shall demonstrate in the concluding remarks, the designation of the name *Malkhut* to the lowest *sefirah* illustrates the self-perception and national attitude of the Spanish kabbalists who maintained a "spiritual monarchy," concealed and supernal.

Moreover, the intensified identification of David with the *Shekhinah* and the attempt to establish the feminine Goddess as a "leg" and foundation of the entire constellation suggest a veiled polemic with Christian theology. As has been recently shown by Ruth Mazo-Karras, throughout the twelfth and fifteenth centuries we find an increase in the Christian depictions of David as a king, prophet, priest, and warrior, as well as an overtly masculine portrayal.[59] In contrast with this stance, the Castilian mystics and the circle of Zoharic authors established a feminine heroine with androgynous characteristics. As a female character, this Davidic character has no agency or responsibility for her actions, and so is free of the sin enacted by David in his killing of Uriah the Hittite and adultery with Bathsheba; as a masculine figure, however, he is portrayed as repentant, and as married to the supernal *sefirah* of *Binah* as well as the lower *sefirah* of *Malkhut*. Every culture fashions its heroic figure, thus reestablishing the boundaries of identity and its concept of masculinity and femininity.[60] Since the *Shekhinah* cannot be the focal point of religious ritual, this *sefirah* is therefore represented

---

56 R. Isaac of Acre, *Meirat 'Einayim*, 66b, lines 31–35. The identification of Jerusalem with the attribute of *Malkhut* is prevalent, and it seems that its connection to David lies in the tradition of R. Isaac the Blind and R. Jacob bar Sheshet. According to Yehuda Liebes, the identification of David with the fourth leg as the *sefirah* of *Malkhut* is alluded to already in the talmudic literature in the discussion of the Blessing of the Rebuilding of Jerusalem; Liebes 1984.
57 On "the symbolic correlation of David and *Shekhinah*" as an expression of the assimilation of the feminine into the masculine, see: Wolfson 2004, 84, 458–459 n. 250; Wolfson 2001.
58 Liebes 2009, 145.
59 Mazo-Karras 2018, 201–218.
60 Connel 1995.

by the messianic figure of David.[61] In addition, interpreted through the lens of national identity, the figure of the *Shekhinah* may represent the fragile reality of the Jews, who, though deprived of political sovereignty, might find in the fantastic realm of the divine *sefirot* a sense of power and an imaginary kingdom.

7 From Lurianic Kabbalah to Shabbateanism

It seems that in Safedean Kabbalah the perception of David as feminine figure influenced ideas of messianic redemption, sin, and heretical thought, through the identification of the savior with psychological characteristics and personality traits, such as dark side, depression, and "absence," that are symbolizing already in the Zohar "feminine nature." As articulated by R. Hayyim Vital in *Sha'ar ha-gilgulim* (*Gate of Transmigration*):

> Know that a person who has come into the world for the first time will struggle greatly to subjugate his *yetzer* (evil inclination), even if his soul is very high, since it is the beginning of his purification from the *kelipot* (shells, i.e., the forces of evil), since even in the state of *tzelem* (image) he was still enclothed in *kelipot*, as mentioned. *As a result, this person will be sad all of his days and always worry without reason.* However, the true reason is that the *kelipot* cause sadness, as is known. This is the secret of what happened to King David, who was close to God, and yet we find that his *yetzer* overcame him in the incidents involving Bat Sheba and Abigail, which is a great wonder. However, as said, it occurred because it was the beginning of his departure from the depths of the *kelipot*. *You can thereby understand several verses that David said of himself: 'I am sunk in the mire of the shadowy depths,' (Psalms 69:3) and other verses to this effect. Know, therefore, that the sins of someone who has come into the world for the first time do not count before God as they do for others, since he is still affected by the* kelipot, *and it takes great effort to leave them.* This is the secret of our Sages, may their memory be a blessing: 'Had you not been David and he Saul, I would have destroyed many Davids before Saul.'[62] Understand this well. Sometimes the soul of a new person is very lofty but he [still] cannot overcome his *yetzer* – if he could, he would easily be very pious. This is a powerful lesson, for it explains why sometimes a person may only transgress lightly but receive a serious punishment, while someone else may perform a terrible sin, and yet not get punished for it. (*Sha'ar ha-gilgulim*, Introduction, 27; emphasis mine)

Vital draws here a connection between certain exalted souls that are sunk in the depths of the *kelipot*, and worry and sadness, like King David himself. As noted by Lawrence Fine, these ideas were applied by Vital and R. Issac Luria to their own souls, a subject whose personal aspects Liebes examined in relation to the

---

[61] As I show in my article, "King David and Jerusalem: From Psalms to the Zohar."
[62] b. Moed Katan 16b.

Mystery of the Doe and to Luria's messianic self-perception.[63] Indeed, underlying this reading is the messianic identification of R. Hayyim Vital with the redeemer, son of David.[64] "Even though his soul originates from a very high place" hints at the ability of the Messiah to sin grandly. Even though David's soul was from a high place, he was a sinner, due to the circumstances of his soul being in its first incarnation, as it had only now emerged from the shells. Depression therefore stems from the exit of the soul from the husks, so that it exists for the first time on the outside, and not from the state of the soul inside them.

As we have already discussed, according to the Midrash and the Zohar, David was stillborn,[65] and his lifeless state was connected to both the original sin of Adam as well as his father Jesse's problematic coupling with his concubine,[66] motifs that may allude to some biographical elements in Vital's life. On this basis, the kabbalists developed the concept of the "holy deceit." According to this idea, Jesse's sinful act lured the *kelipot* into believing that he was already a lost cause, so that they left him alone, and did not notice how the soul of his newly conceived son arose and escaped from the confines of their world, the world of the husks.[67]

Moreover, according to the Lurianic doctrine, King David is a reincarnation of the first man, Adam (following the letter acronym of ADaM as *Adam, David, Messiah*).[68] Therefore, the sins of David mirror the sin of Adam. For example, in Sefer *ha-Gilgulim* he claims:

> Here David changed his sleep habit, and slept in the day rather than the night, and this caused the chain of events (according to b. Sanhedrin 107a). This is the secret of the verse,

---

[63] Fine 2003, 113–169. Liebes 1992.

[64] On Luria and Vital as the Messiah son of David and Son of Joseph, see: Vital 2006, Introduction, 5a–b, 8a; *Toldot ha-Ari* 1967, 199; Ronit 1988, Ch. 2–3, especially 336–352 and 265, 299–303; Fine 2003, 246; Liebes 1992, 125; Tamar 1970, 115–123. In *Sha'ar ha-gilgulim*, introduction 36, Vital identifies himself also with the suffering son of Joseph: "Shmuel [Vital = his son] said, even though my father, of blessed memory, hid his words in this place, I remember that face to face, he one day revealed to me, that this verse alludes to the intimacy [*korvat*] of his soul ... However, in the time of my father it is possible that, if Israel repents, my father will be the messiah from the line of Joseph."

[65] See n. 32 above.

[66] As brought in an aggadic story in Yalkut Hamikhiri; see Kara-Ivanov Kaniel 2017, Ch. 3.

[67] On the "holy ruse," see: Scholem 1973, 50, 249, 258; Tishby 1992, 131–132; Liebes 1995, 311–312 n. 88–89.

[68] Isaac Luria also explains that Uriah was an incarnation of the primordial snake, while Batsheva was Eve. For some remarkable similarities to the church fathers' reading, see: de-Lubac 2000, Ch. 7, 64–67; Mazo-Karras 2018. On Lurianic exorcism and the role of David in cursing the devil by use of Ps. 109:6, see: Chajes 2003, 72–79. For recitation of exorcistic hymns attributed to King David already in antiquity by Josephus and others, see: Bohak 2008, 98–100.

'David arose from off his bed, and walked upon the roof of the king's house; and from the roof he saw a woman bathing' (2 Samuel 11:2) – washing away the filth of the serpent; 'for she was purified from her uncleanness' (11:4) – of the primordial snake.[69]

The identification of Haim Vital with King David and his own messianic yearnings stands in the foreground of these readings. On the roof of the King's house recurs an archetypal repetition of the scene in the Garden of Eden. Eve and Batsheva are just sparks of one entity, while Vital explains his sorrows and tormented soul through the soul roots of the Davidic line. Moreover, in the first printing of the *Sha'ar ha-gilgulim* that was expunged, the messianic ability of David to repair the sin of Adam was presented in extremely radical way. David's troubled soul and the justifications of his sins were explained by the great size of his soul: wherein his evil deeds "were not considered sins at all," and were even able to "increase his reward" (!).[70] This explanation was printed in the addenda to the volume of *Sha'ar ha-gilgulim* published by Samuel Vital, which also included the subject of his father, Haim Vital's, soul.[71] To be sure, there is a deterministic element here, which aims to soften and ease Vital's conflicts about his own behaviors – despite the grandeur of his soul.

Moshe Idel has emphasized the centrality of the issues of messianism and eschatology to the nascent kabbalistic literature, arguing that already in the Bahir, "theurgic activity causes the descent of the new soul of the Messiah."[72] Whereas all human souls can suffer reincarnation for even up to a thousand generations, the soul of the redeemer is assigned specifically to him, and has never yet been incarnated in a human body.[73] Even if Luria does not directly oppose the Bahir, it is significant that he thinks David's soul is not necessarily new, since it had suffered numerous reincarnations, beginning with the primordial fall of Adam, with subsequent appearances through various personalities. Nevertheless, there is a sense of a newness to David's soul, according to Vital, since it is the first time that the soul of the redeemer emerged from the husks by way of the ruse of the "holy deceit."

---

69 *Sefer ha-gilgulim* 1982, Ch. 62, 63b–64a.
70 *Sha'ar ha-gilgulim*, Jerusalem: Ahavat Shalom, 1917, 160.
71 *Sha'ar ha-gilgulim, Hosafot ha-Rashu* [= R. Samuel Vital], Jerusalem 1902, 64b–65a. I am grateful to Yehuda Liebes and Uri Safrai for the discussion of these sources.
72 Idel 2006; Idel 2012 (citation from page 36 n. 36). Fine 2003, 94–95, 192–193, 321–339. See also in Chajes 2003.
73 See the Book Bahir §126, 209, "And when Israel is good, the souls deserve to exit and come to this world [...] This is the reason why we say the son of David will not come until all the souls that are in the human body will be consumed [b. Nida 13b] and new ones will deserve to exit, then the son of David will deserve to be born. How? Because his soul will exit among the others."

Indeed, in Lurianic Kabbalah we are witness to an expansion of the simple theory of a "one united" soul, which passes from body to body (as promulgated by the school of Nahmanides), to a more complex theory of a tripartite division of the soul, which includes subsidiary particles called "sparks," terms that already appear in kabbalistic works penned in thirteenth- and fourteenth-century Castile.[74] This concept of transmigration resonates with a modern psychoanalytic theory of the "multiple self," which in David's case commits his soul to pass through various personalities (including Vital himself, as he testifies).[75]

In an additional known segment from *Sha'ar ha-gilgulim* referencing the mystery of impregnation and reincarnation in the Zohar, Vital outlines ideas regarding the journey of the souls, and the personal biography of King David.

> Knowing this, you can understand King David's fear [of God] when he said, 'Many have said, "For nafshi (my soul) there is no salvation for it from God." Selah.' (Ps. 3:3) For it is strange that people could have spoken so badly about such a great person as King David ... The *nefesh* (physical soul) of King David was very elevated, but as a result of the primordial sin of Adam it descended into the depths of the *kelipot*, to the feminine side of the *kelipot*. David's birth was its first departure from the *kelipot*. Therefore, it began its rectification only from the level of *Asiyah* (making), which is called *Nefesh*. The reason is that it was a transmigration from the third level. This is the secret of what is mentioned in Sava de-mishpatim and in other discourses as well, *that David was from the feminine side and not the masculine side. Rather, [the origin of his soul was] in the 'World of Death,' which is called Nukva (feminine). Understand this.* It was therefore asked there: 'Why was he called "Obed"?' The tree was lacking, and he rectified it.' (Zohar, 2:103b) [...] When David sinned with Bat Sheba he blemished his *nefesh*. As a result, the one who possesses his *ruah* will merit the completion of its rectification before David rectifies his *nefesh* [...] This is why he said, 'there is no salvation for him [the body],' and not, 'there is no salvation for her [the soul]' [...] 'many say of my soul *(lenafshi)* [God will not deliver him (Ps 3:3)]' since there is only a *nefesh* within me, it indicates that she has no salvation in David's body at the time of the *Resurrection of the Dead*. (*Sha'ar ha-gilgulim*, Introduction, 7; emphasis mine)

According to this homily, following the sin of Adam, David's potential soul descended into the depths of the feminine side of the *kelipot*. When David was actually born, his soul began the process of rectification from the lowest level in the World of *Asiyah*, related to the *sefirah* of *Malkhut* and to the level of *nefesh*. Here Vital relies on the following passage from the Zohar's *Sava de-mishpatim* (*The Old Man*). In this Zoharic homily we learn that David's soul derives from the

---

74 Scholem 1991, 197–250.
75 On the "multiple self" following Mitchel and Bromberg, see Kara-Ivanov Kaniel 2019b.

feminine side. Therefore, like all the heroes of the Judean dynasty, he is capable of overcoming the tragic fate of the *Tikla*, the wheel of souls governed by harsh rules of impregnation and transmigration:

> When David came *he remained in the lower tree of the Female, and had to receive life from another.* [...] in all aspects, transformed by transmigration: so it was with Perez, so it was with Boaz, so it was with Obed [...] But by these, evil was consumed and good eventually emerged – the one of whom is written 'Goodly to look on, and YHVH is with him.' (1 Sam. 16:12, 18). Here, the lower tree stood firm, and '(Ps. 47:9) God reigned over nations.'
> (Zohar II 103b; vol. V, 63–64)

Over the course of the Zoharic *drasha*, David is described as one who, as a result of the restoration (*tikkun*) he performed, is attached to the female tree, echoing the commandment to "work ... and take care of" the Garden of Eden (Gen. 2:15).

In contrast to the rest of the world that is mired in the despair imposed by the forces of evil (as long as man rules man), in the Davidic dynasty there is a mechanism to transform evil to good. Here in *Sava de-mishpatim* the Zohar alludes to the fact that all the men of the Davidic dynasty – Judah, Boaz, Obed, Jesse, and David – are from the feminine side and function as receivers, since they draw sustenance from the inverted supernal tree and receive light and "life from another."[76] This idea appears also in other Lurianic texts, such as the statement in *Sha'ar ha-psukim:* "and it is known that David comes from the feminine side" (*Sha'ar ha-psukim, Psalms*, 63).

In conclusion, according to Vital, David's soul was full of extreme contrasts; on the one hand, David was possessed by the husks, and on the other he had the power to rise above them and repair them – from the bottom of the world of '*asiyah* to the world of '*azilut*. These internal conflicts were the source of David's terrible suffering, as it is said in *Sha'ar ha-gilgulim*, Introduction, number 27, "because depression draws down (its power) from the husks, as is known." This homily would later be adapted and utilized by Nathan of Gaza to explain the nature of Shabbatai Zevi's soul, as it was rooted in David's soul.[77]

---

[76] This idea recurs in many Zoharic homilies, such as Zohar II 232b–233a. On the idea that "the seed of David is inverted," see: *Secret of Secrets* (*Raza de-razin*), a homily that was central in the external identification of Shabbatai Zevi: Zohar II 73a–74a.

[77] On this in the Shabbatean context, see: Scholem 1973; Mark 2003, 293–294 no. 44.

8 Symbolic Chariot – Ma'arekhet ha-elohut and Shoresh Yishai

The Zohar ascribed to the *Shekhinah* classic archetypical and feminine symbols such as the moon, ocean, wellspring, doe, and rose. In the sixteenth century, with the rise of reflective consciousness and early modern notions of identity and selfhood, an additional aspect of David's messianic figure was revealed.[78] As illustrated by Eitan Fishbane, *kawanot* (mystical intentions) create a Throne and Chariot for the Divine, an idea that later evolved in hasidic literature through the view of the Patriarchs as *behinot* (aspects) who are employed when working on one's own traits.[79] In fact, this perception of the *tzaddikim* (the righteous ones) as God's Chariot somewhat replaced the quadrilateral personal Chariot composed of Abraham, Isaac, Jacob, and David.

As Adam Afterman has shown, this process began with R. Asher ben David, who combined traditions from different schools of thought – the school of R. Isaac the Blind, the Bahir, Maimonides' doctrine of *dvekut* (cleaving) to the Active Intellect, and R. Judah Halevi's principle of divine choice and the transformation of man into a vessel – to broaden the doctrine of the Chariot to include *every righteous person* to become a messenger, a "Chariot" or "Throne," for the Divine. In R. Asher's interpretation this process happens only after death, but according to Bar Sheshet, it can take place even during one's lifetime. This idea later took on new forms, such as the enclothement in the tetragrammaton and Holy Spirit in the Geronese and in Nahamanides' Kabbalah, as well as in the narrative-based interpretation prevalent in Zoharic and Castilian Kabbalah, which emphasized the affinity between biblical figures' personal storylines and the *sefirot*.[80]

R. Asher asserts that the Patriarchs "would see that His *Shekhinah* dwelled upon them when He would reveal himself to speak with them, and they became a Throne for the *Shekhinah*... because the attributes of Holy One, blessed be He, *Hesed*, *Din*, and *Rahamim*, are called Patriarchs, every one of them is called 'Throne'"[81] (Ben David 1996, 74). However, according to R. Jacob bar Sheshet, "it is possible that when they said that the Patriarchs are the Chariots they did not intend to refer only to the Patriarchs alone and to David, but rather *to every*

---

78 Weinstein 2011.
79 Fishbane 2009, 385–418.
80 Afterman 2011, 216–219, and more; Scholem 1991, 146; Tishby 1989, 416. Afterman focuses on the cleavage of the soul rather than the idea of the body as a vessel for the unification, while I would like to emphasize the narrative storylines of heroes such as David and the Patriarchs.
81 Afterman 2011, 218.

single righteous person who cleaves to one attribute of the attributes of Holy One, blessed be He" (Bar Sheshet 1964, 397–398; emphasis mine). This reading regards as allegorical the notion that David and the Patriarchs are the Chariot, while the Zohar, and subsequently Lurianic Kabbalah and Shabbateanism, prefer to emphasize the mythic and personal aspects by expanding the narrative plot of the characters. *Ma'arekhet ha-elohut*, for example, goes even further and "invents" a pseudo-Talmudic formula, stating:

> Regarding this matter our Sages, may they be blessed, said that *the righteous are the Chariot*. This means the Chariot of the *Shekhinah*. Because there is a righteous person above in the Chariot, as it is written 'the righteous is an everlasting foundation' (Prov. 10:25), the *Shekhinah* rests on the lower righteous one who likens the form to its creator, according to the principle *matza min et mino ve'na'or* (varieties of like kind find each other).
> (*Ma'arekhet ha-elohut*, Ch. 11, 229; emphasis mine)

It seems that in several instances the Zohar contests the notion that the righteous entail the Chariot and emphasizes that the Patriarchs and David are uniquely chosen:

> Rabbi Abba said, 'There we learned: From four sides, all derives; therein all roots of those above and below intertwine. And it has been taught: One enters, another emerges; one conceals, another expresses; linked with one another – fathers of all!' (Zohar I 216b; Vol. III, 306)

> Rabbi Shim'on said, 'Only your fathers did YHVH desire.' (Deut. 10:15) It is written: *your fathers – precisely, three! As indicated by only – literally, only!* From these, all others branch and intertwine, raising the name to be crowned.'
> (Zohar I, 223b–224a; Vol. III, 345; emphasis mine)

Contrary to the emphasis on the Patriarchs as three, R. Abba argues that the Chariot is made stable by four legs. However, R. Simon bar Yohai insists on a triadic foundation, relying on the verse, "*Only* to your fathers did he show his loving favor" (Deut. 10:16; emphasis mine). The debate regarding the essence of the divine chariot as being combined from three legs or four legs continues to accompany kabbalistic, Shabbatean, and hasidic literature. This debate is not technical, but rather deals with questions of messianic salvation, gender fluidity, identity, and heresy.

Another issue that is connected to the symbolic function of the Chariot is that of transmigration, impregnation, and reincarnation, since the human soul has the ability to transcend into the divine realm, as we have learnt from Vital's identification with King David's place in the Chariot. Even though at first glance it does not appear to be an explicit work of Kabbalah, in the sixteenth-century *Shoresh Yishai* (*Root of Jesse*), Shlomo Halevi Alkabetz sets forth an amalgamation of ideas and traditions on the question of transmigration, combining positions from the

Bahir, the Nahmanidian school, R. Joseph of Shushan, Recanati, and others.[82] In his discussion, Alkabetz dedicates considerable attention to the commandment to be fruitful and multiply. Like the *Sava de-mishpatim* in the Zohar, Alkabetz views the intentional abstention from this commandment as a grave sin, since, as he puts it, the well is filled from the river, and whoever does not procreate causes the supernal river to dry up, "because the unification that is achieved by procreation cannot be interchanged."

> Indeed, Ben Azzai says [...] it is a great thing that must be considered, a great mystery which you will only discover in the depths of the great sea, the *Book of the Zohar*, and in the *Tikkunim* (*Tikunei ha-zohar*) in particular. It [the mystery] is what we have said previously, that whoever is without sons has no rectification (*takkana*). You should know that this is the case when one comes to procreate and did not procreate. However, if one comes to this world to fulfill another commandment that he had previously lacked, or to receive *karet* or another punishment, or to do kindness for his generation – that person does not require sons, and will not be punished if he does not procreate, and if he does procreate his seed will not live on through them [...] and she is not his wife and they are not his sons. Rather that woman belongs to he who was not blessed to reproduce. (Alkabetz 1978, 77–79)

Alkabetz justifies Ben Azzai's statement in the Talmud, that anyone who does not engage in the mitzva to be fruitful and multiply "is considered as though he sheds blood and also diminishes the Divine Image."[83] Then he adds that in certain transmigrations, one can return without being required to procreate – and in those cases, avoiding the commandment to be fruitful is not deemed sinful. We thus already find a creative process, one that will be developed by subsequent kabbalists, of open transmigrations that incorporate a variety of options. In closing, Alkabetz quotes Karo's *Maggid Mesharim* (*Preacher of Righteousness*) as though quoting the Talmudic sages (!): "Furthermore, it has been said that we have found *tzaddikim* who in their death procreate because they already died pre-

---

82 On *Shoresh Yishai*, see: Zak 2018, 40. The kabbalistic sources in *Shoresh Yishai* mostly refer to subjects relating to levirate marriage and transmigration; Zak 2018, no. 50. According to Alkabetz there are three levels of transmigration: the highest level is that of Moses, Abraham, and *Raya Meheimana* (the Loyal Shepherd) who returned "to do kindness for their generation." The next level reinstates the person to transmigrate as "punishment for certain sins that cannot be rectified ... since for every transgression of *karet* (excision) the person will return." Here, the author combines the Bahir's idea of a thousand transmigrations with the three transmigrations posited by Nahmanides, along with the transmigration of animals and beasts as set forth by R. Joseph Hamadan. This level is connected to the fear of punishment and to the attribute of Isaac, as well as to the negative commandments (*mitzwot lo ta'aseh*). The third level, conversely, is connected to Jacob and the attribute of *Tiferet*, and is meant to fulfil the positive commandments (*mitzwot 'aseh*) that had been lacking.
83 In the Talmud, *b. Yevamot* 63b.

viously" (*Shoresh Yishai*, 80).⁸⁴ The phrase "*tzaddikim* who in their death" Alkabetz interprets conversely as indicating that they died previously and became righteous through death and returned to rectify their generation. His words do not concern David, but his grandmother Ruth, the Moabite. Like the thirteenth- and fourteenth-century kabbalists, Alkabetz highlights the kindness that Ruth did "for the dead" as an allusion to levirate marriage.

He extensively discusses here and elsewhere (ibid., 14a–16a) the mystery of the soul quivering inside the womb of the widow and divorcee, as described by the *Sava* in the Zohar. In his discourse on the mystery of transmigration, Alkabetz borrows the metaphor used by the thirteenth-century kabbalist R. Joseph of Shushan, of the souls as the image of the supernal family.⁸⁵ Alkabetz goes on to say that levirate marriage of the brother instead of the father is like water drawn from a spring, and "these things are water that have no end." In his discussion Alkabetz frequently employs water imagery, such as "to draw water from a far-away place," as an explanation of Ruth's deeds, which initiates the circle of *Hesed* (both in the literal meaning that appears in the *Book of Ruth*, as well as in kabbalistic doctrines of metempsychosis).⁸⁶ Following the Zohar, *Shoresh Yishai* offers a female perspective on the subject of transmigration while describing Ruth and Tamar as righteous women and broadly illuminating the distinctiveness of the messianic family, without revolving around the personal character of the "son" and the fourth leg of the Chariot. Yet, it is clear that the Zoharic tradition about the "feminized Messiah" is standing at the background of these homilies.

9 Shabbatai Zevi and David as the Feminine Leg of the Chariot

As we have seen, Shabbatai Zevi, the great heretic of the Shabbatean movement, derived his power from messianic kabbalistic trends and, in particular, from his identification with the feminine divinity: the *Shekhinah*. I suggest that the pursuit

---

84 Karo's original phrasing is slightly different: Karo 1960, 47: "The righteous procreate in death more than in life."
85 R. Joseph of Shushan the Capital, MS Jerusalem 597 8o 201b, "Know, that each family of Israel is a tree in the Garden of Eden and a branch in the Tree of Life, and it is one organ of the Heavenly Chariot. Therefore, family relations are a metaphor for the divine unity; for the entire family is one entity ... the dead are like the roots of the tree, and the branches are the living, for it is thanks to the dead that the living exist." See also Scholem 1991, 197–250.
86 On Alkabetz's poetics and mysticism, see: Zak 2018.

of heresy was aimed primarily at *male* Shabbatean figures, while female figures relatively were protected from persecution.[87] Perhaps believers identified Shabbatai Zevi with King David (rooted in Zoharic symbolism) in order to protect their messiah. As feminine figures, whose kingdoms are based on subterfuge, intrigue, and trickery, both David and Shabbatai Zevi represent the "power of the powerless."[88] Because the *Shekhinah* appears not to possess "agency," David and Shabbatai Zevi, as her representatives, are not liable for their sins. Moreover, as a metaphor for the personal messiah, David symbolizes the entire congregation of Jewish men (*Knesset Israel*), who are all absolved of guilt along with him. Therefore, the feminine aspect of the Messiah and its representation as the fourth leg of the Chariot is essential in any attempt to understand their unique heretical behavior.

These opposing tendencies – suffering and a sense of spiritual elevation, melancholy, depression and spiritual enlightenment – all constitute the map to the souls of Shabbatai Zevi and of King David. As described by the Shabbatean believers, at times Shabbatai Zevi is at "a state of alienation [from God] but after a while it [the illumination] came back to him and this went on until he was hidden from us."[89] In times of spiritual elevation, Shabbatai Zevi would frequently sing psalms in the street, accompanied, like David, by musical instruments and song. Scholem noted that this musicality is among the most prominent traits in Shabbatai Zevi's character, one that drew hearts to him. Even during the periods of his weekly fasts and asceticism, Shabbatai Zevi led the feast of *Melave Malka* (escorting the queen) between his fasts from Sabbath to Sabbath. Attributed to King David, this "fourth" meal originated in fourteenth-century Kabbalah, appearing, for example, in *Ma'arekhet ha-elohut* and in later customs developed in Lurianic Kabbalah. Influenced by Shabbatean tradition, this meal became known as the "Meal of the Messiah."[90] As written in *Hemdat Yamim* (*The Beloved of Days*):

> We have prepared the feast of faith, we have prepared the feast, this is the feast of King David the anointed one (*meshihah*), and Abraham, Isaac, and Jacob come to take part [...] My teacher would break off a morsel of bread, [to eat it] as a poor man would, in the spirit of the aspect of *Malkhut* (David) and did not leave any for us.
>
> (*Sefer Hemdat Yamim*, The Holy Sabbath I, Ch. 18)

---

[87] Elisheva Carlebach defined Shabbateanism as a movement that inspired a "pursuit of heresy" within the pre-modern Jewish world: "This exclusive focus on combating heresy as a mainstay of a rabbinic career is a virtual novum in early modern Jewish history"; Carlebach 1994, 7.
[88] See: Doniger 2000; Fonrobert 2006; Ashley 1988; see also: Boyarin 1999, 67–92.
[89] Scholem 1973, I, 132–133.
[90] On the development of this tradition, see: Hallamish 2006, 504–508.

It is clear that Shabbatean authors sought to strengthen the affinity between Shabbatai Zevi, on the one hand, and David as the Messiah and as a feminine figure connected to the *Shekhinah*, on the other.[91] The decision to call the fourth meal the "Meal of the Messiah" references their current redeemer, Shabbatai Zevi, who was saved and "graced with life" as David was. Both protagonists are identified with "the bread of the poor" (*lechem oni*), because of their ordeals and the internal and external persecution they experienced. It may be that this meal grew out of Talmudic traditions regarding the death of David on the Sabbath.[92] When the Patriarchs arrive at David's fourth meal, they come to honor the attribute of *Malkhut* identified with him. Shabbatai Zevi, who has plenty of feminine characteristics, attracted a similar tradition. Thus, the departure of the *neshama yetera* (the additional soul) and the *Shekhinah* at the conclusion of the Sabbath are attributed to Shabbatai Zevi by way of the *Melave Malka*, and allude to his feminine persona.[93] This is a cyclical ritual that may refer to the rebirth of the redeemer, just as the days of the week are reborn again and again from the Sabbath.

According to the author of *Hemdat Yamim*, the Patriarchs come to David's meal: "This is the meal of David the King Messiah; Abraham, Isaac, and Jacob are coming to dine with us." The Babylonian Talmud in tractate *Pesahim* discusses the wording of the prayer and the placement of the blessing of *Matzmiah Keren Yeshu'ah* (Who Causes the Horn of Salvation to Flourish) adjacent to the *Magen David* (Shield of David) blessing which completes the blessings of the Patriarchs. The homily of the sages in *Pesahim* 117a based on God's words to David, "I will make your name great like the name of the greatest men" (2 Sam. 7:9) alluding to the Patriarchs.[94] This homily, alongside the description of David as one superior to the Patriarchs in *BT Moed Katan*, points to his unique role in the Chariot. His supremacy over the Patriarchs coupled with his jealousy of them may elucidate Shabbatean messianic motifs, but also illuminate the conflictual perception of the fourth leg which represents, as noted above, imperfection and instability.[95]

---

91 The topic of Shabbatai Zevi's feminine characteristics is discussed by Idel, Liebes, Elqayam, Papo, and others. I will expand on the subject elsewhere (El Prezente, forthcoming).
92 *BT Shabbat*, 30a (following Ps. 39:5, "Show me Lord, my life's end."). According to *Ruth Rabbah* 3:2, David died on *Shemini Atzeret* on Sabbath. According to *BT Ketubot* 103b, "If one dies on Shabbat eve it is a good sign for him; at the conclusion of Shabbat it is a bad sign for him." The question of the Shabbatean nature of *Hemdat Yamim* was discussed by Ya'ari, Tishby, Liebes, Huss, Elqayam, Fogel, and others.
93 Scholem expounded on the subject of Shabbatai Zevi as the Sabbath. In the Idra Rabbah, Zohar III 144b, Rashbi also symbolizes the Sabbath. See also below after n. 99.
94 b. Pesahim 117a. For the Judeo-Christian messianic context of this blessing, see: Liebes 1984.
95 On the legs of the *Shekhinah* and her faults, see: Roi 2017, Ch. 2.

Nonetheless, the Zohar suggests that the *lechem oni* (the attribute of *Malkhut*) is superior to the stable legs of the Patriarchs that are engraved in the Chariot.[96]

I suggest, therefore, that Shabbatai Zevi viewed himself as the fourth leg of the Chariot, like King David before him. Accordingly, he wished to rectify the three *regalim* and celebrate them, *consecutively in one week*, in order to join them as the fourth *regel* which both incorporates and transcends them. As is stressed in the addition to the apocalyptic vision of Nathan of Gaza, *Mar'ah le-Avraham* (*Vision of R. Abraham*), in the book *To'ey Ruah* (*The Apocalyptic Vision of Rabbi Abraham the Hasid*), this was a recurring custom for Shabbatai Zevi before his death in exile in Ulcinj (Passover 1676).

> And in the year 5418 (1657) there will be three *regalim* in one week to atone for all the sins committed by Israel during the *regalim*. To him the Holy one, blessed be He, will give a new Torah and new commandments to rectify all the worlds. In the year 5418 he will recite the blessing "*matir asurim*" ("He permits the forbidden"). (Scholem 1942, 182)

The image of the Chariot that was completed with the appearance of Shabbatai Zevi and his request to seat the King upon his throne joins with the testimonies of his companions that describe his unification with the Patriarchs who anointed him with the *shemen ha-mishha* (anointing oil): "a voice called out three times night after night, 'do not touch my anointed Shabbatai Zevi.'"[97] In *Sefer ha-beriah* (*The Book of Creation*), and *Raza de-ma'aseh merkavah/Raza de-malka meshiha* (*The Mystery of the Workings of the Chariot/The Mystery of the King Messiah*),[98] Nathan expounds on Shabbatai Zevi's figure as engraved in the Chariot. It is from these discourses that we learn the extent to which Shabbatai Zevi was connected to sanctified ritual – both with the cyclical week in his identification with the Sabbath (he even asserted that his "name is Sabbath" and he is referred to as "*Shabbat ha-gadol*" [Great Sabbath]), and in the yearly cycle and the holidays of the month of *Tishrei*. Again, the basis for this identification can be found in the Zohar: "'God included in the seventh day His work that He had made.' [Gen 2:2] This is Sabbath, fourth leg of the Throne" (Zohar I 5a; vol. I, 31). It seems that the

---

96 Zohar I 250b. On David's pauper's prayer which bypasses the rest of the prayers, see: Zohar I 168b. For an alternative tradition, see: Zohar III 195a.
97 Sasportas 1973, 94; Scholem 1973, I, 111–112. According to Coenen and Sasportas, this transpired in 1648, when he was about twenty-four years old.
98 On this composition, see: Tishby 1964, 320 no. 110; Scholem 1973, II, 693 no. 3; Liebes 1995, 281 no. 77; Elqayam 1993, 99–106; and in Noam Lefler's PhD dissertation (forthcoming). In *Sefer ha-beriah* (*Book of Creation*) Nathan describes the service of God through spiritual love as a tool for the transformation of man into a Chariot for the Divine (as in Wirszubski 1990, 291). For Nathan's attestation to having looked upon the Chariot, see: Scholem 1973, I, 168; Scholem 1991, 308.

influence of Bar Sheshet theology led the Zoharic kabbalists to transform Talmudic midrash into a new structure, one that emphasizes the role of the Patriarchs and David with them, as an embodiment of the divine chariot. In addition, this myth enhances the dependence of the three legs of the Chariot on the fourth leg, and evokes an image of two messiahs that were not meant to be born, in the sense of "*bar niflei*" (stillborn).[99]

Shabbatai Zevi depends on the Patriarchs to anoint him and join him to them as the Chariot, resembling the once-stillborn David's reliance on the Patriarchs for his very life. Despite this dependence, both characters are nonetheless superior to the Patriarchs. Zevi sees himself also as the fourth New Year – *Tu bi-Shvat*, the new year of the trees, a festival that became ritualized because of the influence of *Hemdat Yamim*.[100] By the believers he was perceived to be the sanctified *ilan* (tree) and the one who "will deliver us to the Tree of Life."[101] He was called "The Pleasant Tree Son of Jesse Lives upon the Earth," a phrase, as Boaz Huss demonstrates, that is numerically equal to his own name in Gematria. Like the Shabbatean poems, the prayers that precede *Seder Tu-bishvat* in *Hemdat Yamim* also strengthen the messianic link between David and Shabbatai Zevi: "Therefore, swiftly cause the offshoot, Your servant David, to blossom and raise up his horn through Your salvation. And His glory will be lifted and be delivered upon the whole world in its entirety."[102] Like David, Shabbatai Zevi's identification with the fourth leg of the Chariot alludes to his affinity for the spiritual *heikhal* (palace), which is the "*mikdash adam*" (human temple).[103]

Conclusions

This paper demonstrates the links between David as a feminine figure and Shabbatai Zevi, and shows how their symbolization as the fourth leg of the Chariot further developed the connections between femininity and heresy. In both cases

---

99 See n. 32 above. On Shabbatai Zevi's companions who called him *Bar Naflei*, see: Scholem 1973, I, 107; II, 511, 693, 774. On nature which hesitates and becomes impregnated, wishing to compensate for an essential lack in their existence, see: Pedaya 2002, 216, 226.
100 Huss, "*The Pleasant Tree Son of Jesse Lives upon the Earth*" – *On the Shabbatean Origin of Seder Tu bi-Shvat*.
101 As stated in the Shabbatean poem translated from Ladino by M. Attias.
102 *Sefer Hemdat Yamim*, The Holy Sabbath, Ch. 1.
103 These traditions reinforce Maoz Kahana's assertion that Shabbatai Zevi represents "sacred time" and "sacred place"; Kahana 2016. This is how Kahana explains the eating of the forbidden animal fat and the rest of the prohibitions that were permitted in the new Torah.

the characters' imperfections "allow" them to sin as they do, for as "feminine" figures they do not bear full responsibility for their actions and deeds. The feminine Messiah may be regarded as weak, ill, or mad – without losing his appeal as a deviant seducer and brave, heretical hero. To put it differently, the identification of David with the *sefirah* of *Malkhut* was one of the main reasons for the Shabbatean fascination with the Zohar. Not only did the Zohar place the feminine Messiah at the heart of its homilies, but it glorified the sins of David and in so doing created a precedent for Shabbatai's own behavior. In the case of David and Shabbatai Zevi, heresy indeed accompanies femininity. If the present order and its law are typically gendered as masculine, the threatening, disruptive forces that attempt to bring forth redemption are identified as feminine.

Beyond the *kitzutz* and heresy, the keys to redemption are related to the *Shekhinah* as well, precisely because unification with her is not constant and she moves and connects between the worlds, as Nathan states in *Sefer ha-beriah* regarding the designation of *Malkhut* as *Yirah* (fear): "The serpents have a claim on her, for she [*Malkhut*] is not united in the entire sacred *Yihud* [unification], because, God forbid, she is *kelo* [as not]."[104] This statement ascribes to the serpents a claim of ownership over the divine feminine, marking her as a figure that requires protection because of her liminal state as a gateway to the divine world – a state that renders her vulnerable to the powers of the *sitra aḥra* (the other side) that lie in wait. Since it is impossible to avoid encountering the forces of evil that seek control over the feminine, it is necessary to strengthen her through the serpents of the *kelippah*, as a kind of vaccination: "Since in the serpent of *kelippah* the feminine power is greater than the masculine" (Nathan of Gaza, *Derush ha-taninim*, 47). This statement is key to understanding the central theme of women in Shabbatean thought, and the double-sided game that allows for the identification of masculine leaders with the divine feminine, while simultaneously avoiding the actual threat involved in placing real women at the heart of messianic activism.

In more general sense I would propose that this feminized version of David that was innovated and remarkably developed by the Zohar may have been rooted in an anti-Christian polemic: as a rebellion against the Christian concept of messianic redemption and the idea of Original Sin; as the humiliation through feminization of an archetypically male Christian hero; or, rather, as the internalization of Christian attitudes by the kabbalists, as happens with the veneration of

---

[104] Wirszubski, *Between the Lines*, 218. The word "*kelo*" appears to be a mistake, and it may be that the intended meaning was "*kilayon*" (annihilation) by the *sitra aḥra*, or the word "*be-lo*" (without). Since the *zivug* union between her and *Tiferet* is not constant, the *kelipot* have a claim and a place to grasp her when she is "without" *zivug*.

Mary.[105] David's centrality in medieval art, and his influence on the royal dynasties and kings in developing European religious culture, exposed the kabbalists to overt images that challenged them and their assumptions regarding sin, repentance, and salvation. The phenomenon of a feminized David might also have been influenced by the perception among Christians during the High Middle Ages that Jesus and leaders such as Bernard of Clairvaux were feminine and motherly figures.[106] In the Middle Ages, the kabbalists resisted Christian ideas of asceticism, martyrdom, and suffering, substituting extreme sexuality, the reversal of roles, and gender fluidity. In addition, symbolizing David through the *Shekhinah* may be an indication of how kabbalists turned Christian accusations of "feminized" Jewish men into advantage.[107]

The Zohar embraced the dichotomous David (sinner turned saint, hated turned chosen, jester turned king), as presented in the Bible and the Talmud, but enhanced this David in its own image. Through a process of creating "counter-history," the Zoharic David underwent a process of transgenderization, as the medieval kabbalists indeed saw themselves as "female" and powerless (despite their heightened mystical awareness, given the un-redeemed world in which they lived). Yet by identifying themselves with David and the *Shekhinah*, both of which represented the simultaneous power and vulnerability of the Jewish nation, these (male) kabbalists transformed the shameful situation into a virtue.

Bibliography

Primary Sources

Alkabetz, Shlomo. *Shoresh Yishai (Root of Jesse)*. Jerusalem, n.p 1978.
Azriel of Gerona. *Commentary on the Talmudic Aggadoth*. Tishby edition. Jerusalem: Magnes, 1982.
Baer Gottlober, Avraham. *Memories and Journeys*. Jerusalem: Dorot, 1976.
Bar Sheshet, Jacob. "*Sefer ha-emuna ve-habitahon* (Book of Faith and Trust)." *Kitvei Ramban*, Vol. 2. Ed. Hayyim D. Chavel. Jerusalem: Mosad ha-Rav Kook, 1964.
Ben David, Asher. *Perush yud gimel middot (Commentary to the Thirteen Attributes)*. Abrams edition. Los Angeles: Cherub Press, 1996.
Emden, Jacob. *Sefer Shimush*. Amsterdam, n.p, 1758.
Frances, Emmanuel. *Divan*. Tel Aviv: Devir, 1932.

---

[105] This is an idea that was discussed intensely by Art Green and Peter Schäfer.
[106] Bynum 1982.
[107] Cuffel 2007; Resnick 2012.

Genesis Rabbah. Albeck edition. Jerusalem: Shalem Books, 1995 (second print).
Gikatilla, Josef. *Sha'arei Orah (Gates of Light)*. Ben Shlomo edition. Jerusalem: Bialik Institute, 1981.
Isaac of Acre. *Meirat 'Einayim*. Goldreich edition. Jerusalem: Hebrew University, 1980.
Karo, Yoseph. *Maggid Mesharim (Preacher of Righteousness)*. Jerusalem: Shemot, 1960.
Ma'arekhet ha-elohut. Jerusalem: Becker, 2013.
Meier, Menachem. "A Critical Edition of 'Sefer Ta'aamei ha-Mizwoth' by Joseph of Shushan." PhD dissertation. Brandeis University Press, 1974, 232–233.
Moses de Leon. *Mishkan ha-Edut (The Tabernacle of the Covenant)*. Bar Asher edition. Los Angeles: Cherub Press, 2014.
Moses de Leon. *Perush le-ma'aseh merkavat yehezkel (Commentary on the Ezekiel's Work of the Chariot)*. Farber edition. Los Angeles: Cherub Press, 1998.
Moses de Leon. *Sefer ha-rimon (The Book of the Pomegranate)*. Wolfson edition. Atlanta: Brown Judaic Studies, 1988.
Moses de Leon. *Shekel ha-kodesh (The Holy Shekel)*. Mopsik edition. Los Angeles: Cherub Press, 1996.
Nahmanides. *Nahmanides on the Torah*. Shavel ed. Jerusalem: Mosad Rav Kuk, 1960.
Nathan of Gaza. *Derush ha-taninim (Treatise on the Dragons)*. Ed. Gershom Scholem, *Beikvot Mashiach – Anthology of Sources from the Early Days of the Development of the Sabbatean Faith*. Jerusalem: Tarshish, 1944. 9–22.
Sasportas, Jacob. "*Sefer Tzitzat Novel Tzevi* (Book of the Decaying Deer's Fringes)." *Sabbatai Ṣevi: The Mystical Messiah, 1626–1676*. Ed. Gershom Scholem. Trans. R. J. Zwi Werblowsky. Princeton: Princeton University Press, 1973.
Sha'ar ha-gilgulim. Jerusalem: Ahavat Shalom, 1917.
Sefer ha-gilgulim; Sefer Torat ha-Gilgul. Jerusalem: Ahavat Shalom, 1982.
Sefer Hemdat Yamim (The Beloved of Days). Kushta, n.p 1735.
The Book Bahir. Abrams edition. Los Angeles: Cherub Press, 1994.
Toldot ha-Ari. Meir Benayahu editon. Jerusalem: Ben Zvi Institute, 1967.
Vital, Hayyim. *Sefer ha-hezionot (The Book of Visions)*. Faierstein edition. Jerusalem: Ben Zvi Institute, 2006.

Secondary Sources

Abramson, Sheraga. *Issues in Geonic Literature*. Jerusalem: Rav Kuk Press, 1974. [Hebrew]
Afterman, Adam. *Devequt: Mystical Intimacy in Medieval Jewish Thought*. Los Angeles: Cherub Press, 2011. [Hebrew]
Ashley, Kathleen. "Interrogating Biblical Deception and Trickster Theories: Narratives of Patriarchy or Possibility." Semeia 42 (1988): 103–116.
Barnai, Jacob. *Two Works about Shabbatai Zevi*. Jerusalem: Carmel, 2017. [Hebrew]
Bohak, Gideon. *Ancient Jewish Magic*. New York: Cambridge University Press, 2008.
Boyarin, Daniel. *Dying for God: Martyrdom and the Making of Christianity and Judaism*. Stanford: Stanford University Press, 1999.
Butler, Judith. *Gender Trouble: Feminism and the Subversion of Identity*. New York: Routledge, 1990.
Bynum, Caroline W. *Jesus As Mother: Studies in the Spirituality of the High Middle Ages*. Berkeley: University of California Press, 1982.

Carlebach, Elisheva. *The Pursuit of Heresy: Rabbi Moses Hagiz and the Sabbatian Controversies*. New York: Columbia University Press, 1994.
Chajes, J. H. *Between Worlds: Dybbuks, Exorcists, and Early Modern Judaism*. Philadelphia: University of Pennsylvania Press, 2003.
Chajes, J. H. "In a Different Voice: The Non-Kabbalistic Women's Mysticism of Early Modern Jewish Culture." *Zion* 76, 2 (2002): 139–162. [Hebrew]
Connell, Raewyn. *Masculinities*. Berkeley: University of California Press, 1995.
Connell, Raewyn, & James W. Messerschmidt, "Hegemonic Masculinity: Rethinking the Concept." *Gender and Society* 19, 6 (2005): 829–859.
Cuffel, Alexandra. *Gendering Disgust in Medieval Religious Polemic*. Notre Dame: Notre Dame University Press, 2007.
Dan, Joseph. "Rabbi Judah the Pious and Caesarius of Hiesterbach." *Scripta Hierosolymitana* 22 (1971): 18–27.
De-Lubac, H. *Medieval Exegesis, Vol. 2: The Four Senses of Scripture*. Michigan: Grand Rapids, 2000.
Doniger, Wendy. *The Bedtrick: Tales of Sex and Masquerade*. Chicago: University of Chicago Press, 2000.
Elior, Rachel. "Divrei haAadon leYaacov Frank," *The Sabbatean Movement and its Aftermath, Jerusalem Studies in Jewish Thought* 17 (2001): II, 471–548.
Elqayam, Avraham. "The Burden of Silence: Queen Esther as a Messianic Prototype of Fluid Identity in Sabbatean Mythopoesis." *Conceal the Outcasts: Jews with Hidden Identities*. Eds. A. Elqayam and Y. Kaplan. Jerusalem: Ben Zvi Institute, 2016. 173–249.
Elqayam, Avraham. "The Mystery of Faith in the Writings of Nathan of Gaza." PhD dissertation. Ramat Gan: Bar Ilan University, 1993. [Hebrew]
Elliott, Dyan. *Fallen Bodies: Pollution, Sexuality, and Demonology in the Middle Ages*. Philadelphia: University of Pennsylvania Press, 1999.
Fishbane, Eitan. "A Chariot for the *Shekhinah*: Identity and the Ideal Life in Sixteenth-Century Safed Kabbalah." *Journal of Religious Ethics* 37/3 (2009): 385–418.
Ferziger, Adam S. "Feminism and Heresy: The Construction of a Jewish Metanarrative." *Journal of the American Academy of Religion*, 77.3 (2009): 494–546.
Ferziger, Adam S. "Feminism, Heresy, and the Boundaries of American Orthodox Judaism." *A New Spirit in the Palace of Torah: Jubilee Volume in Honor of Professor Tamar Ross on the Occasion of her Eightieth Birthday*. Eds. Dov Schwartz and Ronit Irshai. Ramat Gan: BIU Press, 2018. 327–372. [Hebrew]
Fine, Lawrence. *Physician of the Soul, Healer of the Cosmos: Isaac Luria and His Kabbalistic Fellowship*. Stanford: Stanford University Press, 2003.
Fonrobert, Charlotte. "The Handmaid, the Trickster and the Birth of the Messiah." *Current Trends in the Study of Midrash*. Ed. Carol Bakhos. Leiden: Brill, 2006. 245–275.
Goitein, S. D. "A Report on Messianic Troubles in Baghdad in 1120–21." *JQR* 43 (1952): 57–76.
Goldreich, Amos, "R. Isaac of Acre's Meirat *'Einayim*." Master's thesis. Jerusalem: Hebrew University of Jerusalem, 1981. [Hebrew]
Green, Arthur. "Shekhinah, the Virgin Mary, and the Song of Songs: Reflections on a Kabbalistic Symbol in Its Historical Context." AJS Review 26, no. 1 (2002): 1–52.
Hallamish, Moshe. *Kabbalistic Customs of Shabbat*. Jerusalem: Orhot Press, 2006. [Hebrew]
Heinemann, Joseph. "The Blessing for the Rebuilding of Jerusalem." *Iunei Tefila*. Jerusalem: Magnes, 1981. 93–101. [Hebrew]

Huss, Boaz. *The Pleasant Tree Son of Jesse Lives upon the Earth – On the Sabbatean Origin of Seder Tu bi-Shvat.* 39–50 [forthcoming, Meir Benayahu book. Hebrew].

Idel, Moshe. "Commentaries on the 'Secret of '*Ibbur* in 13th Century Kabbalah and their Significance for Understanding of the Kabbalah at its Inception and its Development." *Da'at* 72 (2012): 5–49. [Hebrew]

Idel, Moshe. *Messianic Mystics.* New Haven: Yale University Press, 1998.

Idel, Moshe. *Recanati.* Vol. II. (forthcoming).

Idel, Moshe. *The Privileged Divine Feminine in Kabbalah.* Berlin: De Gruyter, 2019.

Idel, Moshe. "The Secret of Impregnation as Metempsychosis in Kabbalah." *Verwandlungen. Archäologie der literarischen Kommunikation IX.* Eds. A. Assmann & J. Assmann. Munich: Wilhelm Fink, 2006. 341–379.

Joseph of Shushan. *Sefer Ta'amei ha-mitzvot, Mitzwat Aseh (The Book of the Reasons; Positive Commandment)* 57. In Menachem Meier, A Critical Edition of the "Sefer Ta'aamei ha-mizwoth," (PhD diss., Brandeis University, 1974). 232–236.

Kahana, Maoz. "Cosmos and Nomos: Rabbi Joseph Karo and Shabtai Zvi as Portable Heavenly Temples." *El Prezente* 10 (2016): 143–153.

Kara-Ivanov Kaniel, Ruth. *Holiness and Transgression: Mothers of the Messiah in the Jewish Myth.* New York: Academic Studies Press, 2017.

Kara-Ivanov Kaniel, Ruth. "King David and Jerusalem: From Psalms to the Zohar." *Perspectives on Jewish Texts and Contexts.* Eds. Ophir Muntz-Manor and Ilana Pardes. Berlin: De Gruyter, 2019a. 67–107.

Kara-Ivanov Kaniel, Ruth. "'Sefirot in the Image of Man': Multiple Self in Kabbalistic Literature." *Pe'amim* 157 (2019b): 135–175.

Liebes, Yehuda. *God's Story: Collected Essays on Jewish Myth.* Jerusalem: Carmel, 2009. [Hebrew]

Liebes, Yehuda. "Long Live the King: The Weakness of the King and his Strength." *Jubilee Vol. presented to A. Ravitzky.* Eds. B. Brown, A. Rosenack, et al. Jerusalem: Israel Institute for Democracy, 2012. 452–489. [Hebrew]

Liebes, Yehuda. "Matzmiah Keren Yeshu'a." *Mehkarei Yerushalayim be-Mahshevet Yisrael* 3 (1984): 313–348.

Liebes, Yehuda. *On Sabbateanism and its Kabbalah: Collected Essays.* Jerusalem: Bialik Institute, 1995. [Hebrew]

Liebes, Yehuda. "Two Young Roes of a Doe: The Secret Sermon of Isaac Luria before his Death." *The International Conference for the study of Jewish Mysticism* 4 (1992): 113–169. [Hebrew]

Mark, Zvi. "Dybbuk and Devekut in Shivhe ha-Besht: Toward a Phenomenology of Madness in Early Hasidism." *Spirit Possession in Judaism.* Ed. M. Goldish. Detroit: Wayne State University Press, 2003. 257–301.

Mazo-Karras, Ruth. "King David as a Figure of Masculinity in Christian and Jewish Medieval Culture." *God's Own Gender? Religions and their Concepts of Masculinity.* Eds. Daniel Gerster and Michael Krüggeler. Würzburg: Ergon Verlag, 2018. 201–218.

Melammed, Renee Levine. "Visionary Experiences Among Spanish Crypto-Jewish Women" (Translations with Commentary). *Judaism in Practice: From the Middle Ages through the Early Modern Period.* Ed. Lawrence Fine. Princeton: Princeton University Press, 2001. 348–352.

Meroz, Ronit. "Redemption in the Lurianic Teaching." PhD dissertation. Jerusalem: Hebrew University of Jerusalem, 1988. [Hebrew].

Neumann, Erich. *Eranos Lectures – Mensch und Sinn.* Trans. Tamar Kron and David Viller, with introduction and commentary. Tel Aviv: Resling, 2013.

Neumann, Erich. *The Origins and History of Consciousness*. Princeton: Princeton University Press, 1973.
Pappenheim, Bertha. "Zur Sittlichkeitsfrage." Lecture given at the 2nd Delegates Day of the Jewish Women's Association in Frankfurt am Main on 2–3 October 1907. Hamburg: Jüdischen Frauenbundes, 1907.
Maciejko, Pawel. *Jacob Frank and the Frankist Movement 1755–1816*. Philadelphia: University of Pennsylvania Press, 2015.
Pedaya, Haviva. *Nahmanides: Cyclical Time and Holy Text*. Tel Aviv: Am Oved, 2003. [Hebrew].
Pedaya, Haviva. *Name and Sanctuary in the Teaching of Rabbi Isaac the Blind*. Jerusalem: Magnes, 2001. [Hebrew]
Pedaya, Haviva. "Ve-Ima Hashata Let Lan – A Geneology of the Shekhina as a Mother." *As a Perennial Spring: A Festschrift Honoring Rabbi Dr. Norman Lamm*. Ed. Bentsion Cohen. New York: Downhill, 2013. 87–151.
Pedaya, Haviva. *Vision and Speech*. Los Angeles: Cherub Press, 2002. [Hebrew]
Rapoport-Albert, Ada. "From Prophetess to Madwoman: The Displacement of Female Spirituality in the Post-Sabbatian Era." *Hasidic Studies: Essays in History and Gender*. Liverpool: Littman Library of Jewish Civilization in association with Liverpool University Press, 2011a. 269–317.
Rapoport-Albert, Ada. "On Women in Hasidism: S. A. Horodetsky and the Maid of Ludmir Tradition." *Hasidic Studies: Essays in History and Gender*. Liverpool: Littman Library of Jewish Civilization in association with Liverpool University Press, 2017. 318–367.
Rapoport-Albert, Ada. *Women and the Messianic Heresy of Shabbatai Zevi, 1666–1816*. Oxford and Portland: Littman Library of Jewish Civilization, 2011b.
Resnick, Irven M. *Marks of Distinction: Christian Perceptions of Jews in the High Middle Ages*. Washington, DC: Catholic University of America Press, 2012.
Roi, Biti. *Love of the Shekhina – Mysticism and Poetics in Tiqqunei ha-Zohar*. Ramat Gan: Bar Ilan University, 2017.
Schäfer, Peter. *Mirrors of His Beauty: Feminine Images of God from the Bible to the Early Kabbalah*. Princeton: Princeton University Press, 2002: 147–172.
Scholem, Gershom. *Major Trends in Jewish Mysticism*. New York: Schocken Books, 1941.
Scholem, Gershom. *"Mitsvah haba'ah be'aveirah": Studies and Texts Concerning the History of Sabbateanism and its Metamorphoses*. Jerusalem: Bialik Institute, 1982. 9–67. [Hebrew]
Scholem, Gershom. "New Sabbatian Documents from the Book 'To'ei Ruah'" *Zion* 7.3 (1942): 172–196. [Hebrew]
Scholem, Gershom. *On the Mystical Shape of the Godhead: Basic Concepts in the Kabbalah*. New York: Schocken Books, 1991.
Scholem, Gershom. *Origins of the Kabbalah*. Princeton: Princeton University Press, 1991.
Scholem, Gershom. *Sabbatai Ṣevi: The Mystical Messiah, 1626–1676*. Trans. R. J. Zwi Werblowsky. Princeton: Princeton University Press, 1973.
Sedgwick, Eve Kosofsky. "Epistemology of the Closet." *Theory and Critique* 37 (2010): 284–304.
Shapiro, Judith. "Transsexualism: Reflections on the Persistence of Gender and the Mutability of Sex." *Body Guards: The Cultural Politics of Gender Ambiguity*. Eds. J. Epstein & K. Straub. Routledge: New York, 1991. 248–279.
Shinan, Avigdor, *"Al Demuto shel ha-Melekh David be-Sifrut Hazal." David: From Shepherd to Messiah*. Ed. Y. Zakovitch. Jerusalem: Ben Zvi Institute, 1995. 181–199. [Hebrew]
Stone, Sandy. "The Empire Strikes Back: A Posttranssexual Manifesto." *Camera Obscura* 10 (1992): 150–176.

Tamar, David. *Studies in the History of the Jews in Palestine and Italy.* Jerusalem: Reuben Mass, 1970.
Tishby, Isaiah. *Paths of Faith and Heresy: Essays in Kabbalah and Sabbateanism.* Ramat Gan: Masada Publishing, 1964. [Hebrew]
Tishby, Isaiah. *The Doctrine of Evil and the "Kelipah" in Lurianic Kabbalism.* Jerusalem: Magnes, 1992.
Tishby, Isaiah. *The Wisdom of the Zohar: An Anthology of Texts.* 3 vols. Oxford: Littman Library of Jewish Civilization, 1989.
Van der Haven, Alexander. *From Lowly Metaphor to Divine Flesh: Sarah the Ashkenazi, Sabbatai Tsevi's Messianic Queen and the Sabbatian Movement.* Ramat Gan: Idra Press, 2018. [Hebrew]
Warner, Michael. *The Trouble with Normal: Sex, Politics, and the Ethics of Queer.* Cambridge: Harvard University Press, 2000.
Weinstein, Roni. *Kabbalah and Jewish Identity.* Tel Aviv: Tel Aviv University, 2011. [Hebrew]
Weiss, Tzahi. *Cutting the Shoots: The Worship of Shekhina in the World of Early Kabbalistic Literature.* Jerusalem: Magnes, 2015. [Hebrew]
Wirszubski, Chaim. *Between the Lines: Kabbalah, Christian Kabbalah and Sabbateanism.* Jerusalem: Magnes, 1990. [Hebrew]
Eliot Wolfson. *Language, Eros, Being: Kabbalistic Hermeneutics and Poetic Imagination.* New York: Fordham University Press, 2004.
Eliot Wolfson. "*Min u-minut be-heker ha-kabbalah.*" *Kabbalah* 6 (2001): 231–262.
Zak, Bracha. *Solomon had a Vineyard.* Beer-Sheva: Ben-Gurion University Press, 2018. [Hebrew]

Moshe Idel
Abraham Abulafia: The Apotheosis of a Medieval Heretic in Modern *Me'ah She'arim*

> Our sages, the fools of the Jews... the majority of the sages of our generation are fools.
> Abraham Abulafia, *Sefer Ge'ulah*

1 Who was Abraham Abulafia?

In the short list of Jewish heretics, the name of Abraham Abulafia is rarely mentioned. Though ostracized by Kabbalists for centuries, he did not enjoy the fate of Maimonides, whose Halakhic writings saved him from oblivion in Jewish traditional culture, despite the fiery polemics against the *Guide of the Perplexed*, and whose philosophical writings ensured his prominent status in the "enlightened" Judaism through centuries. Spinoza, ostracized by his contemporaries, Jews and Gentiles, made his way back to recognition as a central figure in European philosophy and then slowly also as an important figure among the "enlightened" Jews. Living between the time-lines of the two, the Kabbalist perhaps also mediated between them.[1]

Quite different is the fate of Abraham ben Samuel Abulafia (1240–c. 1291), a mystic, a Kabbalist, and a self-proclaimed prophet and Messiah. Born in Saragossa, educated in Tudela, travelling to the land of Israel when he was scarcely twenty, studying some forms of medieval philosophy for almost a decade sometimes between 1260–1270 in South Italy, especially Maimonides' *Guide of the Perplexed*, then turning into a Kabbalist in Barcelona in 1270 he made claims about his being a prophet and a Messiah. In the following two decades, he propagated his ecstatic Kabbalah (tightly connected to these two claims) in Spain – both in the Kingdom of Aragon and in Castile – in some towns in the Byzantine empire, and afterwards in Southern Italy but especially in Sicily since 1281.[2]

---

[1] For a survey of some of my claims as to Abulafia's mediation between the two great philosophers see Harvey (2008).
[2] See Idel (1987, 1993a), Wolfson (2000), Sagerman (2011), and Hames (2007). For a survey of scholarship in the field see Kiener (1993) and Huss (2007, 2008a). The earlier work appears in English in *BGU Review* (2008b).

A perusal of his writings shows a rare and surprising mixture of medieval philosophy, mostly Maimonidean, with radical types of exegesis, like permutations of letters and *gematria'ot*, some stemming from Ashkenazi sources, accompanied by pretensions as to his ecstatic experiences. He composed rather detailed handbooks of techniques conducive to those experiences. To be sure, his adoption of Maimonides and of the Ashkenazi techniques of interpretation and paths to mystical experiences is quite selective. An elitist figure, Abulafia nevertheless attempted to disseminate a series of esoteric topics to young followers in those countries; in his writings, he departs from the traditional understanding of those topics.

As we shall see below, already in the early 1270s Abulafia confesses that he was persecuted because of his ideas. In the second part of the 1280s, while teaching in Sicily, some erudite persons from Palermo appealed to Rabbi Shlomo ben Abraham ibn Adret – known by the acronym *Rashba'* [1235–c. 1310] – then the preeminent Halakhic figure in Spain, to ask advice concerning Abulafia's prophetic and messianic claims. Rashba's negative answers triggered a fierce controversy between him and the ecstatic Kabbalist, which included several epistles, most of them now lost. This culminated, it seems, in a formal ban on Abulafia and his writings.[3] Because the written documents of Rashba's critiques and his hypothetical ban are no longer extant, most of what we know stems from Abulafia's responses to these critiques, which reached us in many manuscripts. Nevertheless, the result of these critiques was the disappearance of Abulafia's views and writings from the main line of development of Kabbalah in the Iberian Peninsula for two centuries, until the expulsion of the Jews in 1492.

2 Some "Problematic" Thoughts of Abraham Abulafia

Let me briefly present the problematic nature of Abulafia's thought, as seen from the perspective of both Rabbinic Judaism as well as many Kabbalists. I shall address only a few of the aspects in order to illustrate the sharp discrepancies between his views and the more standard understandings of those topics in the dominant Rabbinic forms of Judaism. Those more anthropological views are

---

[3] Idel (2000a). Interestingly enough, this controversy, as in other critiques of Abulafia, did not engage with his techniques grounded in various types of pronunciation of divine names. Compare, however, to Gribetz (1991).

coupled with a variety of theological and cosmological claims that will not be surveyed here; those claims inseparably constitute the conceptually naturalistic framework of Abulafia's techniques to achieve mystical experiences.

[a] Who is a Jew? An Inclusive/Exclusive Vision

Unlike the widely accepted Halakhic description of who is a Jew, which is matrilineal,[4] Abulafia defines Jewishness as predominantly a matter of spiritual activity. He defined Jewishness less by genetic criterion, as in the matrilineal Rabbinic approach, but as a matter of a personal "confession". Though some trends in Rabbinic Judaism and in Jewish philosophy are more inclusive,[5] I wonder if there are parallels to the following passages:

> And the Jew who thinks that because he is Jewish and can trace his ancestry to the seed of Yehudah, he is of the seed of royalty, if he does not confess in the truth his similarity with the tribe of Yehudah is only [the matter of] a name. For Yehudah is [etymologically] related to *hodayah*.[6]

Abulafia bases his discussion here on the Biblical etymological allusion in Genesis 49:8. Yet there the "confession" is on the part of biblical Yehudah's brothers to Yehudah. The Kabbalist alters the meaning and has it referring to God. The genetic extraction is conceived to be merely nominal, insufficient for a fullfledged Jewish identity. In an untitled fragment, Abulafia describes the nature of the Jew as follows:

> The name *'Eheyeh* suffices, since the comprehension of the Jew will be the comprehension of the Name and this is the way [the name] *Shadday* was interpreted to the effect that for us it suffices the name *'Eheyeh*, and likewise *YeHUDY, YHW DaY, 'Ehad 'Ah 'Ehad*, and by the comprehension of *YHWH 'Ehad*, and redemption will come to us.[7]

---

4 See Lavee (2018).
5 For the more universalist Rabbinic approach, see Nehorai (1992). For a discussion of earlier, missionary vectors in Rabbinic Judaism that were later eradicated, see Lavee (2010). See also Jospe (1994), Novak (1995), and Frydman-Kohl (1992). See also Kellner (1996, 2008).
6 See Abulafia's epistle entitled *Matzref la-Kesef* (2014, 1: 90).
והיהודי שחושב להיותו יהודי ומיוחס לזרע יהודה שהוא מזרע המלוכה אם אינו מודה על האמת אין לו משבטו של יהודה כי אם השם המשותף בלבד. והנה יהודה מלשון הודיה.
7 MS Firenze-Laurentiana II, 48 fol. 89a: די בשם אהיה כי תהיה השגת יהודי השגת השם וכן פירשו שהיה
לנו לומר די בשם אהיה וכן יהודי. יהו די, אחד אח אחד, ובהשגת יהוה אחד תהיה לנו גאולה.
On this treatise and its authorship, see Idel (2008). The treatise was later printed by Munteanu as *Sefer Peras Ha-Sefer, Book of the Reward of the Number* (2011), and more recently by Torgeman as *Sefer Pardes ha-Sefar* (2008).

The word *YeHUDY*, Jew, contains the same consonants that constitute also the locution *YHW DaY*, which means that the three consonants that constitute the Tetragrammaton (*YHW*) are sufficient (*DaY*). In other words, confession in and the understanding of the consonants of the Tetragrammaton suffice in order to be a "real" Jew. Abulafia predicates redemption, in a spiritual sense, on the recognition of the divine name, its technical use and its understanding.[8]

Elsewhere in his writings, we read again about a connection between the nation and the divine name: "You, oh nation of God, Supernal Holy Ones who look to the Name and to the source of your intelligence, and have seen the form of YHVH within the form of your hearts."[9] It seems to me that the expression *mabbitei shemo*, namely those who look to His Name, explains the name *Yisra'el* by dividing the word *Yisra'el* into *yishar* (etymologically related to the word *yashur* [He will look to]) and *'El*[God].[10]

Ironically, this marginalization of the genetic factor in favor of a spiritual one is reminiscent of the attitude of Christianity, a religion Abulafia sharply critiqued. Moreover, the recognition of the centrality of the divine names, a basic component of Abulafia's Kabbalah, is conducive to personal redemption, which in his view is the real redemption. Such derivations of the meaning of Jewishness from letters of the divine name have hardly any parallel in Jewish traditional literature, and ignore the Halakhic approach to sensitive topics concerning identity.[11] In such a view, which is at least implicitly inclusive, "true" Judaism is open also to non-"genetic" Jews, namely those who confess and understand the divine names. The centrality of the divine name and of comprehension represent a synthesis between the Ashkenazi and the Maimonidean modes of thought. Both the operations related to the divine names and the rational religion influenced by Maimonides proved problematic for many medieval Jewish thinkers.[12]

---

8 די אהיה = גאלה = 39 = אחד את אחד = יהו די = יהוה אחד
9 See "'*Sefer Ha-Ot*'. Apokalypse des Pseudo-Propheten und Pseudo-Messias Abraham Abulafia" (1887, 80).
10 Regarding the non-genetic meanings of the term *Yisra'el* in Abulafia's writings, see Idel (1990c, 36, 38, 40, 110, 120, 166–167, 197). Nota bene: *Israel* is for this Kabbalist an allegory for the seekers of God. See also below n. 13.
11 Compare to the much more traditional historical-theosophical interpretation *YHWDH* in the writings of a Kabbalistic who was acquainted with Abulafia's Kabbalah, R. Isaac of Acre, in his yet unidentified treatise found in MS New York, JTS 1853, fol. 1a. I hope to elaborate on this untitled text elsewhere.
12 For the more general view of philosophers as heretical in the Jewish Middle Ages, see Kasher (2012) and Valabregue (2016).

By understanding it as a form of more comprehensive and spiritual religion, Abulafia attempted to reinterpret the term *Yahadut* in a way that is unparalleled in the Middle Ages. He even attempted to discuss this type of religion with the Pope, intending "to speak with him in the name of the principle of *Yahadut*."[13] The term כלל here is essential for a proper understanding the passage: in the Middle Ages, it means, inter alia, "principle," as in the following passage of Abulafia's:

> The person who realizes the knowledge of the Name as it is in truth in accordance to Kabbalah, will realize that this principle is the principle that announces that the four Names are exchanging their place.[14]

In the Arabicized medieval Hebrew of the Tibbonian philosophical jargon (and Abulafia was using this type of Hebrew), the term *Yahadut* – though it existed earlier – was understood as having an abstract meaning. The same is true of other Hebrew terms ending in *–ut*, as for example, *mahut, 'ammitut, kamut, peshitut, 'ahdut, hit'ahdut*, etc. For Abulafia, *Yahadut* means quintessentially the knowledge of the divine name. This is what he attempted to discuss with the Pope. He did not intend to act as a representative of Jewry (namely of ordinary Jews) in his abortive encounter with the Pope. Given what he regarded as the foolishness of so many of the "genetic" Jews, including Rabbis, this would be absurd. As we shall see in section 3, Abulafia had felt persecuted by Jews for several years beforehand. This makes it unlikely that Abulafia would indulge in fantasies being a

---

13 שאם יבא שם רזיאל לדבר איתו בשם יהדות כלל שייקחו אותו מיד ולא יראה פניו כלל אבל יוציאוהו חוץ לעיר וישרפוהו באש

This is the full Hebrew context found in *Sefer ha-'Edut*, printed in *Matzref ha-Sekhel* (2001b, 57). See Idel (1982–1983), especially pp. 6–7. See also his *Sefer ha-Melitz*, printed in *Matzref ha-Sekhel* (2001b, 9). See also Abulafia's *'Otzar 'Eden Ganuz*, II:9 (2000b, 190). In a seminal passage in his *'Imrei Shefer* (1999, 104), Abulafia later connects the term *Yahadut*, as one of the three crowns, to kingdom [*malkhut*] and to Abraham, then the crown of Mosaic Torah with Moses, and finally priesthood, namely the ritualistic approach to Judaism, which is the crown of Aharon. In my opinion, for Abraham Abulafia, the first among the three crowns he mentions, that of *Yahadut*, connected to the patriarch Abraham, is the more comprehensive and higher one, while the two others are not only later but also more limited in scope, as I shall elaborate elsewhere.

14 See Abulafia's Epistle entitled *Matzref la-Kesef ve-kur la-Zahav* (2001c, 7).
המשיג ידיעת השם כאשר היא על האמת לפי הקבלה, ישיג כי זה הכלל הוא כלל מודיע שארבעה שמות אלה מתחלפים.

See also the occurrence of כללי in the passage quoted in n. 30 below.

representative of this community (a rather Zionist reading of the encounter).¹⁵ As I've suggested in a number of studies, a spiritualist reading is more plausible.¹⁶

Abulafia occasionally wrote in three different conceptual registers for different types of readers. The highest and superior register is what we would call the allegorical one. This is the case in Abulafia's use of *Yahadut*.¹⁷ The occurrences of *Yahadut* as an abstract religious system should be taken seriously in considering later, abstract metamorphoses of *Yahadut*.

[b] An Inclusive Approach to Alien Speculative Thought

I claim that Abulafia's view of "authentic" Judaism, which he deems to include an intellectual approach to reality, is much more inclusive than Rabbinic views of Judaism. This is illustrated by his openness toward the metaphysics – basically of Aristotelian extraction – as developed by Gentile philosophers:

> You know what happened to the four sages of Israel, as it was said of them: Four entered the *Pardes*,¹⁸ which is a name for the divine science [*Hokhmat ha-'Elohut*] which is from the existence of the delight [*Mi-qiyum ha-Ta'anug*], and so did the Gentiles call the Garden of Eden, *Paradiso*, whose meaning is self-evident, that it a place of delight. It means that everything that someone desires to attain, and he attains it, he remains some time with

---

15 Compare, however, the claims of Boyarin (2018, 85–87), based solely on a deficient citation of the Hebrew passage of Abulafia's as I adduced it in my article mentioned above, and quoted in the previous footnote. In Boyarin's quotation, the critical term for his thesis כלל – which I translated "principle" – mysteriously disappears from the Hebrew original as I quoted it and elaborated at length on it, while the term יהדות was spelled היהדות. Boyarin must have had a corrupted version of my article, otherwise unknown to me; if this is indeed the case, I deeply apologize for inducing him into such a significant error. Moreover, Boyarin refers only to a part of the available material in the writings of the ecstatic Kabbalist. He follows Elliot Wolfson's particularistic reading – in my opinion misreading – of Abulafia, to be discussed below in this article. See also below n. 47. The particularistic reading of *Yahadut* by these two scholars flatly contradicts Abulafia's basic assumption that the real sense of a religious term is the allegorical one, while the plain sense is destined to the *vulgus*, as we have seen earlier in this paragraph. I hope to return to this issue in a separate study, citing more Abulafian parallel texts, in addition to what is found and brought earlier, but ignored by both Wolfson and Boyarin. See also below notes 28, 30. They ignore the existence of rather seminal concepts, exceptional in Judaism, including in its philosophical forms, like "universal religion", "universal Kabbalah", and "universal Torah" found in Abulafia's writings. See my *Abraham Abulafia's Esotericism* (2020, chapters 12 and 14).
16 See, e.g., Idel (1982/1982, 98–99).
17 Idel (2014). See also below note 28.
18 BT., *Hagigah*, fol. 15a.

this attainment and [then] he is disgusted by it.¹⁹ This happens to everything that has some deficiency, either from the side of someone that realized it or from the side of what he realizes.... But anyone who enters the *Pardes* has to enter in peace and exit in peace.²⁰ He has to be careful of the sparks of light in order to see whatever he has to see, not to peer and be damaged or dead. And if things appear to him to be one, it is not worthwhile that he should think that this is one and the other is one, and he should [not] say in his heart that there are two powers, since this is really a heresy and an ignorance of reality. And if [the archangel] Metatron sits on high and writes down the merits of Israel once a day,²¹ this sitting on high is not a truth, but the sitting is existence [קיום] as it is written "He that sits on the circle of the earth,"²² "He that sits in the heavens shall laugh, the Lord shall have them in derision,"²³ and those similar to them, should be studied by [the means of] the many words of the sages of the world, since by those [forms of] knowledge the quandaries will be resolved as well as the doubts on many of the imaginative issues, and the man will remain with his intellect in perfection and with his Torah in truth, and the plain senses of the scriptures will not cause his removal from the appropriate path.²⁴

Abulafia's conceptual openness is indubitably of Maimonidean extraction, probably augmented by the philosophical sources he studied in Southern Italy in the 1260s. Yet the Kabbalist does not invoke Maimonides' name in this interesting passage. Instead, he argues rather explicitly that the study of the Gentile wisdom is the clue for a proper understanding of esoteric topics in Judaism. He resorts to Maimonides' hermeneutical strategy of equivocal terms, interpreting the "sitting on high" as meaning existence,²⁵ one of the many cases when the allegorical

---

19 Compare to the later dictum found in Crescas's book *The Light of The Lord*: תענוג תמידי אינו תענוג
20 BT., *Hagigah*, fol. 15a. For Abulafia's understanding of the Paradise as a matter of divine names, see Idel (2011b).
21 I could not find a precise source for the claim of the daily writing of Metatron.
22 Isaiah 40:22.
23 Psalm 2:4.
24 *'Otzar 'Eden Ganuz*, II:9, MS. Oxford 1580, fols. 131b–132a (2000b, 288–289): כבר ידעת מה שקרה לארבעה חכמי ישראל כמו שאמרו עליהם ארבעה נכנסו לפרדס. והוא שם לחכמת האלהות שהוא מקיום התענוג וכך קראו הגוים לגן עדן "פרדיסו", ועניינו שהוא ניכר מאליו שהוא מקום עדון. וזה כי כל דבר שהאדם תאב אליו להשיגו ומשיגו, והוא עומד קצת זמן בהשגתו עמו כבר מואס בו. וזה יקרה לכל דבר שיש בו חסרון השלמות הראוי לו בין מצד המשיג, בין מצד המושג... ואמנם כל מי שנכנס לפרדס צריך להיותו נכנס בשלום ויוצא בשלום, וצריך שיזהר מניצוצי האור כדי שיראה מה שצריך לראות ולא שיציץ ויהיה נפגע או מת. ואם יראו לו עניינים שהם דבר אחר אין ראוי לו שיחשוב שזה אחר וזה אחר ויאמר בליבו שיש שתי רשויות, כי יש בזה כפירה באמת וסכלות במציאה, ואם מטטרון יושב וכותב זכויותן של ישראל פעם אחת ביום, ואין יש ישיבה למעלה הוא אמת אבל הישיבה ההיא קיום כמו "היושב על חוג הארץ" (ישעיה מ' כב') "יושב בשמים ישחק אדני ילעג למו" (תהלים ב' ד'). וכיוצא באלו הדברים כך ראוי ללומדים ברוב דברי חכמי העולם, כי באלו הידיעות יותרו הקשרים והספקות ברוב העניינים המדומים וישאר האדם עם שכלו בשלמות ועם תורתו באמתות, ולא יביאוהו פשטי הכתובים אל הרחקה מהדרך הנכונה."
25 For Maimonides' analyses of the occurrences of the verb *YShB* in connection to God as equivocal see *The Guide of the Perplexed* I (1963, 37–38). Maimonides already resorted to the two biblical verses mentioned in the two previous footnotes. For an interesting parallel to the view that philosophy can save someone from a misunderstanding of the Bible, see Albalag (1973, 83–84).

sense is superior. Abulafia relates the plain-sense understanding of the biblical passages, with their anthropomorphic overtones, to the power of imagination (in his eyes inferior to intellect).²⁶ Those issues are the real secrets Abulafia recommends keeping from the *vulgus* (which includes the "genetic" Jews), and are the very same issues he confesses to having discussed with Christian sages:

> It is appropriate to safeguard it together with the *vulgus*, who are the righteous in the nation, that it is appropriate to safeguard the three ways since all three are true, but there are three different degrees and each of them completes what is appropriate in order to complete those [individuals] who safeguard it and know it. And there is no doubt that among the Christians, there are some sages who know this secret, and they spoke with me secretly and revealed to me that this is indubitably their position. And I considered them to be in the category of the pious men of the Gentiles.²⁷ And one should not care as to the words of the fools in any nation, since the Torah was not given but to those who possess knowledge.²⁸

---

26 Idel (1987, 137–138, 144–145).
27 The "pious men of the Gentiles" is a Rabbinic category. From the linguistic point of view, the term is problematic for Abulafia's conceptualization of anthropology, since in his books "pious" stands for a lower category. See also Wolfson (2012, 200 n. 41 or 207, n. 76). Wolfson presents a particularistic (and in my opinion erroneous) interpretation of Abulafia, followed recently by Boyarin, in a non-critical manner, as mentioned above. On problems of Wolfson's sheer misunderstanding of medieval philosophical terminology and thus grounding his particularistic interpretation on erroneous reading of relatively simple texts, see Idel (2015). As I pointed out there, Wolfson mistranslated a Maimonidean term related to a distinguished person as being universal, as if pointing to being particular or individual. This mistake is repeated also most recently in his article "Deceitful Truth and Truthful Deceit: *Sod ha-Hippukh* and Abulafia's Divergence from Maimonides" (2018), without any explanation for reiterating such an obvious mistake.
28 Introduction to *Mafteaḥ ha-Ḥokhmot* (2003, 48–49).

שההדרך הראשונה כלה המונית. ואעפ"כ ראוי לשמרה עם ההמון שהם הצדיקים שבעם כמו שזכרתי תמיד שראוי לשמור שלשת הדרכים ששלשתם אמת. אבל להם שלש מדרגות מתחלפות וכל אחת משלמת מה שראוי לה לפי מהותה להשלים שומריה ויודעיה. ואין ספק שיש מהנוצרים קצת חכמים שיודעים זה הסוד ודברו עמי בסוד וגלו לי שזו היא דעתם בלא ספק. ואז דנתים אני גם כן מכלל חסידי אומות העולם. ואין לחוש על דברי הפתאים בשום אומה שלא נתנה תורה אלא לבעלי הדעת.

See Scholem (1967, 129, 379, note 33). On triple exegetical and anthropological hierarchies, see Idel (1990c, 109–114). The anthropological distinction between common people (the multitude), the philosophers, and the prophets is a seminal and recurring theme in Abulafia's writings; it may reflect an earlier source because the similar position of ibn Falaquera in *Sefer ha-Ma'alot* (1894, 77), as well as ibn Kaspi. See Mesch (1975, 86). For the ironic phrase "our sages, the fools of the Jews, [...] the majority of the sages of our generation are fools," see Abulafia's early work *Sefer Ge'ulah* (2001d, 45): ויאיר לבות חכמינו הפתאים היהודים [...] רוב חכמי דורנו פתאים. Thus, even sages who fall under the second rank of the triple anthropology are conceived to be foolish Jews. See also above note 17. Those foolish Jews did not disappear in our generation, as we will see in the later part of this study.

The closing sentence, with its claim that the Torah was not delivered to the fools of any nation, is quite exclusive, on the one hand, insofar as it concerns fools, including Jewish ones. On the other hand, it is very inclusive toward Gentile intellectuals.

Even more poignant is the following passage, also from Abulafia's preface to his commentary on the Torah:

> It is incumbent on every illuminate to conceal what has been revealed to him regarding the general principles[29] of the secrets of the Torah, and even more so of its details, from the multitude of our sages, even more so from all the other ignoramuses.[30]

Such passages suffice to show that Abulafia's attitude to the "other" differs dramatically from the Rabbis and Kabbalists who adduced a difference based on a genetic criterion. Abulafia adopted an intellectual criterion. The attempt to harmonize his Kabbalah to quite different trends is to read Abulafia (to use his term) "vulgarly" rather than "esoterically." Herein lies a quandary: why have these texts been ignored or perhaps suppressed in the scholarship?[31]

[c] The Possibility of Prophecy in the Present

Abulafia's great concern with divine names and redemption is not just a matter of pure gnosis, but of concrete experience. So, for example, he relates:

> When I arrived at [the knowledge of] the Names, by my loosening of the bonds of the seals, "the Lord of All" appeared to me and revealed to me His secret and informed me of the end of the exile and of the time of the beginning of redemption. He compelled me to prophesy.[32]

---

29 See above in the text referred to in n. 14.
30 Abulafia's introduction to *Mafteaḥ ha-Ḥokhmot* (2003, 6): כל משכיל מחויב להסתיר מה שנגלה לו מכללי סתרי התורה וכל שכן מפרטיהם מעין המון חכמינו וכל שכן משאר עמי הארץ.
31 See Wolfson's earlier book on Abraham Abulafia, *R. Abraham Abulafia – Kabbalist and Prophet, Hermeneutics, Theosophy, and Theurgy* (2000). More recently, in "Deceitful Truth and Truthful Deceit: *Sod ha-Hippukh* and Abulafia's Divergence from Maimonides" (2018), Wolfson comes much closer to my position than earlier in his studies, a laudable shift no doubt. He nevertheless ignores some of the material I deal with here in this section, a strong example of scholarly exclusivity in order to create the image of Kabbalistic exclusivity. See also above n. 15. See, however, the Pythian passage found in this latter article (Wolfson, 2018) on p. 103: "Israel's election is predicated on an exclusiveness inclusive of its own others, but the inclusiveness of this exclusive that it still depends on the exclusiveness of its inclusiveness. The inclusion of the excluded in the claim of exclusivity thus only renders the inclusivity more exclusive."
32 See Abulafia's epistle *We-Zot Li-Yhudah* (1853, 18–19), corrected according to MS New York, JTS 1887. More on the issues dealt with in this passage see Idel (2000b, 155–186). See also Idel (1993b, 108–113).

Note the first-person singular locutions which underscore the claim of his own status as a prophet. To be sure, nascent Rabbinism assumed that prophecy had already ceased, as part of the emergence of the new legalistic elite.[33] For this reason the sage was considered higher than the prophet.[34] Elsewhere Abulafia states:

> We and all those who follow our intellectual Kabbalah[35] [attaining] prophecy by means of the combinations of letters, it will teach us the essence of reality as it is, in an easier way in comparison to all the ways in existence in the world, despite the fact that the knowledge of the essence of reality is apprehended by much thought. What brings it [knowledge] about is the combination [of letters], and this combination induces it [knowledge] as immediately as a youth studies the Bible, then the Mishnah and Gemara; he will certainly achieve it quickly, with perseverance, being better than any thought.[36]

Here, as in many other cases, the linguistic technique of Kabbalah is described as superior to any other technique, the nomian one included, because it alone guarantees achievement of the highest religious objective. The anomian technique is not described as continuous with the nomian topics of studies mentioned in the passage. It is faster, and was probably ranked mystically higher than any other form of human activity, as we learn from another passage from the same book:

> The path of the combination of letters, [but] not anything else,[37] since any another path is impossible by nature to bring man to this rank, which is the rank of the holy spirit and the rank of prophecy.[38]

Indeed, in a fragment of a lost work by a student of Abulafia, whom I propose to identify as R. Nathan ben Sa'adyah Har'ar, we read:

---

33 See *BT, Megillah*, fol. 17b; Efraim E. Urbach (1988, 1999), Alexander (1995), Yadin-Israel (2014, 94–105), Dan (2007), and especially Sommer (1996). See also Glatzer (1945), Bamberger (1941), and Goldreich (2010, 9 n. 1).
34 See Goshen-Gottstein (2006, 2:37–77), Huss (1999), and Wolfson (2009).
35 *Qabbalah sikhlit*. This rather rare term occurs as well in *Sha'arei Tsedeq*, fol. 26a. There he refers also to the Kabbalah by a more widespread phrase as "inner Kabbalah" [*Kabbalah penimiyt*].
36 *'Otzar 'Eden Ganuz*, MS Oxford-Bodleiana 1580, fol. 90a (2000b, 182) and fol. 136a: "We have Kabbalistic ways which bring us to the *intelligibilia* easily [*be-qalut*], without their [the philosophers'] ways." On easiness, see also Vital (1973, 97). For the claim of easy access by means of Kabbalah, using exactly the same term *be-qalut*, see already in a passage of his predecessor R. Yehudah ben Shlomo ha-Kohen of Toledo, printed by Sirat (1979, 50 n. 22).
37 Is able to bring about revelations.
38 *'Otzar 'Eden Ganuz*, MS Oxford-Bodleiana 1580, fol. 49b (2000b, 98).

The wise and illuminated R. Nathan, blessed be his memory, told me[39]: "Know that the perfection of the secret of prophecy for the prophet is that he should suddenly[40] see the form of his self, standing in front of him. He will then forget his own self and it will disappear from him. And he will see the form of his self in front of him, speaking with him and telling him the future."[41]

Rabbinism regarded prophecy at present obsolete, a threat to its own Halakhic control of Jewish life and would indeed respond to those claims.

[d] Spiritual Messianism

Abulafia's interpretations of the term Messiah likewise depart dramatically and explicitly from the Rabbinic worldview. In a seminal passage that represents the different registers mentioned above, he writes:

> The term *Mashiyaḥ* is equivocal, [designating] three [different] matters; first and foremost, the true Agent Intellect is called the *Mashiyaḥ*... and the man who will forcibly bring us out of the exile from under the rule of the nations due to his contact with the Agent Intellect – he will [also] be called *Mashiyaḥ*. And the material human hylic intellect is called *Mashiyaḥ* and is the redeemer and has influence over the soul and over all elevated spiritual powers. It can save the soul from the rule of the material kings and their people and their powers, the lowly bodily desires. It is a commandment and an obligation to reveal this matter to every wise man of the wise ones of Israel in order that he may be saved because there are many things that oppose the opinions of the multitude of the Rabbis, and even more differ from the views of the *vulgus*.[42]

Abulafia sees in the vulgar and rabbinic notions of the Messiah only the plain and thus the inferior sense of what the Messiah really represents. His pejorative attitudes toward Rabbis, evident in the phrase *hamon ha-rabbanim* [the multitude of Rabbis], appears therefore in an early treatise, a commentary on a prophetic book he himself wrote, composed not later than 1282.

The quintessence of Abulafia's approach is that he allegorized both the Messiah and Jesus as two inner faculties that play a central role in his intellectual worldview: what Neoaristotelians in the Middle Ages called intellect and

---

39 Presumably to R. Isaac of Acre.
40 The assumption that the prophetic experience starts suddenly recurs in R. Isaac of Acre; if this text indeed represents R. Nathan's stand, then R. Isaac was influenced by R. Nathan.
41 Preserved in R. Moshe of Kiev (1784), fol. 69b; Scholem (1991, 253, 259–260, 314 n. 22; 1924–25; 1930, 289–290).
42 See his *Commentary on Sefer ha-Melitz*, MS. Rome-Angelica 38, fol. 9a; MS Munchen 285, fol. 13a; Idel (1989, 66; 1987, 127, 140; 1998, 58–100) and Berger (1959, 55–61).

imagination, respectively. He internalized these two redemptive figures as part of the ongoing oscillations of an intense spiritual life.⁴³ More than the religious distinction between Jews and Christians, the distinction concerning the inner faculties was conceived of as much more robust intellectually and existential. It radiated upon religious distinction. Living more in the inner spiritual world and its alleged faculties, some of the Jewish elite figures projected the details of inner life and its conflicts onto the external religious tensions. They dramatically reinterpreted them, casting the religious distinction in accordance to the spiritual one. This projection of the later, spiritual axiology onto the earlier Jewish forms of religious one, reflects the imposition of the axial upon a preaxial vision. This double subversion was accomplished by someone who adopted for himself another type of sonship, an intellectual one conceived of as the peak of religious life.

[e] Negative Attitude to Rabbis

The phrase *hamon ha-rabbanim*, mentioned above, occurs in the epistle Abulafia wrote to R. Yehudah Salmon, his student in the early 1270s. In the late 1280s, Salmon became the associate of ibn Adret in the Halakhic court in Barcelona. In response to ibn Adret's assault against him, Abulafia writes:

> This Kabbalah is concealed from the multitude of Rabbis who are preoccupied with the wisdom of the Talmud. It is divided in two parts in general, and they are the parts of the knowledge of God by the way of the ten *sefirot* called branches...and they reveal the secret of the union [of God], and the part [dealing with] the knowledge of God by means of the twenty-two letters, out of which, and of their vocalizations and their cantillations, the names and the seals are compounded, and they are speaking to the prophets in dreams, and by means of 'Urim and Tummim, and by means of the Holy Spirit, and in prophecy.⁴⁴

Note the sarcastic overtone of the recurring phrase "multitude of Rabbis", which is indubitably part of a rivalry between Abulafia and the representative of the primary elite. The sense that prophecy has returned is therefore coupled with the feeling of a dual superiority: over ordinary rabbis, who ignore Kabbalah in general, but also over those rabbis like ibn Adret who, as a disciple of Nahmanides, adopted the

---

43 See Idel (2000b, 155–186; 1989, 45–62).
44 *We-Zot Li-Yhudah* (1853, 15): כי הקבלה הזאת הנעלמת מהמון הרבנים המתעסקים בחכמת התלמוד נחלקת תחלה לשני חלקים בכלל, והם חלקי דעות השם על דרך עשר ספירות הנקראות נטיעות... והם המגלים סוד הייחוד וחלק ידיעות השם על דרך כ"ב אותיות אשר מהם ומנקדותיהם ומטעמיהם הורכבו השמות והחותמות והם המדברים עם הנביאים בחלומות ובאורים ותומים וברוח הקדש ובנבואות.

For the context of this quote see Idel (1993b, 106–108). For more on this topic, see my preface to *Natan ben Sa'adyah Har'ar, Le Porte della Giustizia*, a Cura di Moshe Idel (Idel 2001, 130–144).

first type of Kabbalah. Abulafia considered himself superior, as he imagined that his type Kabbalah belongs to the higher form of this lore, as it deals with divine names, which revealed themselves to prophets. Ibn Adret's sharp polemic against Abulafia only exacerbated the latter's negative approach to the Rabbis, honing it into a sort to Jewish anticlericalism.[45] In the same epistle, Abulafia describes those Kabbalists who believe in the ten *sefirot* as theologically inferior to Christians, who believe in the Trinity.[46] I have no doubt that he refers to ibn Adret's specific type of Kabbalah, which assumed the divinity of the ten divine powers. In any case, Abulafia elsewhere contests Rabbinic myths as to the superiority of the Jews and speaks about Rabbis whose souls did not stand on Mt. Sinai; thus their "brain is polluted."[47]

There can be no doubt that Abulafia conceived himself as someone offering an alternative to Rabbinic axiology. In his commentary on the book of Deuteronomy, he writes:

> You should know in truth that even if you know the twenty-four books that are the entire Torah, and you know also the six treatises of the Mishnah by heart, and the [Midrahim of] *Sifrei* and *Sifra'* and the entire Talmud, together with their commentaries by heart, together with all their details, you will not be able to attain any rank of the ranks of prophecy, but if you will study the wisdom of combination of the letters and their paths.[48,49]

Here we have a clear example of a conflict between two forms of elites, gravitating also around the question of the possibility of present-day prophecy. This conflict can be illustrated by the manner Abulafia appropriated Nahmanides' description of the transmission of Kabbalah in an oral manner, assuming that in fact this

---

45 For some Christian forms of anticlericalism in Western Europe in Abulafia's lifetime see Wakefield (1973).
46 *Ve-Zot Li-Yhudah* (1853, 19).
47 See Idel (2012b; 2020, chapter 9). Some of the texts dealt with in these studies regarding the negative attitudes to Rabbis have been systematically ignored in the particularistic interpretation of Abulafia. See also n. 15 above.
48 On the importance of paths [*Netivot*] for entering an ecstatic experience, a term found already in *Sefer Yetzirah*, see the Abulafian treatise *Ner 'Elohim* (2002, 31).
49 *Mafteah ha-Tokhehot*, his commentary on the Deuteronomy (2001a, 242):
ודע באמת ובאמונה שאם לא תדע אלו הדרכים הנקראים בכלל צירוף האותיות ואפילו אם תדע ארבעה ועשרים ספרים שהם תורה בכללה. ותדע ששה סדרי משנה גם כן על פה וספרי וספרא וכוליה תלמודא עם פירושיהם בגירסא על פה בכללם בפרטי פרטיהם, לא תוכל עם כל זה להגיע אל שום מדרגה ממדרגות הנבואה עד שתלמוד צירוף האותיות ונתיבותיהם.

For the eschatological significance of remembering the classical texts of Judaism, see Idel (2003a).

description deals with the transmission of prophetic Kabbalah.⁵⁰ According to him, a redemptive experience can be achieved even in the present. When describing the effect of the application of his technique, he claims that the aspirant will undergo a transformative experience:

> It will appear to him as if his entire body, from head to foot, has been anointed with the oil of anointing, and he was "the anointed of the Lord" [Mashyiah YHWH] and His emissary, and he will be called "the angel of the Lord"; his name will be similar to that of his Master, which is Shaddai, who is called Metatron, the prince [namely the angel] of the divine Face.⁵¹

Let me attempt to describe Abulafia in other terms: his concern with prophecy as attainable in the present, and with techniques to reach it, stems to a degree from Ashkenazi sources. That concern differs from Maimonides' very cautious approach to this phenomenon as an actual possibility.⁵² Though it draws from late philosophical sources and from linguistic speculations, however, Abulafia's definition of prophecy in conspicuous intellectual terms, and the analysis of its components, stems predominantly from Maimonides's *chef d'oeuvre*, the *Guide of the Perplexed*.⁵³ This philosophical cargo is also discernible in his descriptions of the Messiah. This attitude to Rabbis reflects his critical understanding of the historical aspects of Judaism.

3 Accusations of Heresy

The topics dealt with above are coupled with the criticism of Abulafia addressed to him quite early in his Kabbalistic career. Given his positions as to major topics in Rabbinic Judaism, there is no wonder that he was persecuted. So, for example, he writes:

> Behold, the good is discerned by [means of] evil and evil is discerned by good, and all this is interpreted in *Sefer Yetzirah*.⁵⁴ On this issue the power of my fear was overcome, and I compelled my will and I sent my hand to [deal with]⁵⁵ what is somewhat higher than

---

50 *Mafteah ha-Tokhehot* (2001a, 122–123).
51 *Sefer Hayyei ha-ʿOlam ha-Ba*', MS Paris BN 777, fol. 109. For an analysis of the context of this passage, see Idel (1989, 15–16; 1990b, 236; 1989, 116–119).
52 See Idel (2018).
53 See Idel (2009). There I point out the mixture of the Maimonidean and linguistic aspects of prophecy in Abulafia.
54 Cf. VI:5. See also Pines (1990, 124–125, note 88).
55 A Hebrew idiom which means "I dared."

my capacity, seeing as I did that my generation is calling me an heretic and an Epicurean because I worshipped God in truth and not according to the fantasy of the nation[56] that walks in darkness, since they and those like them were immersed in the abyss, [and] were glad, and they were [also] glad to cause my immersion in their vanities and in the darkness of their deeds, too.[57]

In the same book, Abulafia claims that if Maimonides would have explained the commandments in accordance to philosophical spirituality he would now be considered "heretical and Epicurean" by Jews.[58] Some years later, in his *Commentary on Sefer ha-Melitz*, he describes the following situation:

Nowadays, because of our being in this lengthy exile that we are [...] this name[59] was hidden from the sages who are members of our nation, *a fortiori* from their multitude,[60] so that everyone that searches for the knowledge of this name or other holy names similar to it, for the sages of this generation he turns to be a heretic and an Epicurean.[61]

---

[56] Though the term *ha-'am* can be also translated as populace (as it is in Maimonides' *Guide of the Perplexed* III:54, [Pines 1990, 638, following Isaiah 9:1]), I prefer to use the word "nation" here. There is no good reason to doubt that he is referring here to those Jews who persecuted Abulafia.

[57] MS Jerusalem NUL, 8° 1303, fol. 73a, printed with several errors which I correct below, in Cohen's edition of *Sefer Ge'ulah* (2001d, 5–6):

והנה הטוב מבחין את הרע, והרע מבחין את הטוב, וכל זה מפורש בספר יצירה. על זה נצחתי כח פחדתי והכרחתי רצוני והשלחתי ידי במה שהוא למעלה מיכולתי מעט בראותי דורי קוראים אותי מין ואפיקורוס בעבור הייתי עובד אלהים באמת ולא כפי דמיון העם ההולכים בחשך ובעבור היותם הם ודומיהם נשקעים בתהום היו שמחים וכאשר היו שמחים כשהיו יכולין להשקיעני גם אני בהבליהם ובמחשך מעשיהם.

See also Scholem (1967, 129–130, 380, note 40) and Idel (2011c, 530).

[58] *Sefer Ge'ulah* (2001d, 14–15). I have already corrected the reading of this text in my study (Idel 2011c, 530–531), where I printed the improved Hebrew passage on the ground of the unique manuscript. This text should be compared to the much later (though equally important) discussion found in his *'Imrei Shefer* (1999, 20–21), where he claims that Maimonides dealt with only the "plain" sense of the commandments, while the secret meanings of the commandments are interpreted as referring to Hokhmah and Binah, Love and Understanding, and *limmud* (study). The epistemologies of Maimonides and Averroes influenced Abulafia's understanding of the emergence of the ideal of mystical union without an accompanying antinomianism, as it was the case of the extreme mysticism in some Christian circles in Central Europe, known as the "Free Spirit." See Lerner (1972, 61–68).

[59] Namely, divine name.

[60] The plural form מהמוניהם is not clear. Is this term connected to the locution המון הרבנים mentioned in the preceding paragraph?

[61] *Sefer ha-Melitz*, printed in *Matzref ha-Sekhel* (2001b, 36):

ואמנם אנחנו היום מפני היותנו בגלות הארוך הזה שאנו בו...נעלם זה השם מחכמי אנשי עמנו כל שכן מהמוניהם עד ששב היום אצל חכמי דורנו זה, כל המבקש שום ידיעה בשם כזה או בזולתו מן השמות הקדושים הדומים לו כמין ואפיקורוס.

It is hard to miss the precise identity of the person who in that generation sought knowledge of the divine names and, consequently, was branded a heretic and an Epicurean: for it was Abulafia himself who regarded the disclosure of the unknown divine name *'hwy* as the peak of his revelatory achievements. Likewise, in one of his latest books, *Gan Na'ul*, Abulafia claims that he was accused of believing in the pre-eternity of the world, like Aristotle, an accusation tantamount in the Middle Ages to heresy.[62]

However, much later criticisms of Abulafia are much more severe, amounting to the most intensive and virulent assault on the views of this controversial Kabbalist. R. Yehudah Hayyat, an accomplished Spanish Kabbalist who arrived in Northern Italy after the expulsion from Spain, admits that he has seen there "many books" by Abulafia, but refers to only three by name: *Sefer 'Or ha-Sekhel*, *Sefer Hayyei ha-'Olam ha-Ba'*, and one of Abulafia's commentaries on the *Guide of the Perplexed*. He describes the founder of ecstatic Kabbalah as "mad," and his books as "replete with imaginary things and fakes invented by his heart."[63] Two centuries later, when dealing with one of Abulafia's principal works, *Hayyei ha-'Olam ha-Ba'*, the noted paragon of Jewish culture and a mystic by himself, R. Hayyim Joseph David Azulai (1724–1807), better known as the *Hid"a*, noted:

> This is a book written by R. Abraham Abulafia, concerning the circle of the seventy-two letter [Divine] Name, which I saw on the manuscript parchment. And know that the Rashba [R. Solomon ben Adret] in his Responsa, sec. 548,[64] and Rabbi Yashar [R. Joseph Solomon del Medigo of Candia], in *Sefer Matzref le-Hokhmah*,[65] expressed contempt toward him as one of the worthless people, or worse. However, I say that in truth I see him as a great rabbi, among the masters of secrets, and his name is great in Israel, and none may alter his words, for he is close to that book mentioned, and his right hand shall save him.[66]

These remarks of the Hid"a aptly summarize the problematic involved in Abulafia's thought and his role in the development of the Kabbalah.

But Abulafia's prophetic and messianic claims, understood or misunderstood by his critics, contemporary or later, are not the only important reason

---

[62] *Gan Na'ul* (2000a, 40) and Scholem (1967, 383, note 92). Compare to *'Otzar 'Eden Ganuz* (2000b, II:1) and to *Sitrei Torah* (2001g, 91–92). Also see Dan (2013, 409), who argues that Abulafia believed in pre-eternity, this being the reason why language did not play a role in the creation of the world.
[63] See Hayyat's Introduction to his *Minhat Yehudah* (1558, fol. 3b).
[64] See vol. I no. 34 *Teshuvot ha-Rashba'*, edited by Dimitrovsky (1990, 107).
[65] Ch. 12 fol. 31b. In practice, Yashar of Candia copied the attack of R. Yehudah Hayyat, found in the introduction discussed above. It is astonishing that a person as expert in Kabbalistic literature as R. Azulai saw fit to mention Yashar's copy of this attack rather than the original.
[66] See *Shem ha-Gedolim*, Ma'arekhet Sefarim, VIII, section 76 (Azulai 1992).

for Abulafia's marginalization. His Kabbalah differed from the theosophical-theurgical content of a vast majority of other (mainly Sefardi) Kabbalists, whose works were printed in the first wave of Kabbalistic books. This is also the case of an Italian like Menahem Recanati). Their dissemination contributed much to Abulafia's relegation to the margins from the point of view of printing by traditional Kabbalists. The publishing of Kabbalistic books was dominated by the theosophical-theurgical Kabbalah, with books of Menahem Recanati, *Zohar*, Joseph Gikatilla, *Ma'arekhet ha-'Elohut* and its commentaries, printed mainly in Italian printing houses since the second quarter of the sixteenth century. Only a few short excerpts from Abulafia's writings were printed, always anonymously, in some collections of Kabbalistic texts.[67]

4 The Post-Abulafian Quest for Prophecy in Jewish Mysticism

Kabbalists in the Iberian Peninsula did not adopt Abulafia's emphasis on the importance of prophecy as an ideal and also a possibility in the present; they preferred the theosophical-theurgical approach or the magical one. However, this ideal did not disappear, as Abraham J. Heschel showed in his sustained efforts to discover how that ideal came to influence various Jewish authors in the Middle Ages.[68] Here is not the place to elaborate upon this current, but I shall adduce a few references to prophecy in some Safedian Kabbalists, which will serve the background of the conclusions drawn later on in this essay.

Despite the ban Shlomo ibn Adret put on Abulafia, which was very effective in Spain, Abulafia's writings were disseminated in many copies in Italy and in the Byzantine Empire; there exist more than a hundred manuscripts. Some substantial passages from his writings were copied anonymously in influential Kabbalistic works. The anonymous late fourteenth century *Sefer ha-Peli'yah*, for instance, includes discussions about prophecy and the techniques to reach it taken from Abulafia's writings.[69] His impact is obvious also in Italy, at the end of the fifteenth century in Florence and in Venice, on R. Yohanan Alemanno[70] and on R. Asher

---

[67] See, e.g. the *Polyglota* on the Psalms printed by Augustino Giustiniani, or *Liqqutei Shikhekhah u-Fe'ah*.
[68] See Heschel (1996) and Idel (2003c).
[69] See Kushnir-Oron (1980, 75–80).
[70] See Idel (2011a, 343–462 n. 46).

Lemlein of Reutlingen,[71] an Ashkenazi figure active in Northern Italy who declared himself the Messiah. Though we may assume that the fierce critiques of ibn Adret drastically diminished Abulafia's impact in Spain, it hardly affected the preservation of his writings and their influence in other centers of Jewish culture. The ban lost its strength a generation after the expulsion from Spain, along with the fears of prophecy as a present possibility. For example, R. Moshe Cordovero, who was acquainted with Abulafia's writings and quotes them,[72] writes:

> The sons of the prophets, when they used to prepare themselves for prophecy, brought themselves [to a state of] happiness as in the verse, "Take me a musician, and when the musician plays…"[73] And they would concentrate in accordance with their ability to do so, in attaining the wondrous levels and divesting the material, and strengthening the mind within the body, until they abandoned matter and did not perceive it at all, but their mind was entirely in the supernal orders and subjects. And they concentrate, and divest [themselves] from the physical, and go away, and this matter is man's preparation on his own part.[74]

R. Hayyim Vital – one of his students and a great Kabbalist in his own right – was even more interested in prophecy. He wrote a short description of this ideal and techniques to reach it, entitled *Sha'arei Qedushah:*

> The ancient Hasidim come after them, and were called Perushim, and they sought to follow the path of the prophets and their practice and imitate them in caves of cliff and in deserts and they separated themselves from the ways of men. And some of them were separated in their houses as if they were walking in a desert, and day and night they were not silent, praising God by their study of the Torah and the psalms of King David, blessed be his memory, which are enjoying the heart, until their thought was cleaving forcefully and with a strong desire to the supernal lights. And they steadily continued this [practice] all their life until they reached the Divine spirit, and prophesied.[75]

The prophecy described here relates to some sort of ascetic life, not to the classical prophets of the Hebrew Bible. Here, as in Abulafia and Cordovero, the initiative is that of the aspirant. It is a rather interesting pun that the *perushim*, the ancestors of the rabbis who decided that prophecy ceased, are described here as ascetics who practice a way of life intended to reach prophecy.

Elsewhere in this book Vital distinguishes between ecstasy (or what he calls the "divestment of the corporeality," when the soul leaves the body) and prophecy (a state in which the soul is aware and receives a message):

---

71 See Idel (2011a, 216–217, 225, 297–298)
72 See Idel (1990a, 179–184).
73 2 Kings 3:15.
74 See Cordovero (1885, fol. 30d); on this passage see Ben-Shlomo (1965, 40).
75 See Vital's edition of *Sha'arei Qedushah* (1973, 7).

> Behold, when someone prepares himself to cleave to the supernal root, he will be able to cleave to it. However, despite the fact that he is worthy to this [achievement] he should divest his soul in a complete manner, and separate it from all matters of matter, and then you should be able to cleave to her spiritual root. And behold, the issue of divestment that is found written in all the books dealing with issues of prophecy and divine spirit, a real divestment that the soul exits from his body really, as it happens in sleep, because if it is so this is not a prophecy but a dream like all the dreams. However, the dwelling of the Holy Spirit upon man takes place while his soul is within him, in a state of awareness, and she will not exit from him.[76]

Vital's popular booklet, which saw many printings, had a huge impact in Hasidic circles[77] but also among their opponents[78] (a topic that still awaits inquiry). It became a conduit of the idea that prophecy is possible in the present. Below we shall introduce another obvious example, but they can be easily multiplied, not all of them quoting explicitly the source. R. Joseph Ashkenazi reports a conversation with his relative R. Israel Ba'al Shem Tov:

> Rabbi Joseph asked him: "Why was I privileged to see him?" The Besht said to him: "Because you recited [aloud] to me, and I recited before you, and my words purified you. We were united as one, and because of that, you were able to see him. If your mind had been stronger, you would have heard what he said to me, and you, too would have been able to ask him whatever your heart wished. Moreover, you would have been made known to him, you would be able to envision him at any time." Rabbi Joseph grieved about this matter very much because seeing the soul of a righteous man is at the level of prophecy,[79] as it is said in the book *Sha'arei Qedushah* of Rabbi Hayyim Vital.[80],[81]

---

[76] See Vital (1973, 102–103). On this passage, see Werblowsky (1977, 66–70). For an interesting reference to prophecy in the Lurianic corpus, see the view of a later follower of Luria, R. Jacob Hayyim Tzemah, *Sefer Qehilat Ya'aqov*, MS New York, JTS 2146, fol. 90a, corresponding to Vital's *Sha'ar ha-Yihudim*, ch. 4. On the question of attributing the fourth part of *Sha'arei Qedushah* to Vital, see bar-Asher (2013).

[77] See Idel (1995, 38, 105, 278 n. 74, 297 n. 255, 346 n. 95, 378 n. 35).

[78] See, for example, R. Eliahu Pinhas Horowitz's late eighteenth-century *Sefer ha-Berit* (1897), which is a long commentary on *Sha'arei Qedushah*. Earlier in his career this Kabbalist wrote a short commentary on Abulafia's *Hayyei ha-'Olam ha-Ba'*. See Idel (1976, 65; 2004, 65–67) and Ruderman (2014, 40, 145 notes 2, 3).

[79] This is an interesting reference to those in the immediate vicinity of the Besht who envisioned him as a prophet. This passage should be added to the material I adduced in my "The Besht as Prophet and as Talismanic Magician" (2006, 122–133) and "On Prophecy and Early Hasidism" (2004, 65–70).

[80] See 3:7 in Vital (1973, 112–114).

[81] See Ben-Amos and Mintz (1984, 124–125). See also Idel (2012a, 79–106).

Those texts, together with Abulafia's additional influences on later Kabbalists, form part of a modest quest for types of experiences that differ from what we find in theosophical-theurgical Kabbalah, especially the Lurianic ones, but also in the Zoharic literature. This dimension of Kabbalistic literature shows simply discarding the mystical aspects of Kabbalah is quite problematic. Their importance for understanding the new wave of appropriation of Abulafia is not just a matter of adducing formal testimonies as to his status in the eyes of some Kabbalists, but as a source that supplied something vital but missing in other forms of Kabbalah.

5 Printing Abulafia's Writings in Ultra-Religious Circles[82]

In 1855, a Hasidic printer in Koretz, R. Yehudah Leibush Rappoport, compiled a list of books. He mentions Abraham Abulafia's book *Hayyei ha-'Olam ha-Ba'* as one of the manuscripts that he intended to print,[83] but this project never materialized.

The modern printing of Abulafia's writings began in 1984 with the critical edition of Abulafia's anonymous commentary on *Sefer Yetzirah*. The editor, Israel Weinstock, correctly identified the anonymous author as Abraham Abulafia.[84] The subtitle of his edition is "one of the classical books of the well-known Kabbalist."[85] This is indeed quite a surprising description of Abulafia, given that the publishing house was Mossad ha-Rav Kook, a strictly Orthodox religious institution. This edition includes a critical apparatus, based on several manuscripts and valuable comparisons of the context to views of Abulafia's teacher, R. Barukh Togarmi, and an attempt at decoding the meaning of the text. Sometimes, this decoding conflates Abulafia's views with the theosophical Kabbalists. Weinstock,

---

82 I do not refer below to the printing of some few of Abulafia's writings by those who do not belong to Orthodox communities in Israel, like the 19th century Adolph Jellinek, and in the 20th century Gershom Scholem, Aryeh Kaplan, Adam Afterman, Raphael Cohen, Avi Solomon, and Arieh Krawsik. Nor do I refer to the Latin, English, French, or Sicilian/Italian translations of Abulafia's writings in the Renaissance period.

83 See the verso of the first, unnumbered page of *Sefer Sha'ar ha-Yihudim* in Vital (1855). The plan of printing was done under the aegis of the Hasidic leader R. Israel of Ryzhin.

84 See the *Perush Sefer Yetzirah 'Almoni' mi-Ysodo shel Rabbi Avraham Abulafia* [*ha-Meyuhas le-Rabbi Avraham ibn Ezra*], edited by Weinstock (1984). For the identification of the author of this anonymous treatise as Abulafia, see pages 25–26 of my 1976 thesis, *Abraham Abulafia's Writings and Doctrines*, and the accompanying endnotes.

85 אחד מספרי-המופת של המקובל הנודע

a more historically oriented Orthodox thinker than the others mentioned below, assumes that the text was circulated anonymously in order to allow its identification with the lost commentary on this book by Abraham ibn Ezra. I find no reason to accept this assumption.[86]

The next significant instance of religious interest in Abulafia's thought is the 1989 printing of two works belonging to ecstatic Kabbalah, R. Yehudah Albotini's *Sullam ha-'Aliyyah* and *Sha'arei Tzedeq* by Joseph Eleazar Elimelekh Porush.[87] Though not a critical edition, the volume brings forth hitherto unprinted traditional texts practically unknown by most of the Kabbalists in the last centuries. The edition carries the imprimatur of one of the towering figure of ultra-Orthodoxy: Rabbi Hayyim Yehudah Leib Auerbach.[88] In his introduction, Porush assumes that R. Isaac Luria had accepted the importance of Abulafia's Kabbalah. He argues this is evident in R. Hayyim Vital's preface to *Sha'arei Qedushah*, a work that addresses the importance of prophecy, which Vital considered as representing Luria's own view.[89] Luria's authority was thus invoked in order to neutralize ibn Adret's ban; Abraham Abulafia's name is explicitly mentioned. This is part of the harmonistic understanding of the nature of Kabbalah in general and the attenuation of Abulafia's idiosyncratic messages. The book was received very coldly in the Kabbalistic academy, and the author himself died relatively young several years afterward. It should be mentioned that initially, this Yeshivah is related to a Hasidic figure.

A decade later, Rabbi Matatyahu Safrin – a Komarno Hasid living in Jerusalem – printed an abridged version of Abulafia's *'Or ha-Sekhel* and his *Sefer ha-Ḥesheq*. The printing carried the imprimatur of Rabbi Israel Yacov Fisher, a prominent Halakhic figure in *Me'ah She'arim* and head of the High Court of the Haredi community. Rabbi Fisher, stemming from a *mitnagged* line, described Abulafia as "one of the great [figures] among the ancients,"[90] and referred to the greatness of both the author and his book. He claims that the printing of this book will bring about "a bright light to the wisdom of Kabbalah." In his introduction to *'Or ha-Sekhel*, the editor Mattityahu Safrin reiterated Porush's claim (without attribution) about the alleged consonance of Luria's Kabbalah with Abulafia's thought. Though I do not grant too great a significance to such an imprimatur

---

86 *Perush Sefer Yetzirah 'Almoni'*, edited by Weinstock (1984, 51–62).
87 Both were published by *Makhon Sha'arei Ziv*, beside the *Yeshivah* of *Sha'ar ha-Shamayyim*, Jerusalem.
88 The founder of the Lurianic Yeshivah, *Sha'ar ha-Shamayim*, who died in 1954 (Meir 2010).
89 See Vital (1973, 15).
90 On the front page of *Sefer ha-Ḥesheq*, Abulafia is described by Safrin as "one of the powerful among the ancients" (1997, 4).

(I do not assume that Rabbi Fisher actually read the books), the very fact that the books were sold out in *Me'ah She'arim* and that a second edition, published by Amnon Gross, followed immediately afterwards, is nevertheless emblematic.

Indeed, between the years 1999–2003 Amnon Gross printed almost all the known books of Abulafia and has continued to do so in the years since. He studied Abulafia's books in a group in *Me'ah She'arim*, in the ultra-Orthodox Hasidic school known as the disciples of Rabbi Aharele [Aharon] Rotte. The leading figure in this group was Rabbi Avraham Yurovitz (1948–1993), a major Halakhic figure in one of Jerusalem's most extreme ultra-Orthodox communities. He was, from some points of view, an outstanding figure, but at the same time a dissident type of personality in his original milieu. In the 1980s, we had several nocturnal discussions in my apartment in Jerusalem. I delivered to him photocopies of some of the manuscripts of ecstatic Kabbalah, and I understood from him that he assembled a small group in order to exercise Abulafia's techniques. This seems to me the first modern and significant presence of Abulafia's writings in *Me'ah She'arim* as an active lore, and it was ultimately instrumental in the publication of most of Abulafia's writings (a project with which I was not connected at all).

Amnon Gross printed a series of thirteen volumes, including not only most of Abulafia's original writings but also those of his disciples, sometimes attributed to him.[91] Gross added laudatory prefaces to most of those volumes, some of which have been reprinted in more than one edition in the same year, though by now no imprimatur was thought necessary. Maybe the authority of Yurovitz, who passed away already in 1993, was sufficient. This series has been sold for almost two decades, alongside series of volumes of classics of Judaism and Kabbalah, Bible, Talmud, Lurianic volumes, in most of the bookshops in *Me'ah She'arim* and in the neighborhood of *Ge'ulah*. More recently, Gross printed a book from Abulafia's school, *'Or ha-Menorah* (2017), and reprinted two books from his school: *Sha'arei Tzedeq* and *Sullam ha-'Aliyyah* (2008).

The first page of each of the thirteen volumes introduces the author as "the perfect and comprehensive sage; the luminary, the great genius, the well-known, the Hasid, the humble,[92] the divine Kabbalist, the honorable, our teacher and Rabbi, Abraham Abulafia... whom everyone called Abraham the visionary."[93]

---

91 This is the case of *Sefer ha-Tzeruf* and *Sefer Ner 'Elohim*.
92 How humble Abulafia was is indeed a great quandary. See, e.g., his view that the Messiah, and he considered himself to be a messianic figure, was higher than Moses. Cf. Idel (1989, 50–51). Compare also above n. 13 above, the passage from *Sefer 'Imrei Shefer*, where Abraham's Judaism is, if the text is understood correctly, potentially higher and earlier than the Mosaic Judaism.
93 The Hebrew formula is "החכם השלם והכולל, המאור הגאון הגדול, המפורסם, החסיד והעניו, המקובל האלוהי כמהר"ר אברהם אבולעפיה...שהיה נקרא בפי כל אברהם הרואה."

Gross too relies on the approach of Vital's *Sha'arei Qedushah,* presented as reflecting Luria's view, in order to vindicate Abulafia's approach in general and the printing of his works in particular.[94] In the last year, a young Kabbalist, Ohad Torgeman, printed an untitled anonymous text of Abulafia's, which I identified some years ago, under the title *Pardes ha-Sefer* (2018). All these books are regularly sold in more than one bookshop in *Me'ah She'arim* for many years.

None of those editions include a critical apparatus or a conceptual analysis, but short laudatory prefaces that praise Abulafia's Kabbalah, with all the superlatives of traditional expressions in Judaism. Neither do they mention the academic sources through which they discovered theses writings. Let me mention that I identified a manuscript of Abulafia's *Ḥayyei ha-'Olam ha-Ba'* in a box which included the original autograph writings of R. Menahem Mendel of Shklov, one of the outstanding pupils of the Gaon of Vilna, and a founder of *Me'ah She'arim* in the early 19th century. One of his descendants, Mr. Sh. A. Stern showed me the anonymous manuscript, found together with R. Menahem Mendel's writings.[95] Indeed this late figure had been strongly influenced by Abulafia's Kabbalah,[96] as was R. David ha-Kohen (known as *ha-Nazir*), who had prophetic claims, and was interested in Abulafia's books and manuscripts.[97] According to some evidence, and also oral traditions, Abulafia's books were studied in the famous Kabbalistic Yeshivah of Beit 'El.[98]

Today, some of the most important databases in the field of Judaica, most of them compiled by Jewish religious organizations or institutions, have made Abulafia's books available in electronic formats.

6 Why Were Abulafia's Books accepted in Me'ah She'arim?

At first glance, the special attention Abulafia's writings attract in some circles in *Me'ah She'arim* raises quite a quandary: Why do groups from a stronghold of Jewish ultra-Orthodoxy adopt the writings of the *bête noire* of Jewish mysticism? When formulated in such a way we face a paradox. However, the situation can be

---

[94] See Gross's introduction to *'Imrei Shefer* (Abulafia 1999, 2–3).
[95] See Mendel (2001).
[96] See Idel (2003b).
[97] See Idel (2005).
[98] This interesting affair deserves a separate analysis, which cannot be offered in this framework.

analyzed in a more lucid manner. To be sure, most of the *Me'ah She'arim* groups are not concerned with Abulafia, in any form, at all. Yet many of the neighborhood's bookshops have been selling the set of his books for a long time, without any significant protest I am acquainted with.

Attempts to address changing attitudes of circles toward theories and practices shaped centuries beforehand by resorting to a single answer are, at best, simplistic. There is no precise repetition in history, even more so when Abulafia offered more than one technique in several different books. We may better describe this as a case of "selective recuperation." Later thinkers adopt parts of the earlier traditions in accordance to their specific concerns. In other words, we should speak in this context about "selective affinities." Most of the authors mentioned above are related to one or another Hasidic group. The introversive dimension of Hasidism – an acute concern with inner processes – that played an active role in this selective type of affinities.[99]

Hasidism's departure from earlier strong metaphysical speculations, as found especially in Lurianic Kabbalah, created the space for a selective recuperation of aspects of Abulafia's thought. That recuperation remained indifferent to the metaphysical cargos of philosophical origins and privileged his techniques as conducive to an individual experience. Less concerned in theosophical or even in a shared theology, Hasidism embraces a variety of stands, from theism to immanentism, pantheism or panentheism, an approach that puzzled scholars in the field. Hasidim put emphasis on the experiential dimensions, or on subjective experiences, earlier framed by broader systems of thought imported from non-Jewish speculative sources, which contributed to the more general worldview and psychology. These were conceived now as unnecessary for the articulation of Hasidic thought, as it was in Rabbinic Judaism in the case of Halakhah, deemed to be free of comprehensive and systematic ideologies or theologies

Abulafia's complex thought has been selectively adopted in recent times; those elements highlighted above, conceived of as problematic in earlier forms of Judaism, were marginalized or not acknowledged at all.[100] This entailed overlooking what in my view is the most interesting intellectual achievement of this Kabbalist: bringing together the logocentric-philosophical and the linguocentric-magical approaches. Overemphasizing the technical, linguistic aspects of his Kabbalah has entailed ignoring the centrality of the intellectual Neo-Maimonidean apparatus so pivotal in Abulafia's writings. This reductive reading amounts to a return to

---

99 On the psychological interpretation of the ten *sefirot* in Kabbalah in the context of impact on Hasidism, see Idel (1995, 227–238; 1988, 146–153) and Margolin (2004, 2011).
100 See Idel (2020).

the non-philosophical dimensions of *Sefer Yetzirah* and to its Ashkenazi commentaries, by removing the quintessential philosophical apparatus that the ecstatic Kabbalist added from mainly Maimonidean sources. Interestingly enough, this is done mainly by contemporary Ashkenazi authors who are less acquainted with medieval philosophy. In contrast, most of the Sefardi Kabbalists with whom I am acquainted remained reticent as to the ecstatic Kabbalist and the printing of his books.

Some technical aspects of Abulafia's books which have been printed in the last generation for the first time were adopted practically. They supplied something modern readers did not find in Lurianic or even in Hasidic literatures: a structured and detailed path toward a personal experience, in a manner reminiscent of other types of mystical techniques found in other religions to be practiced *de facto*. At the same time, other aspects of Abulafia's works have been basically neglected: the cosmological and theological frameworks, as well as the strong eschatological tendencies as he understood them, which together with the linguistic techniques created idiosyncratic understandings of the topics we discussed above. His books became a mirror of the modern authors' needs. The aspects that from the Jewish traditional point of view appeared radical, aspects hinted at in those books and illustrated above, did not attract their attention.[101] Such a phenomenon parallels the adoption of the Yogi practices in the 20th century in the West, a trend known as "transcendental meditation," which is mostly devoid of the metaphysical and psychological elaborations of the Sanskrit original texts.[102]

No doubt, we witness here an invention of a tradition, based on the writings of quite a rebellious figure, whose radical views have been dramatically tamed and adapted, before being adopted. Those who have read Abulafia as part of the broader Kabbalistic tradition have not only misunderstood his specific sort of Kabbalah (especially by attempting to harmonize it with the theosophical-theurgical Kabbalah), but have also changed the latter type of Kabbalah in the process.[103]

---

101 This is also the case of the English books popularizing Kabbalah authored by Kaplan (1995) and Pearl Epstein.
102 See also Persico (2016).
103 Some forms of scholarship on this Kabbalist have taken a similar turn. See the very title of Wolfson's book, *R. Abraham Abulafia: Kabbalist and Prophet, Hermeneutics, Theosophy, and Theurgy*. A related misreading has understood the *Zohar*, basically a variegated and complex homiletic literature, as a reflection of mystical experiences. This misunderstanding emerged more recently in scholarship, perhaps influenced by Abulafia's ecstatic stance. See, e.g., Wolfson (2004, 112); and compare to Huss' claims in his two studies mentioned in n. 2 above. See also Abulafia's mispresentation as a particularist, as discussed in section 2a above. Recently Abulafia is [mis]understood as a theosophist, and the Zoharic literature became more ecstatic than ever.

To offer just one recent example: A new edition of a Kabbalistic book written in the first part of the sixteen century in Jerusalem or in Aleppo, R. Joseph ibn Tzayyah's *'Even ha-Shoham*, which has little to do with ecstatic Kabbalah, carries a subtitle absent in the original: הקבלה הנבואית – the prophetic Kabbalah.[104] In November 2018 I asked the editor, Ohad Torgeman, why he added this subtitle. His answer was quite astonishing: "This is the way books are sold in *Me'ah She'arim*." Though this may be an exaggeration, or just the impression of an individual (albeit an informed Kabbalist), it may nevertheless contain more than a grain of truth. The continuous sale of Abulafia's books for years corroborates Torgeman's assessment. It is true not only of a specific individual, Amnon Gross, but also of many buyers that have acquired hundreds of sets of the volumes he printed and the participants of his classes on Abulafia.

Let me conclude with a quote from Gross's preface to his edition of Abulafia's *Sefer ha-Maftehot*, the commentary on the Pentateuch:

> In the preface to *'Imrei Shefer* I have already expressed my being moved and affected by the strength of the secrets and the revelations that our Rabbi,[105] R. Abraham Abulafia informs us.[106] And many of the readers that are standing at my entrance, thinking that all the awesome secrets and the ways of prophecy, are found in my possession, [but] like many of those that peruse those writings I too am thirsty for the word of God, since there is no one closer than the prophet to announce the actual word of God. And whoever has already tasted the words of our Rabbi and feels that there is no one that opens the doors and explains the secrets, which is greater than our Rabbi. Many times the author causes our spirit to tremble by the moving opening "behold this is a great secret" and "now I shall reveal to you the secret", and many similar ones, and we, like a beast of prey, are drawn up to jump on its prey, drawn up in silence and digesting each and every word and letter, "let me swallow some of that red broth"[107] and expect to see the voices, to hear the lightings, but suddenly we feel that the tension calmed down, the prey disappeared and the secret dissipated.[108]

---

104 See ibn Tzayyah (2018).
105 See the preface to *SImrei Shefer* (Abulafia 1999, 1–2).
106 See also two other occurrences of this phrase, referring to Abulafia, later in this passage.
107 Genesis 25:30. The use in this context heir of the words of Esau to his brother Jacob is quite surprising.
108 Preface to *Mafteah ha-Hokhmot* (Abulafia 2003, 2):

כבר הקדמתי ב"אמרי שפר" להביע מהתרגשותי ומהתפעלותי מעוצם הסודות והגלויים שמודיע לנו רבינו הרב אברהם אבולעפיה. ורבים מן הקוראים נצבו על פתחי בחושבם כי כבר מונחים בכיסי כל הסודות הנוראים ודרכי הנבואה כולם כמו רבים מן המעיינים באלו הכתבים צמא גם אני לדבר השם שהרי אין לנו יותר קרוב מן המתנבא להודיע דבר השם ממש. ומי שכבר טעם מדברי רבינו יודע ומרגיש שאין לנו בבחינת פותח דלתות ומגלה סתרים גדול מרבינו. רבות הפעמים מרעיד רוחנו המחבר בפתיחותיו המרגשות "הנה זה סוד גדול" "ועתה אגלה לך סוד" וכהנה רבים. ואנו כחית-טרף הדרוכה לזנק על טרפה דרוכים בדממה ובולעים בלעט כל מלה ואות בבחינת "הלעיטני מן האדום האדום הזה". ומצפים לראות את הקולות לשמוע את הברקים ולפתע מרגישים כי המתח פג הטרף נעלם והסוד פרח הלך לו.

Gross evidently understands the nature of the secrets in Abulafia's texts as related to some form of revelation or synesthetic experience; their author is identified as a reliable prophet. Still, Gross confesses that despite his fascination with the writings of the ecstatic Kabbalist, he does not understand some of the Kabbalist's resort to combination of letters.[109] This offers a clue for understanding Abulafia's revival: his secrets are not understood. If they were understood – as I explicated some of them above – he would once more be ostracized in ultra-Orthodox communities. So far, we've seen no polemic related to the printing of those books and their sale in *Me'ah She'arim*, at least not in a written form. But Abulafia's detailed and diverse techniques to reach prophecy supply something now considered necessary in some of those communities, though missing in canonical Kabbalistic literature: detailed instructions as to how to reach prophecy, namely some form of ecstatic experience. Ultra-Orthodox groups, now more confident than ever, can afford the danger of an alternative source of authority. The New Age interest in Abulafia thus bears some similarity to ultra-Orthodox interest: a mystical path, reminiscent of the Oriental techniques, but one endowed now with the aura of Kabbalah, is imagined to enrich the spiritual experiences of recent seekers.[110] In both cases, techniques to achieve ecstasy have been disassociated from the more general worldview. They can then be practiced while ignoring the conceptual framework.

This type of selective reception, in religious and scholarly circles, is hardly a unique phenomenon in religion. As mentioned above, the practice of transcendental meditation has been detached from any acquaintance with underlying Hindu or Buddhist worldviews. Likewise, the celebrated French philosopher Pierre Hadot, who conceived ancient philosophy more as a mode of life than a mode of thought,[111] argues that a contemporary retrieval of spiritual exercises from ancient philosophy requires that the exercises be shorn of their underlying conceptual commitments. Addressing such a possible retrieval of ancient spiritual exercises of the Greeks, Hadot writes of the schools of ancient philosophy:

> The models they offer can be actualized only if they are reduced to their essence or their most profound significance. They must be detached from their antiquated cosmological and mythical elements, so that their fundamental positions, which the schools themselves considered essential, can be brought out.[112]

This statement is reminiscent of Rudolph Bultmann's demythologization project of early Christian myth. But I have my doubts if a retrieval of older traditions that

---

109 See his preface to *'Or ha-Sekhel* (Abulafia 2001f, 2).
110 See, e.g., Meilicke (2002).
111 See Hadot (2002a).
112 See Hadot (2002b, 278).

did not enjoy a continuous practice can be as significant today as in the past. In the case of Abulafia, it means a reception by small groups in Me'ah She'arim and by other groups in Jerusalem and in some other places in Israel, a reception that amounts to a de-philosophization of his thought without the editors and the aspirants being aware of the more general framework of his thought and the meaning of this revamping. In other words, we may consider Abulafia's reception as part of the dissolution of earlier Rabbinic/Kabbalistic traditions that were antagonistic to him and his writings, of selective affinities and of *ad hoc* spiritual choices. This adoption has violently disassociated his techniques from their conceptual context, including his understanding of the intellectual nature of the ideal experience.

The contents of those writings of the ecstatic Kabbalist have been adapted and adopted in the last two decades because they were strongly repackaged, reinterpreted, and often radically misunderstood. But this is the way tradition, and in many cases even culture in general, works: a figure considered in medieval Spain to be a Jewish heretic, whose books were banned and relegated to remain in manuscripts for centuries, may nevertheless become for some groups in contemporary ultra-orthodox Jerusalem "the perfect and comprehensive sage; the luminary, the great genius, the well-known, the Hasid, the humble, the divine Kabbalist, the honorable, our teacher and Rabbi." These small ultra-Orthodox groups in the most particularistic stronghold of the Mosaic-ritual Judaism unwittingly celebrate an "Abrahamic" (basically a "prophetic") understanding of Judaism,[113] as Abulafia proposed it: universalist, mentalist, and conceived of as higher than the "Mosaic" one, and also higher than the "ritualistic" Judaism of Aharon.[114] From this limited point of view, Abraham Abulafia was indeed a "prophet": the majority of the sages of "our generation" are, as he put it, "fools." It seems they did not change with time.

Bibliography

Abulafia, Abraham. *Commentary on Sefer ha-Melitz*, MS Rome-Angelica 38, fol. 9a. N.D.
Abulafia, Abraham. *N.T.* MS Firenze-Laurentiana II, 48 fol. 89a. N.D.
Abulafia, Abraham. *Sefer Hayyei ha-'Olam ha-Ba'*. MS Paris BN 777, fol. 109. N.D.

---

[113] It may well be that such a view is related to Abulafia's assumption, already found in several earlier sources, that Abraham wrote *Sefer Yetzirah*, one of the major sources of Abulafia's techniques. See Idel (2011c).
[114] See above n. 15.

Abulafia, Abraham. *We-Zot Li-Yhudah*. Ed. A Jellinek. *Auswahl Kabbalistischer Mystik*. Leipzig, 1853.
Abulafia, Abraham. *Sefer ha-Hesheq*. Ed. Matatyahu Safrin. Jerusalem, 1997.
Abulafia, Abraham. *'Imrei Shefer*. Ed. Amnon Gross. Jerusalem, 1999.
Abulafia, Abraham. *Gan Na'ul*. Ed. Amnon Gross. Jerusalem, 2000a.
Abulafia, Abraham.*'Otzar 'Eden Ganuz*. Ed. Amnon Gross. Jerusalem, 2000b.
Abulafia, Abraham. *Mafteah ha-Tokhehot*. Ed. Amnon Gross. Jerusalem, 2001a.
Abulafia, Abraham. *Matzref ha-Sekhel*, ed. Amnon Gross. Jerusalem, 2001b.
Abulafia, Abraham. *Matzref la-Kesef ve-kur la-Zahav*. Ed. Amnon Gross. Jerusalem, 2001c.
Abulafia, Abraham. *Sefer Ge'ulah*. MS Jerusalem NUL, 8^0 1303, fol. 73a. Ed. R. Cohen. Jerusalem, 2001d.
Abulafia, Abraham. Sefer 'Or ha-Sekhel. Ed. Amnon Gross. Jerusalem, 2001f.
Abulafia, Abraham. *Sitrei Torah*. Ed. Amnon Gross. Jerusalem, 2001g.
Abulafia, Abraham. *Ner 'Elohim*. Ed. Amnon Gross. Jerusalem, 2002.
Abulafia, Abraham. *Mafteah ha-Hokhmot*. Ed. Amnon Gross. Jerusalem, 2003.
Abulafia, Abraham. *Sefer Peras Ha-Sefer, Book of the Reward of the Number*. Ed. Alexandru Munteanu. Providence: Providence University, 2011.
Abulafia, Abraham. Matzref la-Kesef. MS. Sassoon 56, fol. 30b. A Fifteenth-Century Manuscript of Jewish Magic, MS. New York Public Library, Heb. 190, (Formerly Sassoon 56): Introduction, Annotated Edition and Facsimile. Vol 1. Ed. Gideon Bohak. Los Angeles: Cherub Press, 2014.
Abulafia, Abraham. *Sefer Pardes ha-Sefer*. Ed. Ohad Torgeman. Jerusalem, 2018.
Albalag, Isaac. *Tiqqun ha-De'ot*. Ed. Y.A. Vajda. Jerusalem: Israeli Academy of Sciences and Humanities, 1973.
Albotini, R. Yehudah. *Sullam ha-'Aliyyah*. Ed. Y.E. Porush. Makhon Sha'arei Ziv: Jerusalem, 1989.
Alexander, Philip S. "A Sixtieth Part of Prophecy: The Problem of Continuing Revelation in Judaism." *Words Remembered, Texts Renewed: Essays in Honour of John F.A. Sawyer*. Eds. J. Davies, G. Harvey and W.G.E. Watson. *Journal for the Study of the Old Testament: Supplement Series*, 195. Sheffield: Sheffield Academic Press, 1995. 414–433.
Azulai, R. Hayyim Joseph David. *Shem ha-Gedolim ha-Shalem*. Ed. Isaac Benjacob. Jerusalem: 'Otzar ha-Sefarim, 1992.
Bamberger, Bernard. J. "Revelations of Torah After Sinai." *HUCA* 16 (1941): 97–113.
bar-Asher, Avishai. "'This Fourth Part has been Neither Copied nor Printed": On the Identification of the Last Part of *Sha'are Qedusha*." *'Alei Sefer* 23 (2013): 37–49. (Hebrew)
Ben-Amos, D. and J. R. Mintz, editors and translators. *In Praise of the Baal Shem Tov [Shivhei ha-Besht]*. New York: Schocken Books, 1984.
Ben-Shlomo, Joseph. *The Mystical Theology of Moses Cordovero*. Mossad Bialik: Jerusalem, 1965. (Hebrew)
BT. *Hagigah*, fol. 15a.
BT. *Megillah*, fol. 17b.
Berger, Abraham. "The Messianic Self-Consciousness of Abraham Abulafia – A Tentative Evaluation." *Essays on Jewish Life and Thought Presented in Honor of Salo Wittmayer Baron*. New York, 1959. 55–61.
Boyarin, Daniel. *Judaism: The Genealogy of a Modern Notion*. New Brunswick, NJ: Rutgers University Press, 2018.

Crescas, R. Hasdai. *The Light of the Lord (Or Hashem)*. Trans. Roslyn Weiss. Oxford: Oxford University Press, 2018.
Cordovero, Moshe. *Shi'ur Qomah*. Warsaw, 1885.
Dan, Joseph. "The End of Prophecy and its Significance to Jewish Thought." *Alppayyim* 30 (2007): 257–288. (Hebrew)
Dan, Joseph. *History of Jewish Mysticism and Esotericism*. Vol. 9. Jerusalem: Merkaz Shazar, 2013.
Dimitrovsky, Ch. Z., editor. *Teshuvot ha-Rashba'*. 2 Vols. Mossad ha-Rav Kook: Jerusalem 1990.
Frydman-Kohl, Baruch. "Covenant, Conversion and Chosenness: Maimonides and Halevi on 'Who is A Jew?'" *Judaism* 41.1 (1992): 64–79.
Glatzer, Nachum N. "A Study of the Talmudic Interpretation of Prophecy." *Review of Religion* 10 (1945): 115–137.
Gribetz, Arthur. "The Sama' Controversy: Sufi vs. Legalist." *Studia Islamica* LXXIV (1991): 43–62.
Goldreich, Amos. *Automatic Writing in Zoharic Literature and Modernism*. Los Angeles: Cherub Press, 2010. (Hebrew)
Goshen-Gottstein, Alon. "'The Sage is Superior to the Prophet': The Conception of Torah Through the Prism of the History of Jewish Exegesis." *Study and Knowledge in Jewish Thought*. Ed. Howard Kreisel. Beer Sheva: Ben-Gurion University of the Negev, 2006. 2:37–77.
Hadot, Pierre. *Exercices spirituels et philosophie antique*. Nouvelle éd. Albin Michel: Paris 2002a.
Hadot, Pierre. *What Is Ancient Philosophy?* Trans. Michael Chase. Cambridge, MA: Harvard University Press, 2002b.
Hames, Harvey J. *Like Angels on Jacob's Ladder: Abraham Abulafia, the Franciscans, and Joachimism*. Albany: SUNY Press, 2007.
Harvey, Warren Zev. "Idel on Spinoza." *Essays in Honor of Moshe Idel*. Ed. Sandu and Mihaela Frunza Cluj-Napoca: Provo Press, 2008. 99–101.
Hayyat, Yehudah. *Minhat Yehudah*. Fol. 3b. Mantua, 1558.
Heschel, Abraham J. *Prophetic Inspiration After the Prophets, Maimonides and Other Medieval Authorities*. Ed. Morris M. Faierstein. Hoboken: Ktav Publishing House, 1996.
Horowitz, R. Eliahu Pinhas. *Sefer ha-Berit*. Wilna, 1897.
Huss, Boaz. "'A Sage is Preferable Than a Prophet': Rabbi Shimon Bar Yohai and Moses in the Zohar." *Kabbalah* 4 (1999): 103–139. (Hebrew)
Huss, Boaz. "The Mystification of the Kabbalah and the Myth of Jewish Mysticism." *Pe'amim* 110 (2007): 9–30. (Hebrew)
Huss, Boaz. "The Formation of Jewish Mysticism and Its Impact on the Reception of Rabbi Abraham Abulafia in Contemporary Kabbalah." *Religion and Its Others*. Eds. Heicke Bock, Jorg Feuchter, and Michi Knechts. Frankfurt: Campus, 2008a. 142–162.
Huss, Boaz. "The Mystification of the Kabbalah and the Myth of Jewish Mysticism." *BGU Review: A Journal of Israeli Culture* 2 (2008b): 9–30. (English)
ibn Tzayyah, R. Joseph. *'Even ha-Shoham*. Ed. Ohad Torgeman. Jerusalem, 2018.
Idel, Moshe. *Abraham Abulafia's Works and Doctrine*. Ph. D. Thesis. Jerusalem: Hebrew University, 1976. (Hebrew)
Idel, Moshe. "Abraham Abulafia and the Pope: The Meaning and the Metamorphosis of an Aborted Attempt." *Association of Jewish Studies Review* 7–8 (1982–1983): 1–17. (Hebrew)

Idel, Moshe. *The Mystical Experience in Abraham Abulafia.* Trans. J. Chipman. Albany: SUNY Press, 1987.
Idel, Moshe. *Kabbalah: New Perspectives.* New Haven: Yale University Press, 1988.
Idel, Moshe. *Studies in Ecstatic Kabbalah.* Albany: SUNY Press, 1989.
Idel, Moshe. *Chapters in Prophetic Kabbalah.* Jerusalem: Akademon, 1990a. (Hebrew)
Idel, Moshe. "Enoch is Metatron." *Immanuel* 24/25 (1990b): 228–231.
Idel, Moshe. *Language, Torah and Hermeneutics in Abraham Abulafia.* Albany: SUNY Press, 1990c.
Idel, Moshe. "The Contribution of Abraham Abulafia's Kabbalah to the Understanding of Jewish Mysticism." *Gershom Scholem's "Major Trends in Jewish Mysticism" 50 Years After.* Ed. P. Schäfer and J. Dan. Tübingen: Mohr, 1993a. 117–143.
Idel, Moshe. "Defining Kabbalah: The Kabbalah of the Divine Names." *Mystics of the Book: Topics, Themes, and Typologies.* Ed. Robert A. Herrera. New York: Peter Lang, 1993b. 108–113.
Idel, Moshe. *Hasidism: Between Ecstasy and Magic.* Albany: SUNY Press, 1995.
Idel, Moshe. *Messianic Mystics.* New Haven: Yale University Press, 1998.
Idel, Moshe. "R. Shlomo ibn Adret and Abraham Abulafia: For the History of a Neglected Polemic." *Atara L'Haim, Studies in the Talmud and Medieval Rabbinic Literature in Honor of Professor Haim Zalman Dimitrovsky* Eds. D. Boyarin, et al. Jerusalem: Magnes Press, 2000a. 235–251. (Hebrew)
Idel, Moshe. "'The Time of the End': Apocalypticism and Its Spiritualization in Abraham Abulafia's Eschatology." *Apocalyptic Time.* Ed. Albert Baumgarten. Leiden: Brill, 2000b. 155–186.
Idel, Moshe. Ed. *Natan ben Sa'adyah Har'ar, Le Porte della Giustizia.* Trans. Maurizio Mottolese. Milan: Adelphi, 2001.
Idel, Moshe. "*Memento Dei* – Remarks on Remembering in Judaism." *Il senso della memoria: Atti dei convegni Lincei.* Rome: Accademia Nazionale dei Lincei, 2003a. 162–167.
Idel, Moshe. "Menahem Mendel of Shklov and R. Avraham Abulafia." *The Vilna Gaon and His Disciples.* Eds. Moshe Hallamish, Yosef Rivlin, and Raphael Shuhat. Ramat Gan: Bar Ilan University Press, 2003b. 173–183. (Hebrew)
Idel, Moshe. "On Prophecy and Magic in Sabbateanism." *Kabbalah* 8 (2003c): 7–50.
Idel, Moshe. "On Prophecy and Early Hasidism." *Studies in Modern Religions, Religious Movements, and the Babi-Baha'i Faiths.* Ed. Moshe Sharon. Leiden: Brill, 2004.
Idel, Moshe. "Abraham Abulafia, Gershom Scholem and R. David ha-Kohen (ha-Nazir), on Prophecy." *Derekh ha-Ruaḥ: Jubilee Volume in Honor of Eliezer Schweid.* Vol. 2. Ed. Yehoyadah Amir Jerusalem: Hebrew University and Van Leer Institute, 2005. 787–802. (Hebrew)
Idel, Moshe. "The Besht as Prophet and as Talismanic Magician." *Studies in Jewish Narrative: Ma'aseh Sippur, Presented to Yoav Elstein.* Eds. Avidov Lipsker and Rella Kushelevsky. Ramat Gan: Bar Ilan University Press, 2006.
Idel, Moshe. "A Unique Manuscript of an Untitled Treatise of Abraham Abulafia in Biblioteca Laurentiana Medicea." *Kabbalah* 17 (2008): 7–28.
Idel, Moshe. "Definitions of Prophecy – Maimonides and Abulafia." *Maimonides and Mysticism, Presented to Moshe Hallamish on the Occasion of his Retirement.* Eds. Avraham Elqayam and Dov Schwartz. Ramat Gan: Bar Ilan University Press 2009. 1–36. (Hebrew)
Idel, Moshe. *Kabbalah in Italy.* New Haven: Yale University Press, 2011a.

Idel, Moshe. "On the Paradise in Jewish Mysticism." *Journal for the Studies of Religions and Ideologies* 10 (2011b): 18–27.

Idel, Moshe. "Sefer Yetzirah and Its Commentaries in the Writings of Rabbi Abraham Abulafia." *Tarbiz* 79 (2011c): 471–556. (Hebrew)

Idel, Moshe. "'The Besht Passed His Hand Over His Face': On the Besht's Influence on His Followers: Some Remarks." *After Spirituality: Studies in Mystical Traditions*. Eds. Philip Wexler and Jonathan Garb. New York: Peter Lang, 2012a. 79–106.

Idel, Moshe. "On the Secrets of the Torah in Abraham Abulafia," in *Religion and Politics in Jewish Thought: Essays in Honor of Aviezer Ravitzky*. Vol. 1. Eds. Benjamin Brown, Menachem Lorberbaum, Avinoam Rosenak, and Yedidyah Z. Stern. Jerusalem: Shazar Center, 2012b. 418–421. (Hebrew)

Idel, Moshe. "The Pearl, the Son and the Servants in Abraham Abulafia's Parable." *Quaterni di Studi Indo-Mediterranei* 6 (2014): 103–135.

Idel, Moshe. "'Higher than Time': Observations of Some Concepts of Time in Kabbalah and Hasidism." *Time and Eternity in Jewish Mysticism*. Ed. Brian Ogren. Leiden: Brill, 2015: 185–194.

Idel, Moshe. "Prophets and Their Impact in the High Middle Ages: A Subculture of Franco-German Jewry." *Regional Identities and Cultures of Medieval Jews*. Eds. Javier Castano, Tayla Fishman, and Ephraim Kanarfogel. Newark: Littman Library of Jewish Civilization, 2018. 285–337.

Idel, Moshe. *Abraham Abulafia's Esotericism: Secrets and Doubts*. Berlin: de Gruyter, 2020 (forthcoming).

Jellinek, Adolph. "'*Sefer Ha-Ot*'. Apokalypse des Pseudo-Propheten und Pseudo-Messias Abraham Abulafia." *Jubelschrift zum siebzigsten Geburtstage des Prof. Dr. H. Graetz*. Ed. A. Jellinek. Breslau: 1887.

Jospe, Raphael. "The Concept of the Chosen People: An Interpretation." *Judaism* 170.43 (1994): 127–148.

Kaplan, Aryeh. *Meditation and Kabbalah*. New Jersey: Aronson, 1995.

Kasher, Hannah. "'The Philosophers Never Believed in Anything' (R. Isaac Arama): Notes on the Accusation that Philosophers are Heretics in Medieval Jewish Philosophers." *Jewish Thought and Jewish Belief*. Ed. Daniel J. Lasker. Beer Sheva: Ben Gurion University Press, 2012. 57–70. (Hebrew)

Kasher, Hannah. *High Above All Nations (Deut 26, 19): Milestones in Jewish Philosophy on the Issue of the Chosen People*. Tel Aviv: Idra, 2018.

Kellner, Menachem. "On Universalism and Particularism in Judaism." *Daat* 36 (1996): v–xv.

Kellner, Menachem. "Maimonides' 'True Religion': For Jews or All Humanity." *Meorot* 7.1 (2008): 2–28.

Kiener, Ronald. "From 'Baal ha-Zohar' to Prophet to Ecstatic: The Vicissitudes of Abulafia in Contemporary Scholarship." *Gershom Scholem's "Major Trends in Jewish Mysticism" 50 Years After*. Ed. P. Schäfer and J. Dan. Tübingen: Mohr, 1993. 145–159.

Kushnir-Oron, Michal. *The Sefer Ha-Peli'ah and the Sefer Ha-Kanah: Their Kabbalistic Principles, Social and Religious Criticism and Literary Composition*. Ph. D. Dissertation. Hebrew University. Jerusalem, 1980. (Hebrew)

Lavee, Moshe. "Converting the Missionary Image of Abraham: Rabbinic Traditions Migrating from the Land of Israel to Babylon." *Abraham, the Nations, and the Hagarites: Jewish, Christian, and Islamic Perspectives on Kinship with Abraham*. Eds. Martin Goodman, George H. van Kooten, Jacques T.A.G.M. van Ruiten. Leiden: Brill, 2010. 203–222.

Lavee, Moshe. "Either Jews or Gentiles, Men or Women: The Talmudic Move from Legal to Essentialist Polarization of Identities." *JSQ* 25 (2018): 345–367.
Lerner, Robert. *The Heresy of the Free Spirit in the Later Middle Ages.* Notre Dame: Notre Dame University Press, 1972.
Maimonides, Moses. *The Guide of the Perplexed.* Trans. Shlomo Pines. Chicago: Chicago University Press, 1963.
Margolin, Ron. *The Human Temple: Religious Interiorization and the Inner in Early Hasidism* Jerusalem: Magnes Press, 2004. (Hebrew)
Margolin, Ron. *Inner Religion: The Phenomenology of Inner Religious Life and its Manifestations in Jewish Sources (From the Bible to Hasidic Text).* Ramat Gan and Jerusalem: Bar Ilan University Press, Shalom Hartman Institute, 2011.
Meilicke, A. C. "Abulafianism among the Counterculture Kabbalists." *Jewish Studies Quarterly* 9.1 (2002): 71–101.
Mesch, Barry. *Studies in Joseph ibn Caspi.* Leiden: Brill, 1975.
Moshe of Kiev. *Shushan Sodot*, fol. 69b. Koretz, 1784.
Meir, Jonathan. "The Imagined Decline of Kabbalah: The Kabbalistic Yeshiva Sha'ar ha-Shamayim and Kabbalah in Jerusalem in the Beginning of the Twentieth Century." *Kabbalah and Modernity.* Eds. Boaz Huss, Marco Pasi, Kocku von Stuckrad. Leiden: Brill, 2010. 197–220.
Mendel, R. Menahem. *Kitvei ha-Grm"m.* 2 Vols. Jerusalem, 2001. (Hebrew)
Nehorai, Michael Zevi. "Righteous Gentiles Have a Share in the World to Come." *Tarbiz* 61 (1992): 465–87. (Hebrew)
Novak, David. *The Election of Israel, The Idea of the Chosen People.* New York: Cambridge University Press, 1995.
'Or ha-Menorah. Ed. Amnon Gross. Jerusalem, 2017.
Persico, Tomer. *The Jewish Meditative Tradition.* Tel Aviv: Tel Aviv University, 2016. (Hebrew)
Pines, Shlomo. "Truth and Falsehood Versus Good and Evil, A Study of Jewish and General Philosophy in Connection with the *Guide of the Perplexed*, I,2." *Studies in Maimonides.* Ed. Isadore Twersky. Cambridge: Harvard University Press, 1990. 124–125.
Porush, Y. E. E., editor. *Sha'arei Tzedeq.* Sha'arei Ziv: Jerusalem, 1989.
Ruderman, David B. *A Best-Selling Hebrew Book of the Modern Era: The Book of the Covenant of Pinhas Hurwitz and its Remarkable Legacy.* Seattle and London: University of Washington Press, 2014.
Sagerman, Robert J. *The Serpent Kills or the Serpent Gives Life: The Kabbalist Abraham Abulafia's Response to Christianity.* Leiden: Brill, 2011.
Scholem, Gershom G. "Sha'arey Zedeq, a Kabbalistic Text from the School of R. Abraham Abulafia, Attributed to R. Shem Tov (ibn Gaon?)." *Qiryat Sefer* 1 (1924–25): 127–139. (Hebrew)
Scholem, Gershom G."Eine Kabbalistische Erklaerung der Prophetie als Selbstbegenung." *MGWJ* 74 (1930): 285–290.
Scholem, Gershom G. *Major Trends in Jewish Mysticism.* 3rd Revised Edition. New York: Schocken, 1967.
Scholem, Gershom G. *On the Mystical Shape of the Godhead.* Trans. J. Neugroschel. Ed. J. Chipman. New York: Schocken Books, 1991.
Sha'arei Tzedeq and *Sullam ha-'Aliyyah.* Ed. Amnon Gross. Jerusalem, 2008.
Sirat, Colette. "Juda b. Salomon Ha-Kohen – philosophe, astronome et peut-être Kabbaliste de la premiere moitié du XIIIe siècle." *Italia* 1.2 (1979): 39–61.

Sommer, Benjamin D. "Did Prophecy Cease? Evaluating a Reevaluation." *Journal of Biblical Literature* 115.1 (1996): 31–47.

Tzema<u>h</u>, R. Jacob Hayyim. *Sefer Qehilat Ya'aqov.* MS. New York, JTS 2146, fol. 90a.

Urbach, Efraim E. "When did Prophecy Cease?" Tarbiz 17 (1946): 1–11. Rpt. In *Me-'Olamam shel <u>H</u>akhamim.* Jerusalem: Magnes Press, 1988. 9–20. (Hebrew)

Urbach, Efraim E. "Prophet and Sage in the Jewish Heritage." *Collected Writings in Jewish Studies.* Eds. Robert Brody and Moshe D. Herr. Jerusalem: Hebrew University Magnes Press, 1999. 393–403. (Hebrew)

Valabregue, Sandra. "Philosophy, Heresy, and Kabbalah's Counter-Theology." *HTR* 109 (2016): 233–256.

Venetianer, Ludwig, editor. *Sefer ha-Ma'alot* (The Book of Degrees). Berlin, 1894.

Vital, R. Hayyim. *Sha'arei Qedushah.* Benei Beraq, 1973.

Vital, R. Hayyim. *Sefer Sha'ar ha-Yihudim.* Lvov, 1855.

Wakefield, Walter L. "Some Unorthodox Popular Ideas of the Thirteenth Century." *Medievalia et Humanistica* NS 4 (1973): 25–35.

Weinstock, Israel, editor. *Perush Sefer Yetzirah 'Almoni' mi-Ysodo shel Rabbi Avraham Abulafia [ha-Meyuhas le-Rabbi Avraham ibn Ezra].* Jerusalem: Mossad ha-Rav Kook, 1984.

Werblowsky, Raphael J. Zwi. *Joseph Karo, Lawyer and Mystic.* Philadelphia: JPS, 1977.

Wolfson, Elliot. R. *Abraham Abulafia: Kabbalist and Prophet Hermeneutics, Theosophy, and Theurgy.* Los Angeles: Cherub Press, 2000.

Wolfson, Elliot. R. "Hermeneutics of Light in Medieval Kabbalah." *The Presence of Light: Divine Radiance and Mystical Experience.* Ed. M. Kapstein. Chicago: Chicago University Press, 2004. 105–118.

Wolfson, Elliot. R. "'Sage is Preferable to Prophet': Revisioning Midrashic Imagination." *Scriptural Exegesis – The Shapes of Culture and the Religious Imagination: Essays in Honour of Michael Fishbane.* Ed. Deborah A. Green and Laura S. Lieber. Oxford: Oxford University Press, 2009. 186–210.

Wolfson, Elliot. R. "Textual Flesh, Incarnation, and the Imaginal Body, Abraham Abulafia's Polemic with Christianity." *Studies in Medieval Jewish Intellectual and Social History: Festschrift in Honor of Robert Chazan.* Ed. David Engel, Lawrence H. Schiffman and Elliot R. Wolfson. Leiden: Brill, 2012. 189–226.

Wolfson, Elliot. R. "Deceitful Truth and Truthful Deceit: *Sod ha-Hippukh* and Abulafia's Divergence from Maimonides." *A Tribute to Hannah: Jubilee Book in Honor of Hannah Kasher.* Eds. Avi Elqayam, Ariel Malachi. Tel Aviv: Idra, 2018. 91–126.

Yadin-Israel, Azzan. "*Bavli Menahot* 29b and the Diminution of the Prophets." *Journal of Ancient Judaism* 5 (2014): 85–105.

Part 3: **Literature in Jewish Modernity**

Robert Alter
The Authentic Paganism of Saul Tchernikhovsky

Certain twentieth-century writers were drawn to introduce pagan themes and images in their work as a gesture of rebellion against Judeo-Christian values and as an affirmation of the life of the body in nature. A paradigmatic instance is D. H. Lawrence's memorable story, *The Man Who Died*, in which Jesus emerges from the crucifixion to a true resurrection, a resurrection of the flesh, in an act of sacred sex with a priestess of Isis. A salient expression of this trend in Hebrew literature is the work of the so-called Canaanite poets, a group in part inspired by Saul Tchernikhovsky, that became active at the beginning of the 1940s, Yonatan Ratosh being its leading figure. There is something *willed*, I would say, about most of these literary imaginings of paganism, which seem framed to make a polemical point. That is palpably the case of the Canaanite poets, impelled as they were by an ideological program to assert their identity as Hebrews, not Jews, who belonged to what they referred to as the Semitic Sphere and who attached themselves to the mythology and cult of the ancient Semitic world that stood outside the biblical texts which in their view had led to the repressive world of Judaism. Although the Canaanite poets did trigger considerable discussion and controversy in Hebrew literary circles as late as the 1950s, they proved to be a transient phenomenon, and it is fair to say that the model of Tchernikhovsky has not left a lasting imprint in Hebrew literature. In any case, paganism in his own poetry, as we shall see, is rather different from the expression given to pagan themes by the Hebrew Canaanites.

His upbringing was quite unlike that of the other Hebrew writers who came of age in the last part of the nineteenth century.[1] He was born in 1875 not in a predominantly Jewish *shtetl* but in a small town of perhaps 8,000 people, most of them Russian, in the Ukrainian steppes. Russian was the language spoken in his home, though he acquired Yiddish from his grandparents (he would later express disdain for the flawed Russian of his fellow Hebrew writers). His father was a relaxed kind of Orthodox Jew, more or less observant out of motives of cultural loyalty rather than piety, and his mother was, it seems, scarcely a believer. He learned Hebrew not in a traditional *kheyder* but with a private teacher imported

---

[1] The details of Tchernikhovsky's life are available in Ido Bassok's large Hebrew biography, *Layofi vanisgav libo er* (2017). The facts of the poet's life are established there through scrupulous research, although the readings of the poems are bit thin.

from Odessa who offered instruction to a small group of children including, at least for a while and quite exceptionally, girls. Hebrew was taught as a modern language, and the level of instruction must have been quite high, for this gifted student by the age of eleven was already composing poems in Hebrew. Tchernikhovsky, after going on to secondary schooling in Odessa and medical training in Heidelberg and Lausanne, would remain a staunchly secular Jew, though the term "secular" needs to be qualified because there was a deeply religious current in his poetry that was not monotheistic.

Tchernikhovsky wrote explicitly pagan poems from an early moment in his career. The titles speak for themselves: "A Song for Ashtoreth and for Bel," "The Death of Tammuz," "Weavings for Ashtoreth," and, perhaps the most celebrated of these texts, "Before the Statue of Apollo," which extols the Greek god as the embodiment of beauty, that supreme value rejected by the Jews, who are called "living corpses and the rot of human seed, / rebels against life." As even these few phrases will suggest, "Before the Statue of Apollo" is a militant manifesto, and it is not, in my view, the best of Tchernikhovsky's pagan poems, though it became a rallying cry for some Hebrew readers while it shocked many others. What it does do is to offer a transparent revelation of Tchernikhovsky's stance as a vehement rebel against Jewish tradition, all the way back to and including the Bible. Being a Jew and expressing his Jewishness in the Hebrew language were at the core of his identity, but he rejected Judaism's fundamental orientation toward reality. He is in this way an unabashed heretic, repeatedly demonstrating in his poetry that it is possible to achieve strong cultural expression as a Jew without the baggage of Jewish tradition.

The real power of Tchernikhovsky's neo-pagan poetry is its ability to enter into the vividness and felt immediacy of the pagan world in all its sensuality and in its embrace of the primordial forces of nature. Perhaps surprisingly, he often did this through the pre-eminently Renaissance form of the sonnet, and since both the brief and the extended texts we will be considering are sonnets, a comment is in order about why Tchernikhovsky was drawn to this demanding form. To begin with, the sonnet is inseparable from the humanism and the universalist perspective that pervade his work. The fourteen-line structure, comprising an octet and a sestet, emerged in Italy in the thirteenth century and would become a prominent poetic form of the Renaissance. The first sonnets in a language other than Italian, it is worth noting, were written in Hebrew, just a few decades after the form's introduction, by Immanuel of Rome (1261–1328), a poet whom Tchernikhovsky admired and to whom he devoted a monograph. The sonnet, then, is testimony to the enriching interaction between Hebrew and other cultures that Tchernikhovsky repeatedly advocated and manifested both in his poetry and in his translations from many languages, ancient and modern. But he also cherished the sonnet for its poetic concision and its musicality, values that he celebrated in one of his own sonnets, "To the Hebrew Sonnet" (1920). In his pagan sonnets, he clearly reveled in the paradoxical fusion of raw archaic energies and beautifully polished form. His poem on the Hebrew sonnet flaunts in its opening line the ingenious Hebrew epithet for this form, *shirat zahav*, "poetry of gold," where the letters of the word meaning "gold" have the numerical value of fourteen, the number of lines in the sonnet. He was also attracted to a composite form that compounds the intricacies of this poetry of gold, the corona of sonnets (*kelil sonetot*), in which the last line of each poem becomes the first line of the next, with the fifteenth sonnet made up of all the first lines in sequence. It is this form he used for "To the Sun," one of the great longer poems of the twentieth century. Why he should have chosen the demanding corona of sonnets in the war-torn Odessa of 1919 to synthesize his views on art, science, history, violence, and religion is a question I shall take up when we look more closely at "To the Sn." First, I would like to consider a sonnet written in that same soul-trying year, "Astarte Mine, Will You Not Say to Me."

Here is the poem in my necessarily inadequate English approximation:

> Astarte mine, will you not say to me: from whence
> You came in the vale to us? Was it by a Sidon merchant
> From the city stronghold of the sea, through agate and chalcedony waves?
> Did Dan's chieftains lie in wait for it on the mountains in the night?
>
> Were you borne in linen packs on camels of Dedan
> And she-camels raising golden sand in their swaying gait
> With a caravan from Sheba armed with lifted spears
> While before it jingled pomegranate bells, and crescent bangles sang?
>
> Wondrous to me you are, O wondrous, your eyes are emeralds.
> Why, you are fashioned all of ivory, your limbs linked together so.
> And no man reveals the secret, who gave you to me – no man.
>
> A basket of figs for you – I have scooped up finest flour,
> A *log* of my olive oil – to you have I prayed:
> "Lead him, a shining lad, bring him to me quick."   (Tchernikhovsky 1990–2003, 1: 200)[2]

The most palpable absence in this English version is the wonderful musicality of the Hebrew original. The rhyme scheme is ABBA AABA CCD EED, and Tchernikhovsky flaunts his virtuosity in the way he handles these rhymes. The most notable instance is the second and third line, where "Sidon" (*Tsidon*) rhymes with "chalcedony" (*kaltsidon*), yielding a doubled *rime riche* and the linking of

---

[2] This and subsequent translations of Tchernikhovsky's poems are mine.

the Phoenician city-name with a word, rare in Hebrew as in English, for a precious stone. Tchernikhovsky means to highlight the bejeweled nature of the poetic landscape, in keeping with his understanding of the sonnet as a "poem of gold," and so the waves with their white foam and their blues and greens are figured as chalcedony and agate, and the exquisite statuette of Astarte is ivory with emerald eyes. A noteworthy feature – quite characteristic of Tchernikhovsky – of this poem set in the ancient Near East is its total avoidance of actual allusions to the Bible. This is a remarkable departure from the practice of most Hebrew poets, down to the Statehood Generation of Yehuda Amichai, Dahlia Ravikovitch, and Natan Zach. Tchernikhovsky by and large does not want to *remember* the biblical world (with the exception of a few poems that take up and rewrite biblical stories) but rather to construct an alternative world in Hebrew to that of the Bible. The diction of this poem is conspicuously biblical, apart from the names for two of the three precious stones and the verb for "say" in the first line. This archaic diction gives the poet direct access to the ancient – and manifestly pagan – setting, and it is hard to imagine a modern poet in another language doing this because in Hebrew it is still possible to write perfectly comprehensibly in a diction and grammar that are three millennia old. The fourteen rhyming lines of the sonnet impose a necessity for compression on the poet, but within these confines he succeeds in evoking a broad expanse of cultures: Phoenician Sidon to the north, the tribe of Dan in the mountainous border region between ancient Israel and Lebanon, Dedan and Sheba in the Arabian Peninsula to the far south. One should note that the sole hint of an Israelite presence here, the tribe of Dan, is hostile, threatening to ambush the bearers of the statuette of the goddess and seize it.

The speaker is clearly a young woman, perhaps a Canaanite, perhaps an Israelite following the cult of the surrounding cultures, a common enough practice abundantly confirmed in the Bible as well as by archaeological evidence. She is a sensual woman, rhapsodizing over the beauty of the likeness of the goddess that she has acquired. She is also linked to the world of growing things, as her offering to Astarte of figs, fine flour, and olive oil will suggest. What she may be entreating the goddess to give her in return for this offering might be a child, for Astarte is a fertility goddess, but it is more likely that she is asking for a handsome lover – *tsah*, the adjective that I have translated as "shining," is attached to the lover in the Song of Songs, though I think this amounts to a small lexical clue, not really an allusion. What makes this sonnet so remarkable, beyond its beautifully wrought form, is the poet's ability to inhabit the mind and sensibility of a young woman living in the ancient pagan world. Unlike "Before the Statue of Apollo," this is not a poem that pleads an ideological case but rather a concrete imagining of the charm and naturalness of the pagan relation to reality.

Before we consider the details of "To the Sun," some comment is in order about why Tchernikhovsky should have tackled this large subject through the difficult form of the corona of sonnets in the Odessa of 1919. Conditions at that time and place were horrendous. The Reds and the Whites were battling over possession of the city. There was little food to be had, and Tchernikhovsky barely had the wherewithal from his intermittent work as a physician to acquire it for his Russian wife and their young daughter. He had served three years as an army physician caring for maimed and wounded soldiers not far from the front (though evidently he was not actually in the trenches, as he seems to imply in the seventh sonnet of the cycle). After the revolution of 1917, with which he had little sympathy, Russia, having withdrawn from the war, was torn by violent conflict, destined to conclude in the imposition of a violently oppressive regime, the signs of which were already visible in 1919. In these conditions of disruptive turmoil, one might think Tchernikhovsky would scarcely have had the composure to write a haiku, no less an architectonically intricate cycle of fifteen sonnets.

Art, I would suggest, was Tchernikhovsky's constant bulwark against the upheavals of history. At this dark moment, when he was in his mid-forties, with a substantial body of poetic achievement behind him, he chose a form of poetry associated with what he no doubt regarded as the luminous Renaissance to produce a kind of *summa* of his personal beliefs. There are some themes in the cycle one might associate with modernism (others with Romanticism), but Tchernikhovsky throughout his career rejected the formal iconoclasm of modernist poetry, its cultivation of free verse and fragmentation – his corona was composed just two years before T. S. Eliot's *The Waste Land*, and the two poems are formally poles apart, though they both reflect something of the trauma of the Great War. For Tchernikhovsky, poetry must always be musical and harmonious, a verbal testimony to the very possibility of harmony in an often seemingly chaotic world. He meant "To the Sun" to be many things – an autobiography of the poet and his sense of being summoned to his vocation (the first word of the poem is "I," in the Hebrew, the verb "to be" conjugated in the first person singular), a grand gesture of reverence to the sun god and the celebration of vitalistic energy embodied in the solar cult, a paean to nature in all the glory of its colors and music and enlivening flux and its perennial powers of growth, an evocation of the multifaceted worship of nature in remote historical eras and in far-flung cultures, an effort to account for the exercise of murderous violence in this overarching picture of cosmic beauty and integrated being, the reaching for a bridge between the scientific investigation of the world and the vision of it through the prism of the many religions and of art, and an affirmation of poetry. All this, I should add, is cast in rather challenging language, with some relatively rare terms and at points somewhat convoluted syntax, a reflection both of Tchernikhovsky's general stylistic bent and of the constraints of the sonnet form. He taps several different historical layers of the Hebrew language, but, following his general predisposition to exploit the dignity and archaic power of biblical Hebrew while avoiding allusion, the language of the Bible predominates. Given the scope of the poem's imaginative achievement, the challenge is one that Hebrew readers should be motivated to embrace.

The boldest conceptual aspect of "To the Sun" is the theological affirmation that runs through it from beginning to end, but it is a theology that is not easy to pin down. The first word of the cycle, as I have noted, is "I-was" (*hayiti*), and the second Hebrew word is *le'lohai* ("to-my-god"). The question is what precisely is meant by "my god" in this poem. The word is equated from the first sonnet onward with the sun (the poem's epigraph, a quotation from the Mishnah Sukkah, is a reference to the ancestors of the rabbinic Jews who worshipped the sun), and the sun is repeatedly conceived as a deity, surely a heretical gesture. I do not think that Tchernikhovsky, a twentieth-century man of scientific training, literally believed in the existence of a sun god in the way the ancient Egyptians, Mesopotamians, and Canaanites did. Nevertheless, he assumed that imagining the sun as a divine presence was the best way to account for the role it played in the large cosmic picture drawn in the cycle of sonnets. There was in his view a poetic truth in how the various ancient cultures conceived the sun, but that poetic truth was also, he felt, an existential one. The evidence of Tchernikhovsky's poetry argues strongly that he had an immediate sensuous experience of the flow of vital energy in the world that for him was exhilarating, enrapturing, and sustaining, and he saw the worship of solar deities in far-flung ancient cultures, north and south, east and west, as fitting responses to that flow of energy. It is this that makes the paganism of "To the Sun" authentic and not merely an ideological gesture or a thematic ploy.

"To the Sun" is at once an intensely personal, autobiographical poem and a poem that traces a sweeping cosmic panorama, and I think that unusual combination embodies the authenticity of its pagan vision of reality. The cycle begins with an evocation of the poet's organic connection with the natural world that he first experienced growing up in the Ukrainian steppes. "I was to my god like a hyacinth or mallow / who has nothing in its world but this sun gleaming bright" (Tchernikhovsky 1990–2003, 1: 204–214).[3] The second of these two flowers, a rare term of problematic identity taken from the Mishnah, evidently indicates a swamp flower that opens to the sun by day. More significantly, the hyacinth is associated

---

[3] My translation of the entire cycle can be found in Alter (2001). In several instances, that translation has been modified for the present article.

in Greek myth with the beautiful young man loved by Apollo, who accidentally kills him with a discus; from his blood the flower springs up, crying out "Ai, Ai." This mythological background is worth recalling because it links the seemingly pacific image of the hyacinth with violence and establishes a connection between the sun and blood that will play out in the subsequent sonnets.

The poet from the outset feels torn in his vocation. The sun god has made him a "priest" and "prophet" but has taken him from the green world of village and field to the great city – clearly, Odessa – where he longs for the sun-drenched blessings of his early years and wonders whether his god may have betrayed him (Sonnet 2). The third sonnet then swings from doubt to affirmation as the speaker senses in himself as poet an ability to envision the world's grandeur wherever he is:

> For me to be the axis of the world that he fashioned,
> Its essence, its utter center, he aboundingly stored up
> For the present and what's to come, for the past that has vanished.
>
> And in the abundance of all charm in color he did not shame me.
> And he abundantly enriched me – by his power, which is strong –
> with symphonies of light and shade, and kohl and rouge and crimson.

Though outside the larger context of the poem, this declaration of being the world's axis might sound like overweening egotism, it is borne out by the cycle – the poet's gift of imagination enables him to encompass the wide world in all its throbbing variety.

The fourth sonnet then introduces the theme of blood hinted at in the hyacinth, linking it, surprisingly, with growing things. Here is the second quatrain:

> And the network of wood-veins in the crosscut of mahogany,
> trees bloodlogged that spurt up in fierceness,
> and hues of near-daybreak and of evening washed in blood
> that sloughs off golden treasures and will never be impoverished.

What is startling here is the substitution of blood for sap in the trees and their association with "fierceness." It is a choice that tells us a great deal about Tchernikhovsky's vitalistic vision of reality. In his sense of things, blood is intimately associated with the sun. The chlorophyll coursing through the veins of tree leaves is what converts the energy of the sun into the power of arboreal growth. Tchernikhovsky substitutes blood in order to underscore the connection between vegetal and animal as living things and also in order to imbue the realm of green things with the vitality of the moving, even ravenous creatures that have actual blood in their veins. Blood also has a long-established cultural association with violence, and, as we shall see, violence plays a role in Tchernikhovsky's vitalistic scheme. In this quatrain, the red of sunrise and sunset is evoked as "washed in blood," which is another reinforcement of the link between blood and sun.

The next sonnet in the sequence will pick up this link in the prayer that begins in the first tercet and concludes in the initial line of the second tercet: "You who dwell in being's recesses, pray, keep for me the blood. / Quench not your fire that you lit in me in your mercy. // Liquid fire guarding fire, one spark from your flames!" The blood flowing through the veins of the trees, these lines suggest, is also the liquid fire with which the divine sun suffuses all things. Tchernikhovsky thus swerves away both radically and consistently from the world-view manifested in the preponderance of biblical texts. The biblical perspective is pre-eminently hierarchical. As it is expressed in the beautiful Psalm 8, there is a splendid harmonious order in which God is at the pinnacle, the divine entourage of celestial beings below Him, and below them man, who holds sway over the other living creatures of the sky, earth, and sea. This hierarchy is in effect a corollary of monotheism. Our poet, by contrast, conjures up a thoroughly anti-hierarchical vision of the world, and one might regard this as the core of his heresy, in which he not so much debates with the values of Judaism (as in "Before the Statue of Apollo") as zestfully moves beyond them. All things participate through a kind of cosmic egalitarianism in the surging life-force. The second quatrain of the eighth sonnet strikingly expresses this idea,

> For beside you there is nothing, O sun that has warmed me!
> Sun-children you are to me, the cocoons hanging high.
> Sun-children – the elephant tree, the peel of each garlic,
> Avatars of light and heat – the combustible coal.

One should note that in rabbinic Hebrew the garlic peel, *qelipat hashum,* is an idiom for something utterly worthless, but in Tchernikhovsky's universe nothing is worthless – there is no great chain of being but rather a vast, intense swarm of things interconnected through the animating energy of the sun. The through-and-through consistency in which this view is maintained is a reflection of what I have been calling Tchernikhovsky's neo-paganism. The corona of sonnets is addressed to one particular deity, but other gods are invoked more than once. Thus, the thirteenth sonnet begins, "A vanished world's idol seized me – there was no escape." The sundry polytheisms cited in the cycle, from ancient Greece and Egypt and Canaan to China and Scandinavia, embody for the poet a fitting sense of the teeming variety of existence, not harmonious in the manner of Psalm 8 but pulsating with energy and vivid in beauty. Astarte, Apollo, the moon goddess, and other deities alongside the sun god are worthy of worship because they are manifestations of this energy and this beauty, even if the poet does not exactly believe in them in the same literal manner that the ancients did.

He is perfectly aware of the disparity between the archaic world he celebrates and his own historical location in 1919. At a couple of points in the cycle, he expresses a troubling doubt as to whether he may have been born in the wrong era. The first quatrain of the eighth sonnet puts this doubt sharply but follows it by a grand affirmation:

> Did I come too soon or was the Rock late who created me?
> Gods are around me and fill all existence.
> The stars are my gods, I pray to them bewitched
> By your faces, light of day and pale moon.

The slightly odd phrase "Did I come too soon" suggests a notion that if the twentieth century lacks all sense of reverence for the cosmic presences, that worship will return at some future time because it is the appropriate, and indeed necessary, response to the nature of existence.

Tchernikhovsky's own historical moment emerges explicitly in the sixth and seventh sonnets. I will mention the former briefly and then turn for a closer look at the crucial seventh sonnet. At the beginning of the sixth sonnet, the poet feels himself struggling in "A realm of sheer doubt, doubt of what is certain." The concrete reference of the realm of doubt is spelled out in the second quatrain:

> And in the upheavals of the living who cling to each decree
> Piercing decree, undermining Shaddai,
> A shield of innocent faith I donned over my battle-garb
> And in the everydayness of each day some bit remained with me.

Shaddai (in the King James Version, "the Almighty") is invoked not as a monotheistic notion but as an archaic-poetic name for the deity: "undermining Shaddai" means subverting the established world order. The sonnet then goes on to evoke the nurturing soil and the stifling warmth of the granary filled with the chaff that the poet recalls from his childhood. In the quatrain just quoted, there is a telescoping of the poet's experience in the Great War and in Odessa in 1919. The battle-garb (*madim*) takes us to his service near the front as a medical officer, which will be the subject of the next sonnet. The chain of decrees cancelling each other reflects not so much the war as the contested Odessa after the Russian Revolution, with the Bolsheviks imposing a series of draconian and sometimes contradictory measures while the struggle between them and the counter-revolutionaries goes on.

Then, in the seventh sonnet Tchernikhovsky introduces himself – his presence is surely more than would be indicated by the primly cautious "speaker in the poem" – as army surgeon:

> When I stood between the living and the already dying
> (What a terrible craft), a sharp scalpel in my hand,
> Some would weep out of joy, some curse me roundly,
> I soaked up the last light in a dying stranger's pupil.
>
> By the thunder of potent cannons rolling through the meadow,
> By the fire flashing in my bunker's pitch-black to me alone
> I traced the last line, erased the living from my page,
> From a bejeweled goblet thus a precious stone is torn out.
>
> And yet in the spark of the guttering eye,
> In the light soaking up light before blanking out forever;
> And yet in that fire-flash burning and shrieking,
>
> In the fire calling to fire that bids disaster and doom –
> It was you who were in them, this your glory that stunned me –
> Did I come too soon, or was the Rock late who created me?

The octave explicitly represents Tchernikhovsky's experience as an army surgeon, perhaps dramatizing it by placing it literally in the trenches – *minharah*, the word I have translated as "bunker," generally means "tunnel," but in this battlefield context would have to designate a trench or bunker. These lines strongly express the anguish of the combat physician, caring for wounded men, many of them grievously wounded and beyond any medical help. Light, elsewhere in the poem equated with the life of the cosmos, is here the last glimmer of life in the eyes of the dying soldier. The cannons thundering over the field are called *tothei on*, and I have chosen "potent" as an English equivalent for the second of those two words because the Hebrew term is associated with sexual potency. The implication of that association will become clear in the concluding tercet of the sonnet.

The horrors of war pose a challenge to the overarching vision of the sonnet cycle, which is, after all, an affirmation of the fertility and vitality of all sorts of life benignly energized by the sun. The poet's response to this challenge is bold and even shocking, and some reflection on what he is saying here is in order. The last spark in the guttering eye is bracketed with the flash of the artillery, "the fire calling to fire that bids disaster and doom." The first phrase here is modeled on the pattern of "abyss calling to abyss" in Psalms. What follows it is the startling assertion "It was you who were in them, this your glory that stunned me." The onomatopoeic force of this line in the Hebrew is arresting. Here is an approximation in transliteration of how Tchernikhovsky meant it to sound (upper-case letters indicate the accented syllables): *hawYEEsaw ATaw BAWM, zeh HODkhaw HamawMAWni*, with *BAWM*, "in them," in the middle of the line echoing the thunder of the cannons. But what could Tchernikhovsky possibly mean when he sees the presence of the sun god in the flash of artillery fire? I do not think that he is adopting a view like that of the Italian Futurist poet Filippo Marinetti, who famously, or notoriously, celebrated the orgy of violence he witnessed in the Great War as a theater of beauty. Granted, Tchernikhovsky was a militant Zionist, and on occasion the militancy would be given pronounced expression, especially after his immigration to Palestine in 1931. What he envisages, however, in the devastating power of these modern weapons is something quite removed from what some have excoriated as "Jewish fascism." As we have seen, pulsating energy, linked to the sun, is the key to the cosmos as he sees it. It is an energy that produces life, impels action and enterprise. It is also an energy that can be wild as well as sustaining, that knows no moral restraints. The closest poetic expression in Hebrew to this sense of reality is the Voice from the Whirlwind at the end of the Book of Job. "To the Sun" employs no allusions to Job, in keeping with Tchernikhovsky's general avoidance of biblical allusion, but there is a certain kinship between his vision at this point and that most heterodox of all biblical texts. The panorama of creation unfurled in the Voice from the Whirlwind is one of great beauty that also incorporates elements of violence: the eagle on the crag brings back prey for his chicks who "lap up blood, / where the slain are, there he is," and even the gentle gazelles do not merely foal but "burst forth" (*tifalahna*) with their babes, a verb Tchernikhovsky enthusiastically adopts in the eighth sonnet for she-jackals giving birth to their whelps. For the Job-poet, creation is dazzling to contemplate but also uncanny, defying the conventional moral norms of humankind, incorporating seeming ruthlessness and explosive force as well as harmony. Tchernikhovsky proposes something akin: violence, and especially the insane collective violence of warfare, is terrifying, appalling; yet the energies manifested in it are continuous with the energies that plow fields, erect grand structures, build civilizations, engender life in all its multifarious forms. When the devastating artillery roars and flashes, "It was you who were in them." The cannon-fire is frightening and destructive, yet it is also a kind of soul-trying epiphany – "this your glory that stunned me."

The sun till now has figured in the cycle as a nurturing, beneficent god – never, by the way, called Apollo in order to make room for the Mesopotamian Shamash, the Egyptian Re, and other avatars of the solar deity. But Tchernikhovsky would have been perfectly aware that the various gods often exhibit fierce aspects, like the Canaanite warrior-goddess Anat, the Greek Ares, and the major Canaanite weather-god Baal, who rides in a chariot of clouds, hurling thunderbolts; and this fierceness, an intrinsic component of the reality we inhabit, was also, he imagined, a property of the fiery god of the sun. Thus, quite strikingly, the sestet of the next sonnet joins birth and war in a grand cosmic chorus:

> And all existence becomes a voice of prayer, the prayer of all.
> To you the mother jackals call as they burst forth with their whelps,
> To you the battle trumpet as light breaks in the camp.
> The suns in the sphere above as the voice sweeps them up.
> In the chorus of the infinite I'll sing and not be still:
> In my heart the dew yet lodges that descends on Edom's steppes.

Tchernikhovsky's music of the spheres is not the medieval monotheistic one (though he uses a term from medieval astronomy, *galgal*, for "sphere") – there is a cosmic melody, but it incorporates the sound of the battle trumpet summoning soldiers to arms. And in a move characteristic of the imaginative fluidity of the cycle, the last line of this sonnet pivots from a spatial scanning of the celestial realm to a temporal move three millennia backward to dew falling on ancient Edom, picked up in the ninth sonnet when peoples of the desert respond in worship and song to the sacred presence of the moon and stars.

With this transition, the poet moves back in time in the ninth and tenth sonnets, as his ear picks up the melodies of "primeval lays," *neginot minei qedem*, as he imagines each people bowing to the mystery of night and the desert, his own people, when in exile, preserving something of this primeval reverence in its monthly ritual of sanctifying the new moon. The tenth sonnet spins out a narrative of the gods in which the insistent monotheistic deities of Judaism and then Islam drive out the many gods of the Mediterranean world and of Scandinavia to the north. And yet, the poet affirms an irresistible necessity for the gods of nature because it is they who manifest the true character of reality. Thus the tenth sonnet concludes:

> And yet there's a vision ... an age that will fashion, like the refiner,
> Its god to come – and we shall worship him in gladness –
> For my heart utters song to Orion and the sun.

The eleventh sonnet then offers an experiential grounding for this affirmation: the poet will pour no libation to the imageless "god of the vulgar people" because he has been swept up in "a wave of sacred ecstasy," "joyous trembling ... in the flood of heartlife taking part in all mystery." From this point, as the cycle builds toward its grand conclusion, it swings in the twelfth sonnet both back in time to the prehistoric era and forward to the end of all ages:

> ... till time's ending when the earth's climate changes, and its forest fragrance fades
> With the remnant of structures on poles, rot's survivors,
> And in the graves of great princes, amphoras and jars.

Against this panorama of evanescence, he imagines the fire of the sun god, which cannot be extinguished, surging up again in every particle of the living world from the brain of the genius to the mosquito's buzzing song. The last two sonnets before the concluding one then leap from the ancient realm of idols – "the sun-shrines of On," "Danite icons," "sacred groves" – to the world as modern science understands it – "The minute atom's permutations in gold and in tin" – which equally registers the animating presence of the sun, however different its language from that of the archaic cults.

The fifteenth sonnet, in accordance with the requirement of the corona, is a recapitulation of all the first lines of the cycle in the order they have appeared. This artifice of conclusion has a splendid resonance here that may not be the case for many other coronas. The fourteen sonnets, after all, have conducted a poetic voyage that carries us from the individual experience of the poet in his native rural setting through eons and across seas and continents. Thus, the first quatrain of the concluding sonnet evokes the growth of the poet in fields of golden grain, rain and fog, open to nature's symphonies of light and shade. The second quatrain introduces his experience in the war as he clings to the mesmerizing song of every nation. The first tercet carries us back to the ancient world with its gods that have nurtured the poet. Finally, the concluding tercet of the fifteenth sonnet and of the whole cycle traces the link between the burgeoning of vegetable and fruit and "a vanished world's idol" that has ineluctably seized the poet, leaving him at the very end to wonder – the cycle concludes with a question mark – whether he may be a worshipper of the "the last age's icon in the kingdom of the idol."

The architectonic structure of "To the Sun" in a sense bears witness to the authenticity of the pagan world-view that is articulated in the cycle. The address throughout to the sun god and the invocation of the sundry gods of Canaan, Egypt, Mesopotamia, and of other more remote regions are not isolated flourishes. The way that Tchernikhovsky is able to make sense of reality is by seeing it everywhere as the manifestation of these multifarious divine presences. He surely did not believe in a sun god or a moon goddess as an actual personal entity, any more than a sophisticated monotheist would believe in the one and only God as an old man with a beard speaking perfectly intelligible human language to his adherents. What he did believe, intoxicated as he was with the enchantment of nature and the potency of the life-force in all things, from garlic peel to the roar of cannons, was that the many gods were the most plausible representations of this wondrous reality, giving it faces and, indeed, bodies that monotheism had lamentably erased. The remarkable thing about this paganizing project is that it is consummated in Hebrew, which makes it a vigorously Jewish expression of heresy. The rich language of the poem, as I have noted, is by and large conspicuously biblical, although there are interwoven elements of post-biblical

Hebrew (more rabbinic than modern). But the poem consistently builds a world that is antithetical to what one finds in the Bible, advancing on its pagan trajectory almost as if the Bible had never existed. Tchernikhovsky would afterward try again, never with quite the same success, to reach for this golden ring of the sun, coming closest in the long cycle of poems about bees (and much else), *Ama dedahava,* that he wrote in the early 1940s toward the end of his life. "To the Sun" remains his ultimate achievement, an imaginative integration of disparate realms through an exquisitely wrought sequence of interlocked rhymed poems that is a profession of faith in the sustaining light of life at an ominous moment of historical darkness.

Bibliography

Alter, Robert. "Saul Tchernikhovsky: To the Sun: A Corona of Sonnets." *Literary Imagination* 3.2 (2001): 159–178.

Bassok, Ido. *Layofi vanisgav libo er.* Jerusalem: Carmel, 2017.

Tchernikhovsky, Shaul. *Kol kitvei Shaul Tchernikhovsky.* 8 vols. Tel Aviv: Am Oved, 1990–2003.

David Suchoff
Heretical Canines: Kafka's "*Forschungen eines Hundes*" (Investigations of a Dog)

> If the earlier generations were like angels, we are like men; if they are like men,
> we are like donkeys.
> *Shabbat* 112b, Fromer, *Organismus des Judentums*

The resolve of Kafka's research dog, in his story of 1922, is to "water the ground as much as you can," in keeping with the sayings of the "first fathers" of his tradition. "In this opinion," as he puts it, "I am at one with the vast majority of the dog community," a position he takes since he "must firmly dissociate myself from all heretical views on this point," and so introduces the theme of what he calls "*ketzerische Ansichten*," or the "heretical viewpoints" of non-standard scholarly positions in his text (Kafka 1971, 287; 1992, 437).[1] This heresy concerns concrete nourishment: a fact that did not escape some of Kafka's first Hebrew-speaking readers, as Kafka's childhood friend Hugo Bergmann recalled from pre-state Palestine, where German-speaking readers were offended by the "*Befremden*," or "estrangement" of its tongue-in-cheek portrayal of canonical forms (Bergmann 1972, 4). Kafka's use of the "dog," in this early Jewish reception, with references to the "spells, songs, and ritual movements" of his community did not miss what Benjamin Harshav in *The Meaning of Yiddish* later called the story's "veiled allegory on the Jewish condition," including the role of heresy in its constitution. "Questioning itself," as Harshav notes, and traditional forms, was Kafka's canine mode for using Jewish material in translation. "Investigations," as it moves from the singing canines at its start to the hunting dogs of its conclusion, places heresy – the role of otherness in traditions – at the center of the most confessional of Kafka's late-life works (Harshav 1990, 115).

Kafka's canine "Investigations" makes heresy felt through the rule that governs this research account: its culture never overtly references any presence of a controlling master's world. Sacvan Bercovitch wisely calls the text a "parable of interpretation as mystification," since the story's frame assumes that its dogs can "in no way perceive human beings," whose superiority is called into question (Bercovitch 1993, 3; Winkelman 1967, 204). At the same time, Kafka's

---

[1] I would like to thank Professor Susan Mizruchi of Boston University for her helpful commentary on this essay. I am also grateful to Professor Ben Fallaw for his incisive reading of an earlier version.

narrator-scholar uses a dispassionate tone to come to terms with his own society's reproduction of inhumanity, in both its higher and lower realms. Through this mask of innocence, "Investigations of a Dog" allows its dog-researcher to act in anything but a canine fashion: offering a heretical view of the Jewish cultural and political movements of his time. "*Lufthunde*" or "air-dogs" suggests lap-dogs or human pets, as well as the Yiddish expression – "*Luftmensch*" – for the beggar who lives on nothing, and hence as thinkers unaware of the implicit dependence in which they are kept. Meanwhile, the dogs who "water the earth" believe their urination and territory-marking, like quasi-Zionists, is the more effective mode of bringing forth the nourishment that sustains the canine community as a whole.[2] In keeping with Kafka's idea of a "small literature" as a forgiving form of self-criticism, this aspect of the story offers a quiet parody of Simon Dubnow's Yiddishist ideal of "internal autonomy" for the Yiddish-speaking Jews of Europe, which is quietly satirized alongside the competing ideal of a return to the Land (Dubnow quoted in Harshav 1993, 34; Kafka 1948, 148).

At its more general level, "Investigations of a Dog" exposes and rejects the nationalism of canonical writing, moving from the particularity of Kafka's Jewish sources to a general re-consideration of the multiple voices from which all traditions are formed.[3] This larger narrative shows the research dog how the principles of mastery function: by swallowing minor voices and digesting them, then fencing off linguistic and literary territory as belonging to one national culture alone. In this broader trajectory of the story, "*Bodenbearbeitung*," or "preparation of the earth," signifies the myth of a separate national tradition the narrator learns to question, and finally de-identify with from a heretical point of view. A similar scene takes place in "Ithaka," the homecoming chapter of Joyce's *Ulysses*, where the Jewish but non-circumcised Leopold Bloom and the culturally heterodox Stephen Dedalus perform a ritual of co-urination in the garden, outside of the latter's Dublin home (Joyce 1986 [1922], 577). At the culmination of Kafka's canine homecoming, the narrator encounters a troupe of musical canines – led by a "*Jagdhund*," or hunting dog – who spur him into joining their performance, and enacting a ritual of national self-purgation of his own. After this visceral

---

[2] For an account of these canine meanings in this national context, see Bruce (2007), 188–95.
[3] Other canonical texts where dogs speak against their masters include Baudelaire's "chiens saltimbanques"—canine acrobats—and later more disputatious canines, often hiding in the mask of servility: from Cervantes "The Dialogue of the Dogs," to E.T.A. Hoffmann's *Nachricht von den neuesten Schicksalen des Hundes Berganza* (1814), to Heine's "Disquisition of the Dogs" and on to canines who expose a de-colonizing process in Samuel Beckett's work. See Chambers (1971), 313–314 and 317; and David Suchoff, "De-Colonizing Dialect: Beckett's Palestinian and Irish Canines," forthcoming.

expulsion of his previous training, the ending of "Investigations of a Dog" leaves the researcher transformed. Kafka's narrator begins to study foreign voices as the hidden but nourishing center of literary and cultural traditions. He discovers heretical music, that life-giving force at the heart of canonical norms.[4]

1 Partial Thievery: The Heresy of Canonical Creation

> Why do I not do as the others: live in harmony with my people, and accept in silence whatever disturbs the harmony (*Eintracht*)?
> Kafka, "Investigations of a Dog"

The specifically Jewish tradition of heresy evoked in "Investigation of a Dog" appears in Kafka's diary entry of October 29, 1911, on the Talmudic passages that explicate *pardes*, an acronym that also suggests the original garden, as a paradise of linguistic fertility (Kafka 1948, 96; 1994b, 163–64; *Hagiga* 14b; *Tosefta Hagiga* 2:3–4). In the Talmudic model of interpretation, the Hebrew consonants *P-R-D-S* pronounce the flourishing garden of interpretation that canonical tradition imagines in its allegory of reading: the Hebrew for *P* stands for "*peshat* or plain meaning," the *R* for "*remez* or hint, sometimes designating allegorical interpretations," the *D* for "*derash*, or homiletic exposition," and the *S* for "*sod* or secret (namely symbolic) interpretation of the text" (Idel 2002, 430). In the Talmudic parable, four sages enter the "garden" or *pardes*: Rabbi Akiba, the canonical sage, along with Ben Azzai, Ben Zoma, and Elisha ben Abuya, the Talmud's heretic, also known as "*akher*," or the "other" in the tradition's terms. Kafka reports having received his version of this tradition from Yitzkhak Löwy, the Yiddish theater actor whose troupe Kafka helped bring to Prague, and whose production he famously introduced in his "Introductory Talk on the Yiddish Language." In Kafka's diary, however, the Talmudic version of *akher* is changed. While the canonical text has only Rabbi Akiba entering the garden and leaving intact – "R. Akiba went up whole, and came down whole" (*Hag*. 2:3–4) – Kafka effectively places *akher*, or the heretic, within another character. Rather than describing Elisha ben Abuya as having "cut the shoots," and figuratively halting the growth of tradition, he replaces him with Eliezer: a sage who becomes a "*Freidenker*," or free-thinker, in Kafka's text (Kafka 1948, 96; 1994b, 163).

---

4 The idea of "betrayal" as "*Tradierbarkeit*," in Walter Benjamin and Gershom Scholem's notion of tradition, is discussed in a related manner in Bielik-Robson (2019), 10, 21–22.

Karl Grözinger suggests convincingly that this version was a conflation of traditional elements. In Kafka's version, Eliezer is said to have become a "free-thinker" at "age forty," rendering him similar to the most canonical figure in Kafka's parable: Rabbi Akiba himself who, as his diary accurately notes, "had not begun his studies" until that age, and who "achieved complete knowledge" nonetheless (Grözinger 1994b, 37–38). Kafka's version of *pardes*, that garden of infinite interpretation, rethinks the role of *akher*, or the other in the process, as heretical knowledge ceases to be "other," or a scapegoated source of illicit knowledge, at least in any locatable human sense. "Complete knowledge," in the canonical figure of Akiba, finds a different kind of parallel voice: as Elisha becomes his hidden alter ego who, at the "age of forty," both recapitulates and revises the classical development that Akiba's non-scholarly beginnings set forth. The *sod*, or secret reading in Kafka's model of interpretation, is transformed in the process, as the figurative "cutting of the shoots" that charges the "other" with destruction of tradition is seen in a different light. The "other," or *akher*, in Kafka's critical constellation, is represented instead as hidden within a version of traditional reading. The "free-thinker," in his model of interpretation, is the scholar who very much resembles Kafka's research dog in a crucial respect: a figure who carries heretical, already digested knowledge forward in his transmission of the traditional texts.

"*Forschungen eines Hundes*" develops this notion of internalized heresy with a quiet humor. In terms of *pardes*, the "*Resh*" or Remez level of interpretation – that of allegory, as Harshav suggests – makes heretical knowledge the foundation, or open *sod*, or secret of the human, in Kafka's canine world. The "question" of "what the canine race nourished itself upon," and hence the founding question of the story's "investigations," centers on an already swallowed form of difference. An absent humanity thus appears in the text in the idea of "others" who – as a form of pre-digested heresy – signify a nourishment that passes through the mouth without investigation: "with slop in your snout," as the story's adage has it, "all questions disappear for now."[5] That the other's contributions are swallowed, and then neglected, is the story's governing – and literalized – metaphor, as well as its unspoken rule for an eloquence that originates from above as well as below. As "Eliezer" in Kafka's reading of *pardes* has figuratively swallowed *akher*, the heretical other, so the research dog of Kafka's "investigations" – while becoming a "free-thinker" in the process – seeks to confront an otherness his "community" of "scholars" as

---

5 Kafka (1992): "*Hast du den Fraß im Maul, so hast du für diesemal alle Fragen gelöst,*" 462, my translation; cf. Kafka (1971), 303.

well as average canines refuse to acknowledge, or even see. "The basic fiction on which this whole story and its interpretation depend," in Winkelman's sense, is also the quite visible process of submission to unnamed masters, on whom the nourishment and sustenance of the canine tradition of scholarship most often depends (Winkelman 1967, 204).

This absence of humanity in "Investigations of a Dog" therefore works in many different ways at once. It is identified with an unspeakable harm and unspoken exploitation: the community is ruled by "laws that are not those of the dog world, but are actually directed against it," and which go without an explicit name (Kafka 1971, 280). Whether a materialist "scholar," or a cultural determinist in the story's terms, canines share an implicit agreement on what counts as heretical honesty. As a result, the "mystery of food," as Winkelman calls it, and whether it appears "on the ground" or "descends from above," in either case rests on a common blindness to naturalized forms of otherness suffered by the "childlike" narrator, as well as by any "old dog" (Winkelman 1967, 205; Kafka 1971, 286). Such obedience appears as the consequent affliction of every national and linguistic tradition, whose forms of sustenance, since Herder, have been conceived of as embodying a "sometimes neglected" but unique "ancestral inheritance" or *"längst bessessenem Gut,"* as the story calls it, which "must laboriously be rehabilitated anew" (*ergänzt werden muß*) (Kafka 1971, 287; 1992, 436–37). In so far as the narrator eats and "waters the earth" with his own impurities, as canine law demands, his approach to "heretical views" is limited. He assumes, in other words, that his cultural – and figuratively agricultural – sustenance has been kept within the borders, in this Germanic sense of *"Boden,"* of his own linguistic ground. "I began to inquire into the question of what the canine race nourished itself upon," the narrator reports, questioning this implicit boundary, and so becomes a form of Kafka's *Freidenker*, a free-thinker who undergoes Judaism's *Gilgul Ha-Nefashot*, or the transmigration of souls, from Elisha ben Abuya's human form (Kafka 1971, 286; 1992, 436).

The hidden *akher*, in this cultural sense, is already embodied in the *"Forscher,"* or the investigator who begins to discover these sustaining contributions of the foreign voice within himself. "All knowledge, the totality of all questions and all answers," he begins, in this translation of the *homo mensura* – man as the measure of all things – doctrine, "is contained in the dog" (Kafka 1971, 289–90; 1992, 441). Knowledge that is heretical to pronounce in its original accents – as this translation from the Latin suggests – begins a process of revelation in the story, as otherness is gradually uncovered as present within the community's own linguistic norms. Kafka's model for this process in minor literary terms was the Yiddish theater: in particular, a performance of Gordin's *Elisha ben Avuya* on

October 28, 1911, given by a theater troupe he helped bring to Prague.[6] Sparked by the play, his diary then reconstructs the Talmudic parable of such appropriation: a process in which the "other" is treated as heretical and shunned, while traditional authority learns from – and in a manner plagiarizes – the material it deems heretical in translated form. "Once, on a Saturday," as Kafka's diary entry of 28 October, 1911 retells the parable – when the religious scholar was forbidden to ride on horseback, and his number of steps was severely limited, "Rabbi Meier followed on foot, the Talmud in his hand" (Kafka 1948, 96). In this recounting of *Hagiga* 2:1, the bearer of official commentary – the interpretation of the law, as well as the law of interpretation – stays within the nation's bounds. "Aher was riding his horse on the Sabbath, going on his way," as the other bringing new viewpoints to tradition, and as Kafka accurately notes: "R. Meir was walking after him to learn Torah from his mouth."[7]

Kafka's "Investigations" deconsecrate the sovereignty of this magic, as the tradition reveals its intellectual sustenance as obtained from heretical, non-canonical mouths. As Rabbi Meir in the Talmudic parable keeps his steps carefully within the bounds of tradition, so the research dog sniffs out the path of otherness, while remaining within the canonical prescriptions of his community. The story traces the shape of what remains *akher* or heretical in the narrative of an autonomous tradition, while the classical story remains on the path, or halakha, of normative interpretive terms. In modern terms, this gambit could be called a form of cultural appropriation, in a Talmudic form of borrowing the other's voice. "And from this walk," Kafka's diary continues, "emerged a symbolic demand, and the reply to it. Come back to your people, said Rabbi Meyer," a gesture that signifies his translation of akher's teachings for the tradition (Kafka 1948, 96). The *sod*, or "symbolic" demand, as Kafka calls it in the terms of *pardes*, is the same kind of translation that occurs in "Investigations of a Dog." Knowledge and sustenance appropriated from the other of human traditions are translated in a plagiarism of zoological proportions, while the foreign source of that otherness magically disappears. "*Denn was gibt es außer den Hunden?*" as Kafka's narrator asks – "What is there actually besides our own species?" – is less a question than a statement of the mode in which tradition hides its exploitation of the other's voice (Kafka 1971, 289; 1992, 441).

This heretical reference, of course, to sources outside a canine tradition also tells us that the nagging questions of Kafka's narrator are anything but

---

6 See Beck (1971), 215.
7 Cf. Kafka's version with the one quoted and discussed in Rubenstein (1999), 67. A version of this Talmudic material that Kafka saw performed also appears in Gordin (1999 [1910]), 34 ff. Translations from the Yiddish text are my own.

contained. His interest in art is spurred by a group of canines who re-stage his people's scholarly and folkloric practices, recapturing the foreignness behind these canonical rules. "Great magicians though they might be," as the researcher describes their musical performance, "*das Gesetz galt auch für sie*," or "the law was valid for them too" (Kafka 1971, 283; 1992, 431). The self-exposure the narrator notes could be called the partial magic of smaller traditions, described by Kafka in his diary entry of December 25, 1911. These practices of national cultures became acutely visible in the dynamics of "small" or minor literatures, in which the rules of more powerful literary traditions are brought into view. "What in great literature," as Kafka described the heretical sources its tradition, "goes on down below, constituting a not indispensable cellar of the structure, here," in the writing of a small people, "takes place in the in the full light of day" (Kafka 1948, 150).[8] "*Diese Hunde*," as the narrator calls this troupe of vaudeville dogs, display precisely the appropriation and cancelation by the canon of the material it captures from them: "blowing fanfares so near that they seemed far away (Ferne) and nearly inaudible" (Kafka 1971, 282; 1992, 429). And in this transitory art that "*vergeht*" – "these dogs committed a serious offence against the Law" (*diese Hunde vergingen sich gegen das Gesetz*) – these performers "*ver*," or un-do, the *sod*, or secrecy about the foreign that allows a canine society to persist in its illusion as an essentially separate realm.

These dogs who were "violating the law" – placed before it, as in "*Vor dem Gesetz*," Kafka's most famous parable – are also fulfilling the exposure function of a minor literary traditions: resembling in part the *Lufthunde*, or soaring air-dogs of the story. Kafka's German word "Lufthunde" is a loan-translation of the Yiddish term "*Luftmensch*," meaning in small literary terms the *batlonim*, or beggars, who live from "air," and at the expense of the community. Such canine practices illuminate the otherness – and the original destitution – of dominant traditions: *Luftmensch* can mean "charlatan, idle boaster," or "an irresponsible person," with lofty claims exposing an impoverished, dependent state (Winkelman 1967, 210). "The strong light of the canonical," as Gershom Scholem calls it, consists of its ability to hide its translated, as well as well as stolen origins, which then appear as "*das Licht, das zerbricht*" – that is, "the light that breaks" in exposing a spectrum of otherness of which the tradition was built (Biale 1985, 88). Kafka's diary thus reports that the heretic responds to "Come back to your people" with a "*Wortspiel*," or play on words, which – like "*Vor dem Gesetz*," or "Before the Law" – suggests that the "other," as he is called, has never left (Kafka

---

[8] Kafka's notion of "small literatures" exposing the dynamics of major literary processes is discussed in Suchoff (2012), 29 ff.

1948, 96). Canine music plays out this verbal *Spiel* of tradition, in which a multitude of foreign sources tells the fuller story of a tradition which, like Akiva, was impoverished at its start.

2 Necessary Others: The Music of Cultural Resistance

> Hast thou found honey? Eat so much as is sufficient for thee, lest thou be filled therewith, and vomit it.
> Proverbs 27:16

The other tradition of Elisha ben Abuya standing behind the research of Kafka's narrator concerns one of Israel's "Ten Martyrs": the translator figure known as "Hutzpit Ha-Meturgeman." This story was available to Kafka as part of the larger narrative of Elisha ben Abuya he learned about: since it was also performed in Prague, in Gordin's Yiddish, a performance he attended and commented upon – which is to say in the writing of a small people that appears on the far-from-classic stage. The heretic explains his departure from canonical tradition as a response to empire, and ultimately to translation as a resistant force. While the Romans "slaughtered Akiva and all of his students like sheep," ben Abuya concludes his explanation to the head of the House of Study with the fate of the "Meturgeman," a term defined in a source Kafka possessed as a synonym for one of the "Amoraim," or latter-day sages: "Amora=Meturgeman=*Dolmetscher oder Erklärer*," according to Kafka's source, with the latter meaning "translator," glossed as an exegete, or literally an "explainer" of the law (Gordin 1999 [1910], 142). Kafka's emphasis on interpretation – as a form of translation – follows this anti-imperial agenda of Kafka's animal stories: of re-claiming the authority of the colonized voice. Thus, where "Rotpeter" (Red Peter) in "Report for an Academy" will report that he was looking only for an "*Ausweg*," or "way out" from the condition of conquest, he is at the same time transmitting a more open view of dominant tradition, by defining its authority as based in its translation of an earlier and foreign source (Kafka 1994a, 301).

Faced with the "*Notwendigkeit*," or "necessity" of a tradition based on angelic messengers, "*der einzige Ausweg bot die Auslegung*," – that is, "the only way out was offered by interpretation," according to Fromer's *Organismus des Judentums*: "now I am reading Fromer," Kafka notes in 1912 (Kafka 1948, 173). Elisha ben Abuya represents a similar escape from imperial authority in Gordin's drama: particularly in his reaction to the fate of otherness in the person of Hutzpit, the translator who dies a brutal death under Roman rule. Explaining this tradition in terms of imperial crime and punishment, Elisha gives an early version of the task of the translator, one of the sages who is murdered by the Romans while trying to keep a minor voice alive:

> After Rav Hutzpit spent his entire life expounding and clarifying the meaning and significance of the Law [Torah], and the Romans ripped out his tongue and threw it to the dogs, why didn't He send his thunder and lightning crashing down, to punish the hangmen and murderers himself! (Gordin 1999, 40, my translation)

Heresy emerges, as the Other declares in this Yiddish drama, during the incipient consolidation of a "new" testament, or imperium: killing the translator, Roman authority defines the leftovers of the foreign sources it conquers and subordinates as fare fit only for the dogs. This ripped-out "tongue," as an image of the translator's voice, signifies what Kafka meant in his statement that a small literature "creates a literary history out of the records of its dead writers," a comment that stands for the underlying force of his texts as a whole (Kafka 1971, 149). Remnants of the past treated as fit only for canine humiliation, as this passage suggests, can be read from the perspective of *akher*, or the other. In this dogged voice, Kafka's source taught him a writing that could be used against imperial conquest, and to indict its "hangmen" and "murderers" instead.

It is this heretical tongue that nurtures the hidden force of a dominated people: clever enough to know, as Walter Benjamin said of the "tradition of oppressed," which of its voices must be preserved for history, when survival in the present makes such truths impossible to speak (Benjamin 1968c, 257). "I must admit that I was less surprised by the artistry of the seven dogs – it was incomprehensible to me," the research dog notes from his beaten-down position, "and quite definitely beyond my capacities – than by their courage in facing so openly the music of their own making," as they re-make the dominant culture in forms of their own. Such an art – "I was a child," he realizes of his first efforts to comprehend it – must emerge from its definition by the colonizing masters: from the assumption imposed on smaller literatures and languages, that they are unworthy of artistic expression at all. "Canine artistry" therefore makes the narrator feel "as if I myself were one of the musicians, instead of their victim" (*Opfer*), a statement of how much he has already liberated himself from this distorted vision of minority art (Kafka 1971, 282; 1992, 430). "I only want to be stimulated by the silence that rises up around me as the ultimate answer," he concludes in response, so that the submissive attitudes of his fellow canines can be fully undone.

"*Wunderte ich mich*," or "I was astounded," is therefore the way the research dog expresses his astonishment at this multiple perspective. Courage, or "*Mut*" as Kafka puts it in German, is expressed at the "*Wunder*," or miraculous absence of any angels, necessary or otherwise, that fail to erase the minor artists of his tale. According to rabbinic narrative, and the Yiddish drama that Kafka viewed in Prague, Elisha the Other or *Akher* overcame precisely such censorship as a "gnostic"; that is, a believer in "two powers in heaven," and thus a heresy in the House of Study and its terms. In this version, "heretical books fell from Elisha's lap when he arose to leave the Beit Midrash," translatable here as the house of literary interpretation, committing a sin of exposure in both a linguistic and cross-cultural sense (Goshen-Gottstein 2000, 105). Subsequent scholarship, as Goshen-Gottstein notes, has construed these books of the parable quite broadly: "the heretical books are taken as Greek philosophical works (Jellinek and Back), as Philonic speculation (Siegfried), as gnostic works (Grätz), or as Christian books (Heimann)," any one of which would expose trans-linguistic connections meant to be silenced, especially at the site where students are tested on their knowledge, and the cultural continuity of the canon is assured (Goshon-Gottstein 2000, 105). Rather than scorn this tradition, Kafka's "*Musikanten*" claim the "*Mut*" – otherwise known as *chutzpah* – to re-perform the canonical definitions of their culture, and grasp its co-formation through foreign terms (Kafka 1971, 282; 1992, 430).

"What they produced," or "*was sie erzeugten,*" as the research dog states, requires that such *nerve* remain under the surface: at least in a linguistic sense. In order to come to terms – "*sich auszusetzen*" is the reflexive German verb Kafka uses – with their own artistic potential, these performers must "set out," and re-capture strangeness in their own performance, and figuratively begin their culture anew. In the process, an account that is "*völlig*" and "*offen,*" or "complete" and "open," can be given of what tradition has always hidden, and what small literatures have always exposed to critical view (Kafka 1971, 282; 1992, 430). The silence that remains an integral part of their performance points to a failed erasure in this sense: the musicality that pertains to canines – "*nur dem Hundegeschlecht verliehen,*" or "bestowed only upon the canine race" – satirizes such notions of racial enclosure, by acting out the foreignness very much alive in their art. The trumpeted norms of any dominant culture appear boldly in their performance, while making clear their overwriting of the other's voice. The "*noch Fanfaren blasende Musik,*" or coveted harmonies "still blaring in fanfare," thus permit the audience to detect "*kaum hörbar,*" or "scarcely audible," sounds of these non-national traditions that the research dog easily perceives (Kafka 1971, 282; 1992, 430).

One such "*hörbar*" voice of the other in Kafka's sources concerned Metatron, the recording angel in heaven, whose punishment Elisha ben Abuya, or *akher*, the tradition's audible other, brings about. Fromer's version in *Organismus des Judentums*, Kafka's source, describes how Elisha sees "*den obersten der Engel,*" or the most exalted of the angels, and explains the dual scene of writing that ensues:

He saw Metatron, who had been given permission to sit and record the merits of Israel. Upon which he (the other) declared: 'it is taught that there is no sitting in heaven, no posterior and no back, and that tiredness is not present. Could there possibly be two powers in heaven?

At this they led Metatron out and gave him sixty fiery lashes. To him they declared: why did you not rise when you saw him (the other)?

Then permission was given him (Metatron or another Angel) to erase the merits of the other.[9]

Er sah Metatron, dem die Erlaubnis erteilt war, zu sitzen, und die Tugenden Israels aufzuschreiben. Da sagte er (Acher): "Es wird gelehrt, das oben kein sitzen, keinen Hinterteil und keinen Rücken gibt und keine Müdigkeit vorhanden ist. Vielleicht gibt es gar zwei Herrschaften im Himmel?

Darauf führten sie Metatron heraus und gaben ihm sechzig feurige Prügel. Sie sagten zu ihm, warum bist du ihm (Acher) nicht aufgestanden, also du ihn gesehen hast?

Dann wurde ihm (Metatron oder einem anderen Engel) die Erlaubnis erteilt, die Tugenden Achers auszulöschen. (Fromer 1909, 62)

While "two powers in heaven" – the gnostic heresy – cannot exist according to canonical doctrine in this version of parts of Tractate *Hagiga* 15a–b, the speech of *acher* portrays heavenly writing as a darkly comic act of multiple meanings. However perfectly the scene of writing is arranged, the ascent of Elisha exposes heaven's hidden plurality: with the "other" present, the recording angel is placed in an impossible situation no matter how he behaves at his desk. Were he to rise and show his fealty to the Highest One, he might not only write with less clarity – "God forbid," as Elisha says in the fuller Aramaic – but act as if hailing the arrival of the "other," when writing his human version of the "merits of Israel," and hence a nominally nationalistic text (Goshen-Gottstein 2000, 106).

Attempted erasure stands at the center of this parable: as Metatron – the power behind the throne – produces his script, his failure to wipe the other's story from history proves inevitable, since it is structured into the two permissions—רשויות—that ultimately tell the foreigner's tale. The first "*Erlaubnis*" he read of permits "sitting" in heaven – going against the demand that the Highest One be continually honored, as Elisha notes. One consequence of this "permission" suggests that writing cannot be accomplished without resting, and hence rendering invisible what Kafka's source calls the "*Hinterteil*" or "backside." This reference, of course, has already backfired: an otherness intimate to the writer is not only present, as the imagery suggests, but also persists as the grounding condition of angelic writing being produced. The second "permission" granted the writing angel is to scorch the merits of the Other from his account of the "merits

---

[9] For a modern translation of this passage, see Rubenstein (1999), 66. Here, I have translated as literally as possible the German version that Kafka read in Fromer (1909).

of Israel": a clause that already bites back at Metatron, as censorship only reinforces the position of the foreign within national voice. This "permission," as Goshon-Gottstein notes, is already "secondary and playful" in the Talmudic parable: since the erasure of the "gnostic" possibility of "two powers in heaven" is simply realized in another area of the text. These "two permissions ... granted Metatron" – to sit on his *Hinterteil*, and to scorch the merits of the "other" from his writing – thus make it possible to assert, with national and textual honesty, that "two domains exist on high" after all (Goshon-Gottstein 2000, 111).

This heresy is reflected in Kafka's "Investigations," as his researcher translates nationalism into his own recalcitrant and doggish voice. "The hardest bones, containing the richest marrow," as the narrator puts it, "can be conquered only by a united crunching of the teeth of all dogs"; a "figure of speech," as the narrator himself calls it, that imagines the "*Mark*," or blood-producing essence of a nation, in explicitly narcissistic terms. "If I remain faithful to this metaphor," he admits, "I want to compel all dogs to assemble together, I want the bones to crack upon under the pressure of their collective preparedness ... while all by myself, quite alone, I lap up the marrow." Kafka's canine imagines such loyalty as linguistic egotism, and therefore as an "*ugeheuerlich*," or monstrous dream. Such collective definition is imagined as deadly: not just as premature autopsy of language of the nation, but as search for the *Mark* or essence of its expression: as a "*Versammlung*" or assembly of canine mouths that would remain "*innerhalb des Bildes*," or within any pre-decided and limiting picture that would define the language and traits they share (Kafka 1971, 291).[10]

And as Metatron could not write his nation's "merits" without a *Hinterteil* noticed by the "other," Kafka's scholarly narrator rejects any wish for the establishment of a normative accent for his people and their voice. "That sounds monstrous," as he confesses of his own earlier canine ambitions: "almost as if I wanted to feed on the marrow, not only of a bone, but of the whole canine race [*Hundeschaft*] itself." In Kafka's careful linguistic usage, of course, the word "race" never appears: *Hundeschaft*, the neologism he uses instead, formed from the word for "dog," or "*Hund*," with the Germanic suffix "-*schaft*," corresponding to the English "-hood," instead unveils, and begins to reject, the essentializing linguistic move that excludes foreign content from the essence of the national language and its forms. Such a definition, he points out, is only a "*Bild*," or a

---

10 As Capar Battegay notes, this strong critique of nationalist essentialism was banished by the "so-called Critical Edition" ("*die sogenannte* Kritische Ausgabe") to its "*Apparatband*"; see Battegay (2011). Kafka's German in this section is therefore quoted from *Beschreibung eines Kampfes: Novellen, Skizzen, Aphorismen aus dem Nachlaß, Gesammelte Werke*, ed. Max Brod, Fischer (1976 [1936]), 192.

"metaphor": the idea of collective expression is thus described as a form of the angel Metatron's task, to record "the merits of Israel," or of any other "-hood," or supposedly essential expression of any linguistic group. Researching and eventually writing down the national inheritance – that "united crunching of all the teeth of all dogs" – appears as a noxious and implicit form of cannibalism – with its subsequent silencing of linguistic others and their forms. "The marrow," the narrator therefore concludes from his consideration of a "united" dogdom, "is no food," or *"Speise,"* but *"das Gegenteil,"* as he tells us, or just the opposite: a poison, or a *"Gift,"* ingested in the desire to expel foreign nourishment from the *Mark*, that center and distinction of national expression (Kafka 1976, 192).

This "poison" or – at least to the English ear – the ironic *Gift* of essential meaning is recast by the "Investigations" in the idea of *"das wahre Wort"* (the true Word), nurtured in the un-marked territory of the linguistic boundary zone (Kafka 1992, 456). Such, of course, is the more archaic meaning of the German *Mark* in what we might call the first place: the *Grimm Dictionary* cites this form as derived from the aggressive attempt to mark, and thereby claim, in an *"erweiternd"* or "extending" gesture the resources of a *"Grenzland"* of value, as the later usage of *Mark* as national currency suggests ("mark," *Deutsches Wörterbuch*). Kafka's canine is much less obedient: the "true Word" in his usage refers instead to the zone of linguistic formation. It was in this era when a fuller language could "still have intervened," not yet hindered by the most threatening linguistic group. *Das wahre Wort* thus hails from a period of pre-canonical diversity, when "the Word was there, was very near, at least, at the tip of everyone's tongue" (Kafka 1971, 300). Expressive richness, in this time of linguistic development, flourished precisely because no *"Spitze"* – that peak or most desirable form of the "native" tongue – had yet been marked: when the *"Zunge"* or tongue, meaning language, was set free, in other words, to deepen its eloquence through its mutual relations with not yet "other" forms (Kafka 1992, 456). Without the *Spitze* or peak language enforced by the canonical spear, "planning or re-planning of the structure" of language, as the dog suggests, was still possible (Kafka 1971, 300, 1976, 192). The "true Word" flourished, in other words, as what Walter Benjamin called "pure language": when the question of which accents might be stigmatized, or which foreign usages might be considered heretical solecisms, was impossible to name (Benjamin 1968b 260).

After this lost era of linguistic formation, the "true Word" was open to its *Gegenteil* or contrary forms. The *"Schweigen"* or active silence of dogdom preserves a memory of this period of consolidation, when correct pronunciation, known as the standard accent, is separated from the false. As a defense against blasphemous utterances about their linguistic back-formations, such silence is impossible to separate from canine culture as whole. This large-scale prohibition makes good sense, especially for the performing canines, who stand up on their "*Hinterbeine*," or "hind legs," and expose themselves to the charge of imitating an implicitly more human culture, on which the oral nourishment of their own might depend. "Raising their front legs," as the researcher notes, they are "committing a sin" (*Sünde begehen*): performing a "*gestus*," as Walter Benjamin defined the concept, by acting out a gesture from beyond their own linguistic realm (Kafka 1971, 283–84; Benjamin 1968a, 121).[11] Their silence is in this sense darkness made visible: like the prohibition on pronouncing foreign words in their accent of origin – a spoken heresy – in any upstanding culture: the demand, for instance, in English that "restaurant" be pronounced with an "aunt" at the end, rather than in a French that might suggest better taste. "They had good grounds for remaining silent," as the researcher describes this omnipresent form of linguistic censorship, "that is, assuming they remained silent from feelings of guilt (*Schuldgefühle*) at all" (Kafka 1971, 283–84).

This shameless art performs eloquence as explicitly drawn from foreign sources. Its "power" is derived, as the narrator describes it, from the "not unconquerable" sound "of a clear, piercing, continuous note which came without variation from literally the remotest distance" (*förmlich aus großer Ferne*), with their result of "forcing" him to his "knees" (Kafka 1971, 284; 1992, 433). In this subjected position, the narrator conquers his own desire for subjection. The process at work is in keeping with Kafka's adage that "what is intended to be actively destroyed must first be fully grasped," suggested in Kafka's earlier fiction by the "Jäger Gracchus" of the "Black Forest", whose longing is to bury the imperialism of his name (Kafka 1991, 95; 1992, 133). This purgation of linguistic purity thus means re-enacting its assumptions, performed in the fasting the researcher has already undergone. The result is his rejection of collective identity as an essence, in any linguistic or national terms. "It seemed to me," as the researcher realizes in his confrontation with the "Jäger" late in his investigations, "that I saw something more of him," taking the measure of the beautiful creature he encounters: "there was blood under me, at first I took it for food (*Speise*); but I recognized immediately it was blood (*Blut*) that I had vomited," or "*dass ich ausgebrochen hatte*" (Kafka 1971, 312; 1992, 476).[12] Crucial here is the narrator's rejection of the principle he had formerly swallowed without question: "blood," as the idea of unity, originally

---

11 Cf. Walter Benjamin, "Franz Kafka: On the Tenth Anniversary of his Death": "the gestures of Kafka's figures are too powerful for our accustomed surroundings, and break out into wider areas."
12 In German the full passage reads: "unter mir lag Blut, im ersten Augenblick dachte ich, es sei Speise, ich merkte aber Gleich, das es Blut war, dass ich ausgebrochen hatte."

taken for *Speise*, or food – is identified as the undergirding assumption of his earlier investigations, then cast aside as a form of the *Gift*, or poison taste. Any notion of the linguistic "marrow" or essence of a nation is now understood as a mortal danger instead.

3 Music and Vomit: The Silence of the Dogs

> These things hast thou done, and I kept silent; thou thoughtest I was altogether such a one as thyself.
> Psalms 50:21

Kafka's research dog vomits – an action traditionally linked to heresy – with a significant difference at the high point of the story. Where Maimonides, as James Diamond notes, defined unbounded appetite and oral expulsion as signifying a heretical move beyond acceptable knowledge, the research dog experiences purity as the mode of linguistic thought that needs to be expelled and rethought (Diamond 2007, 63). "Who are you?" he therefore asks the final singing dog he encounters, at the culmination of the narrative, in the purgation of nationalism with which the story concludes. "I'm a hunter" – "*Ich bin ein Jäger*," the final singing dog replies. The unnamed *Meister* here is not simply Germanic, in the "Black Forest" sense of Kafka's "Jäger Gracchus," but a mode of linguistic patriotism that must be expelled. Canine vomit is in this sense the narrator's *Ausbrechen or vomiting as a gesture* against such definitional violence: the destructive hunting down of a single language that expresses the national spirit (Kafka 1992, 476). "The worst," as the researcher says of the culminating music he encounters, "was that it seemed to exist solely for my sake, this voice before whose sublimity (*Erhabenheit*) the woods fell silent." At this "worst" moment of his potential elevation, the dog hears poetry accurately: as the silencing of other voices in the forest. At this moment of sublimity, he discovers the sublime elevation of a national voice as the ground for unspeakable acts to occur (Kafka 1971, 314; 1992, 479).

Instead, the researcher excavates and revels in these differences. "Who was I," as the dog puts it, "that I could dare to remain here," in this poetic forest, "while lying brazenly, *mich breitmachte*, in my own filth and blood?," or "*Schmutz und Blut*"(Kafka 1992, 479). In the place of sublimity, *Schmutz* as a High German word is enlarged by sensing its relation to the other's voice. Made "*breit*," or broad – or "brazen" in English translation – this High German word effectively overlaps with its kindred Yiddish noun. In philosophical parlance, the *Schmutz* is a duck-rabbit: a word in the "*Hoch*" or high language which can appear as an entirely different linguistic animal at once (Kafka 1971, 314). In a word, this "*breitmachend*" expression does just what his phrase says: it prevents *Blut*, and thus the "*Blutlache*" or limiting "blood-puddle" of national identity in which he finds himself from becoming the organizing limit of his experience (Kafka 1992, 479). As a result, his scholarship moves to the study of a "*Grenzgebiet*," or border-zone, "*der beiden Wissenschaften*," or of the study of both nourishment and the musical voice. In terms of literary modernism, he creates a field in which the "watering the earth" that suggests national demarcation – a pissing contest, as Leopold Bloom recalls it in "Ithaca," the nostos or homecoming chapter of *Ulysses* – overlaps with music, and thus the study of sounds that move across the borders of linguistic norms (Kafka 1971, 314; 1992, 479; Joyce 1986 [1922], 577).

Hidden nationalism – wearing the emperor's new clothes of poetry – is therefore rejected. "*Ich glaubte zu erkennen*," as the researcher puts it – "I believed myself to understand" that music, like literature, nourishes itself from foreign sources, not any original voice. The singer is silent, like the earlier "musical dogs," who were "ostensibly quite calm when they played, but were in reality in a state of intense excitement," as their performance acts out and explodes any national myth (Kafka 1971, 314; 1992, 479). As a result, the narrator perceives "something such as no dog before me had ever seen, at least there is no slightest hint of it in our tradition": silence is therefore read not merely as a sign of submission to laws, but as an indication that obedience – to "laws ... not those of the dog world, but [to those that] are actually directed against it" – is being transformed in a critical sense. "We are those," as he puts it, "who are oppressed by the silence"; yet every dog who feels compelled to repeat the same ideas, the narrator suggests, also experiences "*einen Drang zu fragen*:" that is, a compulsion to question what is repeated, and hence to think in new and different ways (Kafka 1971, 280; 1992, 426). Winfried Kudszus is thus correct that the hunting dog figures death, as the researcher turns the "*Jäger*" against deadly self-censorship: a break already apparent in the fact that the hunting dog was "singing, without knowing it yet," as the text reports (Kudszus 1983, 306–7). The researcher hears silence not as absence in this scene, but as the silencing of domination itself. Such is the declaration of the final line of the story, that "such freedom as is possible today is a wretched business," when its more traditional tones are heard. In German, "freedom" is everyone's business, as Kafka suggests: not "*Geschäft*" or trade, but "*ein kümmerliches Gewächs*" – a struggling plant, to be nurtured with the linguistically allied expression of Yiddish *Kummer*, into new forms of life (Kafka 1971, 316; 1992, 482).

"You disturb me ," the hunting dog therefore tells the researcher, who rightfully interrupts his obedience: "I can't hunt while you're here," he tells him, since the narrator's questions have already broken his servitude to the masters of the hunt (Kafka 1971, 314; 1992, 478–9). This break in organized, if unnamed, service is crucial: "Why won't you let me keep lying here?" – the narrator's earlier question – finds its answer in a "*Musik*" that is silent: devoid of the grandiosity of any human masters, because it wells up instead from the lower realms of canine life. The hunting dog sings without hunting, separating his song from any privileged sense of human origins, while departing from both the adulation of unnamed masters and the conformity of the pack. "And besides," as the narrator puts it, "it is a particularity of dogs (*die Hundeschaft*) to be always asking questions," as the narrator noted early on: "they ask them confusedly all together: it is as if the track (*Spur*) that leads back to the asker of the correct question is meant to be wiped away" (*verwischt*) (Kafka 1971, 297; 1992, 452). This culminating scene validates and values otherness as creative: in the disruption of the hunt, as well as the music of the silenced that appears as if from nowhere, when in fact conjured from the trials of doggish life. Here, Kafka's "Investigations" value questioning without worship: an activity he called the "most unbridled individualism of faith" (*zügelloseste Individualismus des Glaubens*), and named in his aphorism as the crucial element of messianic thought (Kafka 1946, 80–81).

In the end, the research dog returns to this search for foreignness as a multiplicity that was there from the start. The instinctive questioning practiced by his community, drenched in irony, provides a case in point: every question, as Kafka notes in his diary, can be used "like a spear," pointed in a number of different directions at once (Kafka 1948, 423). "Where then are my real colleagues," he asserts of this questioning and unbridled spirit: "that is the burden of my complaint" (Kafka 1971, 298). In this search for a freedom that his fellow canines regard as heresy, Kafka's researcher is indeed in pursuit of what Theodor Adorno called a "relation, not identity," and hence in quest of a difference that refuses to be buried: in his case under the well-gnawed bones of a canonical and national point of view (Adorno 1997, 348). "I am afraid that the last thing by which I will be able to recognize my real colleagues," he declares, "is by their successes," a statement of his relentless pursuit – "because I'm a dog" – of "freedom," which he ends his narrative by declaring, with the tenacity accorded to his species, to be a "possession nonetheless" (Kafka 1971, 298, 291, 316; 1992, 453, 433, 482). The precise ground of that freedom is uncertain, best compared by the narrator to the "thousandth forgetting of a dream dreamt a thousand times," and so a heretical goal to pursue in this dog-eat-dog world. "The story is not ended, it has not yet become history," however, as Gershom Scholem points out of this longing, "and the secret life it holds can break out tomorrow in you or in me" (1946, 350).

Bibliography

Adorno, Theodor. *Aesthetic Theory*. Trans. Robert Hullot-Kentor. Minneapolis: University of Minnesota Press, 1997.
Battegay, Caspar. *Das Andere Blut: Gemeinschaft im deutsch-jüdischen Schreiben 1830–1930*. Köln: Böhlau Verlag, 2011.
Beck, Evelyn Torton. *Kafka and the Yiddish Theater*. Madison: University of Wisconsin Press, 1971.
Benjamin, Walter. "Franz Kafka: On the Tenth Anniversary of His Death." *Illuminations*. Trans. Harry Zohn, ed. Hannah Arendt. New York: Schocken Books, 1968a.
"The Task of the Translator." *Illuminations*. Trans. Harry Zohn, ed. Hannah Arendt. New York: Schocken Books, 1968b.
Benjamin, Walter. "Theses on the Philosophy of History." *Illuminations*. Trans. Harry Zohn, ed. Hannah Arendt. New York: Schocken Books, 1968c.
Bercovitch, Sacvan. *The Rites of Assent: Transformation in the Symbolic Construction of America*. New York: Routledge, 1993.
Bergmann, Hugo. "Franz Kafka und die Hunde." *Mitteilungsblatt der Irgun Olej Merkas Europa* 40.34/35 (September), 1972, 4.
Biale, David. "Gershom Scholem's Ten Unhistorical Aphorisms on Kabbalah: Text and Commentary. *Modern Judaism* 5.1 (February), 1985, 67–93.
Bielek-Robson, Agata. "The Marrano God: Abstraction, Messianicity and Retreat in Derrida's 'Faith and Knowledge.'" *Religions* 19, 2019, 1–23.
Bruce, Iris. *Kafka and Cultural Zionism: Dates in Palestine*. Madison: University of Wisconsin Press, 2007.
Chambers, Ross. "The Artist as Performing Dog." *Comparative Literature* 23.4, 1971, 312–324.
Diamond, James. *Convicts, Heretics, Lepers: Maimonides and the Outsider*. South Bend: University of Notre Dame Press, 2007.
Fromer, Jakob. *Der Organismus des Judentums*. Charlottenburg: Selbstverlag des Verfassers, 1909.
Gordin, Jacob. *Elisha ben Avuya*. Amherst: National Yiddish Book Center, 1999 [1910].
Goshen-Gottstein, Alon. *The Sinner and the Amnesiac: The Rabbinic Invention of Elisha Ben Abuya and Eleazar Ben Arach*. Stanford: Stanford University Press, 2000.
Grözinger, Karl Erich. *Kafka und die Kabbalah: Das Jüdische im Denken Franz Kafkas*. Frankfurt/M: Fischer Taschenbuch Verlag, 1994.
Harshav, Benjamin. *The Meaning of Yiddish*. Stanford: Stanford University Press, 1990.
Harshav, Benjamin. *Language in Time of Revolution*. Berkeley: University of California Press, 1993.
Idel, Moshe. *Absorbing Perfections: Kabbalah and Interpretation*. New Haven: Yale University Press, 2002.
Joyce, James. *Ulysses*. Ed. Hans Walter Gabler, with Wolfhard Steppe and Claus Melchior. New York: Vintage Books, 1986 [1922].
Kafka, Franz. *Parables and Paradoxes in German and English*. New York: Schocken Books, 1946.
Kafka, Franz. *The Diaries 1910–1923*. Trans. Martin Greenberg, with the cooperation of Hannah Arendt. New York: Schocken Books, 1948.
Kafka, Franz. "Investigations of a Dog." *The Complete Stories*. Ed. Nahum N. Glatzer. New York: Schocken Books, 1971. 278–316.

Kafka, Franz. "Forschungen eines Hundes." *Beschreibung eines Kampfes: Novellen, Skizzen, Aphorismen aus dem Nachlaß. Gesammelte Werke*. Ed. Max Brod. Frankfurt/M: S. Fischer, 1976. 180–215.

Kafka, Franz. *The Blue Oktavo Notebooks*. Ed. Max Brod, trans. Ernst Kaiser and Eithne Wilkins. Cambridge: Exact Change, 1991.

Kafka, Franz. "Forschungen eines Hundes." *Nachgelassene Schriften und Fragmente II*. Ed. Jost Schillemeit. Frankfurt/M: S. Fischer, 1992. 423–482.

Kafka, Franz. "Bericht für eine Akademie" (Report to an Academy). *Drucke zu Lebzeiten I*. Ed. Wolf Kittler, Hans-Gerd Koch and Gerhard Neumann. Frankfurt/M: S. Fischer 1994a. 299–314.

Kafka, Franz. *Tagebücher I: 1909–1912 in der Fassung der Handschrift*. Frankfurt/M: Fischer Taschenbuch Verlag, 1994b.

Kudszus, Winfried. "Musik und Erkenntnis in Kafkas *Forschungen eines Hundes*." *Erkennen und Deuten: Essays zur Literatur und Literaturtheorie: Egar Lohner In Memoriam*. Eds. M. Woodmansee and W.F.W. Lohnes. Berlin, Schmidt, 1983.

"Mark." *Deutsches Wörterbuch von Jacob und Wilhelm Grimm*, 16 volumes, Leipzig 1854–1961. Online version Leipzig 1971, consulted 08.08.2018.

Rubenstein, Jeffrey L. *Talmudic Stories: Narrative Art, Composition, and Culture*. Baltimore and London: Johns Hopkins University Press, 1999.

Scholem, Gershom. *Major Trends in Jewish Mysticism*. New York: Schocken Books, 1946.

Suchoff, David. *Kafka's Jewish Languages: The Hidden Openness of Tradition*. Philadelphia: University of Pennsylvania Press, 2012.

Winkelman, John. "Kafka's 'Forschungen eines Hundes.'" *Monatshefte* 59.3 (Fall), 1967, 204.

Noam Gil
Isaac Bashevis Singer and the Poetics of Negativity

> The Jew is the impious man in the widest sense. Piety is not something near things nor outside things; it is the groundwork of everything.   Otto Weininger (1906, 322)

> I had read Otto Weininger's 'Sex and Character' and resolved never to marry ... I lusted after women yet at the same time saw their faults, chief of which was that they (the modern, not the old-fashioned kind) were amazingly like me – just as lecherous, deceitful, egotistical and eager for adventure.   Isaac Bashevis Singer (1984, 66)

Isaac Bashevis Singer remained faithful throughout his life in his admiration of the Austrian philosopher Otto Weininger,[1] although the affinity between the two is rarely mentioned and never fully discussed in studies of his work. The source of this admiration lies mainly in Singer's fascination with Weininger's character – a young Austrian idealist, the embodiment of the self-hating Jew, committing a romanticized suicide at a young age – and with his ideas concerning both women and "womanly men"; i.e. the Jews.

Weininger's notorious *Sex and Character* (*Geschlecht und Charakter*) provides an unflattering portrayal of women, identified mainly by their inherent inability to grasp the laws of identity. Women are devoid of logical thinking and rational introspection and unable to form any consistent judgment. They are amoral, deceptive and dependent, have no self-awareness and are confined solely by their sexual urges. Weininger's women also dwell in negative spaces, since negation in the female's psyche is "eternal as existence" (300). Furthermore, they have no individual will; they are indifferent to their past and foolishly celebrate the present. Alongside women, Weininger dedicated a chapter of his book to defining Jews and Judaism in similar terms – their shared absence of concern for personal and geographical property, their mutual lack of dignity and honor, their nonexistent awareness of questions of morality, their dependence on the "stronger" sex and the "stronger" race, and their inherent unreliability. In short, both women and Jews are identified as "the strongest opposition to the male nature" (306).[2]

---

1 It is repeatedly and explicitly illustrated in his autobiographies (Singer, 1981, 5; 1984, 66), his biographies (Goran, 1994, 29–30; Noiville, 2006, 57), and stories (*Enemies, A Love Story*, for example).
2 Weininger was not unique in his pairing of women with Jews, defining them both as an obstacle to aesthetic and political aspirations. For example, Shulamit Volkov (2006) situates this derogatory point of view in a Germanic tradition. This same analogy is part of an alliance between

However, women differ from Jews in the amount of "oppositions" each group entails: the female's negativity relates to her own (mis)understanding and character, unlike Jewish negativity, which relates both to them and to others. The Jew is defined as a "parasite, a new creature in a different host, although remaining essentially the same," unlike the passive affiliation of the woman's psyche to "any form impressed on it" (320); accordingly, while women do not believe in themselves, relying on the authoritative (male) figure, Jews do not believe in others either. In fact, Weininger's Jew is the eternal disbeliever and an all-encompassing heretic:

> The Jew takes nothing seriously; he is frivolous, and jests about anything... the Jew does not really believe in knowledge, nor is he skeptic, for he doubts his own skepticism.   (321–2)

The Jewish individual is identified here, more than anything else, through negative attributes: he is a "nothing," an "opposition," a "less" ("worldless," "baseless," "shameless"), a "dis" ("disloyal," "dishonest"), a "lack" that will forever remain emptied out, an "I" which resists its incorporation into a bigger "we."

Weininger's book typifies the familiar trope of the Jew as an immediate antithesis to several forms of cultural or political ideals in pre-world-wars Europe, when the values which the Jew was associated with were often essentially negative.[3] Zygmunt Bauman famously used the term "Conceptual Jew" to identify this abstract figure as

> a semantically overloaded entity, comprising and blending meanings which ought to be kept apart, and for this reason a natural adversary of any force concerned with drawing borderlines and keeping them water-light ... [the Conceptual Jew was] an image construed as compromising and defying the order of things, as the very epitome and embodiment of such defiance.   (1989, 39)

This same defiance of the Jew became quite fashionable also in post-Holocaust discourse as well; several theorists have used similar ideas to Weininger and other anti-Semites, only in a positive frame of mind. The Jew, or more specifically the "right" kind of Jew (i.e. the diasporic Jew), in studies by scholars such as Judith Butler, Jacques Derrida, Julia Kristeva, Daniel Boyarin, Maurice Blanchot, Jean

---

anti-Semitic and anti-feminist discourse at the end of the 19th century and the first half of the 20th century. Sander Gilman also discussed this analogy in his *The Jew's Body* (1991), between Jewish and female hatred through the psychological and anthropological discourse on hysteria.
3 See, for example, Sara Hammerschlag's *The Figural Jew: Politics and Identity in Postwar French Thought* (2010, 6–9), or Zygmunt Bauman's essay "Allosemitism: Premodern, Modern, Postmodern" (1998).

François Lyotard, Giorgio Agamben, Gilles Deleuze and Felix Guattari,[4] among others, was often depicted as a subversive entity which dismantles, deconstructs or challenges several forms of Identitarian thinking (be they national, cultural, geographical, spiritual, sexual). In both cases, in anti-Semitism and post-structuralism, the Jew has been conceptualized and re-conceptualized as the quintessential "other," the "stranger," the "forgotten," the "repressed," the one who is "left out," or "left over," the "abjected," the "stateless," the "placeless," the "foreigner," the "wanderer," the "liminal," the "dejected" and other adjectives, some of which also resonate in Singer's poetics.

1 The Radical Particularity of the Negative "Jew"

Singer was committed throughout his life to the dying language he wrote in, Yiddish, and its folklore, situating many of his novels and short stories either in the place where he grew up, Warsaw, or the place he emigrated to before the war, New York. His characters, by and large, where the "un-adaptables," Polish Jewish citizens, immigrants, Holocaust survivors. Some of them are alive, some are dead (and reappear as ghosts), and many are in-between, unwilling or unable to assimilate to a modernized world. Reading many of Singer's texts, I argue that Singer employs a form of characterization which does not resist Weininger's obnoxious illustrations but rather turns Weininger's "womanly Jewish vices" into (for a lack of a better word) virtues. Singer, I further argue, makes use of negativity to undermine several perceptions that are mostly associated with pre-war European (masculine) ideals. Many of his characters, mostly women, almost exclusively Jewish, embody a form of negativity which serves also as a critical foil, as "the strongest opposition to the male nature"; i.e. the strong, logical, rational, loyal, cultured, and refined "man." In novels such as *Enemies, A Love Story* or *Shosha*, *The Slave* and *The Magician of Lublin*, as well as numerous short stories,[5] Singer has introduced characters who are identified in negative terms, as, to use Weininger's words, "the hardest and most formidable enemy not only

---

4 See, for example, Judith Butler's *Parting Ways: Jewishness and the Critique of Zionism* (2012), Jacques Derrida's *Acts of Religion* (2001), Julia Kristeva's *Powers of Horror: an Essay in Abjection* (1984), Daniel Boyarin's *The Radical Jew: Paul and the Politics of Identity* (1997), Maurice Blanchot's essay "Do Not Forget" (published in his posthumous *Political Writings: 1953–1993*, 2010), Jean François Lyotard's *Heidegger and "the Jews"* (1988), Giorgio Agamben's *Remnants of Auschwitz: The Witness and the Archive* (2002), and Gilles Deleuze and Felix Guattari's *Kafka: Toward a Minor Literature* (1975).
5 See Gil, 2016.

of the [enlightened] views that I have developed ... but of the entire stand point that makes these views possible" (273). For Weininger, the Jewish psyche, or, as he calls it, the Jewish "psychic constitution" (274), is highlighted in antagonistic terms, simply as the opposite against which the true non-Jewish, masculine European Enlightened man must align himself. In contrast, in several of Singer's stories, the Jewish characters provide in many cases a critical disposition that highlights the potential of negative perspectives as some sort of liberating force.

These are not narratives of dissent but of a refusal. The characters, many of whom are Holocaust survivors or emigrants who were victimized by their own given identity as Jews of a specific (Nazi) kind (clearly enumerated in the Nuremburg Laws in 1935), do not follow or seek a way out of a tragic predicament, but endeavor to affirm a radical particularity which will never be reduced to any form of collectivity. They do not offer in their life stories an alternative construction over general perspectives, but a gradual withdrawal. This form of particularity is also manifested through their refusal to be recognized, or to be interpreted by a reader, as well as even to be characterized by an omnipotent narrator. This chapter explores Singer's poetics of negativity through his arguably most memorable novel, *Enemies, A Love Story*, a representative text which highlights this aspect in Singer's poetics. His heresy is manifested not necessarily through defiance of an omnipotent God or of a modernized Jewish community, since defiance implies an active reaction to forms of social or spiritual orthodoxies. His unique heretic standpoint is manifested, rather, through an affirmation of avoidance.

To put this somewhat differently, Singer's writings are immersed in the "lost causes" of the world. Many of his stories chronicle the life of the excluded and their banishment from some sort of a political and social order. His protagonists frequently identify with – or even assume – the "weaker" and the depreciated roles in several of his stories, such as "The Woman," "The Jew," "The Animal," "The Dead," "The Inhuman," "The Primitive," and other diverse and vilified roles. They embody weakness and negativity – whether it is spiritual, cultural or sexual – insisting on remaining anonymous, unassimilated and unidentifiable.[6] Even though Singer wrote mainly between the 1940s and the 1970s and explored themes that were familiar in these post-world-war years, he was not associated with a group of individuals (authors, painters, poets, playwrights, film makers, philosophers) who dedicated many of their works to highlight the negative outcome of the wars on European culture. These writers and artists (Paul Celan, Samuel Beckett, Eugène Ionesco, Francis Bacon, Michelangelo Antonioni, Emil

---

6 See Gil, 2018.

Cioran, Marguerite Duras, and others) reflected upon humanity's self-destructive tendencies and thus were repeatedly discussed in negative terms. Samuel Beckett is repeatedly mentioned as the high priest of this aesthetic style, "late modernism," which highlights an existential/ontological/epistemological dead-end with no prospects on the horizon. Singer's immediate suspicion towards humanity's self-destructive tendencies sounds familiar in the context of this form of post-Holocaust modernism. And yet, Singer's poetics stands out in its recurring defiance of any sensibility tinged with even a bit of modernism. He was consistent in his "old-fashioned" attitude – a traditional story-teller living in the past, refusing to align himself with any manifestation of modernism and identifying himself as a devout folklorist.[7] Singer was, I believe, an author who found it difficult to give up the role of a *kegner* – a Yiddish "againstick" – who was almost pathological in his refusal to belong.

2 Going Backwards – a Yiddishist in the City

In reading Singer's protagonist's life journey in *Enemies*, I intend to selectively address two significant aspects that embody the protagonist's condition in post-World War II America: the city and the Yiddish language. In Singer's texts these categories, the geographical and the linguistic, signify at the same time multiplicity and decay, abundance and disintegration. They designate in his stories an absent center, or a missing "cosmic destination" as Singer calls it in one of his stories (Singer, 1982 [1964])– the same destination which each assimilated Jew within each text yearns for. As Singer himself commented in his autobiographical *Lost in America* (1981), the metropolis (New York) was to him a "mental catastrophe ... some mutation for which there was no name in my vocabulary, not even a beginning of a notion" (107). Singer repeatedly characterized himself as an uprooted person in a place devoid of roots, America, without a unifying history, origin or language, where a "father speaks one language and the son another" (128). The same unnamed and undefined "mental catastrophe" of the city (be that Warsaw, New York, Buenos Aires or Miami) correlates to the condition of many of his protagonists in many of his stories, especially in their efforts to adapt to this new reality. This frequent juxtaposition between the individual and his or her city reveals a radical urban understanding that literally fuses the subject with his background. Singer's *Enemies*, I will show, defies oppositional perceptions of both spaces and character, as the focal point is almost solely directed towards the marginalized

---

7 Singer, 2006 (1943), 86–8.

ingredients of the city: the rats, the ghosts, the soon-to-be-dead emigrants and Holocaust survivors, the New York tunnels and many more. However, these elements in Singer's texts do not create a new understanding of modern urban life in a literature that includes the excluded, but in a literature that deals with endless exclusions.

This process is also evident in Singer's approach to the Yiddish language and culture. Dan Miron has pointed out that Singer's Yiddish is "a language with no territory, no protection, no cultural political alliances, no prestige and no army or any military terminology – the language of the weak, the victims" (338).[8] Additionally, in his famous essay "What is Proper Ground for Literature" ("Vos is der boden far literatur?" 1943), Singer defined his old (Yiddish) language in contrast to the new (American) world: its "backwardness" in opposition to America's technological and cultural modernity, its inadaptability and anachronism in a place that constantly develops and progresses, its old and dying ingredients in a place of constant renovation. All of these, according to Singer, signify both an existential circumstance of Yiddish-speaking emigrants, stranded in a foreign country, and an aesthetic helplessness, of writers writing in an outdated language, destined to "dine on leftovers [since] only food prepared in the old country can nourish [them] in the new" (9).

This "out-datedness" is manifested in Singer's own exilic point of view, as a writer in isolation from his god and from his (Yiddish) community (Landis, 1996, 129). His Yiddish-speaking characters epitomize various claims that were raised in studies about the language's "weakened" characteristics: the female qualities of this *mameloshen* (mother's tongue) and its opposition to the paternal Hebraic language (Sherman, 1996, 192–3); its defiance of order, as a language that prospers from stolen words, from a broken grammar, a language of withdrawal and dissolution (Deleuze and Guattari, 1986, 60), a language of resistance and of rejection of the new world's linguistic and cultural norms (Norich, 2002). Singer himself explicitly compared the language's and its speaker's shared fate, when stating that their mutual "severe disorientation [in America] ... remain forever helpless and not quite themselves" (Burgin, 1986; 8). Furthermore, Singer explicitly criticized modernists' and rationalists' perceptions of Yiddish, stating that this language was perceived "as a jargon, a diasporic mish-mash of words, lacking in grammar, without rules for constructing a sentence" (2006, 89), "a vulgar

---

[8] Miron relies in his claims on Bashevis Singer's own comments in his Nobel Prize acceptance speech, stating that the Yiddish language is "a language of exile, without a land, without a frontier, not supported by any government, a language which possesses no words for weapons, ammunition, military exercises; a language that was despised by both gentiles and emancipated Jews"; www.nobelprize.org/nobel_prizes/literature/laureates/1978/singer-lecture.html.

language ... [like] an old wrinkled and indigent grandmother whose presence is a source of shame and disgrace" (87). These same debasing perceptions are utilized in Singer's stories when this slandered "grandmother" (his metaphor for the Yiddish language and culture), the one who the modernized characters are ashamed of, is repeatedly situated at the forefront of his narratives. It is a deliberate contamination in his stories of an "enlightened" world, a reminder to his readers that the Yiddish language and its speakers will not cease in haunting a modernized Jewish universe.

Here I go back to Otto Weininger in claiming that Singer's views encapsulate these "negative" factors within the subjective (Jewish) psyche. It is exactly the negative components of the Jewish "female man" (as Weininger defines the Jews), his dying language and his intimidating surroundings, that create an elusive protagonist, devoid of any positive aspects.

3 Enemies, A Love Story

With all its twists and turns, *Enemies, A Love Story* is first and foremost a story about a man who cannot make up his mind. Herman Broder, the protagonist, has three women: Yadwiga, his current wife and former Polish servant, who saved his life during the Holocaust by hiding him in her hayloft; Masha, his lover, a suicidal survivor whose fate will be determined by Herman's obligation to her; and Tamara, his first wife, who was supposed to have died in Poland with their two children but suddenly resurfaced alive in New York. All of these women are completely devoted to Herman, but he "wants to have all three" (1972, 85). He has two apartments but refuses to "commit" to one location even though his boss urges him to choose: "Either you are in the other world or you're in this world. You can't stand with one foot on the ground and the other in the sky" (28). Furthermore, throughout the narrative Herman holds numerous and often contradictory worldviews and philosophies: he turns from being a complete nihilist in "pre-suicidal gloom" (23) to embracing a religious piety and affirming his spiritual background; from gratifying his egotistical sexual urges to assuming responsibilities as a newborn family man; from his need to be a part of the American community to his contempt for assimilated Jews in America. Tamara, his first wife, says: "People like you are incapable of making decisions for themselves" (219). This indecision is best exemplified in the final stages of the novel, when Herman decides to worship God again; to be a devoted father to his as-yet-unborn son; to be faithful to Yadviga; to acquire a new job and assume responsibilities; to return to his mistress, Masha, and thus to leave Yadviga; to abandon his future son and again abandon the responsibilities he assumed a few pages before; to move to California or Florida; to stay in New York; to quit his newly acquired job and commit suicide; to embrace life again and then to escape. These inconsistent journeys back and forth are the embracing and disavowing of contradictory points of view, the acquiring and abandoning of various identities, whether they are spiritual, sexual, matrimonial, communal or intellectual. As the plot develops, there is a growing number of frequently opposed "faces" that Herman wears simultaneously: as "the husband," "the Jew," "the lover," "the father," "the writer," "the rabbi," "the American," "the Pole," "the survivor," and finally even "the protagonist."

In *Enemies, A Love Story*, Herman's journey serves as a constant defiance of any form of regulation, a refusal to assume the same identities he is constrained to wear. As Singer himself commented, Herman Broder is both his author's incarnation and the most uninvolved character he had ever written (Burgin, 1986, 27). Throughout the novel he is defined as a weary and exhausted man, working as a ghostwriter for a rabbi who "had neither the time nor the patience to study or write" (23). He is selling to his naïve readers "phrases like 'a better world' and 'a brighter tomorrow' [which] seemed to him blasphemy on the ashes of the tormented" (22). He is a self-confessed liar, a fraud, a deceiver, a heretic who has abandoned his set of beliefs. He is a riddle to himself and to others, a coward that still lingers outside of reality's domain. Early on, his consciousness is deadened, his memory choked and his hope extinguished. Even in his relationships with his three women, Yadviga, Tamara and Masha, his two wives and his mistress, he creates an illusion of love and devotion that he cannot abide. During the Holocaust and afterwards he abandoned his god and religion, his wife and dead children in Poland, his old country, his intellectual beliefs and his responsibilities. Broder's relation to his Jewish people, similar to other Singer survivors (Dr. Solomon Margulin in "A Wedding in Brownsville," "Alone"'s unnamed narrator, Herman Gombiner in "The Letter Writer") is practically non-existent since he had "torn himself away from the community" (107). He is the ideal example of Weininger's "idea of Judaism" (1906, 306); the incarnation of unreliability and deceit, the lack of concern for geographical property, its persistent disrespect for the powers of progress. This is conveyed, for example, in his refusal to supply residential addresses for his boss. In that sense, Broder also exemplifies, in his (lack of) personal property, Weininger's claims about the Jews' (lack of) individuality and independence. He is also characterized as an intellectual who still remains absorbed in Otto Weininger, who to him is "the most consistent philosopher" (33).

Unlike the energetic characters, the "choice makers" who demand that Herman produce an address, a child, a marriage, a faith, an alliance with an existing community, Herman refuses to act.⁹ As the choices multiply, the refusals intensify as well. They are not only private concrete dilemmas – which woman to love, which job to commit to, where to live – but political conflicts as well:

> In the hayloft he had had the illusion that some basic change would take place in the world, but nothing had changed. The same politics, the same phrases, the same false promises. Professors continued to write books about the ideology of murder, the sociology of fortune, the philosophy of rape, the psychology of terror. Inventors created new deadly weapons, the talk about culture and justice was more revolting than the barbarism and injustice. (245)

Throughout the novel Herman addresses numerous ideological political and aesthetical "phrases" and "promises" – communism, capitalism, Zionism, humanism, Judaism, Christianity, fascism, democracy, modernism, existentialism – and specifically rejects them all. This scorn of the various "isms" is reflected also in Singer's approach towards Yiddish, a language without prospects or army to defend it. In his non-fiction writings Singer attacked the modernized movement of the Haskala, with all its assimilationists, communists or Zionist successors, and blamed them for the liquidation of Yiddish, a language whose speakers are "ignorant of isms" (2006, 91). This specific "ignorance" of which Yiddish speakers were frequently criticized by the Maskilim – as primitive and uneducated folklorists, unable to adapt to the developments of a modernized world – becomes here a subversive element. Any discussion, in *Enemies*, on the Jews' aspiration towards a Jewish state or to fulfill the Marxist ideal, any attempt to intellectual rationalization of current conditions or to support religious reaffirmation, is angrily dismissed by a survivor who, like his language, gradually "ceases to be a part of the world" (95). Herman, thus, is Singer's heretic protagonist in, arguably, the most radical form of the term. He does not take a stand because he excludes himself from the discussion. His point of view is not that of an oppositional critic but of an eternal dissenter to the discourse itself: "lacking the courage to commit suicide, Herman had to shut his eyes, stop up his ears, close his mind, live like a worm" (23).

Herman's wormlike tendencies are best expressed through his perceptions of the city. In his aimless wanderings, the protagonist senses endless amounts of smells, faces, colors, simultaneous actions of people that to him signify that "decay hovered over the city … as if the earth has entered the tail of a comet"

---

9 Dan Miron rightly identifies Singer's poetics with passivity, which "is not the result of a malfunction in the social or the cosmic mechanism; rather it is the only correct stance in the face of the essential order (or disorder) of things" (1996, 154).

(34). It is both a source of fascination and terror as expressed mainly in Herman's subway rides:

> A dense crowd was waiting, bodies pushed against one another. The train rode into the station with a shrill whistling, as if it would fly right past the platform ... an irresistible force shoved Herman into the car. Hips, breasts, elbows pressed against him. Here, at least, the illusion of free will had vanished. Herman was tossed about like a pebble or like a meteor in space ... Jews must have been packed together like this in the freight cars that carried them to the gas chambers. (84)

New York is the venue for the new apocalypse where the snow-covered streets remind Herman of Pompeii "after the eruption of Vesuvius" (161). For Herman the diversity with all its technological merits is not a representative of the American Dream but a symbol of Jewish nightmare, a place that lacks a unifying center where spatial and temporal boundaries crumble. It is the same nightmarish New York that Singer described in "A Wedding in Brownsville" and "The Cafeteria."

The city is, indeed, a place for Jewish destruction, since "there were Nazis roaming about New York" (20). For many survivors and emigrants, as Herman perceives it, the city is a place of integration, where Jews find the opportunity to belong to a new community. The modernized Jews wish to establish a new Judaism adaptable to America. This notion of association is detestable to Herman. The city, with all its multiplicity and opportunities, does not function as a means of accommodation but rather of gradual disintegration "for the achievement of a state of selflessness" (208).

And yet, in *Enemies* these same "threats" provide an ironic way out for the protagonist, as a means of disappearance – the perfect place "to hide himself from the Nazis here in Brooklyn" (15). The urban landscape functions, with all of its threats, as the perfect place to vanish, to simply disappear. *Enemies*, thus, is a story of assimilation but in the most literal sense, to that of complete evaporation. It is an "achievement" of true anonymity of the survivor and his unburdening himself from the numerous identities imposed upon him throughout his life. Again, reading of the protagonist underscores the challenge, throughout the novel, of the inherent futility of Identitarian thinking in post-Holocaust America. This development of a non-identity in the making intensifies as the plot continues until the end, where Herman decides to quit the job Tamara has arranged for him; to abandon his pregnant wife, Yadviga; to leave Masha; to commit suicide (and abandon life) and simply to disappear, leaving his own creator/author helpless after losing him. He is an object that resists its own literary constitution.

Leslie Fiedler recognized Herman's disappearance as Singer's literary leitmotif of "lostness," the only fate left for his Jewish American protagonists. Herman's "removal" is characterized as the final stages of his turning into a ghost (81). It is a process that starts as a metaphor, being a "ghost writer" for an opportunistic boss, and ends as a concrete reality. As the narrator informs us, the protagonist turned into "a missing person," perhaps dead or perhaps alive; might have committed suicide; or might have hidden, as he did during the Holocaust, in an obscure hayloft. He becomes "deregulated," an adversary to any systematic characterizations of positive terms. His disloyalty enables the achievement of true anonymity, perhaps the only true ideal left in his world. He is a character who could not be characterized, literally existing all over the place and in no place at the same time, disorienting in his movements until his own author, Singer himself, has given up on depicting him.

4 The Burden of Identity

Singer repeatedly concludes his stories about Jewish Holocaust survivors or emigrants with a sense of helplessness that surrounds the characters as well as their narrator. Singer's characters are consistent in disappointing their families, their relatives, their community and their employers: they refuse to supply an answer, to succumb to others' analysis or to simply commit.

Broder affirms Singer's long-lasting determination to write works of art that embody, to use Theodor Adorno's words in his *Negative Dialectics*, a "[detachment from the empirical world which] brings forth another world, one opposed to the empirical world as if this other world too were an autonomous entity" (2006, 1). It is a world from which Singer's protagonists, in similar fashion to Beckett's or Kafka's characters, to use Adorno's words once more, "blissfully or unhappily seal themselves off" (6). They resist their own interpretation and epitomize an interpretative darkness that should not be replaced by "the clarity of meaning" (5).

However, unlike Beckett or Kafka, Singer's stories are not narratives of despair, nor do they always relish an existential anguish. They celebrate this "negativity of life" in a form of a twisted and grotesque happy ending; they die a happy death, disappear to a better world. Either way, they remain eternal enemies of the new world, affirming a disposition of negativity, relieved from the burden of identity.

Bibliography

Adorno, W. Theodor. *Negative Dialectics*. London and New York: Routledge, 2006.
Agamben, Giorgio. *Remnants of Auschwitz: The Witness and the Archive.* New York: Zone Books, 1999.

Bauman, Zygmunt. "Allosemitism: Premodern, Modern, Postmodern." *Modernity, Culture and "The Jew"*. Ed. Cheyette, Bryan, Marcus, Laura. Cambridge (England): Polity Press, 1998.

Bauman, Zygmunt. *Modernity and the Holocaust*. Cambridge: Polity Press, 1989.

Blanchot, Maurice. "Do Not Forget." *Political Writing: 1953–1993*. New York: Fordham University Press, 2010.

Boyarin, Daniel. *The Radical Jew: Paul and the Politics of Identity*. Berkeley: University of California, Berkeley, 1994.

Burgin, Richard. *Conversations with Isaac Bashevis Singer*. New York: Farrar, Straus and Giroux, 1986.

Butler, Judith. *Parting Ways: Jewish and the Critique of Zionism*. New York: Columbia University Press, 2012.

Deleuze, Gilles, and Guattari, Felix. *Kafka: Toward a Minor Literature*. Minneapolis: University of Minnesota Press, 1986.

Derrida, Jacques. *Acts of Religion*. Ed. Anidjar, Gil. New York: Routledge, 2002.

Fiedler, Leslie. *Fiedler on the Roof: Essays on Literature and Jewish Identity*. Boston: D. R. Godine, 1991.

Gil, Noam, *The Burden of Identity: on Holocaust Survivors in Jewish American Literature* (Dissertation, Tel Aviv University), 2016.

Gil, Noam. "In Praise of Vulgarity: On Yiddish in Isaac Bashevis Singer's 'Di Makhsheyfeh,'" *Prooftexts*. Vol. 37, No. 1 (2018), pp. 86–101.

Gilman, Sander L. *The Jew's Body*. New York: Routledge, 1991.

Goran, Lester. *The Bright Streets of Surfside: The Memoir of a Friendship with Isaac Bashevis Singer*. Kent: Kent State University, 1994.

Hadda, Janet. *Isaac Bashevis Singer: A Life*. Wisconsin: University of Wisconsin Press, 1997.

Hammerschlag, Sara. *The Figural Jew: Politics and Identity in Postwar French Thought*. Chicago: The University of Chicago Press, 2010.

Kristeva, Julia. *Powers of Horror: Essays on Abjection*. New York: Columbia University Press, 1982.

Landis, Joseph C. "I. B. Singer – Alone in the Forest." *Critical Essays on Isaac Bashevis Singer*. Ed. Farrel, Grace. Athens: University of Georgia, 1996.

Lyotard, Jean-François. *Heidegger and "the Jews."* Minneapolis: University of Minnesota Press, 1990.

Miron, Dan. "Passivity and Narration: The Spell of Bashevis Singer." *Critical Essays on Isaac Bashevis Singer*. Ed. Farrel, Grace. Athens: University of Georgia, 1996.

Noiville, Florence. *Isaac B. Singer: A Life*. New York: Farrar, Straus and Giroux, 2006.

Norich, Anita. "Translation and Transgression: Isaac Bashevis Singer in America." *Isaac Bashevis Singer: His Work and His World*. Ed. Denman, Hugh. Leiden and Boston: Brill, 2002.

Sherman, Joseph. "Upside Down in the Daytime: Singer and Male Homosexuality." *Critical Essays on Isaac Bashevis Singer*. Ed. Farrel, Grace. Athens: University of Georgia, 1996.

Silverman, Max. "Re-figuring the 'Jew' in France." *Modernity, Culture, and "the Jew."* Eds. Cheyette, Bryan, and Laura Marcus. Cambridge: Polity Press, 1998.

Singer, Isaac Bashevis. *Enemies, A Love Story*. New York: Farrar, Straus and Giroux, 1972.

Singer, Isaac Bashevis. *The Collected Stories of Isaac Bashevis Singer*. New York: Farrar, Straus and Giroux, 1982.

Singer, Isaac Bashevis. *Love and Exile: An Autobiographical Trilogy*. New York: Farrar, Straus and Giroux, 1984.

Singer, Isaac Bashevis. *Lost in America*. New York: Doubleday, 1981.

Singer, Isaac Bashevis. "What Is the Proper Ground for Literature?" *Yiddish: Modern Jewish Studies*. Vol. 14, No. 2–3 (2006 [1943]), pp. 86–8.

Singer, Isaac Bashevis. *"Wedding in Brownsville," The Collected Stories of Isaac Bashevis Singer*. New York: Farrar, Straus and Giroux, 1982 (1964).

Volkov, Shulamit. *Germans, Jews, and Anti-Semites: Trials in Emancipation*. Cambridge: Cambridge University Press, 2006.

Weininger, Otto. *Sex and Character*. London: Heinemann; New York: G. P. Putnam's Sons, 1906.

Part 4: **Modern Jewish Thought**

Willi Goetschel
Spinoza, Heresy, and the Discourse of Modernity

Spinoza, early on, was considered an atheist, an irreverent spirit whose abominable rejection of religion had no bounds. For many, Spinoza was either a Jewish heretic or the hero of a Jewish modernity that would celebrate him as its inspirational guide. Alternately dubbed heretic, apostate, renegade, or saint, blessed, and God-intoxicated Spinoza and his controversial identity have become a litmus test regarding the way we understand modernity – and Jewish modernity in particular.[1]

In his provocative essay *The Non-Jewish Jew*, Isaac Deutscher offers an intriguing lineage of the modern Jewish heretic:

> The Jewish heretic who transcends Jewry belongs to a Jewish tradition. You may, if you like, see *Akher* as a prototype of those great revolutionaries of modern thought: Spinoza, Heine, Marx, Rosa Luxemburg, Trotsky, and Freud. (Deutscher 1968, 26)

For Deutscher, there is no doubt that Spinoza is at the heart of the tradition of modern Jewish heresy as the foundational figure of a lineage, inaugurating a long line of "non-Jewish Jews." But this lineage does not exactly "exit" Jewish existence. An apostasy of sorts, it would nevertheless be hard to ignore as part of what it seems to have left behind and deny: the Jewish tradition that brought it forth and of which, Deutscher suggests, this line of Jewish heretics presents such formidable examples. As he continues:

> You may, if you wish to, place them within a Jewish tradition. They all went beyond the boundaries of Jewry. They all found Jewry too narrow, too archaic, and too constricting. They all looked for ideals and fulfillment beyond it, and they represent the sum and substance of much that is greatest in modern thought, the sum and substance of the most profound upheavals that have taken place in philosophy, sociology, economics, and politics in the last three centuries. (Deutscher 1968, 26)

With rapture and exaltation, Deutscher argues the paradox that these champions of universality all hail from a minority group whose particularism they overcame but whose particular background, oddly enough, prepared them for this move. In other words, the paradox of modernity expressed itself in these figures as the

---

[1] For a discussion that the "scandal" of Spinoza's Jewishness poses see my introduction to Goetschel 2004.

breakthrough to a universal vision that owed itself to the particular tradition from which they seemed to sally forth. So Deutscher wonders:

> Did they have anything in common with one another? Have they perhaps impressed mankind's thought so greatly because of their special 'Jewish genius'? (Deutscher 1968, 27)

But quick to resist being carried away completely, he answers his own questions in a more non-committal fashion:

> I don't believe in the exclusive genius of any race. Yet, I think that in some ways they were very Jewish indeed. They had in themselves something of the quintessence of Jewish life and of the Jewish intellect. They were *a priori* exceptional in that as Jews they dwelt on the borderlines of various civilizations, religions, and national cultures. They were born and brought up on the borderlines of various epochs. Their mind matured where the most diverse cultural influences crossed and fertilized each other. They lived on the margins or in the nooks and crannies of their respective nations. Each of them was in society and yet not in it, of it and yet not of it. (Deutscher 1968, 26)

What exactly makes Spinoza the progenitor of a long line of modern Jewish heretics, however, remains unclear. Deutscher does not offer much more than a certain "je ne sais quoi" of Jewish borderline existence in the style of Georg Simmel's description of the Jew as the paradigmatic stranger that Simmel portrayed solely in terms of social marginalization as the Other.[2]

If Deutscher's rhetoric disappoints in offering any illumination of the problem at hand, his discussion captures some of the buzz and excitement palpable in the portrayal of Spinoza as heretic, apostate, renegade, or crypto Jew – a portrayal that continues to circulate in contemporary discourse. While Deutscher was simply interested in identifying the paradox in the construction of universalist visions of modernity, his observation has assumed new meaning in the postsecular age, which has seen a striking surge of interest in Spinoza as heretic. The thrill of Spinoza's heresy highlights the desire to be part of a modernity we still conceptualize along the lines of conventional distinctions, whereby the heretic continues to instill the excitement of the illicit as if the institution of organized religion were still intact. But the desire to understand Spinoza's modernity in terms of heresy might turn out to be more problematic than previously imagined, for it recycles distinctions whose underlying theological-political commitments have long become obsolete.

This essay examines the desire to present Spinoza as a heretic, an urge curiously at odds with Spinoza's own philosophical disposition vis-à-vis heresy.

---

[2] See the excursus on the stranger in Simmel 2009, 601–605.

While often construed as an act of heresy undermining any claim to the validity of religious tradition, Spinoza's argument articulates a rather different concern suggesting that the exercise of genuine hermeneutic transparency does not lead to heresy but instead to understanding the lack of any cognitive as well as religious legitimation of the accusation of heresy.

In the last few decades, however, there has been a remarkable proliferation of publications featuring Spinoza as a heretic. While historical accounts of Spinoza's contemporaries had already presented him as apostate, renegade, or heretic, this is an altogether new phenomenon in more recent Spinoza research and popular accounts alike. This occurs at a moment of an advanced stage of secularism and at the cusp of the emergence of the debates around the postsecular as a concept of late modernity. In the context of this development, the discussion about Spinoza as a heretic becomes symptomatic for the struggle to grasp the meaning of his life and thought at the intersecting point in the crosshairs of the secular and postsecular. The striking interest in the anachronistic concept of heresy at that juncture deserves critical attention because it is indicative of Spinoza's role in the narrative of heresy.

While Spinoza enjoyed a great renaissance in Germany in the 1920s (Lazier 2008), and in France from the 1960s onward (Peden 2014), a new interest beyond the circle of Spinoza scholars was sparked in the Anglophone world by Yirmiyahu Yovel's two-volume study *Spinoza and Other Heretics* in 1989. The Jewish dimension of Spinoza's existence and thinking was all of a sudden openly and unapologetically addressed in its challenging complexity. Yovel's study signaled a new emphasis on Spinoza's connection with the world of Marranos as the subtitle of volume 1, *The Marrano of Reason*, suggested. It was not so much the specific arguments Yovel advanced that made his study so seminal as the effect it had by inserting Spinoza into the wider debates on modernity while insisting on the critical significance of his controversial Jewishness. Yovel captured the concerns of a generation that came to understand Spinoza's significance in the broader context of the need to rethink the terms of modernity. In recognizing the paradigmatic role that Marrano and other Jewish sensibilities can play in this project, Yovel returned the Jewish dimension of Spinoza to the contemporary debate, front and center.

In his illuminating study *The Courtier and the Heretic: Leibniz, Spinoza, and the Fate of God in the Modern World* (2005), Matthew Stewart presented a double portrait contrasting Spinoza with Leibniz that broached the question of heresy in a novel fashion. Stewart captured the problem of casting Spinoza as a heretic as a questionable form of typification that reduced the philosopher and his thought to the dubious status of his social marginalization that would obscure the critical significance of his philosophical project. Stewart's book offered a compelling account of the challenge Spinoza presented, such that even a sophisticated philosopher like Leibniz found himself so profoundly conflicted in his attraction and affinity to the thinker that he ended up running for cover, making sure to conceal the traces of his sympathy. Too radical for Leibniz to embrace him openly, Spinoza proved no less seminal for his thought. Rather than just a quirk, Spinoza's heresy became the mark – or "wound" to paraphrase Adorno – of a modernity unable to recognize the full significance of the challenge it confronted.

A year, later, Rebecca Goldstein's *Betraying Spinoza: The Renegade Who Gave Us Modernity* (2006) presented a picture of Spinoza that seemed to starkly contradict Yovel's notion of Spinoza as the first modern Jew, declaring he "calmly removed himself from any further form of Jewish life" (Goldstein 2006, 5). Rather, Goldstein argued, "Spinoza opted for secularism at a time when the concept had not yet been formulated" (Goldstein 2006, 5). A very different approach can be found in Rachel Kadish's novel *The Weight of Ink* (2017). The novel is a fictional account of the life of a mysterious scribe who, hailing from the Amsterdam Jewish community, shares many interests and concerns with Spinoza, with the exception that she is a woman who is denied any sort of open life as female philosopher. Her greatest desire to correspond with Spinoza is complicated by posing as a male writer. While Spinoza himself does not appear in the novel except by proxy of an elusive epistolary presence, the novel conjures a powerful impression of his inspirational importance both for his time and today's imaginary. While Spinoza's appearance in novels is a literary phenomenon going back to the 19th century,[3] the fictional account in *The Weight of Ink* indicates a new stage in Spinoza's portrayal as a *spiritus rector* of modern Jewish heresy: it highlights the sheer inspirational power that resides in his name and the fetish-like role he has come to play in our contemporary imagination.

As Steve Nadler points out in his 2001 study *Spinoza's Heresy: Immortality and the Jewish Mind,* what is at stake with the controversy over Spinoza's heresy can be summed up this way:

> Spinoza was excluded not by ecclesiastic authorities, but by a community. What he was deprived of was more than just the right to partake in certain liturgical ceremonies. It went, in fact, to the heart of what it means to be Jewish. (Nadler 2001, 4)

What makes Spinoza in the eyes of some a renegade or non-Jew, makes him in the eyes of others the exemplary modern Jew. By emancipating himself

---

[3] See especially the novels by Berthold Auerbach and the discussion in Schapkow 2001 and Rose 2014.

from the old and repressive life forms of a tradition, he recovers the deeper impulse in the face of a modernity that his radical approach helps to reimagine in ways that no longer force Jews to either abandon their tradition or opt out of modernity, but instead offers them a chance to shape and define modernity on their own terms. From Moses Mendelssohn and Solomon Maimon to the exponents of the Wissenschaft des Judentum, Heinrich Heine, Moses Hess, Heinrich Graetz, and Sigmund Freud, Spinoza was seen as the great figure that had shown a way to modernity that would no longer be exclusively Christian. A young Martin Buber identified with Spinoza, as did Adolf S. Oko, a great librarian at the Hebrew Union College and an intellectual who signed some of his early essays with Spinoza's first name, Baruch. This was not unusual. Identification with Spinoza became a common phenomenon for many young Jewish intellectuals of the late 19th and early 20th century.[4] Martin Buber, Margarete Susman, and Leo Baeck celebrated Spinoza as one of the Jewish people's most gifted progenies.[5]

Immanuel Wolf (i.e. Wohlwill) gave classic expression to this view in his programmatic introductory essay of the inaugural issue of the *Journal for the Science of Judaism* (*Zeitschrift für die Wissenschaft des Judenthums*), "On the Concept of a Science of Judaism" (Über den Begriff einer Wissenschaft des Judenthums) when he described Spinoza as a man,

> whose brilliance and depth was centuries ahead, whose most significant impact on the more consequential and deeper philosophy of today is obvious, who parted from the external rite of Judaism but the more vividly grasped its inner spirit.[6]

For the author of the first history of Jewish philosophy, Julius Spiegler, there was no doubt that Spinoza's philosophy bears the imprint of Jewish thought, and can be understood as its distillation (Spiegler 1890). Heinrich Heine gave this fascination with Spinoza striking expression when he described Spinoza as his "fellow-unbeliever" or *Unglaubensgenosse*: a characterization that expresses the

---

4 For Buber's early identification with Spinoza see Friedman 1982, 43; for Oko see the short discussion in Goetschel 2019, 38–40.
5 For a representative comment see Martin Buber's observation in his early "Speeches on Judaism" where he notes that Spinoza is the "greatest philosophical genius that [Judaism] has given the world, who is at the same time the only one among the great philosophers who in truth has no other object of his thought than God." See Buber 1963, 129.
6 See Wolf 1823, 14: "dessen Scharfsinn und Tiefe Jahrhunderten vorauseilten, dessen höchst bedeutender Einfluß auf die consequentere und tiefere Philosophie heutiger Tage unverkennbar ist, der sich zwar vom äußern Ritus des Judenthums losgesagt, aber dafür dessen innern Geist um so lebendiger begriffen hatte."

affinity with a thoroughly critical attitude that was to become paradigmatic for Jewish modernity.⁷

For Heine, Spinoza was no lost cause of Jewish tradition but, on the contrary, one of its most inspiring exponents. In an excursus on Spinoza in his *On the History of Religion and Philosophy in Germany*, Heine makes a decisive intervention in the history of Spinoza reception, fleshing out Spinoza's significance in programmatic fashion. He describes the effect of Spinoza as "a certain soft breeze that is inexplicable" and suggestively adds: "The spirit of the Hebrew prophets still rested perhaps on their late descendant" (Heine 2007, 51). This follow-up sentence sends us back to the preceding "certain soft breeze" whose alliterative play is lost in the English translation. Heine uses the German word "Hauch" that intimately resonates with the Hebrew "ruach," which means breeze, wind, and spirit. Heine's subtle yet resolute countering of the accusation of heresy suggests a far deeper, more substantive "inspirational" lineage than the gatekeepers who classify Spinoza as a renegade or heretic could claim for themselves.⁸

Heine's emancipatory approach to Spinoza was formative for Berthold Auerbach and Moses Hess. Auerbach was not only one of the first authors of a fictionalized novel about Spinoza in 1837 but also went on to translate Spinoza's works he published in a two volume edition in 1841. Auerbach concludes his introduction on extolling Spinoza's vision of the free man as embracing "pious knowledge" or *fromme Erkenntnis* (Auerbach 1841, vol. 1, cccv).⁹ Famously, Moses Hess made Spinoza the patron saint first of his philosophy of history, then his philosophy of action, later to be followed by his proto-Zionist vision *Rome and Jerusalem*.¹⁰

Heine's apt description of Spinoza as his "fellow-unbeliever" or *Unglaubensgenosse* highlights the conflictual dynamics at stake in identifying a

---

7 The label gained notoriety thanks to Freud, who gave it currency by lifting it from the first edition of Heine's *Travel Pictures*, the only place where this newly coined term occurs, and which Heine purged from later editions. In *Jokes and Their Relation to the Unconscious*, Freud featured the expression as an illuminating example of how negation operates in the technique of the joke. Freud's psychoanalytical attention to the term sheds light on the crucial role that drives the dynamics of Heine's insight of the critical function of negation for Jewish modernity. Freud famously returned to the term when, a few years later, he called Heine his "fellow-unbeliever" – a pertinent tribute to Heine, given the fact that Heine – one of Freud's favorite poets – was after all spear-heading Spinozist notions in his own heretical way. For Heine's Spinozist commitments and Freud as avid reader of Heine, see Goetschel 2019a, esp. 195–204 and 85–86.
8 For a discussion of Heine's passage see also Goetschel 2019a, 201–202; for the critical significance Heine assigns to Spinoza in his *On the History of Philosophy and Religion in Germany* see Goetschel 2004, 253–265.
9 For Auerbach and Spinoza see Rose 2014, 200–240.
10 For Hess see Avineri 1985 and Rose 2014, 241–271.

heretic. Formative for the identity of a social group, exclusion by claim of one or another's heresy produces an out-group that stabilizes its in-group at the cost of bloodletting. Heine's play on the notion that the true believer is the unbeliever brings out the in-group's problematic desire for a self-immunization that can only be realized at the cost of its auto-immunity – which is the dialectic that keeps community alive. Amounting to an auto-immune condition, heresy is ultimately a self-defeating concept because it entails a claim to authority that undermines the presupposition of the accuser's own claim to faithful adherence to a divine unfathomable wisdom it otherwise second-guesses. This uncanny dynamic haunts the prosecutor of the heretic more than the one presumed to be a heretic. More problematically, the distinction buys into the notion that exclusion establishes stable borders without realizing that border drawing reconfigures the in-group's own form and constitution in unexpected fashion. By calling themselves Spinoza's fellow-unbelievers, Heine and Freud position themselves as self-conscious members of the out-group whose decisive role brings home the dynamics of in- and exclusion as a constitutive nexus of tradition making.

It is no coincidence that these ideas circulate in Heine and Freud. They echo sociological intuitions concerning group dynamics and the function of tradition that find early articulation in Spinoza's work. In his *Theological-Political Treatise*, Spinoza presents a theory of religion, scriptural hermeneutics, and Jewish tradition that offers an approach whose entire ethos is to expose the notion of heresy as a profoundly irreligious, theologically flawed, hermeneutically spurious and politically divisive notion. For Spinoza, heresy belongs like any other theological concept informed by a claim to dogma to the arsenal of psychological warfare that leads only to strife and discord while undermining the very purpose of the biblical dispensation that commands, according to Spinoza's core claim, only two things, "practicing justice and loving-kindness," as emphasized in Spinoza's introduction to the *Theological-Political Treatise* (Spinoza 2016, 73). Religion is for Spinoza primarily a practice rather than a set of beliefs, whose creedal fixation is the prerogative to be the preoccupation of theology, and whose infelicitous nexus with politics the *Theological-Political Treatise* seeks to disentangle.

It is worthwhile to pay close attention to the irenic message of the title page that summarizes the book's purpose to show "that the republic can grant freedom of philosophizing without harming its peace or piety, and cannot deny it without destroying its peace and piety" (Spinoza 2016, 65). Freedom of thinking, in other words, is not merely fully compatible with religion and peace but, more importantly, is the very condition for genuine religion and peace. The hyphen in the titular term *Theological-Political* indicates the balance between the two, as well as the imperative to delineate their respective limits of authority. Conflict and strife in the world, in other words, are the result of the border dispute between them, where there are "rebellions which people stir up under the pretext of religion" which "surely arise only because laws are made about speculative matters, opinions are considered crimes and condemned as wicked, and their defenders and followers are sacrificed, not to the public well-being, but only to the hatred and cruelty of their opponents" (Spinoza 2016, 69). The notion of heresy, in other words, is a recipe for conflict, strife, war, and worse, the very destruction of the community. Heresy is thus nothing other than the result of the self-fulfilling prophecy of a theology that demands unity but creates strife because the very call for submission it imposes produces the conflict that leads to the suffering which it claims to relieve.[11]

It is incumbent on the state to protect citizens against the confusion between its true mission and its instrumentalization for ulterior motives of domination by theological factions that seek to impose their rule. Spinoza thus continues, introducing the operative distinction that underpins his distinction between theological speculation and religion or "piety" (*pietas*). This central term implies action-based religious belief as opposed to theological speculation. The Latin origin of the term emphasizes precisely the connotation that Spinoza seeks to accentuate:

> But if, by the legislation of the state, only *deeds were condemned and words went unpunished*, such rebellions could not be clothed in any pretext of right, nor controversies turned into rebellions. (Spinoza 2016, 69)

This, Spinoza argues, is precisely the framework of the Dutch republic he lives in, where "everyone is granted complete freedom of judgment, and is permitted to worship God according to their mentality [*suo ingenio*: disposition], and in which nothing is thought to be dearer or sweeter than freedom" (Spinoza 2016, 69).[12] Spinoza understands religious practice to be derived from our *ingenium* or disposition. The hyphen in the "Theological-Political" of the Treatise's title marks the line that situates religious practice on the one side in the sphere of theological authority and the right to freedom of thought, and its expression on the other side of that line, in the sphere of the state's authority. More precisely, Spinoza assigns the authority of the political sphere and its legislative power to an order different from that of theological speculations, which operates within the political framework that constitutes it. Put differently, while

---

[11] For a discussion of the function of the hyphen in the *Theological-Political Treatise* see Goetschel 2019b.
[12] For the Latin, see Spinoza, *Tractatus Theologico-Politicus/Theologisch-Politischer Traktat*, 10.

the political determines the laws, religion is bound to act within it. However, in order for political authority to operate properly, it must acknowledge the freedom of opinion regarding matters of religion. In Spinoza's view, any interference by either of the two spheres constitutes an encroachment onto the other's domain.

In other words, Spinoza's approach to theorizing the relationship between the theological and political side of the hyphen – i.e. both the way he views the function of religion and the state and their interaction – has no time for any sort of concept of heresy. With regard to the notorious "worldly arm," to which the Church liked to surrender those it declared heretic, such a move is in political terms unacceptable because, on Spinoza's understanding, it would directly intervene with the functioning of the state. In terms of religion, such surrender would go directly against the very substance and ethos of "piety" and religion. Spinoza's approach systemically excludes any notion of heresy because according to his view religion is no longer understood to be guided by a concern about the truth of its creeds, beliefs, and convictions, but instead by the concern regarding the consequences of the actions to which they lead or which they mandate.

Spinoza argues this point in a two-pronged approach, "theologically" and "politically." The hyphen that connects the two terms in the title signals that peace and piety can only be secured by way of this double-pronged approach, which, as a result, is "theological-political" in a way that now interlinks the two terms accentuating the interlocking function of the two terms through the hyphen.

Whereas Spinoza's argument to justify the framework of his political theory seems in the eyes of our age intuitive and non-controversial, his view of the role and function of religion and theology deserve closer examination. It is ultimately the subtle way Spinoza reinterprets them that provides the framework for advancing a vision of religion and tradition that no longer needs to rely on exclusionary measures to contain differences of opinion, but rather recognizes them as constitutive to the system and necessary for developing a thriving life of body and intellect. We could say that Spinoza moves here in an intellectual space beyond heresy, a place where the notion of heresy itself betrays a certain impiety and irreverence towards the divine as travesty of the very ethos of religion, piety, and the function of tradition.

In a critical aside, Spinoza gives striking expression to this disconnect, which Lessing will echo a century later in his play *Nathan the Wise*, so often misunderstood as a plea for tolerance. The famous question that Saladin poses to Nathan is anticipated by and taken from Spinoza's *Theological-Political Treatise*. Spinoza had already moved away from simply demanding tolerance. Rather, he viewed the traditional attempt at resolving the issue as a category mistake, according to which one demands tolerance in a matter that is no longer about truth claims, but about the realization of one's righteousness[13]:

> I've often wondered that men who boast that they profess the Christian religion – i.e. love, gladness, peace, restraint, and good faith toward all – would contend so unfairly against one another, and indulge daily in the bitterest hatred toward one another, so that each man's faith is known more easily from his hatred and contentiousness than from his love, gladness, etc. (Spinoza 2016, 70)

But while the narcissism of little differences, as Freud would call it, drives its contentious followers apart, creating divisive fault lines in society, those differences do not seem to produce any different sorts of conduct of their lives, as Spinoza adds:

> Long ago, things reached the point where you can hardly know what anyone is, whether Christian, Turk [Muslim], Jew, or Pagan, except by the external dress and adornment of his body, or because he frequents this or that Place of Worship, or because he's attached to this or that opinion, or because accustomed to swear by the words of some master. They all lead the same kind of life. (Spinoza 2016, 70)

This can only lead, Spinoza suggests, to "great dissension, envy, and hatred, whose violence no passage of time could lessen," and he concludes: "It's no wonder, then, that nothing has remained of the old Religion but its external ceremony [*cultus*]. [...] No wonder faith is nothing but credulity and prejudices" (Spinoza 2016, 70).[14] Piety and religion have turned into a travesty, the preaching of love into the practice of hatred, and the grasp of Scripture has vanished. As a consequence, heresy becomes a purely creedal affair that has no meaning with regard to the conduct and behavior of an individual. To advance this line of argument, Spinoza develops a sophisticated theory of hermeneutics that shows not only the wrongful appropriation of Scripture for the purpose of control over the minds of the faithful; it moreover demonstrates that a genuine understanding of Scripture must reject any such pretension of religion to political power. With this turn, the concept of heresy is effectively put out of commission. This argument is developed in detail in chapters 1–15, while chapters 16–20 offer a radical political theory *in nuce* that has a pointedly sharp, democratic edge. The point of Spinoza's detailed discussion, which involves an in-depth examination of the key issues of scriptural interpretation, is to establish his argument with the support

---

13 For a discussion of Nathan as a staged reader of Spinoza, see Goetschel 2012, 151–154. For the argument that Lessing's play does not argue for tolerance, an Augustinian concept that proves too narrow, but rather for freedom of religion, see Goetschel 2004, 231–232.
14 For the Latin see Spinoza, *Tractatus Theologico-Politicus/Theologisch-Politischer Traktat*, 12.

of the very scriptural traditions with which he engages. To do so, Spinoza will also address the basic question of how tradition works.

The upshot of this discussion is that the polysemic character of Scripture proliferates meaning in such a way that heresy is the natural outcome of the hermeneutic process, the hermeneutic default position, as it were, of making sense. The reason is that the Scripture is the product of a primary interpretation that is being produced by the prophets who render what is revealed to them according to their understanding in their own language. As the opening sentence of chapter 1 formulates it:

> Prophecy, or Revelation, is certain knowledge of some matter which God has revealed to men. (Spinoza 2016, 76)

Interpreting Scripture then is a second order interpretation of the interpretation that Scripture presents. Spinoza goes on to say:

> And a Prophet is one who interprets God's revelations to those who cannot have certain knowledge of them, and who can therefore only embrace what has been revealed by simple faith. (Spinoza 2016, 76)

For Spinoza, however, natural knowledge can also be called prophecy:

> For what we know by the natural knowledge depends only on the knowledge of God and of his eternal decrees. (Spinoza 2016, 76)

Declaring prophecy to be a natural epistemological process no different from everyday knowledge (and natural knowledge thereby to be equally divine), Spinoza suggests an interpretative continuum that has profound effects for the conception of scriptural interpretation as both no less and no more divine than any other hermeneutic activity. He works this out in chapter 7, "On the Interpretation of Scripture," which lays out the basic epistemological issues that predicate the hermeneutic process. The key move of the chapter consists in doing away with the distinction of the hermeneutic protocol between the book of God and the book of Nature. Rather, Spinoza argues for the identity of the hermeneutic process for both:

> To sum up briefly, I say that the method of interpreting Scripture does not differ at all from the method of interpreting nature, but agrees with it completely. (Spinoza 2016, 171)

While the Protestant edge of Luther's principle "sola scriptura" articulates a position that addresses the accusation of heresy by preemptively rejecting any claim to theological truth that lacks direct scriptural evidence, Spinoza turns the claim to the authority of determining questions of dogma into a question of the correct grasp of the meaning of Scripture. In other words, this is an exploration of the conditions of hermeneutic reasoning, which builds on but also radicalizes the Protestant approach. For while the Protestant approach gives the individual the authority for unmediated interpretation, thus making them prophets (potential, temporary, and limited though they might be), Spinoza insists that such a solution of the hermeneutic conundrum of accurate Scriptural interpretation remains ultimately circuitous. In the passage discussed earlier at the beginning of chapter 1, Spinoza adds an important remark saying:

> Though natural knowledge is divine, nevertheless those who pass it on cannot be called Prophets. (Spinoza 2016, 77)

This sentence is confusing because the reader might expect Spinoza to put the interpreter of natural knowledge in an equal position to that of the prophet. To clarify, Spinoza adds a footnote to this sentence expanding in the following way:

> That is, interpreters of God. For an interpreter of God is one who interprets God's decrees to others to whom they have not been revealed, and who, in embracing them, rely on the authority of the prophet. But if the men who listened to prophets became prophets, as those who listen to philosophers become philosophers, then the prophet would not be an interpreter of the divine decrees, since his hearers would rely, not on the testimony and authority of the prophet, but on revelation itself, and internal testimony. (Spinoza 2016, 77, note 2)

This passage poses a hermeneutic challenge to the reader and I think the reason for that is that Spinoza seeks to cautiously signal an issue that the Protestant ethos easily confounds, but which to point out in a more direct way would put its author at direct risk, not with his opponents but with the few interlocutors that share the gist of his theological-political agenda, yet who might resolutely part ways at this point. Let's disentangle the point Spinoza presents here in the text's marginal annotation. Though he claims merely explanatory significance for the annotation, it highlights an important distinction.

Unlike other human beings, prophets hold a privileged position not because of superhuman powers but simply because they are the ones who pass revelation on to others. This transmission, however, is not a simple rendering of an intact message or communication "verbatim" passed on "verbatim"; it is rather an act of interpretation or translation of a particular prophet's vision into human language. It presents thus a first order observation. Whether the prophet him- or herself or another exegete hears an oral or reads a written testimony is of no consequence, because at this stage of the hermeneutic process its transmission has become a second order observation. There is, Spinoza's note argues, no privileged position from which a "prophet" or anyone seemingly invested with superhuman (or institutional) powers could claim a higher order knowledge than that which natural knowledge grants according to the normal order of hermeneutic logic, whose many issues Spinoza so painstakingly details in the *Theological-Political Treatise*.

In a next step, the note concludes:

> Thus the sovereign powers are the interpreters of the law of their state, because the laws they pass are preserved only by their authority and depend only on their testimony.
> (Spinoza 2017, 77)

Similarly then to the prophet, interpreter of divine revelation, the state is the exclusive interpreter of its own law simply because it is the legislator. This circular mode of legitimation of authority might be surprising, but it is not justificatory or declarative: it simply describes the logical circle that applies to any form of self-authorization. What it adds to the discussion of heresy is a demonstration of how the figure of theological self-legitimation is an intrinsically political move. And the political mechanism of legitimation can now be understood as a complex process that is in nature guided by neither epistemological nor hermeneutic justification, but by the way power can legitimate itself only self-recursively.

Consequently, the notion of heresy with all its attendant assumptions of a privileged stance on access to understanding, i.e. translation of phenomena, natural or divine, no longer obtains. Remarkably, Spinoza thus subverts the notion of heresy by way of an indirect strategy of argumentation without ever referring to the term heresy directly.

Significantly, the term heretic occurs only once in the *Theological-Political Treatise*, when Spinoza cites the Dutch proverb "Geen ketter zonder letter": "No heretic without text" (Spinoza 2016, 264).[15] In the context of Spinoza's argument, the proverb serves as a stark reminder that heresy is a function of a certain attitude of scriptural tradition. It is a function of a problematic use of hermeneutics that Spinoza's approach exposes as baseless: There is no opinion that cannot claim a textual basis in Scripture for the simple reason that Scripture consists of a wide range of writings whose only common ground is the call for justice and love. The rest is interpretation and therefore full of variables. As Spinoza notes in the opening paragraph of chapter 14 leading up to the citation of the proverb:

> Anyone who indiscriminately accepts everything contained in Scripture as its universal and unconditional teaching about God, and doesn't know accurately what has been

---

[15] The term occurs a second time at the end of the chapter. Cf. Spinoza 2016, 271, which I discuss further below.

> accommodated to the grasp of the common people, will be unable not to confuse the opinions of the common people with divine doctrine, hawk human interventions and fancies as divine teachings, and about the authority of Scripture.
>
> Who doesn't see that this is the principal reason why the sectaries teach as doctrines of the faith so many and such contrary opinions, and confirm them by many examples from Scripture? (Spinoza 2016, 263–264)

At this point Spinoza refers to the proverb that he embeds in the following reasoning:

> That's why it long ago became a Proverb among the Dutch that *geen ketter zonder letter* [There is no heretic without a text.] For the Sacred Books were written not by one person only, nor for the common people of one age, but by many men, of different mentalities, and of different ages. (Spinoza 2016, 264)

For Spinoza then, the folk saying suggests a comically subtle and wry outlook as vernacular proverbs so often do. Rebuffing heresy as a meaningful notion where the proliferation of sectarian views is understood to be the function of the interpretational practice of the study of Scripture in a religiously post-reformatory, free society, the Dutch proverb recognizes religious diversity as the very sign of genuine religious commitment free from any ulterior political pressure. Spinoza thus writes:

> Still, we don't want to accuse the sectaries of impiety just because they accommodate the words of Scripture to their own opinions. For the Scripture was accommodated to the grasp of the common people, so everyone is permitted to accommodate it to his own opinions, if he sees that in that way he can obey God more wholeheartedly in matters of justice and loving-kindness. (Spinoza 2016, 264)

The problem is that many take this freedom as granted for themselves while they are unwilling to see it extended to those with different views. Instead they desire to persecute those as God's enemies, whereas they love all those who agree with them as God's chosen. But "whoever persecutes the faithful is an Antichrist" (Spinoza 2016, 267). For Spinoza, then, there is "no room left for controversies in the Church" (Spinoza 2017, 268). For faith, Spinoza now states explicitly, does not call for adherence to doctrines concerning truth, "but only such doctrines that are necessary for obedience, which strengthen our hearts in love toward our neighbors" (Spinoza 2016, 267). In identifying genuine faith independently from doctrinal subtleties and as being concerned only with the realization of good deeds of justice and loving-kindness, Spinoza defines religion as free from any truth claim and exclusively practice-oriented.

For Spinoza, there is no room for the concept of heresy in the practice of faith and sound religion. By the end of chapter 14, Spinoza has come to a complete reversal of the definition of heresy. A person who suspects someone of heresy is somebody who seeks to create conflict where there is not initially any concerning genuine religion and piety, i.e. what we might call religiosity. While it is clear that since late antiquity heretics have been a product of an ecclesiastic politics of control and domination, an insight that gains wider currency with Montaigne and others, Spinoza's innovative contribution to the debate is to argue this point from a position that operates consistently from within the tradition of Scriptural hermeneutics and faith. This is why it has such a provocative effect on its readers, and why it was maligned with such profound outbursts of virulence. Faith, which for the persecutors of heresy is appropriated and used as recourse to their claims of legitimacy, ultimately defies such instrumentalization, as the penultimate paragraph of chapter 14 notes, because in the final analysis it

> grants everyone the greatest freedom to philosophize, so that without wickedness he can think whatever he wishes about anything. (Spinoza 2016, 271)

But more radical than that, faith rejects any form of doctrinal politics because it represents an encroachment on faith itself that undermines its very nature. Rather than being hijacked by those who wish to persecute others as heretics, faith does not allow for such forms of power politics:

> Faith condemns as heretics and schismatics only those who teach opinions which encourage obstinacy, hatred, quarrels and anger. (Spinoza 2016, 271)

And like a mantra, Spinoza adds:

> On the other hand, it considers faithful only those who encourage Justice and Lovingkindness as far as the powers of their reason and their faculties permit. (Spinoza 2016, 271)

To prove his point, Spinoza's catalogue of seven "dogmas" articulate a minimal doctrinal program Spinoza calls catholic in the literal sense of the word, i.e. pointedly inclusive (Spinoza 2016, 268–269). There has been some wonder about Spinoza's seven dogmas and its tongue-in-cheek catechism. However, its resolutely irenic inclusiveness demonstrates the possibility that indeed Scriptural tradition need not per se be divisive. Rather than automatically calling for conflict, discord, and strife, for Spinoza, the hermeneutic situation that prophecy creates with its interpretative context presents a possibility of grasping the creative openness that informs the very dynamics of tradition.

Spinoza's *Theological-Political Treatise* offers a compelling argument about heresy as a political and "secular" rather than a religious concept; further, its theory of hermeneutics and religion offers some important insights into the function of tradition, shedding some light on what the concept of heresy and the characterization of individual philosophers as heretic means in a secular and postsecular age. For Spinoza, tradition is not to be understood as a monolithic block. It is not a set of fixed beliefs or creeds, nor a set framework to explain the world. Rather, tradition represents dynamics of transmission of meaning that is at every turn of being passed on reconstituted through the effect of interpretation, i.e. the creative negotiation of a hermeneutic practice. This hermeneutic activity suggests that tradition is not a mere handing down of a set of stable meanings, but rather a process of continual negotiation of the hermeneutic challenge to interpret, i.e. to reconstitute meaning in ever new and changing contexts. In a way, tradition is not the result of a straightforward continuity, but rather the result of repetition with a difference. Discontinuity functions as the catalyst for producing a continuity that functions only because of its internally dynamic difference.

Tradition is in other words not a phenomenon of self-identical repetition of the ever-same, because traditions, even where they are not Scripture-based, hinge on a hermeneutic process that rests on the interplay of difference that makes identity possible in the first place. The model of polysemic proliferation of Scriptural hermeneutics implies for Spinoza also, as we have seen, the idea that religious practice might even include a proliferation of a variety of opposed views. In this light, such "heretical" diversity is constitutive for the life of tradition. For this approach theorizes tradition always already in the plural. There is no such thing as a pristine, singular tradition, according to Spinoza. Traditions define and shape each other reciprocally and thus differentially.[16] This differential character of tradition renders each and everybody as it were a heretic from the start and makes the label "heretic" consequently non-distinctive because ubiquitous. For Spinoza, the label no longer makes a critical difference, that is, any distinction has become moot. The continuation of its application only perpetuates – if at best unintentionally – the epistemic commitments of a theological-political complex that, Spinoza's theory of hermeneutic has shown, are profoundly flawed, dangerous, and destructive.

At the current juncture – whether we call it secular or postsecular – this means that we may want to think twice before calling Spinoza a heretic, especially since the term has by now become metaphorically so loose and diffuse that it no longer has much distinctive meaning beyond expressing fandom and admiration. As the *Theological-Political Treatise* argues with compelling urgency – an

---

[16] See Goetschel 1993.

urgency it might be wise to heed now no less than at the time of its publication – heresy is a concept that has no ground in religion, faith, or what Spinoza calls piety. It is a strictly political and "secular" concept. In politics however, calling someone a heretic is to continue the theological warmongering that religion's imperatives of justice and love prohibit, while the only justification of the state is, as Spinoza insists, safety, i.e. peace and guarantee of freedom of thought and its expression. Heresy, then, has become for Spinoza an utterly dubious notion. To claim otherwise will ultimately backfire and obscure the unwarranted epistemic implications the concept entails.

With regard to the role of heresy in Jewish tradition, Spinoza turns here a new page for our understanding as well. This is no coincidence as he developed his approach through examining both Jewish and Christian traditions, focusing on the former in explicit terms but examining the latter no less rigorously, if implicitly and innocuously, out of caution. Spinoza's contribution here is to help us grasp the constitutive role of interpretative difference as a function of Scriptural tradition and its hermeneutics that keep religion alive in the first place. While his discussion of the ins and outs of Scriptural hermeneutics implies on the one hand that doctrinal differences are endemic to the process of interpretation, these differences mandate on the other hand in Spinoza's view an understanding of religion as practice rather than dispute and strife with regard to cognitive matters. The desire to identify heretical strands in Jewish tradition is for Spinoza the result of an interpretative bias that does not easily map onto the history of Jewish tradition if properly examined. Rather, the urge for such identification of heresy carries a normative commitment that the interpretative nature of Scriptural hermeneutic rejects. To suspect or accuse anybody of heresy is then not only wrongheaded and morally flawed but lacks the very Scriptural legitimacy on which its spurious claims are based. It represents a blatant misappropriation of Scripture and its tradition as it privileges what Walter Benjamin will describe as the problem of the victor dictating the terms of writing history.

Albert Memmi's definition of the heretic "as a dissident who has not been successful," (Memmi 2017, 178) highlights the critical significance of Spinoza's diagnosis of heresy as a concept that gets in the way if we wish to understand the function of tradition. Put differently, Spinoza's approach helps us better understand Jewish tradition – just as any other – as a dynamic of continuity and discontinuity, repetition and difference. Tradition, in other words, is constituted by the dynamic of its internal differences. Ultimately, Spinoza suggests, the notion of heresy is the result of a hermeneutic short-circuit that exposes its own epistemological and ethical failure as it fails the tradition to which it appeals.

Bibliography

Auerbach, Berthold. *B. v. Spinoza's sämmtliche Werke*. 2 vols. Stuttgart: Scheible, 1841.
Avineri, Shlomo. *Moses Hess: Prophet of Communism and Zionism* (New York and London: New York University Press, 1985).
Buber, Martin. *Der Jude und sein Judentum: Gesammelte Aufsätze und Reden*. Cologne: Joseph Melzer, 1963.
Deutscher, Isaac. *The Non-Jewish Jew and Other Essays*. Ed. Tamara Deutscher. London, New York, Toronto: Oxford University Press, 1968.
Friedman, Maurice. *Martin Buber's Life and Work: The Early Years 1878–1923*. London and Tunbridge Wells: Search Press, 1982.
Goetschel, Willi. "The Differential Character of Traditions." *Telos* 95 (1993): 161–170.
Goetschel, Willi. *Spinoza's Modernity: Mendelssohn, Lessing, and Heine*. Madison: University of Wisconsin Press, 2004.
Goetschel, Willi. "Inszenierungen einer Figur: Lessing und die jüdische Spinozarezeption." *Lessing Year Book* 39 (2012): 139–154.
Goetschel, Willi. (2019a). *Heine and Critical Theory*. London: Bloombsury, 2019.
Goetschel, Willi. (2019b). "The Hyphen in the Theological-Political: Spinoza to Mendelssohn, Heine, and Derrida." *Religions* 2019, 10, 21.
Goldstein, Rebecca. *Betraying Spinoza: The Renegade Who Gave Us Modernity*. New York: Schocken, 2006.
Heine, Heinrich. *On the History of Philosophy and Religion and Other Writings*. Trans. Howard Pollack-Milgate. Ed. Terry Pinkard. Cambridge: Cambridge University Press, 2007.
Kadish, Rachel. *The Weight of Ink*. Boston and New York: Houghton Mifflin Harcourt, 2017.
Lazier, Bernjamin. *God Interrupted: Heresy and the European Imagination between the World Wars*. Princeton: Princeton University Press, 2008.
Memmi, Albert. *Dictionnaire critique à l'usage des incrédules*. [No place]: Félin, 2017.
Nadler, Steven. *Spinoza's Heresy: Immortality and the Jewish Mind*. Oxford: Oxford University Press, 2001.
Peden, Knox. *Spinoza Contra Phenomenology: French Rationalism from Cavaillès to Deleuze*. Stanford: Stanford University Press, 2014.
Rose, Sven-Erik. *Jewish Philosophical Politics in Germany 1789–1848*. Waltham, Mass: Brandeis University Press, 2014.
Schapkow, Carsten. *"Die Freiheit zu philosophieren": Jüdische Identität in der Moderne im Spiegel der Rezeption Baruch de Spinozas in der deutschsprachigen Literatur*. Bielefeld: Aisthesis, 2001.
Simmel, Georg. *Sociology: Inquiries into the Construction of Social Forms*, trans. and ed. Anthony J. Blasi, Anton K. Jacobs, and Mathew Kanjirathinkal, with an introduction by Horst J. Helle. Leiden and Boston: Brill, 2009.
Spiegler, Julius S. *Geschichte der Philosophie des Judenthums*. Leipzig: Friedrich, 1890.
Stewart, Matthew. *The Courtier and the Heretic: Leibniz, Spinoza, and the Fate of God in the Modern World*. New Haven and London: Yale, 2005.
Spinoza, Baruch de. *Theological-Political Treatise*, in *The Collected Works of Spinoza*. Vol. 2. Ed. and trans. Edwin Curley. Princeton: Princeton University Press, 2016.

Spinoza. *Tractatus Theologico-Politicus/Theologisch-Politischer Traktat*. In Spinoza. *Opera/Werke*, vol. 1. Eds. Günter Gawlick and Friedrich Niewöhner. Darmstadt: Wissenschaftliche Buchgesellschaft, 1979.

Wolf, Immanuel. "Über den Begriff einer Wissenschaft des Judenthums." *Zeitschrift für die Wissenschaft des Judenthums*, vol. 1 (1823): 1–24.

Yovel, Yirmiyahu. *Spinoza and Other Heretics*. 2 vols. Princeton: Princeton University Press, 1989.

Gilad Sharvit
The Dialectics of Heresy: Trauma and History in Freud

There is a long tradition regarding the relationship between heresy and trauma in Judaism. This tradition begins in part in the story about the four who entered the *Pardes* (the orchard of esoteric knowledge) in Masechet Hagigah (14b). In the famous Talmudic account, one of the rabbis who entered the *Pardes*, Elisha Ben Abuya, or Acher, suffered from trauma induced by this mystical experience. "Ben Azzai," we are told, "gazed and died, Ben Zoma gazed and was harmed," and Acher "cut down the plantings," which is usually interpreted as *became heretic*. From the four, only Rabbi Akiva "entered in peace and left in peace."[1]

The story about the *Pardes* is often taken to explicate the danger of the encounter with the divine. Acher is especially important to the tradition I just mentioned because he became a heretic as a result of his traumatic experience. However, in what follows, I would like to suggest a model of heresy that portrays a different kind of relationship between heresy and trauma. While in the Talmudic legend trauma produced death, physical pain and ultimately heresy, I aim to explore how heresy may produce traumas. My argument in this chapter follows Sigmund Freud's monumental *Moses and Monotheism* (1939).[2] I argue that Freud's theory of the murder of Moses offers such a model of *heresy as trauma*. I am particularly interested in the implications of heresy-induced traumas for religious and social realities. Specifically, I show how Freud portrays a dialectics of heresy in Judaism: following his hypothesis of the murder of Moses in the desert and the return of the Israelites to the monotheism after a period of latency, I would argue that in Judaism heresy does not uphold Jewish tradition but rather (a) inaugurated Judaism and (b) informs the dynamic structure of Jewish history.

In the following lines, I will first address the notion of heresy in modernity, by briefly discussing the reception of Freud's book on Moses. My purpose here is to suggest that Freud's *Moses and Monotheism* proposes a model of heresy different from the prevalent notion of heresy in modernity, which Freud's last book is often taken to reflect. Then I will introduce the model of heresy as trauma, as

---

[1] I would like to express my deepest gratitude to Willi Goetschel, Yosef Schwartz, Galili Schahar, Ilit Ferber, Maoz Kahana, Eyal Bassan and Ori Rotlevy for their wonderful suggestions and remarks at different stages of composing the chapter.
[2] For important works on Freud's *Moses and Monotheism*, see Bernstein (1998), Derrida (1996), Paul (1996), Said (2004) and Yerushalmi (1991).

suggested, in my reading, in *Moses and Monotheism*. Lastly, I will show how this model might explain German Jewish reality in early twentieth-century Europe.

1 Freud as a Heretic

Moses and Monotheism, originally published as a series of three essays, offers a speculative argument about the origins of the Jewish people. Inspired by a set of crucial affinities – already well researched in Freud's time – between Judaism and a brief monotheist episode in Egyptian history during the reign of Akhenaton (circa 1350 BC), Freud theorized that while official historiographical accounts insist that this short monotheistic episode ended with the death of Akhenaton, the Egyptian religion was in fact born again in Judaism. One of the crown Egyptian princes named Moses, who was close to the dead Pharaoh, decided to preserve the Egyptian religion by introducing it to a slave nation that lived in Egypt at that time: the Israelites, who were intended to save the dying Egyptian religion, the one the Egyptians rejected. But, Freud continues, this great religious experiment failed: the Israelite slaves, accustomed to the sensual gratification of a polytheistic religion, could not have coped with the restrictions and prohibitions imposed by the Egyptian monotheism, such as the prohibition to make pictures and circumcision.[3] "The savage Semites," therefore, "took fate into their own hands and rid themselves of their tyrant" (*SE*, 23: 47).

The Moses book naturally concerned many around Freud. His claims about Moses' secret Egyptian identity and his murder in the desert by the Israelites troubled many who appealed to Freud and asked him to refrain from publishing his book in such a sensitive time for the Jewish people. Freud's book outwardly echoed anti-Semitic propaganda, for the Jews were, according to Freud, the descendants of despicable slaves, essentially a nation of murderers. Ernest Jones, in his biography of Freud, recounts how "friends suggested to Freud that the publication might cause hurt feelings in certain orthodox quarters" (Jones 1957, 3: 369). Freud himself reported to Arnold Zweig in Palestine in June 1938 about an American Jew who implored him "not to deprive our poor unhappy people of the one consolation remaining to them in their misery" (Freud and Zweig 1970, 163).[4]

---

[3] The Israelites were forced to obey "the harsh prohibitions" of their new religion, for instance the taboo "against making an image of any living or imagined creature" (*SE*, 23: 18).
[4] In the second prefatory note to the second book, Freud noted that in addition "there arrived, with a frequency surprising to a foreigner, communications of another sort, which were concerned with the state of my soul, which pointed out to me the way of Christ and sought to

Freud, an accomplished public figure, was clearly well aware of the danger his work presented. He refrained from publishing the last part of the book while still in Austria, concerned about the increased danger that anti-Semites like the Austrian ethnologist Pater Wilhelm Schmidt and others in the Catholic orthodoxy posed to himself and his family, but also, and perhaps even more worryingly, to psychoanalysis in Vienna. In the second prefatory note to the third part of the book, which Freud wrote only in exile in London, after escaping Vienna following the German *Anschluss*, he admits:

> At an earlier date I was living under the protection of the Catholic Church, and was afraid that the publication of my work would result in the loss of that protection and would conjure up a prohibition upon the work of the adherents and students of psycho-analysis in Austria ... [In London,] I can breathe a sigh of relief now that the weight has been taken off me and that I am once more able to speak and write – I had almost said 'and think' – as I wish or as I must. (*SE*, 23: 57)

Freud, however, did not hesitate to tell his story. Despite all the requests and the pleadings, despite his sincere concern for himself, his family and his life's work, he was utterly devoted to the truth he discovered. His story about the murder of the Egyptian Moses had to be told, even in the most horrific episode of the Jewish people. This, in any case, was the message with which he opened his book:

> To deprive a people of the man whom they take pride in as the greatest of their sons is not a thing to be gladly or carelessly undertaken, least of all by someone who is himself one of them. But we cannot allow any such reflection to induce us to put the truth aside in favor of what are supposed to be national interests; and, moreover, the clarification of a set of facts may be expected to bring us a gain in knowledge. (*SE*, 23: 7)

The damning responses from the Jewish community were naturally not long in coming. For example, Avraham Shalom Yehuda, a scholar of Jewish history, remarked in 1946 in a short review of the book that "the power of assimilation is so immense, that it destroys every good part and plants in the hearts of our greatest thinkers the seed of hatred towards the tradition of their ancestors" (66).[5] Martin Buber, in his own work on Moses half a decade later, completely disregarded the book. In the only footnote he dedicated to Freud, he observed: "that

---

enlighten me on the future of Israel. The good people who wrote in this way cannot have known much about me; but I expect that when this work about Moses becomes known, in a translation, among my new compatriots, I shall forfeit enough of the sympathy which a number of other people as well now feel for me" (*SE*, 23: 57–58).

5 Elsewhere, Yehuda adds "it seems to me that in these words we hear the voice of one of the most fanatical Christians in his hatred of Israel" (60).

a scholar of so much importance in his own field as Sigmund Freud could permit himself to issue so unscientific a work, based on groundless hypotheses, as his *Moses and Monotheism*, is regrettable" (Buber 1958, 7 fn. 1).

I dwell on the reception of Freud's book because it echoes how we usually think of Freud as a hero of modern heretical secularism. Very shortly, Freud, the secular scientist, who uncompromisingly uncovers truth and insists on its value, despite personal and public sacrifices, symbolizes, for many, the modern struggle against religious illusions of Marx, Nietzsche, Feuerbach and many others. In this line of reading, *Moses and Monotheism* only reaffirmed Freud's earlier anti-religious *The Future of an Illusion* (1927): in both texts, Freud exposed the absurdity of the religious way of life.

Yet, for our purposes, it is important to emphasize that this modern conflict between truth and falsehood, science and religion, which Freud has often come to represent, seemingly reverberates with another logic: inner-religious logic. In battling against the religious *Weltanschauung*, Freud is reminiscent of a "heretic" as Yehuda condemned (66). Freud, like the religious heretic, is willing to face ostracism, boycott or exclusion. Freud proclaimed a truth, discovered a truth, even if this truth hurt, even if it was destructive, even if it was told at the most difficult time of the Jewish people, just as Jesus, Sabbatai Zevi, the Frankists and many others struggled for a truth, despite the hardships, dangers and sacrifices their truth demanded. Freud's actions echoed those of the religious zealot in style if not in essence. He fought with religious dogma with the same vigor and determination as other heretics who struggled with religious orthodoxy. The Jewish Austrian author Stefan Zweig made note of this zeal in *The World of Yesterday* (1943):

> Long before I grasped the implications of the intellectual revolution [of psychoanalysis] [...] I had yielded to the moral strength and steadfastness of this extraordinary man. Here, at last, was a man of science, the exemplar of a young man's dreams, prudent of statement until he had positive proof, but unshakable against the opposition of the world once he was satisfied that his hypothesis had become a valid certainty. Here was a man of the most modest personal demands, but ready to battle for every tenet of his teachings (*jedes Dogma seiner Lehre*) and faithful unto death to the immanent truth of the theories which he vindicated. (316)[6]

---

[6] Yirmiyahu Yovel fittingly pointed out in his *Spinoza and Other Heretics* (1989) the exact similarities between Freud and Spinoza – the Jewish arch-heretic – in their "heretic" quest for truth. "In the figure of Spinoza Freud could see a reflection of himself – a solitary young revolutionary, adhering to a truth excavated from under the surface of the ruling culture, and facing hostility and scorn as a result. Spinoza is a kind of distant brother to Freud, his brother in the honesty of his thought and the difficulties of his path, in his solitude and his genius. Freud indirectly

Zweig's religious language stresses Freud's heretical position.[7] His Freud battled for "every tenet of his teaching" because he had in his possession clear and absolute truth: a truth beyond any doubt, one that had the potential to uphold the canon and demystify tradition, one that Freud would defend with his life, even at the risk of his life's work.

This is, I would dare argue, the prevalent notion with which we have been accustomed when thinking of Freud as a modern heretic. Still, in what comes, I would like to propose a different model of heresy in Freud, one that portrays a more nuanced understanding of the social function of heresy. My argument is based in part on the growing fascination with *Moses and Monotheism* as a book by a Jew and about Judaism. My reading here follows Yosef Hayim Yerushalmi's (1991) now-famous claim that Freud "carefully and solemnly declared himself [in *Moses and Monotheism*] a Jew" (7). Freud, I argue below, was not simply dispelling Judaism or condemning the Jewish people in *Moses and Monotheism*, as Yehuda and Buber argued.[8] In his last work, Freud reconsidered his own position about religion. And this was not in order to celebrate his previous rebelliousness. Rather than being a self-assured zealot, Freud focused in his last book on the subtle impact of heresy on social reality. He recognized the productive nature of heresy, and, a heretic himself, demonstrated how the heretic may not only destroy and dismantle, but enhance and fortify.

(through Heine) refers to Spinoza as his 'brother in nonfaith [*Unglaubengenossen*],' a Jew who has lost his faith yet continues to bear the trait of the Jew both in his own eyes, and, even more so, in the eyes of the outside world" (139–140).

7 For a critical analysis of the function of truth in Freud's *Moses and Monotheism*, see Blumenberg (2018).

8 Moreover, as several commentators correctly observed, *Moses and Monotheism* was in fact a book disrupted by repetitions, inaccuracies and apologies. Far from the scientific work of the brave and honest scientist, Freud's book reflected reservation and disillusionment. Freud himself admitted to the following: "No less than before, I feel uncertain in the face of my own work; I lack the consciousness of unity and of belonging together which should exist between an author and his work. [...] My uncertainty sets in only when I ask myself whether I have succeeded in proving these theses in the example which I have chosen here of Jewish monotheism. To my critical sense this book, which takes its start from the man Moses, appears like a dancer balancing on the tip of one toe" (*SE*, 23: 58). Edward Said claimed in *Freud and the Non-European* (2004) that the repetitions and inconsistencies reflected the status of the book as a formative example of what he famously termed "late style" (*Spätstil*). For Said, the book was not meant to achieve a "resolution and reconciliation," but, like other last works, to evoke "more complexity and a willingness to let irreconcilable elements of the work remain as they are: episodic, fragmentary, unfinished (i.e., unpolished)" (28).

2 Heresy in *Moses and Monotheism*

In *Moses and Monotheism*, Freud offers a description of the most heinous act of heresy. According to Freud, the Jewish people, Moses' people, betrayed their leader and savior, the man who took them out of Egypt, the one who made them into a people. They rejected the Jewish faith he had offered them, and then went on to murder him. They later repressed the act of murder to the extent that it disappears from the official written record, i.e., the Bible. There is no greater heresy, a harsher, more radical rejection of a religious dogma.

Admittedly, writing his last work, Freud focused on the *traumatic* core of the murder of Moses. He argued, following his previous work on religion, *Totem and Taboo* (1913), that this trauma inaugurated Jewish history. I, however, would like to focus on the theological implications of his work. In his Moses book, Freud, I argue, proposed a theory of trauma that should be read also as a model for understanding heresy. For Freud, heresy is an act of transgression against religious orthodoxy, which the Jewish transgression against Moses reflects. Very simply, one is heretic when one goes against or forcefully renounces an accepted religious dogma or tradition.

I suggest that this model is so productive because it focuses our attention on the violent core of heresy and the psychological pain it produces, which we too often neglect. The heretic resembles, in the Freudian imagination, a murder: the heretic inflicts pain. His or her actions echo a violent act of ideological parricide. Heresy is not an emotionally or socially neutral act, but transgression replete with emotion, pain, shame and even violence. Compared to the apostate who leaves his former religion and converts to another, the heretic struggles with his own religion. Freud's model highlights the end-products of such battles. Essentially, in Freud's understanding, heresy is traumatic. Heresy often produces trauma. A trauma that occurs not only at the level of the individual but also at the social level, a trauma that deeply impacts the heretics. A trauma that the story of Moses reveals, displaying its wide effects.

Note, however, that the proposed model supposedly analyzes heresy from the perspective of the orthodoxy or the hegemony. Heresy is depicted as a betrayal: the Israelites betrayed Moses. This is not necessarily how the heretics consider their actions. In many cases, the heretics, like Freud himself, believe they hold the truth and are certain their actions will save others from grave and consequential misconceptions. This is, for example, how Sabbatai Zevi and his disciples considered their position: they understood some essential truths about the coming of the Jewish messiah which the rabbis were blind to and therefore refused to accept. At times, the heretic does not even see herself as a heretic, but rather views the other, the hegemony, as unbelievers. In other words, heresy is deemed transgressive and violent mostly from the perspective of the religious hegemony.

The proposed model, however, highlights a principle ambivalence in this position of the heretic. While the declared position of the heretic is one of confidence and assuredness, Freud, we will shortly see, identified in *Moses and Monotheism* a latent, different psychic reality. Freud's book portrayed an emotional burden that heresy produces. Freud located behind the conscious declarations of the heretic uncertainty, shame, guilt and even trauma. In other words, with Freud we can argue that Sabbatai Zevi may have suffered, even if only unconsciously, from the dramatic effect of his heresy. He suffered from guilt because he murdered – even if only symbolically – the rabbis.

To explain my claim, we should note that in *Moses and Monotheism* the murder of Moses inaugurated a series of unexpected events. According to Freud, the act of murder did not absolve the Jewish people from Moses and his religion. His description of the next chain of events is largely based on his model of history and religion proposed in *Totem and Taboo* (1913) almost three decades earlier.

In *Totem and Taboo*, Freud famously hypothesized that in the prehistoric period, humankind was initially organized in large groups controlled by an authoritarian primal father with tyrannical control of all material goods. Freud speculated that the sons in this primal tribe, who suffered under the father's control, decided to kill him as the only solution to his cruel dominion. However, the rebellion of the sons against the father, the absolute monarch, ended with unanticipated results. The sons were pleased with and proud of their new freedom. But they also felt guilt for the deed: "They hated their father, who presented such a formidable obstacle to their craving for power and their sexual desires; but they loved and admired him too" (*SE*, 13: 143). As a result, the sons, struggling to relieve the overwhelming emotional stress the murder initiated, replaced the murdered father with a totem animal. The primeval totem religion helped them remember the murder in a way that unburdened them of their guilt. During the totem meal, a core element of the totem system, the sons consumed the totem animal, once again killing "his" flesh but also commemorating the "criminal deed" (*SE*, 13: 142).

Freud identified the same emotional structure in the beginning of Judaism. Like the sons of the primal father, the Jews, he claimed, also lamented the murder of Moses. They were remorseful for their heresy. However, in contrast to the sons in the primal tribe, who founded the first religion in history to commemorate their father, the Israelites joined another religion: they allied with a second Moses in the desert, a priest from the Midian region. The first murdered Moses was replaced by a Midian priest of a local god, also named Moses. That is, the Jewish people chose to forget the monotheistic religion by means of another Moses, a prophet of an "uncanny, bloodthirsty demon" (*SE*, 13: 34), who allowed them to enjoy the very same things monotheism forbade.

This point is important for the model of heresy I propose, because here we see how Freud moved away in *Moses and Monotheism* from the basic model of trauma in *Totem and Taboo* to develop a model of heresy. Heresy was not only a refusal to accept a certain religious dogma or the rejection of a religious hegemony. Heresy also introduces alternative social values and systems of religious beliefs. The Israelites not only murdered Moses, like the sons of the primal father. Unlike their ancestors, who restored the father's original commandment through the first totem religion, the Israelites sought a different religious ideal, one incompatible with Moses' harsh monotheism.

The Jewish apostasy, however, had unexpected results. After a few generations under the rule of the Midian priests (a period of latency in Freudian terms), the first religion, the Egyptian monotheism, returned to the surface of the Jewish social reality and became the official religion of the Israelites – now, and only now, the Jewish people. In Freud's words,

> This fact is so remarkable that we feel justified in looking at it once again. Our problem is comprised in it. The Jewish people had abandoned the Aten religion brought to them by Moses and had turned to the worship of another god who differed little from the Baalim of the neighbouring peoples. All the tendentious efforts of later times failed to disguise this shameful fact. But the Mosaic religion had not vanished without leaving a trace; some sort of memory of it had kept alive – a possibly obscured and distorted tradition. And it was this tradition of a great past which continued to operate (from the background, as it were), which gradually acquired more and more power over people's minds and which in the end succeeded in changing the god Yahweh into the Mosaic god and in re-awakening into life the religion of Moses that had been introduced and then abandoned long centuries before. (*SE*, 23: 69–70)

Building on his theory of the return of the repressed, Freud argues that the trauma of heresy did not disappear, but was rather repressed and hidden from conscious social reality. At this stage, let me emphasize, the Jewish people completely repressed their guilt and sorrow. They essentially forgot Moses, while still suffering from the trauma of his murder. The Jewish people, in other words, both struggled with the trauma but also never actually recognized its impact on their psychical and social reality, exactly because they were able to successfully repress it. The trauma had life, but only in the unconscious psychical reality. This, I argue, may apply to future heretics. They, too, may have been ignorant of the true and deep psychical implications of their actions.

However, Freud continues, after a few generations under the Midianite Moses the trauma resurfaced. The emotional pain (shame, guilt) surmounted any attempt to repress it. And in returning, the trauma was more powerful than ever. It forced the Jewish people to return to and accept the principles they had previously so forcefully renounced. The Jews, who categorically denied the religion of Moses, embraced the same religion, which now had a much greater psychological and emotional force.⁹ They were "exalted" and proud to be Moses' chosen people (*SE*, 13: 115); proud of the same aspects in monotheism which previously tormented them. Their return to the first Moses engraved the principles of the Egyptian Moses' religion on the Jewish character: rationality and renunciation of pleasures would define them, according to Freud, throughout their history.

> No other portion of the history of religion has become so clear to us as the introduction of monotheism into Judaism [...] we see that that [monotheistic] idea, released from its native soil and transferred to another people was, after a long period of latency, taken hold of by them, preserved by them as a precious possession and, in turn, itself kept them alive by giving them pride in being a chosen people: it was the religion of their primal father to which were attached their hope of reward, of distinction and finally of world-dominion. (SE, 13: 85)

In Freud's story of Jewish history, the traumatic experience upheld the conscious intentions of the heretical Israelites. Heresy did not abrogate the validity or meaning of Moses' religion. On the contrary, it created the necessary psychic conditions for the complete domination of Judaism on the Israelite slaves. The Jewish religion became so powerful only thanks to the betrayal of the Israelites. Heresy, for Freud, consolidated and animated Moses' monotheism. In an early letter from May 1935 to his close friend and follower Lou Andreas-Salomé, Freud openly declared this intuition: "Religions owe their compulsive power to the *return of the repressed*; they are reawakened memories of very ancient, forgotten, highly emotional episodes of human history" (Freud and Andreas-Salomé 1985, 205; emphasis in origin).

In *Moses and Monotheism*, Freud portrayed the dialectical nature of heresy. For Freud, heresy instituted religious reality. Someone needs to refuse, to violently transgress and oppose the hegemony; a murder (real or imaginary) must be committed, shame and guilt must overflow (even if unconsciously), so that religion will securely hold us from within, and force us to obey. Heresy initiates for Freud the transition from formal, external systems of religious norms to internal psychical domination. Up to the moment of his murder, Moses coerced the Israelites to obey. After their heretic act, they happily obeyed. Initially, the monotheistic religion was but a set of laws that would have disappeared if Moses had

---

9 Just as the sons accepted the rules of the murdered father, who had all the women in the tribe to himself, and formed the first law of the human civilization: the prohibition of incest.

simply died. But because of heresy, the monotheistic religion came to dominate the Israelites for eternity.

Freud never attempted to attest to the concrete form of the religious trauma. He insisted that all religions begin in a trauma, and believed that these traumas were deeply connected to the oedipal complex in the individual, but he also accepted the fact that this drama could have played out differently in different religious contexts. And yet, in his study of Judaism, Freud did provide a concrete historical account: in Judaism, heresy produced the original religious trauma. And since there is no religion if there was no trauma, Judaism, according to Freud, had its origins in a heretical act. To put it differently, in his description of Jewish history Freud replaced revelation with heresy. Taking the biblical story at face value, according to Freud, the events surrounding Mt. Sinai were formative not because of the revelation on the mountain but because of the heresy below. It is the idolization of the Golden Calf, not the giving of the *Torah*, that inaugurated Jewish history.

3 Heresy and the Return of the Repressed

In Freud's portrayal of Jewish history, the return of the Israelites to Moses' monotheism did not expiate the mental pain caused by his murder. Similarly to the return of the repressed in the individual, Freud argues that in the social and religious realms the primary trauma must return later in history.[10] The first, original trauma never dies out: it returns again and again in an attempt to heal the emotional pain it originally created. In other words, just as early trauma haunts us throughout our adult life, the first return to monotheism never really solved the emotional distress of the Israelites but only momentarily relieved it.[11] In *Moses and Monotheism*, Freud explains this mechanism as follows:

---

[10] Already in *Totem and Taboo*, Freud argued: "Let us assume it to be a fact, then, that in the course of the later development of religions the two driving factors, the son's sense of guilt and the son's rebelliousness, never became extinct. Whatever attempt was made at solving the religious problem, whatever kind of reconciliation was effected between these two opposing mental forces, sooner or later broke down, under the combined influence, no doubt, of historical events, cultural changes and internal psychical modifications" (*SE*, 13: 152).

[11] For Freud, each return of the trauma symbolized a new attempt to come to term with the (non)experience of trauma. In his words, the return of the trauma in the present "may also be looked upon as an attempt at cure" (*SE*, 23: 77).

> Not until later does the change take place with which the definitive neurosis becomes manifest as a belated effect of the trauma. [...] it happens because the reactions and alterations of the ego brought about by the defense now prove a hindrance in dealing with the new tasks of life, so that severe conflicts come about between the demands of the real external world and the ego, which seeks to maintain the organization which it has painstakingly achieved in its defensive struggle. The phenomenon of a latency of the neurosis between the first reactions to the trauma and the later outbreak of the illness must be regarded as typical.
> (SE, 13: 77)

The trauma, according to Freud, is repeated both in the individual and at the societal level when its initial repression is no longer effective and long-suppressed impulses and memories can therefore resurface. In Freud's historical model, the trauma would break out when something in the historical life of a people changes in such a way that the initial trauma has less effective hold on them. The initial repression is not potent enough, and this allows the trauma to break out. In Judaism, to continue Freud's model, such changes in the historical conditions would facilitate the eruption of a new heretical episode. The reason for that is twofold: first, since in Freud's theory of neurosis every return of the trauma in the individual must echo the initial trauma, in Jewish history the return of the repressed had to take the form of a new heretical act. Second, and in different terms, heresy supposedly offers another way, an alternative dogma, exactly when the original trauma loses its grip. The heretic sees through the religious worldview that the murder of Moses inflicted on the Jewish people. He or she moves beyond the religious dogma, and is therefore able to offer a different religious vision.

Still, this act, because it repeats and re-expresses the first repressed trauma, would also somewhat paradoxically renew its power. That is, because the return of the repressed in Judaism is also traumatic in essence, the future heretical act would re-enforce the power of the initial trauma of that against which the heretic transgressed. Here lies a second dialectic of heresy in Judaism: because in Judaism the repressed returns, in a form of heresy, it inflicts a new trauma of heresy, and thereby re-consolidates the power of Judaism. In other words, the future heretical acts would in fact solidify the domination of Judaism, rather than incite its imminent collapse.

In that, I argue, the suggested model of heresy echoes Gershom Scholem's vision of Jewish Messianism in his *Major Trends in Jewish Mysticism* (1941). Similarly to Scholem's argument about the foundational role of messianism in the dynamic and ever-changing core of Judaism, the model of heresy as trauma explains, in my understanding, the vitality of Judaism in the last two thousand years. I suggest that the continual return of heresy in Jewish history did not undermine the Jewish tradition, but rather re-enforced its power. Heresy was the driving force of Judaism: it resembled an unconscious undercurrent, which held Judaism from behind. Heretical events did not compromise the Jewish tradition: rather, heresy defended and enlivened Judaism.

To demonstrate this claim, let us now turn to heresy in Jewish modernity.

4 Heresy and Jewish Modernity

The figure of Moses is widely regarded in the psychoanalytic literature as Freud's Jewish alter ego. In *The Interpretation of Dreams* (1900), *The Moses of Michelangelo* (1914) and *Moses and Monotheism*, Moses is that through which Freud negotiated his Jewish identity, and his position as a Jew in a Christian world (Goldstein 1992; Grubrich-Simitis 1991; Rice 1990; Robert 1976).[12] In the last years of Freud's life, Moses became important to him for a second reason. Freud identified with Moses as an ideal figure of a leader. He, like "Moses, will lead a people out of bondage" (Goldstein 1992, 8). Freud in fact pictured himself as a Moses betrayed by his people. Abandoned and deceived by Jung, Adler and others in the psychoanalytic society, Freud shared Moses' fate. In this sense, his last book was supposedly written from the perspective of the "Great Man": Freud and Moses, both betrayed by their followers.

Yet, in Freud's last return to Moses, his historical novel narrated a previously unknown heretical act, which echoed Freud's own heretical stance against Jewish tradition. Put simply, Freud's assimilation redoubled his ancestors' heretical crime. Freud, one of the most recognized assimilated Jews of his generation, was in fact part of the Jewish mob who refused Jewish tradition,[13] not the sacrificed leader, as he often regarded himself. Could it be that in describing the first heretical act, Freud in fact provided us with theoretical framework to think of his own heresy, maybe even of heresy in modernity in general?

Indeed, one could argue that the category of heresy does not apply to Jewish modernity. In *fin de siècle* Vienna, Jews like Freud simply left the Jewish tradition rather than actively acting as heretics. Their alienation seemed to be a natural conclusion of predetermined historical processes, and to a large extent both

---

[12] In a memorable note, Harold Bloom (1985) grouped Freud with Scholem and Kafka to claim that they are the most important representatives of Jewish tradition, who are "already larger figures in the ongoing tradition of spirituality than are, say, Leo Baeck, Franz Rosenzweig and Martin Buber [...] because of [the former's] cultural achievements" (14).
[13] Marthe Robert (1976) identifies the same emotional complex already in Freud's *Moses of Michelangelo* (141–145).

desirable and uneventful. There was no trauma, but rather enthusiasm, hope and confidence for those Jews who forsook the traditional ways of life and joined the German secular society. Still, as Freud's clinical work with neurotic patients and his theoretical work on the primal tribe in *Totem and Taboo* clearly demonstrated, we are oftentimes unaware of our unconscious struggles and pains. We are oblivious of our own traumas.

The model of heresy of Freud, the experienced therapist, spotlights a possible emotional turmoil beyond the prevalent description of modern assimilation. In his work on Moses, Freud offers us a new understanding of the price the loss of Jewish identity and the rejection of Jewish tradition demanded. These "natural" processes may not have been as inconsequential or unremarkable as we previously considered. Freud's work may help us uncover that which generations of Jewish society have struggled to repress: their alienation, their betrayal in Jewish tradition, were not meaningless, but difficult, challenging and innately traumatic. See, for example, Gershom Scholem's now-famous description of the meaning of Judaism in his parents' home in Berlin:

> In our home there were only a few perceptible relics of Judaism, such as the use of Jewish idiomatic expressions, which my father avoided and forbade us to use, but which my mother gladly employed, especially when she wanted to make a point. [...] The *Kiddush*, the Hebrew Blessing for the Shabbat, was still chanted but only half understood. That did not keep people from using the Shabbat candles to light a cigarette or a cigar afterwards. Since the prohibition on smoking on the Sabbath was one of the most widely known Jewish regulations, there was a deliberate mockery (*bewußte Mokkerei*) in this act. In the Passover week we set on the table both Masot and bread in two attached baskets. Even in the high holidays, and especially in Yom Kippur, when the vast majority still fast, father went to the printing house. (Scholem 1980, 10)[14]

Scholem's description projects indifference and carelessness. Scholem's father went as if offhandedly to the printing house, even in Yom Kippur, like many other Germans. However, I would argue that with Freud, the master of suspicion, we should read this text quite differently. This text may express not simple disinterest, but rather the emotional consequence, the emotional price Scholem's father and his generation paid for their assimilation, for their heresy. Scholem's family did not simply disregard the Jewish ceremonies; they did so ostentatiously, scornfully. Indeed, they lit the candles, but they also made sure to light their cigars with the same candles. This heretic ceremony within the Jewish ceremony – and Freud himself witnessed similar incidences in his father's house – reveals an emotional

---

[14] For historical surveys of the struggles of the post-assimilatory generation, see Aschheim (1982), Brenner (1998) and Volkov (2006).

tension which Freud encountered numerous times in his therapeutic work. The nonchalant atmosphere exposes deep ambivalence of the heretic regarding his heresy, which Freud, I argue, identified in the Israelites in the desert.

To clarify, I am not arguing that all or even most of the assimilated Jews suffered from trauma. My argument is rather that trauma is one possible outcome of Jewish assimilation, one where, because of the structure of trauma, we are almost unable to identify its direct and immediate effects. The "official" documents of German Jewish modernity would have erased such traumas, just like the Bible did; only the after-effects, the afterlives of the trauma, would be accessible.[15]

In other words, rather than a discussion of the generation of Freud's and Scholem's parents, Freud, an important representative of the post-assimilatory generation, provided us with a tool to understand his own Jewish reality. Specifically, his model explains how the glaring clarity and self-assuredness of the parents' assimilation had dimmed in their children. The older generation was the generation who, following the scheme of the Moses book, committed heresy. They were the one who murdered Moses, and turned to secular German society. This generation did the terrible deed but also carefully hid it in the depths of the collective unconscious. Similarly to their murderer ancestors, they were un-conscious of the emotional torment inflicted by their heresy. According to the scheme proposed in *Moses and Monotheism*, only the next generation, Freud's generation, would be the first to have to deal with the emotional complexity of the traumas of their parents.

The model of heresy I offer explains why the post-assimilatory generation was in constant conflict with their parents. Like Kafka in the famous letter to his father, the children recognized that which their parents wanted to repress and refused to see. The younger generation perceived how the parents, who rejected the Jewish tradition, still strongly suffered from their heresy. However, while the first generation successfully repressed the emotional effects of their deed, the second generation experienced the return of the trauma that the parents repressed. In this generation, the trauma erupted again.

Could it be that it was not so accidental that early twentieth-century Jewish intellectuals struggled to re-conceptualize the place of Judaism and Jewish tradition in modernity, or reverted to Jewish categories to analyze modern experience? Could it be that it was not a coincidence that in 1901, at the height of Jewish assimilation, Buber identified a growing fascination in things Jewish which he

---

[15] We think of traumas as unique devastating events: the murder of Moses, the crucifixion of Jesus, the apostasy of Sabbatai Zevi. But could not trauma be the result of longer, much more complex episodes of historical magnitude?

enthusiastically described as a new "Jewish renaissance" (Buber 1991, 31)? Could it be that this renaissance was not despite the rejection of Judaism by the previous generation, but rather because of their heresy? That the Jewish tradition was re-energized, revitalized precisely because of the attempts to erase it, to betray it, to murder it?

To conclude, Freud suggested in *Moses and Monotheism* a radical model of heresy. In this book, heresy is the original (*urspunglisch*) act; it is the deed that inaugurated Judaism and, equally important, a deed that would return throughout Jewish history, reinforcing in each of these returns the foundational power of the first trauma. In this radical model, no act of heresy would ever eliminate Judaism. On the contrary, Judaism will flourish thanks to such acts.

I propose that thanks to this model, Freud, the Godless-Jew, defended his religion, after betraying it, after his entire generation betrayed it. He showed that he and others who rejected Jewish tradition, and replaced it with the German secular society, never truly compromised it, but rather gave it new life. It is as if Freud, facing the most difficult hour of Jewish history, proudly admitted his and his generation's heresy. However, because of his model of heresy, Freud could have also claimed that this betrayal helped fortify Judaism. Freud had to tell his story, this horrific story of the murder of Moses in the desert, precisely at those troubled times, facing the rise of anti-Semitism and the danger of Nazi occupation, for it was the best defense he could have invented for himself, for the Jews across Europe, and for Judaism. "We have sinned," he would tell them, "but because of our heresy, Judaism will survive. Because of our heresy, the Jewish tradition will thrive."

Bibliography

Works Keyed to Abbreviations

SE Freud, Sigmund. *The Standard Edition of the Complete Psychological Works of Sigmund Freud*. Trans. James Strachey, 24 vols. London: Hogarth Press, 1953.

Other References

Aschheim, Steven E. *Brothers and Strangers: The East European Jew in German and German Jewish Consciousness, 1800–1923*. Madison: University of Wisconsin Press, 1982.
Bernstein, Richard J. *Freud and the Legacy of Moses*. Cambridge: Cambridge University Press, 1998.

Bloom, Harold. "The Masks of the Normative." *Orim: A Jewish Journal at Yale*. 1 (1985): 9–24.
Blumenberg, Hans. *Rigorism of Truth: "Moses the Egyptian" and Other Writings on Freud and Arendt*. Ed. Ahlrich Meyer. Trans. Joe Paul Kroll. Ithaca: Cornell University Press, 2018.
Brenner, Michael. *The Renaissance of Jewish Culture in Weimar Germany*. New Haven: Yale University Press, 1998.
Buber, Martin. *Moses: The Revelation and the Covenant*. New York: Harper, 1958.
Buber, Martin. *The First Buber: Youthful Zionist Writings of Martin Buber*. Trans. Gilya G. Schmidt. Syracuse: Syracuse University Press, 1999.
Derrida, Jacques. *Archive Fever: A Freudian Impression*. Trans. Eric Prenowitz. Chicago: University of Chicago Press, 1996.
Freud, Sigmund, and Lou Andreas-Salomé. *Letters*. Ed. Ernst Pfeiffer. Trans. William and Elaine Robson-Scott. New York: Norton, 1985.
Freud, Sigmund, and Arnold Zweig. *The letters of Sigmund Freud and Arnold Zweig*. Ed. Ernst L. Freud. Trans. Elaine and William Robson-Scott. New York: Harcourt, 1970.
Goldstein, Bluma. *Reinscribing Moses: Heine, Kafka, Freud, and Schoenberg in a European Wilderness*. Cambridge: Harvard University Press, 1992.
Grubrich-Simitis, Ilse. *Freud's Moses-Studie Als Tagtraum*. Frankfurt: Verlag Internationale Psychoanalyse, 1991.
Jones, Ernest. *The Life and Work of Sigmund Freud*, 3 vols. New York: Basic Books, 1957.
Paul, Robert A. *Moses and Civilization: The Meaning behind Freud's Myth*. New Haven: Yale University Press, 1996.
Rice, Emanuel. *Freud and Moses: The Long Journey Home*. Albany: State University of New York Press, 1990.
Robert, Marthe. *From Oedipus to Moses: Freud's Jewish Identity*. Trans. Ralph Manheim. Garden City: Anchor Books, 1976.
Said, Edward W. *Freud and the Non-European*. New York: Verso, 2004.
Scholem, Gershom. *From Berlin to Jerusalem: Memories of My Youth*. Trans. Harry Zohn. New York: Schocken Books, 1980.
Volkov, Shulamit. *Germans, Jews, and Antisemites: Trials in Emancipation*. Cambridge: Cambridge University Press, 2006.
Yehuda, Abraham Shalom. "Sigmund Freud on Moses and His Torah." *Ever v'Arav*. New York: Shulsinger Bros., 1946. 37–73.
Yerushalmi, Yosef H. *Freud's Moses: Judaism Terminable and Interminable*. New Haven: Yale University Press, 1991.
Yovel, Yirmiyahu. *Spinoza and Other Heretics*. Princeton: Princeton University Press, 1989.
Zweig, Stefan. *The World of Yesterday*. London: Cassell, 1943.

Agata Bielik-Robson
Liquid Theology and the Messianism of Life: Marrano Heresy in Benjamin and Derrida

> Religion of the living: is this not a tautology?
> Jacques Derrida (2002, 85)

> The principle of life (*torat hayim*) remains a great intangible Judaic principle.
> Jacques Derrida (2008, 112)

What is heresy if not theology turned liquid – again? If orthodoxy consists of constructing a rigid religious dogma and the hard law, *dura lex*, which issues from the former, then what Walter Benjamin called the 'liquidation of theology' does not have to result in a mere destruction of all theological concepts; rather, it suggests a return to the living religious matrix which, as Bergson has put it, is still capable of "making gods" (Bergson 1977, 317).

If, indeed, in Ernst Bloch's words, "The best thing about religion is that it makes for heretics,"[1] the theology-turned-liquid revivifies and becomes capable of creating new, flexible, and idiosyncratic religious beliefs which inevitably take non-orthodox shapes. But, as I will try to prove here, the connection between heresy or 'liquid theology' and life is even stronger: if Abrahamic religions every now and then shake off their orthodox forms, they do it not only for the sake of their own vitality – they also do it, perhaps more predominantly, for the sake of life itself, which constitutes their hidden messianic message.

1 Back to the Flow

The method of 'liquidating theology' was described by Walter Benjamin in *The Arcades Project* in the metaphor of the ink blotter (*Löschblatt*) which simultaneously erases the theological writing and absorbs its liquidated content:

---

[1] See the epigraph to Ernst Bloch, *Atheism in Christianity* (2009).

Note: An essay written thanks to the support of NCN Opus 13 Grant: The Marrano Phenomenon: The Jewish 'Hidden Tradition' and Modernity, registered in the OSF system as 2017/25/B/HS2/02901

> My thinking is connected to theology like the ink-blotter to ink. It is totally saturated with it. But if it were up to the blotter, nothing that has been written would remain.
> (Benjamin 1999, 471 [N7a, 7])[2]

The 'liquidation of theology' is thus deliberately ambivalent: on the surface it suggests a destruction and supersession of the theological paradigm, now to be replaced by a secularized modern idiom – under that, however, it aims to make the theological message fluid again, before it had congealed into religious dogmas, and letting it flow as an *under*-current, beneath the surface of concepts.[3] Theology turned into liquid ink may thus be used once again to compose a *new scripture* or a *new law* which will reverberate with the stronger original messianic message rather than the official Holy Writ of the orthodox, either Jewish, Christian or Muslim, theologies: a scripture full of unruly undercurrents, similar to what Ernst Bloch used to call the 'subterranean Bible' (2009, 94). In what follows, I will try to prove that this predilection for secret religious undercurrents belongs to one of the most interesting Jewish (or Judeo-Christian) heresies of modernity: the Marrano ferment. Despite his declaration, Benjamin never created any 'philosophy of Judaism,' or any philosophy *of* religion as such.[4] He did not write *about* religion and theology – he rather wrote *with* them, wanting to use their energetic sub-surface potential without feeling obliged by their overt traditional categories. By 'liquidating' theology into an ink, he wished to convey its messianic message which, always remaining in the secret hiding place, eludes overt articulation. For, as his friend Gershom Scholem once declared in the surprisingly Marranesque manner: "Authentic tradition remains hidden" (1973, 235). If revelation, *Offenbarung* – as the message 'made public,' open and clear – necessarily involves a distortion, then the only way to stay faithful to *what* is revealed is to betray the revelation itself, on which the overt tradition is founded, and dive into a hidden,

---

2 It is possible (though not at all certain) that Benjamin might have known the Sayings of the Fathers, which also compares a seasoned practice of studying Torah to the ink written on, but also inevitably sinking in, a blotted paper: "Elisha ben (son of) Avuya said, one who studies Torah as a child, to what is he compared? To ink written on fresh paper. And one who studies Torah as an old man, to what is he compared? To ink written on blotted paper" (Pirke Avot, 4:20).
3 On the ambivalence of Benjamin's 'liquidation' which bears parallels to Hegel's *Aufhebung*, see this comment by Susan Buck-Morss: "Theology, like the flaneur also threatened by modernity with extinction, might well be described as the dialectical *Urform* of Benjamin's method, *negated and preserved at once*" (Buck-Morss 2006, 268; emphasis added).
4 According to Scholem's diary, Benjamin once said to him: "If I ever have a philosophy of my own, it will somehow be a philosophy of Judaism" (Scholem 2008, 138).

authentic one. The secret tradition cannot be talked *about*, but it can nonetheless be practised – undercover.[5]

Irving Wohlfarth described Benjamin's messianism as 'eccentric' (1979, 73): full of anxious anticipations of *olam ha-ba* (the world-to-come), yet deliberately without footing in any central institution of faith and, for this reason, with no clear sense of direction – a portrait which also fits very well the 'Marrano experience.' This disoriented – always radical and restlessly searching – sense of the messianic activity stems in Benjamin from his conviction, also widely shared by the Marrano thinkers before him, that the world is left to its own devices, without any clear hint of revelation.[6] The divine message, which would give an unambiguous hint of where to aim and how to proceed, became lost in the labyrinth of creation. It rather resembles Franz Kafka's "Letter from the Emperor": a word arriving too late, distorted and mediated through too many layers of being to mean anything. Benjamin, who, together with Gershom Scholem, regarded Kafka as the only modern truly kabbalistic mind, agrees with the author of *The Castle* that the

---

[5] Scholem's definition of the secret authentic religion (or *vera religio*) is crucial for what I call here a Marrano heresy, but some help comes also from Yirmiyahu Yovel, who described the Marrano as the prototype of the modern 'free spirit' capable of fluctuating between separate orthodoxies. In *The Other Within*, Yovel tells the story of the actual Marranos from the Iberian Peninsula, but he also wants to "use it as a vehicle for a wider philosophical reflection" (Yovel 2009, ix). He thus presents the Marranos, the Spanish and Portuguese *conversos*, who nonetheless preserved the elements of their hidden Jewish tradition, as the first modern subjects who lost solid footing in their traditions and thus became 'ineradicably other,' not only to those who still enjoyed premodern fixed identities, but also to themselves (Yovel 2009, 58). Split in their identities and loyalties, the Marranos either "confused the two rival religions" or "became equally indifferent to both" (Yovel 2009, 61), thus giving way to the two typically modern tendencies: the pursuit of idiosyncratic forms of religiosity mediating between Judaism and Christianity, on the one hand, and the 'free-oscillating subjectivity' or a 'type that lives beyond the spheres of conventional belief and mentality' (Yovel 2009, 61), which does not identify with any tradition, on the other: "Besides the Law of Moses, Marranos were involved in inward Christianity, ecumenism, universalism, deism, syncretism, some Calvinism, and religious pre-Enlightenment [...] Indeed, the whole mental geography of Marranism [...] was exported with the Dispersion and came into contact with other societies across the globe. The Marrano experience was thus, in a sense, globalized and set on a cosmopolitan course [...] What took place on the macro-European scale in the matter of modernization and secularization had been prefigured by microforms of life and mind that Marranos experienced in Iberia and exported into their Dispersion" (ibid., 337; 339). Yovel, therefore, believes in a generalized 'Marrano experience' which will also be characteristic of the modern assimilatory Jewry and which created a peculiar – secret, fluid and liminoid – self equidistant from any fixed identity. It is precisely this Marrano 'fluid self' which I want to see operating behind Benjamin's 'liquid theology.'

[6] Yovel quotes an anonymous *conversos* interrogated by the Inquisition: "After God had created the world, he left everyone to be on his own, for good or bad" (Yovel 2009, 100).

transcendence (if it exists) does not interact with the immanence: the channels of communication have been broken. Messages coming from the 'up high' – if we can be sure that they come at all – never reach us the way they were intended, that is, as manifestation of the Highest Life addressing itself to the singular living thing; by entering the immanent sphere of being they either perish or get contaminated with alien hardening and deadening forces of materiality, which Benjamin calls the powers of myth. They become distorted, blunted, muted to the extent that the spark of life in them gets *almost* extinguished. This *almost* is crucial here, because on it hinges the whole hope of salvation. In order to be revived again, the divine word cannot simply be accepted as such; it must undergo a process of hermeneutic *liquidation*. It must first be destroyed in its distorted rigid-mythic form and only then recovered in its original vivid fluidity of a sign sent by the infinite Life 'Up High' to the finite living 'Here Below.'[7]

These constant hints to life are not at all accidental: making theology liquid again not only returns it to its living energetic matrix of the Bergsonian 'god-making,' but also removes the deadening distortion which obstructs the message coming from the Highest Life and which Benjamin, in a typically antinomian vein, associates with the hardness of the religious law. While commenting on *Ra'ya Mehemna*, the latest layer of texts in *Zohar*, Scholem demonstrates the central role of the symbol of the Tree of Life as representing the paradisiac *fluxus* of the all-connected and promiscuous aliveness of all things:

> These symbols are the Tree of Life and the Tree of Knowledge, or the Tree of Knowledge of Good and Evil, which, because its fruit brings about death, is also called the Tree of Death [...] Standing in the center of Paradise and representing higher order of things, the trees control a great deal more than just existence in the Garden of Eden. Since the Fall of Adam, the world is no longer ruled by the Tree of Life as it had been in the beginning, but by the Tree of Knowledge/Death. *The Tree of Life represents the pure, unbroken power of the holy, the diffusion of the divine light through all worlds and the communication of all living things with their divine source.* There is no admixture of evil in it, no 'shells' which dam up and choke life, no death, and no restriction. But since the Fall of Adam, since the time when the forbidden fruit of the Tree of Knowledge was eaten, the world is ruled by the mystery of this second tree in which both good and evil have their place.
>
> (Scholem 1971, 22–23; emphasis added)

But even in the postlapsarian world, the Tree of Life does not disappear: the secret undercurrents of life flowing despite the shells and broken channels of communication find their clandestine way to subvert the tyranny of the Tree of Knowledge/

---

[7] Some of this material first appeared in Bielik-Robson, Agata. "Walter Benjamin (1892–1940)" (Bielik-Robson 2017). Reproduced with permission.

Death and liquidate its rigid finite forms, partitions and distinctions. This complex play of subversion, in which theology is not to vanish but become transformed so it can represent the interests of the repressed and distorted life, which "life assumes in oblivion" (Benjamin 1968, 133), betrays Benjamin's penchant for the Marrano type of hiddenness as the true mark of 'authenticity' which he shares with Scholem. Already at this early stage of his thought, Benjamin's younger friend toys with the idea of the secret renewal of the Judaic tradition coming from *der grosse Geheimbund*, 'the secret society' of those who can un-write the tradition, standing simultaneously within and without it, and thus liquidate or liquefy the border which separates it from other messianic idioms. Scholem openly associates this attempt to make the orthodox partitions fluid again with the position of Marrano theology, freely jumping the fences within the Greco-Abrahamic world in order to find the 'authentic' language of the messianic life whose flux knows no bounds and obstacles (Scholem 2000, 164). Irving Wohlfahrt's take on Benjamin's 'liquidation of theology' chimes very close to the Scholemian endeavour to nullify the official theological discourse of Judaism and bring it down to the pure *Erscheinende*, the living fluid origin, still 'in the process of revelation':

> The blotter can only blot theology, it cannot blot it out. It is, however, not content to dry and thereby consolidate holy writ. Its ambition is to liquefy and thereby liquidate it, to transform its canonic forms back into ink, leaving behind a *tabula rasa* [...] *With the unwriting of Scripture re-emerges the original messianic language that preceded the written word, a language of 'ubiquitous and integral actuality' released from all prescription.*
> (Wohlfahrt 1978, 62–63; emphasis added)

According to Wohlfahrt, such liquidation/liquefaction can be regarded as the epitome of Benjamin's method in general, not just in his approach to theology. Governed by the imperative to undo the hardening of life into the hypostases of the law, it attempts to revert everything to the fluid, supple and plastic element of the living undercurrent, seemingly lost in its overt rigid forms. By using the Pauline/Hegelian terminology, we could call this method a *sublation of law into life*, which would once again emphasize the Jewish/Marrano difference: the goal of this dialectic would not be love, as in the Christian version, but most of all life. Life taken out of the realm of distortion and oblivion, where it got congealed, paralyzed and mortified in the *entstellte*, distorted hypostatic form, into a newly recovered plane of fluidity where it can reassume its 'happy untrammelled journey' (Benjamin 1968, 135).

The theme of the undistorted – happy and liquid – life returns again in Benjamin's response to Scholem's letter devoted to his essay on Kafka: while referring to Kafka's *Castle*, he describes the life spent at the foot of the hill, in which the law had completely dissolved into life (just like it gave way to the vitalistic-pagan cult of the 'fattened calf' at the foot of Sinai), as ambivalent: simultaneously regressing down to the 'hetaeric' stage of anarchy and harbouring a messianic promise. The Kafkan 'students' are left with no object to study since the Scripture had become indistinguishable from life. It lost its privileged, external, transcendent status and sank into the living immanence without a trace:

> Whether the students have lost Scripture or cannot decipher it in the end amounts to the same thing, since Scripture without its keys is not scripture but life, the life that is lived in the village at the foot of the hill on which the castle stands. In the attempt to transform life into Scripture I see the sense of the 'inversion' [*Umkehr*] toward which many of Kafka's allegories seem to tend. (Benjamin 1989, 135)

For Benjamin, therefore, this is not a hopeless situation (as it is for Scholem, who despairs over the degeneration of modern Judaism): it is rather the Hölderlinian moment of the highest danger, which also contains a possibility of redemption. What Scholem takes for a simple Bachofenian will-to-regress on Benjamin's part and his naïve belief in the self-rule of liberated life is actually his dialectical vista in which he attempts to 'pluck the living flower' of the prehistoric plastic condition of 'universal promiscuity' and restore the paradisiac *Ur-Leben* to its untrammelled flow. Just like Freud, convinced that nothing ever disappears in the human psyche, Benjamin also believes that the liquid libidinal element is still there, leaking through the partitions of the Law, and now can be used – as a *brake fluid*. To 'activate the emergency brake' (Benjamin 2003, 402) and stop the fake progress of the mythic order, its further hardening into an 'iron cage' of disenchanted instrumental rationality and formal laws,[8] would thus amount to its liquidation through liquefaction. On the other hand, the newly recovered flow of life, achieved through 'un-writing of the Scripture' in its old form, is not to remain amorphic: the Kafkan inversion ultimately aims at the 'transformation of life into [new] Scripture' – a distinctly anti-Christian but equally strong messianic gesture which opens a perspective of a new law and a different relation between law and life, less deadening and more life-affirming (which, as I will show in a moment, is precisely Derrida's messianic agenda). But this de-incarnational messianic procedure, turning Flesh again into a new Word, cannot succeed without the theological ink able to write life into Scripture. Scholem, therefore, has no reason to be so anxious: just as he awaits a new revelation coming 'from above,' or the still active *das Erscheinende*, Benjamin expects the renewal 'from below' to be enacted by the 'students' who, this time without the help of the divine

---

8 On the Jewish-messianic interpretation of this Weberian concept, see Jacob Taubes, "The Iron Cage and the Exodus from It, or the Dispute over Marcion, Then and Now" (2009, 139).

transcendence, just aided by the theology made liquid/alive again, will create a New Law.[9]

Benjamin certainly does not see liquidation as destruction: the liquidated theology/law does not disappear, but merely changes its form, becomes a *cryptotheology* of the seemingly secular world, a fluid undercurrent which dissolves all rigid forms of theological orthodoxy – the transcendent revelation and its outcome in the divine legislation – in order to uncover the more original sacred of the life-in-flow, reflexively studied and written into a new form by the Kafkan 'student' with whom he identifies.[10] The liquidated/liquid theology, therefore, is modern: different, new and Marrano-syncretic, yet at the same time it claims to recover the oldest and most original – messianic – sense of the holy which underlies all articulated orthodoxies, exactly according to Derrida's epigraph, that the religion of the living is nothing but a tautology. The messianic intuition behind these liquid speculations is that – *Life must flow*.

'Sickening of the tradition,' which Benjamin observed in the works of Kafka, can thus also be seen as its liquidation/liquefaction of the religion *as religion*: its inner *Abweichung*, due to which it becomes like the Benjaminian puppet, *klein und hässlich*, exposed to 'decisive reckoning.'[11] Yet still, as in Benjamin's chess-playing metaphor, it pulls the strings of all significant philosophical discourses; not, however, as *religion* with its official cultic language of sanctity and piety, but as that which always constituted the most vital interest of all religions and which now finally comes to the fore as such – *life*. The very cult of life, therefore, should finally give way to life itself, no longer to be sanctified but *lived*. So far, we only had a religion of life, which constantly talked about the 'sacredness of life' as if it were a treasure worthy only of the life divine: the Scholemian Highest

---

9 Compare a great comment of Adam Lipszyc, who in his study of Benjamin's messianic maneuvers stresses the crucial moment of studying-narrating: "The only messianic action that can be undertaken in Kafka's *Vorwelt* is studying [...] Studying makes possible *the turn*; it reverts towards the past and strives against the wind of oblivion. By engaging in this attempt, it wishes to rescue fragments of the broken and alienated existence in order to put together a story. Where there is no longer any doctrine or revelation, and where instead of Torah we have only a deformed, forgotten life spent at the foot of the Castle Hill, the student tries the impossible: in the reversing movement of recall, he attempts to turn his life into writing, into a narrative. The heavy existence in oblivion is to be replaced by an infinitely light-weight story, a 'happy untrammeled journey'" (Lipszyc 2012, 422–423).

10 On the Marrano concept of cryptotheology, see my *Jewish Cryptotheologies of Late Modernity: Philosophical Marranos* (Bielik-Robson, 2014).

11 In the letter to Scholem from June 1938, Benjamin explains: "Kafka's work represents a sickening of tradition" (Benjamin 2003, 326). See also the opening thesis of "On the Concept of History," which involves the metaphor of the puppet and the dwarf.

Life or the Derridean *vie indemne* – now, however, it is a high time, a new *kairos*, to have life pure and simple, or, in Derrida's formulation: 'Life as life – period' (2009, 307). The Rosenzweigian *ins Leben!*, concluding *The Star of Redemption*, which deeply influenced both Benjamin and Derrida, can thus be read as the messianic imperative to bring religion to its completion, which coincides with Benjamin's ambivalent method of liquidation: to end the cult of 'more life' in order to live it, finally – or, in Derrida's words, "to learn to live *finally*" (2011, 1).

2 The Marrano Messianism or the 'Recall' of the Jews

Yirmiyahu Yovel would have most certainly identified this double aspiration – to 'learn to live, finally' and to invest into a new life-affirming law – as characteristic of the modern Marrano. Benjamin's and Derrida's immanentist form of messianism 'from below' is closely connected – if not simply coterminous – with the Marrano shift towards 'this life,' in which the famous *esperanza* (hope) of the Iberian *conversos* located its new vision of salvation. The forced conversion to Christian religion removed the *conversos* away from the Jewish ritual and imposed on them the Pauline emphasis on individual salvation, which they nonetheless expressed in Judaic terms. By claiming that "salvation lies not in Christ, but in the Law of Moses" (Yovel 1989a, 20) the Marranos proved to be neither Jewish, since they could no longer practice the halakhic law, nor Christian, since they also refused to follow Paul's full sublation of law into love and grace.[12] Yet, they were also both: what they took from Christianity was a model of the Pauline *kathargein*, which would abrogate and internalize, or simultaneously negate and preserve the Mosaic Law, by distilling from it a messianic promise of redemption. This redemption, however, was not directed towards the Christian immortal after-life. Oscillating in the nowhereland between the two religions, the Marranos filled this in-between with a renewed interest in the worldly finite existence; having been ejected from both transcendence-oriented religious systems, they

---

12 "This formula was almost definitory of Judaizing Marranos; it was like a dogma of their hidden religion and a succinct description of their faith. This is, however, basically Jewish ingredients filing a Christian formula [...] In turning to salvation as their central religious concern, the Marranos displayed both their Catholic education and the needs of their situation [...] Educated in the Catholic milieu where salvation was a prime issue, they superimposed a Judaic interpretation over this Catholic concept: not Jesus Christ but the Law of Moses is the true way to salvation" (Yovel 1989a, 20–21).

discovered the realm of immanence – and the immanent life – as their new home. The orthodox Jews, therefore, could still cling to their 'life in deferral' (*Leben in Aufschub*), delayed and suppressed by the ritualistic execution of the transcendent legislation, while Christians could cherish their promise of personal immortality; the Marranos, however, found their own promised land in *life finite*, lived in all its riches and to the full, which none of the premodern institutional monotheisms wanted to claim. It was their Kingdom and the Glory, and it was in the finite immanent life where they put their messianic *esperanza*.[13]

The modern Marrano messianic constellation, therefore, is centred around the two stars: on the one hand, 'this life,' which, having escaped all Procrustean beds of the old laws and traditions, regains its liquid meandering form – and on the other the 'new law' which would take 'this life' in protection according to the new doctrine of the immanent salvation. For these two reasons, for Yovel, the most accomplished Marrano was Spinoza: the first modern thinker to lift immanence from oblivion, elevate a singular *conatus* of every living thing to an object of theologico-philosophical reflection, and bestow it with redemptive qualities, where salvation/liberation may be a matter of love, but not only; Spinoza's *amor intellectualis* is less love in the Pauline sense of all-embracing grace and more the 'third knowledge' which gains ultimate understanding of the eternal laws governing the living matrix of *natura naturans*. In this way, the Marrano rule – "The salvation lies not in Jesus, but in the Law of Moses" – finds its most sophisticated revision in Spinoza's science of the natural law of immanence, which at the same time constitutes the creative divine decree.[14]

But this rule proves even more effective in case of Jacques Derrida, whose complex take on 'Judeo-Christianity' constitutes a dynamic relation, never to be reconciled or simply synthetized: Derrida, a self-professed 'Marrano of the French Catholic culture,'[15] is a thinker who wrestled with the problem of the law for the

---

13 That, for the Marrano theology, 'Life' is indeed this secret divine Name, is confirmed by the Frankist sources documenting the rise and fall of this most amazing messianic Marrano movement which, following the apostasis of Sabbatai Sevi, advocated a massive conversion of the Polish Jews to Catholicism. In one of them, reporting on the sacred beginnings of the Frankist ferment, we can read: "On the day, the 3rd of August 1657, the four of us heard a grand voice clamouring from heaven: *Hayim! Hayim!*" (Doktór 1992, 55).

14 This is why, according to Yovel: "[Spinoza's] philosophy of immanence is characteristically a philosophy of emancipation. It assumes that the recognition of immanence as the overall substance of life, when interiorized by the individual and impregnating the dominant culture and society, is likely to become a major liberating force" (Yovel 1989b, 184).

15 "I am a kind of Marrano of French Catholic Culture, and I also have my Christian body, inherited from St. Augustine [...] I am one of those Marranos who, even in the intimacy of their own hearts, do not admit to being Jewish" (Derrida 1993, 160).

most part of his philosophical career, never happy to either leave the law as it is or abandon it completely. Perhaps, some analogy for Derrida's efforts can be delivered by the seventeenth-century Marrano, Isaac La Peyrere (Spinoza's older friend, then adversary), who in his highly controversial – and by no means heretical on all possible sides of the Jewish–Christian divide – *Du rappel des Juifs* (*The Recall of the Jews*), built a vision of a future modern religion based on the Marrano fusion of new Judaism and new Christianity, which will 'recall' the Jews, whom the Pauline religion superseded, now once again needed as the messianic agents of the Holy History. Deeply influenced by the Lurianic kabbalah on the one hand and the Millenarist prophesies of Joachim da Fiore on the other, Peyrere imagined the coming 'third age' as the 'new age of friends': Peyrere's vision of the new global Kingdom with the centre in Jerusalem is also permeated by what Spinoza, influenced by him, calls 'associative friendship.'[16] Derrida's reflections on friendship lead in a similar direction: towards a new Greco-Abrahamic paradigm in which the law will no longer be treated as an enemy or merely a compromise with social reality but will constitute the very redemptive core of the new *torat hayim*, 'this intangible Judaic principle.'

3 Transforming Life into Scripture: Derrida's New Law

Derrida's numerous readings of Saint Paul disseminated in his writings associated with the theme of 'messianicity' – starting with "Faith and Knowledge" and ending with his penultimate seminar on the death penalty – offer a truly Marrano version of the Pauline *kathargein*. While some of the Jewish Judeo-Christians – here most notably Jacob Taubes – follow Saint Paul in his messianic sublation of law into love, and then only negotiate a different understanding of what this love should mean, Derrida carries the sublation further: polemical towards the

---

[16] "God will recall the Jews and bring them to the Promised Land, led by Jesus, the true Messiah, and by the King of France (to whom the work was presented). From Jerusalem the two will rule over the entire world, now utterly redeemed. Here is a mixture of heterodox Christian and heterodox Jewish visions, sprinkled with traces of a belated Crusader spirit, an early ecumenism, and a premature Zionism – and all held together by a Marrano adhesive" (Yovel 1989a, 81–82). See also Richard H. Popkin, *Isaac La Peyrere (1596–1676): His Life, Work, and Influence*, especially the chapter "Le Peyrere's Heretical Theological Theories" (Popkin 1987, 69–79). When I say only "some analogy," it is because Derrida would have been appalled by the contemporary overtones of La Peyrere's political messianism, which could be interpreted as fostering the unholy alliance of the Israeli and American right wing with its obsession over 'Jerusalem liberated.'

Pauline version of antinomianism, he wants to sublate love into a new law which would somehow recollect the old Law of Moses in the 'Law of Christ,' but now with a new focus – on *this* finite life. This 'inversed messianism,' based on the Kafkan–Benjaminian *Umkehr* which consists of transforming life into a (new) Scripture – inversed in regard to the antinomian strain of Jewish messianism, which constitutes the main bulk of Judaic heresies, Pauline Christianity included – puts Derrida in the typical Marrano position of a double non-orthodoxy, which deviates simultaneously from the Christian emphasis on love only, as well as from the rabbinic emphasis on the legalistic heteronomy of Halakhah. Far from representing any form of messianic anarchy and its regulative notion of a 'happy lawless life' (which still appeals to Benjamin), Derrida's purpose is to revolutionize the formula of the law that would preserve in itself the incalculable moment of love which, for him, is always a 'living/loving,' i.e., a love addressing a concrete immanent this-worldly life: only when forming such a dynamic whole, can love and law come close to the ideal of radical justice.[17] Heretic on all possible fronts, what Derrida boldly proposes is a messianic vitalism based on the new law: a Marrano solution which conforms neither to rabbinic Judaism nor to Pauline Christianity.

This has to be stated very clearly: Derrida's re-sublation of 'living/loving' into a new law is *not* a figure of the *katechon* as envisaged by Carl Schmitt.[18] It is a new – Marrano – position which must be acknowledged as such. Saint Paul's reintroduction of the law into Christian community has always been regarded by his followers as a lame compromise: merely a '*katechonic*' concession towards the harsh necessities of being, not something a true Christian would choose as his ideal. Hence the sense of unease in regard to the secular modernity among the Pauline Protestants who created its liberal laws and institutions out of what they perceived as a necessity of compromise in the absence of the apocalyptic Second Coming. For the modern Jews, however, even those messianically minded, this does not have to be a compromise: from Spinoza, via Mendelssohn, then Cohen and Rosenzweig, and finally Levinas and Derrida, the modern liberal law undergoes a messianic transformation which 'seasons justice with mercy' and infuses the general legalistic order with the uniqueness of face-to-face relation of neighbourly love.

---

[17] "*Living-loving* … Life loves itself in the living being, life loves itself, period, it loves to live, it loves itself in living for life" (Derrida 2016, 111).

[18] See Carl Schmitt, *The Nomos of the Earth in the International Law of the Jus Publicum Europaeum*, most of all the chapter "The Christian Empire as a Restrainer of the Antichrist (*Katechon*)," where Schmitt says: "I do not believe that any historical concept other than katechon would have been possible for the original Christian faith" (2003, 59).

The dialectical paradox of the modern law lies precisely in this novelty – the focus on the singularity as its nominalistic *limes*, or what Rosenzweig calls a 'meta-ethical remnant' and Derrida a 'rogue' (*voyou*): an individual who is 'neither this nor that,' who never coincides with any form or identity, but who nonetheless must be defended against any kind of collective coercion, and as such becomes a legalistic avatar of the *tselem*, a singularity emulating the uniqueness of God, the transcendent *echad*, ultimately transcending any order of general categories and laws. The dialectical evolution of the law, therefore, entails a subsumption of the antinomian element: the role of the law is not to create a general *ethos* of 'parts and wholes,' but to protect the 'deviant' meta-ethical singularity in its right not to participate in the totality, to remain 'entirely other' and preserve a distance towards communal belonging.[19] Before, the law always spoke in the name of the ethical whole and preserved its indemnity – now it is supposed to speak in the name of the separated singularity "beyond any social bond" (Derrida 2006, 298) and protect its precarious life. This antinomian 'use of disorder,' which bends and transforms the law from within, is strictly analogical to the dialectical utilization of apocalypsis in Derrida's figure of *differance*. The impatient messianic slogan – "Lo, I make all things new!" – here becomes harnessed to the most patient of works which consists in making new laws. "Lo, I make all laws new!" therefore constitutes the gist of the Jewish-messianic version of Derrida's revision of Paul: not a sad resignation of a *katechon*, but the positive dialectical messianicity written into the structure of the modern process of legislation. The old law

---

[19] According to deconstruction's sacred formula: *tout autre est tout autre*, "every other is entirely other" – see the title of Chapter 4 in *The Gift of Death* (Derrida 1995, 82–88). On the paradox of the modern law, which commands to recognize the transcendent alterity of the other, see Derrida's comment in his *Politics of Friendship*: "In principle this double dimension maintains the absolute singularity of the other and that of 'my' relation to the other, as a relation of the other to the other I am myself, as its other for itself. But the relation to the singularity of the other also passes through the universality of law. This discourse on universality can determine itself in the regions of morality, of law or of politics, but it always appeals to a third instance, beyond the face-to-face of singularities [...] Does not my relation to the singularity of the other *qua* other, in effect, involve the law? Having come as a third party but always from the singularity of the other, *does not the law command me to recognize the transcendent alterity of the other who can never be anything but heterogeneous and singular, hence resistant to the very generality of the law?* (Derrida 2006, 276–277; emphasis added). Derrida formulates this dilemma for the first time in "Force of Law" (in the first version of the essay delivered as a lecture in 1989): "How to reconcile the act of justice that must always concern singularity, individuals, groups, irreplaceable existences, the other or myself as other, in a unique situation, with rule, norm, value, or the imperative of justice that necessarily have a general form, even if this generality prescribes a singular application in each case?" (Derrida 2002, 255).

dies in order to liberate a meta-ethical life which now, patiently and *little by little*, transforms life again into Scripture.[20]

The natural element of the singular living or the meta-ethical remnant is the story, *le récit*: this is the medium where the transformation occurs. In his philosophy of the narrative form, Derrida follows Benjamin's analysis of Kafka very closely, but his version of the messianic antinomianism is even more subtle. The story, which radiates 'from this side of life,' not only meets Halakhah on its way and strikes it with its mighty paw; it truly liquidates it, by dissolving the hardness of the law and bending it according to the living contingency.[21] The haggadic element, therefore, works as a law-bender. Its role as a *récit* is to make singular life visible to the lofty Law: make the Law notice the idiosyncrasy of the singular life, not pass it by, and force it to understand that *lives matter*. The *récit*/ Haggadah, therefore, seasons justice in the form of the positive law, by irrigating

---

[20] The 'rogue,' whom Derrida envisages as the future citizen of the democracy-to-come, also called *voyoucracy*, strongly resembles a Marrano subject who also distances himself from any communal belonging and preserves his sense of 'shadowy inwardness.' Compare in this context a great comment of Shmuel Trigano who, writing against the radical republicanism of the French rebellion in 1968 (not unlike Derrida himself), says: "Against what the Marxists say, the limit which separates interiority and exteriority – one of the distinctive features of the Marrano (non) identity – could be affirmed as a positive quality of great importance in safeguarding the human element in politics [...] provided that the politics does not constitute a totality of what it means to be human [...] The shadowy retreat [*le retrait ombragé*] ('God's image,' *tselem Elochim*) which contains the secret of being a human can never be treated as a pretext to the unleashing of violence of the State which would like to *see* what's there. It is a singular human being which is in the centre of the State, but he/she will always be hidden like the Holy of Holies in the Jerusalem Temple – in the heart of the Polis – and never the other way around. The centre of the individual is unreachable [...] *This is the teaching which was given to us by the modern experience of Marranism, gradually turned from negative into a positive one*" (Trigano 2000, 268–269; emphasis added). This gradual turning of the tables – 'little by little' reorienting the law from its interest in the all-seeing totality of the polis to the protection of the 'secret' core of the individual lives – is also Derrida's agenda, which coincides with his affirmative reinterpretation of the 'Marrano experience.' The *voyou* indeed bears the features of a modern Marrano, which Derrida fully endorses by saying: "For the word *voyou* is itself a suspect word and the *voyou* himself a suspect character. Shady, questionable, of dubious character [*mauvais aim*], which is to say of suspicious origin [...] It is always a question of a suspicious or mixed origin, of *alliage* and alliance, of, this time, some 'alligation' *(alligare)*" (Derrida 2005, 32).

[21] See again Benjamin's letter to Scholem: "Kafka's genius lay in the fact that he tried something altogether new: he gave up truth so that he could hold to its transmissibility, the haggadic element. His works are by nature parables. But their poverty and their beauty consist in their need to be *more* than parables. They don't simply lie down at the feet of doctrine, the way Haggadah lies down at the feet of Halakhah. Having crouched down, they unexpectedly cuff doctrine with a weighty paw" (Benjamin 2003, 3; 326).

it with theology turned liquid or, in Derrida's Marrano idiom, the blood of Christ transformed into an ink capable of overwriting the old law and scripting a new one. Derrida juxtaposes Shakespeare's sentence from *The Merchant of Venice* – "Mercy seasons justice," falling on with a gentle rain of Christ's blood – with a similar line in Victor Hugo's abolitionist speeches, which he reads in the *Death Penalty* seminar: "the gentle [*douce*] law of Christ will finally permeate the legal code and *radiate out from there*" (Derrida 2014, 201; emphasis added). The Law of Christ, therefore,

> is going to irrigate the law, the written legislation. Little by little, Christ, the spirit, the soul, the gentle law, the gentleness of Christ, charity, the blood of Christ, is going to *irrigate the legal code and transform legislative writing*. So he [Hugo] is playing here natural law against written law while hoping, while even being sure that natural law – the heart, finally, Jesus is the heart, the blood is the heart – the heart is going to transform the written and positive, historical law. *Little by little, the legal code, written law, historical law, will be irrigated, inspired, vivified, spiritualized, by gentleness, the gentle law of Christ.*
>
> (2014, 201.; emphasis added)

Hugo, and Derrida after him, does not say *the love of Christ*, which would be the standard syntagma of the Pauline Christianity, but, strangely, *the law of Christ*: a new legal formula, the role of which is to penetrate the existing civil legislation, so far based on the death penalty and the sovereign 'right to kill,' and subvert/transform it from within, so it begins to represent and protect the 'right to live.'[22] What they both hope for is not a liberation of life in the realm 'outside the law,' but an inner transmutation of the law itself, the change radiating from the legal code already permeated by the 'blood of Christ' or theology 'liquidated' into ink: from a death-dealing punitive device sanctioning the capital punishment into a protective shield defending the precarious singular life against all sovereign impositions. The only justification of this new law, which Hugo calls 'natural law,' is the defence of the weaker: the law's power is not to be displayed in all its dark glory, as in the ritual of the death penalty, but to make Christ's 'weakness' effective against all possible powers of this world.

---

22 See Derrida's comment: "When one tackles the death penalty, one does not dispute one penalty among others but law itself in its origin, in its very order. If the origin of law is a violent positing, it manifests itself in the purest fashion when violence is absolute, that is to say when it touches on the right to life and to death [...] The legal system [*l'ordre du droit*] fully manifests itself in the possibility of the death penalty. By abolishing it, one would not be touching upon one *dispositif* among others. Rather, one would be disavowing the very principle of law. Thus is confirmed that something is 'rotten' at the heart of law. The death penalty must testify that law is a violence contrary to nature" (Derrida 2002, 276).

So, just as theology becomes liquid and alive again, by dissolving its rigid dogmas in the undercurrent of life, so does the law, by shedding the form of *dura lex* and becoming 'vivified' by the 'gentle law of Christ,' making each living a goal in itself and protecting it against instrumentalization. The ultimate messianic purpose is not to give up on the law altogether and opt for an absolutely all-forgiving love as well as all-innocent life, but to have the law, which could be less cruel and more 'relaxed,' deriving from the supple and fluid medium of life itself, spontaneously transforming into Scripture:

> Not that one forgive [...] but that *one become benevolent, tolerant, flexible, in order to avoid the rigidity of the ideal* [...] No excessive rectitude in law, in short, no absolute correctness. For inflexibility, rigidity, correction are essential attributes of what is right [...] *Flexibility is incalculable*; it is that for which there is no objective rule, as there is for law [...] without an objective rule, one must be benevolent toward the other as other, by finding each time, and this is perhaps what benevolence is, by each time inventing the flexibility, the form and degree of flexibility, of *relaxation of the law*, the good rule (without rule, then) of flexibility. Otherwise we get cruelty; *the inflexible law is what produces cruelty.*
> (Derrida 2016, 205–206; emphasis added)

The law is thus *almost* liquidated: almost deprived of heteronomy, almost internalized, made 'liquid' and 'relaxed,' but still short of annihilation. For it is still a law: serving not the 'rigidity of the ideal,' but the fallible singular lives in an incalculable difference and variety, which no general norm can overrule. No longer a sovereign law befalling the singular life with the rectitude of death – the ultimate verdict, this is a *biophilic* law in which the Derridean 'living/loving' finds its protective expression.[23]

---

[23] Some commentators have already noticed the affinity between what I call the biophilic thrust of Derrida's conception of the law and the rabbinic jurisdiction which, perhaps in the gesture of opposition to the Pauline identification of law with death, sees itself as life-fostering and life-protecting. Hence, not only the commandment of *Pikuach Nefesh*, 'saving the life,' overrules all other *mitzvot* (with the significant exception of the 'defamation of the Holy Name,' *Chillul Hashem*, with which Derrida as a self-professed Marrano could not have agreed), but the rabbis also stress that Halakhah is a way of life, a *torat hayim* teaching how to live and not how to die. If in Leviticus 18:5 God states that "You shall therefore keep my statuses and my rules; if a person does them, he shall live by them," it means that the law is given for a better life and not as a deadening instrument of inner ascesis (see Hirvonen 2001). This affinity is obviously mediated by Emmanuel Levinas' talmudic writings which Derrida quotes fully approvingly in "Force of Law": "Levinas speaks of an infinite right in what he calls 'Jewish humanism,' whose basis is not 'the concept of *man*' but rather the other [*autrui*]: 'the extent of the other's right' is 'practically an infinite right.' Here *equity* is not equality, calculated proportion, equitable distribution or distributive justice, but rather, absolute dissymmetry" (Levinas 1990, 98, and Derrida 2002, 250). The other's 'infinite right' is precisely his/her/its 'right to live' which can never be

Derrida may not be an antinomian adversary of the law in the Pauline vein, but he also does not endorse the positive jurisdiction *tout court*. The main issue for Derrida is *force de loi*, 'force of law': the element of enforcement which can take semi-mystical forms and, because of that, blur the line between violence and legitimate power, thus making the latter less legitimate that it wishes to appear. "I have always been uncomfortable with the word 'force' even if I have often judged it indispensable" (Derrida 2002, 235) is Derrida's honest account of the aporia which avoids an easy anarchic way out and seeks instead a new sense of justice maintaining a 'strange' relation to the law or

> the possibility of a justice, indeed of a law that not only exceeds or contradicts law but also, perhaps, has no relation to law, or maintains such a strange relation to it that it may just as well demand law as exclude it. (Derrida 2002, 233)[24]

As we have seen, this strange aporetic relation, which simultaneously demands and excludes law, in the latest seminars translates into a positive programme of law's *relaxation*. What 'relaxes' – or 'liquidates' – the law, makes it supple and fluid, is, as in the *Death Penalty* seminar, mercy as an equivalent of earlier justice which, in "Force of Law" and *Specters of Marx*, Derrida simply identifies with deconstruction: mercy and justice understood as extreme attentiveness to every singular living and its idiosyncratic otherness, as unique (*echad*) as the divine Name itself.[25] Just as the Highest Life is the apophatic principle, 'the hidden tradition' of the 'religion of the living' – so is justice the inner 'heart,' the secret

---

circumvented by any law demanding sacrifice, and which Derrida identifies with deconstruction itself: "Invincible to all skepticism [...] this 'idea of justice' seems indestructible in its affirmative character, in its demand of gift without exchange, without circulation, without recognition or gratitude, without economic circularity, without calculation and without rules, without reason and without theoretical rationality, in the sense of regulating mastery. And so, one can recognize in it, even accuse in it a madness, and perhaps *another kind of mysticism* [*une autre sorte de mystique*]. And deconstruction is mad about and from such justice, mad about and from this desire for justice. *Such justice, which is not law, is the very movement of deconstruction at work in law and in the history of law*, in political history and history itself, even before it presents itself as the discourse that the academy or the culture of our time labels deconstructionism" (Derrida 2002, 254; emphasis added).

[24] Derrida routinely ascribes this dubious mystic of the legal power to Kant. "No law without force, as Immanuel Kant recalled with the greatest rigor," he states in "Force of Law" (Derrida 2002, 233), and the same critique of law's rigidity and inflexibility will emerge in the *Death Penalty* seminar where Kant figures as the most determined philosophical defender of capital punishment, treating it as a paradigm of all legislation.

[25] "Justice in itself, if such a thing exist, outside or beyond law, is not deconstructible [...] *Deconstruction is justice*" (Derrida, 2002, 253; original emphasis).

breath 'vivifying' the overt structure of the positive law: "justice, where it is not yet, not yet there, where it is no longer [...] and where it will never be, no more than the law, reducible to laws or rights" (Derrida 1994, xvii). But, as Derrida emphasizes:

> *The necessity of this distinction* [between law and justice] *does not entail the least disqualification of the juridical*, its specificity, and the new approaches it calls for today. Such a distinction appears on the contrary to be indispensable and prior to any re-elaboration. In particular, in all the places where one may remark what is called today, more or less calmly, 'juridical voids,' as if it were a matter of filling in the blanks without re-doing things from top to bottom. There is nothing surprising in the fact that it is most often a question of *the property and proper nature of life*, of its inheritance, and of its generation [...] To believe that it is merely a matter of filling in a 'juridical void,' there *where the point is to think the law, the law of the law, right, and justice*, to believe that it is enough to produce new 'articles of the legal code' to 'regulate the problem,' would be tantamount to turning over the thinking of ethics to an ethics committee. (ibid., 231; emphasis added)

Hence, instead of sublation of the law, Derrida proposes deconstruction as an aporetic oscillation between justice as the infinite right to live of every singular other and the calculability of the general law, only to be 'cut' by the decision which can never leave behind the difficult moment of undecidability: "No justice is exercised, no justice is rendered, no justice becomes effective nor does it determine itself in the form of law, without a decision that cuts and divides [*une décision qui tranche*]" (Derrida 2002, 252). Justice must 'enforce' itself and be 'put into work' [*mis en oeuvre*] through the application of the law (Derrida 2002, 251), but the law must also retain a certain ghostly/spectral unease deriving from the incalculability of justice:

> Deconstruction always finds itself and moves itself between these two poles [...] That is why the test and ordeal of the undecidable [...] is never past or passed, it is not a surmounted or sublated (*aufgehoben*) moment in the decision. The undecidable remains caught, lodged, as a ghost at least, but an essential ghost, in every decision, in every event of decision. Its ghostliness [*sa fantomaticité*] deconstructs from within all assurance of presence, all certainty or all alleged criteriology assuring us of the justice of a decision, in truth of the very event of a decision. (Derrida 2002, 251; 253)

The law, therefore, is necessary; it cannot be disqualified in a dismissive antinomian gesture, but it also must be informed – aporetically, uneasily – by the ethical spirit of justice/mercy which reckons with the infinite 'right to live' of every singular living. Such inspired law – 'enforced' by the power of ghost/spectre/spirit – should not rejoice its 'spiritedness' (as would be expected in the Pauline Christianity) but rather suffer it; the spirit of absolute justice, which refuses to be fully incarnated in the practice of love, must hover over the law in the ghostly, spectral, haunting manner causing the law to be ill at ease, i.e., always on the brink of self-deconstruction for the sake of justice which, by guarding the 'infinite right to live,' constitutes the only 'mystical authority' and as such remains non-deconstructible. The laws, therefore, may be changing – alternately, forming and breaking – as the earthly vessels of the divine message, which simultaneously contain and distort the word of absolute justice, but the message itself, although not fully comprehensible within the conditions of the worldly immanence, stays untouched. Therefore, "the fact that law is deconstructible is not bad news, [for] one may even find in this the political chance of all historical progress" (Derrida 2002, 242), and indeed, this is also the legislative aim of Derrida himself, who wishes to write a new biophilic Law/Scripture, taking into account the interests of singular lives.[26]

It is precisely the unsublatable aporetic tension between the immanent/historical 'justice as law' (Derrida 2002, 242) and the transcendent 'justice in itself' which makes deconstruction possible – and necessary at the same time.[27] No law can ever be perfect, because, as incarnate into a general rule, it can never give justice to the uniqueness of the divine singularity (*echad*) and its creaturely likeness (*tselem*), but it can become better *little by little* – paradoxically, only when it knows that it necessarily lacks perfection. Hence, the *improvement* of 'the structure of right or of the law' lies in its departure from the rigid ideal of semi-eternal *dura lex* (which is not 'bad news') and its embracement of self-deconstructibility: "the founding or the self-authorizing of law as the possibility of the exercise of deconstruction" (Derrida 2002, 243), i.e., the founding which is at the same time foundering. "No excessive rectitude in law" (Derrida 2016, 205), which Derrida sees as the effect of his 'relaxing' techniques, goes here hand in hand with the inner transformation of the structure of the law, no longer perceiving itself as a mystical source of authority soaring above the living and demanding its sacrifice. The self-deconstructive law, which weakens and relaxes its grip for the sake of

---

26 Compare the fragment from "The 'World' of the Enlightenment to Come": "The heterogeneity between justice and law does not exclude but, on the contrary, calls for their inseparability: there can be no justice without an appeal to juridical determinations and to the force of law; and there can be no becoming, no transformation, history, or perfectibility of law without an appeal to a justice that will nonetheless always exceed it [...] On both sides, then, whether it is a question of singularity or universality, and each time both at once, both calculation and the incalculable are necessary" (Derrida 2003, 41).

27 This aporetic tension between the promise of the transcendent law always to come and the deconstructible actualization of every historical law always already gone is also described by Derrida in reference to Kafka's parable "Before the Law": "The law is transcendent and theological, and so always to come, always promised, because it is immanent, finite, and thus already past. Every 'subject' is caught up in this aporetic structure in advance" (Derrida 2002, 270).

life, constitutes the very opposite of the self-sacrificing law which draws its 'force' from the 'rigor of death' (*rigor mortis*). The deconstruction, therefore, is a deferred and delayed destruction, an apocalyptic fire harnessed to the legislative work: while it "stands on the side of the divine violence that destroys the law, we could even venture to say, that deconstructs the law" (Derrida 2002, 290), it does so by shifting the semantics of the Benjaminian 'liquidation': precisely, from destruction to deconstruction, from the wholesale transcendent negation of this world to the patient transformative work which occurs in the immanence of the worldly life and 'for the sake of life' (Derrida 2002, 289). Once again, echoing his praise of Levinas' 'Jewish humanism of the other' in the more radical Benjaminian formulation of the absolute justice as the divine violence which 'liquidates' and, in this manner, founds/founders the new law, Derrida writes:

> 'Thou shalt not kill' remains an absolute imperative once *the principle of destructive divine violence commands the respect of the living being*, beyond law, beyond judgment, for this imperative is followed by no judgment. It provides no criterion for judgment; *one could not find in it the authority to automatically condemn any putting to death*. The individual or the community must keep the 'responsibility' (the condition of which being the absence of general criteria and automatic rules), must assume their decision in exceptional situations, in extraordinary or unheardof cases. That, for Benjamin, is the essence of Judaism, which would explicitly refuse to condemn murder in cases of legitimate selfdefense, and which, according to him, sacralizes life to the point that certain thinkers [most notably Derrida himself] extend this sacralization beyond man to include animal and vegetable.
>
> (Derrida 2002, 288; emphasis added)

So, just as religion should be ultimately 'in life and for life' (Derrida 2002, 289), so should be the law which, because of that reminder – we could call it a *memento vitae* to emphasize the difference with the traditional 'thanatic' concept of the law – cannot imagine itself as the strongest sovereign 'force' in the world of the living or "the inflexible law [which] produces cruelty" (Derrida 2016, 206). Deconstruction will thus always bring law down from its 'lofty scaffolding' (Derrida 2014, 4) to the horizontal community of creatures (animals and plants included, to be properly protected by a legal system to come), where it truly belongs as the immanent/historical, always incipiently distortive actualisation of the absolute justice: in the 'Here-Below' of the precarious plural lives which it, first and last of all, *should* guard. It is not life that must serve the law, but the law which must serve the singular living which now moves from the margins of religious neglect into the very centre of 'another kind of mysticism' (Derrida 2002, 254), lending the law a new 'mystical authority': this is the gist of Derrida's messianic reversal.

In that sense, Derrida's deconstructive method can indeed be regarded as a creative continuation of Benjamin's liquidation of theology: far from killing Judaism, it offers Jewish tradition a unique chance of life – the life which Judaism always had, but buried and 'distorted in oblivion.' As Derrida himself admits, seemingly oxymoronically, but in fact deeply in accordance with his Marrano self-declaration, he represents the "death of Judaism, but also its *one* chance of survival" (Derrida 2004, 42). The whole point here is to see the possibility of the double affirmative reversal on the two different yet closely related planes: within the 'liquidation of theology' which *prima facie* means only destruction, but in fact produces the most vital forms of modern heresy, as well as within the Marrano predicament which *prima facie* appears only tragic, but in fact paves the way towards modern forms of investment in the immanence, world, life, and new law, which blur the line between the religious and the secular. Just as the theology turned liquid reveals new redemptive potentialities of life, so does the forced conversion entail a fruitful potentiality of creating a modern subject of life, for whom the injunction – 'to learn to live finally' and 'to transform life into Scripture' – becomes a new salvific imperative.

Bibliography

Benjamin, Walter. *Illuminations: Essays and Reflections*. Trans. Harry Zohn. New York: Schocken Books, 1968.
Benjamin, Walter. *The Correspondence of Walter Benjamin and Gershom Scholem, 1932–1940*. Trans. Gary Smith and Andre Lefevre. New York: Schocken Books, 1989.
Benjamin, Walter. *The Arcades Project*. Trans. Howard Eiland and Kevin McLaughlin. Cambridge, Mass.: Belknap Press of Harvard University Press, 1999.
Benjamin, Walter. *Selected Writings*. Vols. 1–4. Eds. Howard Eiland and Michael W. Jennings. Cambridge, Mass.: Harvard University Press, 2003.
Bergson, Henri. *Two Sources of Morality and Religion*. Trans. R. Ashley Audra and Cloudesley Brereton. Notre Dame, Indiana: Notre Dame University Press, 1977.
Bielik-Robson, Agata. *Jewish Cryptotheologies of Late Modernity: Philosophical Marranos*. London: Routledge, 2014.
Bielik-Robson, Agata. "Walter Benjamin (1892–1940)." *Religion and European Philosophy: Key Thinkers from Kant to Žižek*. Eds. Philip Goodchild and Hollis Phelps. Abingdon and New York: Routledge, 2017.
Bloch, Ernst. *Atheism in Christianity*. Trans. J. T. Swann. London: Verso, 2009.
Buck-Morss, Susan. "The Flaneur, the Sandwichman and the Whore: The Politics of Loitering." *Walter Benjamin and the Arcades Project*. Ed. Beatrice Hanssen. New York: Continuum, 2006. 33–65.
Derrida, Jacques. *Circumfession. Jacques Derrida*. Eds. Jacques Derrida and Jeffrey Bennington. Chicago: University of Chicago Press, 1993.
Derrida, Jacques. *Specters of Marx. The State of Debt, the Work of Mourning, and the New International*. Trans. Peggy Kamuf. New York and London: Routledge, 1994.
Derrida, Jacques. *The Gift of Death*. Trans. David Wills. University of Chicago Press, 1995.
Derrida, Jacques. *Acts of Religion*. Ed. Gil Anidjar. New York and London: Routledge, 2002.

Derrida, Jacques. "The 'World' of the Enlightenment to Come (Exception, Calculation, Sovereignty)." *Research in Phenomenology* 33. Leiden: Brill, 2003. 10–51.

Derrida, Jacques. "A Testimony Given ..." *Questioning Judaism*. Ed. Elisabeth Weber. Stanford: Stanford University Press, 2004. 39–58.

Derrida, Jacques. *Rogues: Two Essays on Reason*. Trans. Pascale-Anne Brault. Stanford: Stanford University Press, 2005.

Derrida, Jacques. *Politics of Friendship*. Trans. George Collins. London: Verso, 2006.

Derrida, Jacques. *The Animal That Therefore I Am*. Trans. David Wills. New York: Fordham University Press, 2008.

Derrida, Jacques. *The Beast and the Sovereign*. Vol. 1. Trans. Geoffrey Bennington. Chicago: University of Chicago Press, 2009.

Derrida, Jacques. *Learning to Live Finally: The Last Interview*. Trans. Pascal Anne Brault. New York: Melville House, 2011.

Derrida, Jacques. *The Death Penalty*. Vol. 1. Trans. Peggy Kamuf. Chicago: University of Chicago Press, 2014.

Derrida, Jacques. *The Death Penalty*. Vol. 2. Trans. Elizabeth Rotenberg. Chicago: University of Chicago Press, 2016.

Doktór, Jan. Ed. *Rozmaite adnotacja, przypadki, czynności i anekdoty pańskie* [*Various Annotations, Cases, Deeds, and Anecdotes of the Lord*]. Płońsk: Tikkun, 1992.

Hirvonen, Ari. "Promising Justice: Derrida with Jewish Jurisprudence." *Law and Critique* 12 (2001): 159–183.

Levinas, Emmanuel. *Nine Talmudic Readings*. Trans. Annette Aronowicz. Bloomington: Indiana University Press, 1990.

Lipszyc, Adam. *Sprawiedliwość na końcu języka. Czytanie Waltera Benjamina* [*Justice at The Tip of the Tongue. Reading of Walter Benjamin*]. Kraków: Universitas, 2012.

Popkin, Richard H. *Isaac La Peyrere (1596–1676): His Life, Work, and Influence*. Leiden: Brill, 1987.

Schmitt, Carl. *The Nomos of the Earth in the International Law of the Jus Publicum Europaeum*. Trans. G. L. Ulmen. New York: Telos Press Publishing, 2003.

Scholem, Gershom. *The Messianic Idea in Judaism And Other Essays on Jewish Spirituality*. New York: Schocken, 1971.

Scholem, Gershom. "Zehn unhistorische Sätze über Kabbalah." *Judaica 3. Studien zur jüdischen Mystik*. Suhrkamp: Frankfurt am Main, 1973. 235–242.

Scholem, Gershom. *Tagebücher nebst Aufsätzen und Entwürfen bis 1923. 2 Halbband 1917–1923*. Frankfurt am Main: Jüdischer Verlag, 2000.

Scholem, Gershom. *Lamentations of Youth: The Diaries of Gershom Scholem, 1913–1919*. Ed. and Trans. Anthony David Skinner. Cambridge, Mass.: Belknap Press of Harvard University Press, 2008.

Taubes, Jacob. "The Iron Cage and the Exodus from It, or the Dispute over Marcion, Then and Now." *From Cult to Culture. Fragments Towards a Critique of Historical Reason*. Ed. Aleida Assmann. Stanford: Stanford University Press, 2009. 137–146.

Trigano, Schmuel. "Le Marranisme, un modèle multidimensionnel." *Pardes. Etudes et Culture Juives*, nr 29 (*Le Juif caché. Marranisme et modernité*). Paris: In Press Editions, 2000. 260–274.

Yovel, Yirmiyahu. *Spinoza and Other Heretics: The Marrano of Reason*. Princeton: Princeton University Press, 1989a.

Yovel, Yirmiyahu. *Spinoza and Other Heretics: The Adventures of Immanence*. Princeton: Princeton University Press, 1989b.

Yovel, Yirmiyahu. *The Other Within: The Marranos – Split Identity and Emerging Modernity*. Princeton and Oxford: Princeton University Press, 2009.

Wohlfahrt, Irving. "No-Man's-Land: On Walter Benjamin's 'Destructive Character.'" *Diacritics* 2.8 (1978): 47–65.

Wohlfahrt, Irving. "Walter Benjamin's Image of Interpretation." *New German Critique* 17 (1979): 70–98.

Shaul Magid
Is the Academic Study of Judaism Heresy?

> "History is the religion of fallen Jews."
> Yosef Hayyim Yerushalmi, *Zakhor*

1 Heresy and the Double Border-Crosser

Is the academic study of Judaism necessarily, or potentially, an act of "heresy"? At first sight, this question might seem moot. By some accounts, modernity is itself either a heretical field or an era beyond heresy. Peter Berger (1979), for instance, argues that modernity and secularization have resulted in "a pluralization of plausibility structures" that "*ipso facto* subjectivizes religion" (26) – and thus obviates "heresy" precisely by normalizing choice (i.e., the base meaning of the Greek word "*haeresis*"). In Berger's view, "for modern man, heresy typically becomes a necessity" because "modernity creates a new situation in which picking and choosing becomes an imperative" (28).[1]

More recent scholarship, however, has opened up different approaches by focusing less on what "heresy" *is* than what it *does*. Even in antiquity – as Alain Le Boulluec has shown for Christianity and Daniel Boyarin for Judaism – one cannot assume any single normative tradition from which the heretic deviates.[2] Heresy is not a "thing" that defies, denies, or transgresses orthodoxy. Rather "orthodoxy" and "heresy" fluidly constitute one another. Each can only be defined in relation to the other. To accuse someone of "heresy" is an act of exclusion and a means for creating the boundaries from which "orthodoxy" emerges. As a result, as Boyarin stresses, to study heresy is to illumine the making of communal and normative boundaries:

---

[1] Even if one can question Berger's assessment of secularization, his insights do resonate with Jewish Orthodoxy, which emerged sometime in the nineteenth century to resist the hemorrhaging of belief and practice among many European Jews and to erect boundaries of legitimacy and authority. Even inside Orthodoxy, "heresy" remained a weak tool of exclusion with little consequences beyond specific communities. The problem was not the heretic per se, but the modern structures that made what would have once been called "heresy" viable and no longer deviant. See, for example, Ferziger (2005, 2015).
[2] See Meyer (1988).

> 'Heresiology' ... inscribes the border lines, and heresiologists are the inspectors of religious customs. Ancient heresiologists tried to police the boundaries so as to identify and interdict those who respected no borders, those smugglers of ideas and practices newly declared to be contraband. (2006, 2)

From the perspective of their accusers, those who are accused as "heretics" are border-crossers: the problem is not that they cross over to the other side, but that they return and remain inside. They cross back from whence they came and in doing so blur what others see as a boundary. If they took a one-way passage and remained outside the border, no such accusation would be needed. Heretics are considered dangerous precisely *because* they never fully abandon their investment in the community. Accordingly, heretics venture beyond with the intent to return, carrying with them contraband (either methodological or epistemological) with which they can potentially alter the normative beliefs and practices of their community, often under the guise of defending, or correcting, tradition. In contrast to the apostate, who crosses over and never returns, the heretic has the potential to be a radical reformer of sorts, a critic of the very boundaries created to exclude him or her. This may be one way of distinguishing between a heretic and an apostate. The apostate leaves and does not return.

For the purposes of this essay, heresy requires an act that makes claims on basic normative beliefs and practices and seeks to alter them through various means; claims of prophecy, critiques of tradition, and changing historical circumstances that would require radical rather than incremental change in thought, structure, or practice, etc. It is in this sense, I suggest, "heresy" can provide a useful analytical frame for exploring the complicated place of academic Jewish Studies in relation to modern Judaism and contemporary Jewry.

While "heresy" is almost always deployed negatively, in this essay I do not use it as a pejorative term: I use it to describe the act of constructing, describing, disturbing, and policing boundaries that mark Judaism as it moves through history. In addition, following Boyarin, I do not assume that there is an immutable normative Judaism or stasis of tradition – an "orthodoxy" – from which heresy and heretics deviate. Rather, in asking whether the label "heresy" or "heretic" applies to Jewish Studies or its practitioners, my question will be how the academic study of Judaism relates to what has been defended and articulated as normative during a period in which Jewish identity, religion, and culture has been changing to meet the specific challenges of modernity and secularization.

In some way I depart from Boyarin's definition of heresy in that while I too define the heretic as a border-crosser, the operative aspect of border-crossing for me is the return trip to one's original station with a new notion of Judaism culled in part from having crossed to "the other side." I use scare quotes here to gesture to the other side as a Kabbalistic euphemism for the demonic (the *sitra akhra*) or, in more common parlance, *tarbut ra* (evil culture), a term used to define anything outside the normative orbit of Jewish life and practice. The "other side" is where all the bad stuff resides. When one ventures out there and brings it back, what is often produced is heresy. The heretic is thus one who cannot fully sever themselves from their Jewish roots – he or she does not convert to another religion – but seeks to alter Judaism understood through a complex integration of what was learned "outside" that is then brought back "inside." This border-crossing does not always yield heresy; but it almost always evokes "heretical" suspicion. One can see this in the thirteenth-century rabbis of Northern France's polemics against Maimonides' *Guide for the Perplexed*, to Leon of Modena's seventeenth-century critique of Kabbalah in his *Ari Nohem*, to the accusations of heresy of Mordecai Kaplan in twentieth-century America.[3]

The academic study of Judaism is a particular form of the double border-crossing I describe. There is little doubt that the methods and techniques endemic to the academic study of Judaism are drawn from sources outside the normative orbit of the Jewish literary tradition (even though the tradition itself is not void of outside influences).[4] And in many cases, although not all, practitioners of the academic study of Judaism cross back into that Jewish orbit to make claims, sometimes normative, sometimes scientific, sometimes a mixture of both, about their specific subject, or Judaism writ large. Where, then, does the academic study of Judaism fall on the question of heresy?

The academic study of Judaism, known by various names – such as *Wissenschaft des Judentums* (in nineteenth-century Europe), *Hokhmat Yisrael* (Israel), or Jewish Studies (in twentieth-century North America), each with its own nuances – began in Jewish educational institutions in early-nineteenth-century Europe (i.e., the *Verein für Cultur und Wissenschaft der Juden*), and in the twentieth century entered in different ways into secular universities in North America, Israel, and Europe. In the United States, at least, Jewish Studies has become part of the larger conversation about the study of religion in the humanities and social sciences. Even as philosophy and Kabbalah continued their centuries-long battle for the hearts and minds of educated Jews, with Hasidism and Musar later joining the fray, all stood firm on the basic foundation of rabbinic authority (i.e., the Talmud and its expositors) and the template that became known as *halakha*

---

[3] On Maimonides, see Silver (1965). On Modena, see Dweck (2011). On Kaplan, see Gurock and Schacter (1997), esp. 106–107.
[4] For examples, see the work of Yaakov Elman, Isaiah Gafni, Shai Secunda, and others on the Middle Persian/Zoroastrian influence on the Babylonian Talmud, or the work of Yehuda Liebes and Yonatan Benorach on the Christian influences on the Zohar.

(i.e., as codified and disseminated in R. Joseph Caro's sixteenth-century *Shulkhan Arukh*).⁵ Refracted through the prism of the Enlightenment, and its Jewish articulations in the *Haskalah*, the elasticity of rabbinic authority and halakha has been challenged, and a new set of alternatives articulated. Some of these alternatives were fueled or at least inspired by the nascent academic study of Judaism.⁶ The academic study of Judaism certainly helped *produce* what some would call "heresy" in the sense that it destabilized halakhic practice and beliefs by historicizing tradition (e.g., the rejection of Torah from heaven and/or rabbinic authority) and, as Ismar Schorsch put it, by moving "from text to context."⁷ My interest, however, is not in describing or assuming a normative Judaism and asking whether or how Jewish Studies might threaten it. My question is whether the academic study of Judaism is *itself* a heretical enterprise, and in what circumstances – in the sense of an act of double border-crossing that operates inside of Judaism even as it moves outside and smuggles in new elements.

To explore this question, I begin with the case of *Wissenschaft des Judentums*, and specifically Gershom Scholem's critique of Leopold Zunz and others. I suggest that Scholem's critique can be read as an inner-Jewish heretical debate, not about whether or not *Wissenschaft* is heresy, but whether it is the *right kind* of heresy for Jewish modernity. Then, I turn to a series of case studies of contemporary scholarship on Judaism, using the rubric of heresy to highlight the different ways in which four key scholars – Jacob Neusner, Susannah Heschel, Aaron Hughes, and Martin Kavka – have situated Jewish Studies in relation to normative Judaism.

When we speak of heresy in this fashion – following Boyarin rather than Berger – I suggest that it is possible to reconsider some of the challenges of modernity, secularization, and the Enlightenment in a manner that does not treat the premodern past as some mythologized state of immutability or as the

---

5 See, for example, Sagi (1995). The production of the *Shulkhan Arukh* is complicated by Christian censorship and editing. See, for example, Raz-Krakotzkin (2007) and Dweck (2010). While there have been alterative halakhic compendia that emerged after Caro's monumental work, none before modernity seriously challenged the *Shulkhan Arukh*'s basic template but sought to ameliorate some of its decisions and even methods according to regional customs and practice. Three well-known examples are R. Moses Isserles's "Rema," a gloss of Caro's *Shulkhan Arukh*, Yechiel Michel Epstein's *Arukh ha-Shulkhan*; and R. Shneur Zalman of Liady's *Shulkhan Arukh Ha-Rav*.
6 See Feiner (2001); Yerushalmi (1989, 77–104); Schorsch (1994, 9–70); and Litvak (2012, 65–80; 113–130).
7 There has been some important work on biblical criticism and traditional belief. See, for example, Breuer (2004); Shaw (1969); Ross (2105); Farber (n.d.); and Sommer (2015). For Orthodox responses to *Wissenschaft des Judentums* more generally, see Yedidya (2010).

static tradition from which modernity (and modern academic inquiry) uniquely departs. Judaism in modernity is not just a story of "tradition and change," as Mordechai Waxman put it in the title of his 1958 book about Conservative Judaism.[8] Tradition was always undergoing processes of change, just as "orthodoxy" was always formed in part through a discourse about "heresy" and boundaries created in response to challenges posed by those deemed border-crossers. Individuals inside even an ostensibly hermetically sealed tradition are always reacting to the changing world and modifying, altering, and conforming to new realities that emerge.[9] The question of heresy is more about the nature of that challenge and change, its processes, the epistemological breadth and depth of critique, its open or closed confrontation with received tradition, and the practitioners' self-awareness of implemented changes.

Heresy is more than an act of choosing as Berger describes it: it is also an act of cutting, opening a wound in accepted belief and practice that challenges authority and norms – and thus "crosses borders." It often evokes a rupture that cannot be sutured without a significant alteration. Such a rupture can come through a claim of prophecy and redemption, as with Sabbatei Zvi, arguing that the messianic era inaugurates a "new Torah" that redraws boundaries, making the normative obsolete and the heretical the norm.[10] In the case of *Wissenschaft des Judentums* and its correlates, the rupture is more a matter of epistemology and positioning – that is, the historicization of Judaism that requires viewing it from the outside. Each of these cases claims to improve upon the past; that is, on tradition. And both are cases of a double border-crossing that return "home" bearing internal critiques. Both the Sabbateans and practitioners of *Wissenschaft des Judentums* (one could also include Zionists) cross the border and then cross back again, and each returns to the internal Jewish conversation offering new ways of constructing its viability. Thus, in evaluating the academic study of Judaism on the question of heresy, we will consider the extent to which it "crosses back," whether it intends to return to make new normative claims about Judaism or whether it aspires toward something different. If the heretical positions remain outside or beyond the parameters of Jewish life and practice, it may be deviant but it would not be heretical.

---

[8] See Waxman (1958). The desire to ameliorate or conceal such change is common in many hyper-traditionalist societies but such concealment usually only works for those already committed to the myth of stasis in their world. See, for example, Shapiro (2015).
[9] See, for example, Pelican (1984). Haym Soloveichik makes a similar argument in many of his works. See, for example, *Yeinam* (2017).
[10] On the relationship between prophecy and the Sabbatean claims of messianic redemption, see Goldish (2004).

2 *Wissenschaft des Judentums*: Inside or Outside Judaism?

It is conventional to trace the emergence of the academic study of Judaism to *Wissenschaft des Judentums* in Germany, and particularly the publication in 1818 of *"Etwas über die rabbinische Litteratur"* ("On Rabbinic Literature"), a concise prolegomenon for the project of the collection, elucidation, and scholarly analysis of Jewish literature and culture, written by a young Leopold Zunz.[11] As Ismar Schorsch has masterfully shown in his recent biography, Zunz was a deeply committed Jew as well as a champion of Jewish emancipation.[12] Together with his colleagues in the *Verein für Cultur und Wissenschaft der Juden*, he took on the project of the analysis of Jewish materials by Jews, who engaged the scholarship of their time despite the exclusion of Jews from permanent positions in European universities. The academic study of Judaism was thus a European creation, adapting the methods of Christian scholarship (sometimes under the guise of secularism) to understand Judaism and also to criticize Christianity.[13] Early scholars such as Zunz, Abraham Geiger, and Immanuel Wolf resisted the negative portrayal of Judaism in the German scholarship of the time, which was ostensibly academic but shaped by Christian supersessionism and often laced with latent anti-Semitism. But if *Wissenschaft des Judentums* was a creation by Jews who wanted to extend their influence beyond Jews, it also offered a different vision of Judaism to the modernizing Jews in their midst. For this, Hayyim Nahman Bialik deemed them "heretics of the spirit" because of their commitment to doing so in German rather than Hebrew (Scholem 1997, 63).

Part of what Zunz and his colleagues wanted, and to a great extent accomplished, was to unsettle the Christian monopoly on the academic study of Judaism and make a space for Jewish voices and perspectives. At first sight, their project might seem more akin to apostasy than heresy – that is, studying Jewish texts and history in a manner that speaks to a secular or Christian world rather than to the Jewish community and tradition. This is the charge against them that we find among Zionist thinkers like Bialik and Gershom Scholem. Scholem, in particular, was quite hard on Zunz and his contemporary Moritz Steinschneider, calling them "truly demonic figures" and suggesting

---

[11] On this essay, see Schorsch (2016, 14–20).
[12] Schorsch (2016), esp. 156–181.
[13] On the *Verein*, see Schorsch, "Breakthrough into the Past: The *Verein für Cultur fur Culture und Wissenschaft der Juden*," in Schorsch (1994, 205–232).

> their books, the classical works of the Science of Judaism, are a kind of procession around the dead, although at times it seems that the authors themselves are the ghosts of Old Israel, seeking their salvation while dancing among the graves. (Scholem 1997, 58–59)

One cannot understand Scholem's critique of *Wissenschaft des Judentums* without his Zionist orientation: he questioned the very notion that the Diaspora would continue to exist as a viable place not only for Jews but for the heretical rendering of Judaism.[14] Thus the problem for Scholem was not simply *Wissenschaft des Judentums*' refusal to acknowledge the irrational elements of Judaism but also their project of preparing a Judaism for the emancipated Diaspora.[15] Nevertheless, his critique also speaks to where the academic study of Judaism is positioned vis-à-vis the borders of the Jewish tradition. Scholem's concern to counter *Wissenschaft des Judentums* came in part from his belief that the academic study of Judaism challenged this tradition but also had the prospect for "its transfiguration," provided that it could be put toward the re-vivification of Judaism as a "living organism." He makes an argument, in other words, for Jewish Studies as "heresy" in the sense of a border-crossing enterprise that remains committed to – and thus can transform – the very tradition that lies inside of those borders.

It was not that Scholem was opposed to the secularization of Judaism implicit in its opening up to academic inquiry. In fact, he wrote that "the secularized view of Judaism opens up an enormously positive potentiality" and that "seen from a theological point of view, it may in a quite different fashion lead to a new manner of religious inquiry which will then not be determined simply by formulas from an earlier generation" (1972, 312). In his view, Zunz and company failed not because they were heretics but because they were not heretical *enough*. For Scholem, as a self-defined "religious anarchist," the problem with *Wissenschaft des Judentums* was "the removal of the pointedly irrational and demonic enthusiasms from Jewish history, through an exaggerated emphasis upon the theological and the spiritual," and he described this as "the fundamental original sin that outweighs all others" (1997, 63). The problem for him was not so much the emphasis on the rational as much as the erasure of the irrational *as if it never existed*, "distorting of the past by obscuring its disturbing elements, which rebel and break out into history and thought" (1997, 63). For Scholem, heresy requires honesty even or precisely when such honesty destroys rather than builds. Nietzsche wrote in *The Genealogy of Morals*, "If a temple is to be erected, a temple must be destroyed.

---

14 For example, see my "Myth, History, and Mysticism: Gershom Scholem and the Contemporary Scene" (2011). For another study examining Scholem's critique, see Stair (2018).
15 See Hughes (2013, 46). Scholem continues his critique of *Wissenschaft des Judentums* in numerous studies. See, for example, his *Sabbatai Zevi: The Mystical Messiah* (1973, 8–11).

That is the law" (1967, Essay 2, Section 24, 95). Scholem felt a new temple could be built for Jewish modernity but only if one is first destroyed through acknowledging Jewish irrationalism as an integral part of tradition. The early architects of *Wissenschaft* could not do this as their project's intended audience – or at least one of them – was the broader Western society into which they sought admission, part of which (through thinkers from Kant to Hegel) disqualified Judaism precisely on those irrational grounds.[16]

Although influential, Scholem's critiques of the architects of *Wissenschaft des Judentums* may misread the aims and context of Zunz, Abraham Geiger, and others.[17] Scholem is correct that they had their sights set on emancipation and thus projected an inversion of Judaism's isolationism. This inversion – making Judaism universal – was part of a process of making a case for inclusion. Scholem viewed this universalization as a "disembodiment," a liquidation of peoplehood, the death of Judaism as a "living organism." Susannah Heschel has shown, however, how Scholem was mistaken that *Wissenschaft* scholars were not interested in the revitalization of Judaism in modernity and that only he and his fellow Zionists had that as their primary goal. Scholars such as Abraham Geiger were not only intent on re-inventing Judaism, but they also sought to criticize Christianity's view of Judaism that dominated the scholarly world by showing the scholarly supersessionists that Jesus was not only a Jew but actually quite a good Pharisee as well – and the two aims were intertwined. According to Heschel, *Wissenschaft des Judentums* for Geiger was as much about re-inventing *Christianity* as it was re-inventing and reforming *Judaism* since the latter could never be accomplished without the former:

> Jewish studies (in the nineteenth century) was stimulated by a radical impulse to question or even overthrow the standard portrayal of Western history. The study of Judaism was not simply added to history books; rather, assumptions about the course of the Christian West were deliberately undermined by looking at its development from the perspective of Jewish experience. (1998, 101)

Scholem seemed to have a deaf ear to that perspective, and comparative analysis more generally, having already decided that the renewal of Judaism could only come from "Zion" and not from "Berlin."

I would suggest, however, that both *Wissenschaft des Judentums* and Scholem's Zionist historiography were heretical moves. Scholem deviates from

---

16 On Scholem's critique of *Wissenschaft des Judentums*, see Biale (1979), and more recently Hughes (2013, 54–55).
17 See Heschel (1999, 61–85).

the European project of *Wissenschaft*, which he claimed denied, or minimized, the body of the Jews for a sterilized and de-mystified rendering of Judaism. However, he simultaneously draws upon it to deviate from rabbinic tradition *via* Sabbateanism (i.e., as the liberation from halakhic normativity and the beginnings of the nationalization of Jews). Heschel notes how Scholem's "massive study of Sabbateanism was the intellectual climax, with the movement presented as a 'desire for total liberation,' not from Europe, Christianity, or Islam, but from Judaism itself, just as Zionism constituted liberation from Jewish Diaspora history" (1999, 69–70). But Scholem's heresy is even deeper than that. For his Zionist historiography to work, the equation of Torah and Jews needs to be reversed. Traditionally, as Saadia Gaon argued, the Jews exist only because of Torah, thus severing Jews from Torah can only yield the Jews' utter irrelevance with no *raison d'être*. Zionism suggests that the Jews as a collective body exist distinct from Torah, and while Torah can serve as a way to conceptualize their existence, it is not the core of that existence; they can exist outside of it.[18] For Scholem, Torah was an integral part of the people but best served through a process of secularization whereby tradition can be at the service of the people (culture) but the people are never the servants of the Torah (Orthodoxy). Sabbateanism was, for Scholem, a kind of proto-Zionism in that Sabbatei Zvi posited redemption as a moment of the inversion of tradition. To the extent to which Zionism was viewed as redemptive (and Scholem was certainly very wary of religious nationalism and viewed it as dangerous and destructive), Sabbatei Zvi offered a model that would later take a nationalized secular form of heresy against the centrality of halakha as the vehicle of Jewish identity.

Even in this, however, Scholem was a product of *Wissenschaft des Judentums* – crossing its borders while remaining inside of its intellectual project. To the degree that Geiger and others offered a Judaism that was compatible with Protestantism by stressing its rationalism and hiding, or deflecting, its irrationalism, Scholem took issue with them. But to the degree that they sought to re-make Judaism through scholarship by drawing attention to historicism as a frame and epistemology, not only to understand the past but to re-shape the present, he furthered their aims even through his criticism of them. Scholem, in effect, picks up and extends the one element of *Wissenschaft des Judentums* that could be called "heretical" in the sense that it remains committed to the very tradition that it seems to be transgressing.

---

[18] On the "heretical" nature of Zionism more generally and how it uses and subverts religious categories, see Ohana (2017).

Seen through the lens of the assessments of Scholem and Heschel, it is possible to identify three aims of *Wissenschaft des Judentums*: (1) making Judaism palatable to the West, (2) revising Christianity through immanent critique, and (3) articulating a vision of Judaism for modernity. In the first two, *Wissenschaft des Judentums* is not "heretical" inasmuch as the implied audience was not primarily Jews and the subject of critique was not the lived Jewish tradition. To be heresy it must have as its mandate to re-make Judaism; heresy is part of an internal discourse. Reforming the ostensibly secular academy or criticizing its Christian supersessionist agenda may be subversive, but it is not heretical.

These first two aims of *Wissenschaft des Judentums* are what undergirds its dismissal as "actual apostasy" by R. Shimshon Rafael Hirsch and the claims of others such as R. Hayyim Ozer Grodanzski that its proponents were already "beyond Judaism" (Yedidya 2010, 71; 76). These are also the elements with which others have wrestled in the name of Orthodoxy. R. Esriel Hildesheimer and R. David Zvi Hoffman of the Hildesheimer Rabbinical Seminary in Berlin, for instance, adapted certain principles of "objective scholarship" in the hopes that its moderate use would not touch the nerve centers of biblical criticism or a critique of halakhic authority and would cajole those compelled by *Wissenschaft des Judentums* back to Orthodoxy (or keep those compelled by it inside the fold). Finally, a few thinkers such as R. Abraham Kook were willing to go further and acknowledge the historical claims of some of *Wissenschaft des Judentums* yet argue it does not touch the spiritual core of Judaism.[19] Kook was much more reluctant to allow *Wissenschaft* to challenge the divine core of the Written Law (Torah from Sinai) and allegedly only agreed to speak at the inauguration of the Hebrew University on the condition that there would not be a Bible Department, a condition that was ignored.[20]

But there are – as we have seen – the architects of *Wissenschaft des Judentums* who also make a marked attempt to re-draw the boundaries of Judaism in modernity by using scholarship to make normative claims. And it is this third aim that Scholem both criticized and extended. For Scholem, the "heresy" of *Wissenschaft des Judentums* was not sustainable for Jews in his time because it did not put the "nation" at the center and thus would not be strong enough to fend off assimilation.

Another way to see how the third goal of *Wissenschaft des Judentums* evoked negative responses is to examine the reactions of Orthodoxy to *Wissenschaft des*

---

19 See, for example, Kook (1906, 39).
20 On Kook's speech in April 1, 1925 to inaugurate the Hebrew University, see Leiman (1994). Cf. Caplan (2001).

Judentums when it became popularized in the late nineteenth and early twentieth centuries.[21] In an essay tracing Orthodox responses to *Wissenschaft des Judentums*, Assaf Yedidya delineates different approaches taken by Orthodoxy toward this "heretical" phenomenon. One was total rejection, viewing it as a danger to traditional beliefs and practices. Another approach was to selectively adopt a scientific approach to Judaism in order to show that, in fact, *Wissenschaft des Judentums* could be used, if applied judiciously and with caution and in a limited way, to *prove* the legitimacy of tradition and not undermine it. Yet another was a more generous adaption that resulted in various small revisions.[22]

What we see in all these discussions is the extent to which much of the Orthodox community viewed *Wissenschaft des Judentums* as heretical, and responded accordingly. This would change considerably in the twentieth century, as we shall see below. Just as Scholem viewed *Wissenschaft des Judentums* as the *wrong* kind of heresy, or not heretical *enough* to revive a people in its ancestral land, Orthodox thinkers in Europe generally responded to this third aim of *Wissenschaft des Judentums* – that is, its aim to make inroads into Jewish belief and practice and reform it for modern Judaism, or to pursue scholarship for the sake of making normative claims about its subject. Neither Scholem nor the Orthodox addressed the two other goals of *Wissenschaft des Judentums* – namely, to reform the academy by having Jews, and not solely Christians, do scholarly work on Judaism; and to critique Christianity by forcing it to confront the Jewishness of Jesus and Judaism's contribution to Western civilization. Scholem and the Orthodox each addressed the heretical nature of *Wissenschaft des Judentums* and ignored its outward-facing (and thus non-heretical) components.

3 Where are *Wissenschaft des Judentums* and Heresy Today?

The progeny of *Wissenschaft des Judentum* are flourishing today in North America, Israel, and Europe. The three goals of its earlier iteration – finding a place for Judaism in the academy, using scholarship to "reform" Judaism, and criticizing regnant attitudes toward Judaism in the academy – all continue to function, albeit in different ways. In Israel, the academic study of Judaism has

---

21 On the popularization of *Wissenschaft des Judentums* more generally, see Brenner (1998, 100–128).
22 See Yedidya (2010).

had its strongest impact on Jewish Israeli culture, increasingly in intellectually curious religious sectors. *Hokhmat Yisrael* was once deployed to create a vibrant secular Jewish culture in a Jewish country. The Hebrew University was first established in 1924 for precisely those ends, the university being seen as a vehicle of cultural Zionism's scholarly agenda. In many ways the Israeli universities were successful in that endeavor: many of its early graduates were from kibbutzim and its academic/secular approach to Judaism became popularized outside academic circles. People indeed talked of Tolstoy and Kierkegaard and argued about Aristotle and Maimonides while harvesting avocadoes. It was, for a time, truly a utopia-like "New Jew" experience. If one argues that Zionism in this formative, and radical, period was itself a heretical enterprise in shifting the emphasis from Torah to peoplehood or nationalizing Judaism, then *Hokhmat Yisrael* was its intellectual program.[23]

In the past few decades, long after a secular Jewish culture has been firmly established and many young Israelis now look toward other areas of interest in its globalizing economy, Jewish Studies in Israel is becoming more popular with those from the National Religious camp, and even from the *haredi* camp. Haredim have discovered manuscript work and are now producing critical editions of texts the way *Wissenschaft des Judentums* scholars did in the past. National Religious ideology is now being pursued in some Israeli universities as well as *yeshivot*.[24] Contemporary Israeli secularism is less in need of the cultural project of *Hokhmat Yisrael*, and new norms and practices in Israeli religiosity are now emerging in non-Orthodox religious institutions, both formal and informal. *Hokhmat Yisrael* in Israel, perhaps now in a new phase of Israeli "Jewish Studies," is also making strong connections to the European and American academies and in doing so is becoming less invested in its original purpose of devising secular Israeli culture.

I would say, then, in the contemporary Israeli case, which deserves much more attention than I can give it here, Jewish Studies, whether the old-style *Hokhmat Yisrael* or the newly formed Jewish Studies that is being practiced by members of the religious community (nationalist and *haredi*), is "heretical" to the extent to which it remains part of the nationalist project, even for a limited community. Critical editions may not propose normative changes to religious life, but they certainly serve as alternatives to standard editions of sacred texts that have served the community for centuries. There was good reason why R. Abraham Yeshaya Kareitz (1878–1953), known as the Hazon Ish, one of the great luminaries

---

[23] On this, see Ohana (2017), esp. 13–36.
[24] This is especially true in Bar Ilan University, which identifies itself as part of the National Religious community. The work of Avi Sagi is a great example of academia in the service of broader religious concerns.

of the early twentieth century and of the defenders of tradition against the encroachment of modernity, was opposed to Dikdukei Sofrim by R. Raphael Natan Rabinovitz's (1835–1888) a quite moderate and traditional *Wissenschaft*-like work that offered manuscript variants to Talmudic literature. The Hazon Ish argued that once you begin to question the "Vilna *daf*" (the standard Talmudic page), the authority of the text, and tradition, begins to wane. Regarding the National Religious camp, many have become attracted to university-style Judaic scholarship as a way to deepen their knowledge of traditional sources and, in some cases, fortify their national Zionist agenda. We should remember that "heresy" need not always result in liberating mores but can just as easily result in more strident, even maximalist, options. The recent National Religious dominance of the Zionist narrative, and its intellectual activity, is not a return to any traditional framework but its own deviation from traditional norms on the question of the nationalization of the Jews.[25]

Regarding Israeli scholarship, Jacob Neusner has argued that while the state of Israel holds the potential for a true transition of Judaism into the general humanities it has thus far failed in large part because it is unable, or unwilling, to abandon the nationalist agenda which places Judaism at the center of civilization. Here Neusner laconically notes that "where we witness the remarkable realization of Judaism and its rebirth is where we most miss the humanistic exploration of the extraordinary achievement of the Jews' sector of humanity, that is, Judaism" (1981, 146).[26]

In North America, what has become known as Jewish Studies is a sub-discipline taught mostly in universities – and in some cases, still in seminaries – toward the examination of the Judaic library, the tradition and religion of the Jews, and the Jews themselves who live it. There is a history to the rise of this sub-discipline that has been examined by numerous scholars.[27] My narrow interest here is in the role of Jewish Studies in the American Jewish experience: who is its audience, what are its assumptions, and what are its goals in relation to the question as to what aspect of *Wissenschaft des Judentums* remains operative in

---

[25] See, for example, Ravitzky (1996, 79–144).
[26] I would add that in the past two decades this has begun to change as some younger scholars in Israel have made alliances with European and American institutes of Jewish Studies and the humanities. In the field in which I am familiar, scholars such as Jonathan Garb, Boaz Huss, Yonatan Benaroach, Haviva Pedaya, and Avishai ben Asher have been shifting focus beyond the borders of Israel. More Israeli scholars attend the U.S. Association of Jewish Studies conference and take part in the European academy; for example, the Institute of Western Esotericism and other programs in Europe.
[27] In particular, see Ritterband (1994); Bush (2011); Hughes (2013); Blumenthal (1976); and Greenspahn (2000).

American Jewish Studies? Is it the aspect of looking beyond its borders, the one that criticizes the hegemony of the outside to define Judaism, or the one focused on its community? Put otherwise, in what way is contemporary Jewish Studies in America heretical?

To inquire about the heretical nature of Jewish Studies in America requires us to consider when Jewish Studies became an "American" project? Many of those in the yet-non-existent field of Jewish Studies from the beginning the last century through the 1960s (who mostly taught at seminaries, with a few notable exceptions such as Harry Wolfson and Salo Baron) were born and trained in Europe, and thus brought a European mindset of *Wissenschaft des Judentums* to American shores and to an American Jewish community. Many rabbinical scholars in late-nineteenth-century America, such as Kaufmann Kohler and Felix Adler, travelled to Europe to be trained. Others, such as Isaac Meyer Wise and David Einhorn, and later Salo Baron, Saul Leiberman, Nachum Sarna, Alexander Altmann, Simon Rawidowicz, and Steven Schwarzschild, lived in Europe into adulthood.[28] Even a figure who arguably initiated American Jewish thinking and a wholly American Judaism, Mordecai Kaplan, was born in Russia and emigrated to America as a small child, as did Harry Wolfson, who is often viewed as the beginning of the academic study of Judaism in the university.[29] The full severing from Europe would take another few generations, until after Second World War, when there was no European Judaism to go back to.

America was a very different cultural, intellectual, and religious context than Europe in that both Jews and Judaism had less to prove. While anti-Semitism and exclusion existed, America provided Jews with a truly distinctive opportunity to flourish and become full members of society on multiple levels. It is true that through the Second World War, and into the 1960s, Judaism was still being taught mostly in Jewish seminaries, Christian seminaries, divinity schools, or traditional *yeshivot*. But Judaism increasingly became a subject matter that could be taught outside confessional environments and was thus primed to become a subject for the academy, not defensively and not with any emancipatory agenda. What would be its role in the American academy and in addition what role would it play for American Jews looking for religious and intellectual guidance? How much of American Judaism was forged through academic scholarship on Judaism? It is the latter, as we have said, that would truly constitute a heretical enterprise.

---

28 Altman in particular weighed in on the burgeoning field of Jewish Studies. See Altmann (1980).
29 Ritterband (1994) and Greenspahn (2000) delineate others who preceded Wolfson in American universities. And this does not include figures in the colonial period such as Judah Monis, a Jewish convert to Christianity, who taught Hebrew at Harvard in the eighteenth century.

Perhaps the first scholar of Judaica who thought in a university and not a seminary and who wrote extensively *about* Jewish Studies in the American academy was Jacob Neusner. In a series of three volumes, *The Academic Study of Judaism: Essays and Reflections*, published between 1975–1979, and a subsequent volume, *Judaism in the American Universities*, in 1981, Neusner discussed in great detail the nature of Jewish Studies as an academic discipline, its role in the academy and what it can, and in his mind should, contribute to the arts and letters of American society. To consider Neusner's views, especially in relation to the "heretical" potential of Jewish Studies, it is useful to compare them with those of Susannah Heschel in her essay "Jewish Studies as Counterhistory," which offers a very different model of the role of Jewish Studies in the contemporary academy and for contemporary Jewry.

Neusner's project was a wholly American scholarly enterprise. It marked a new era in Jewish Studies as an American sub-discipline. The challenge now was not acceptance as it was for *Wissenschaft des Judentums*, nor the foundation for secular Jewish culture the way it was for *Hokhmat Yisrael* in Israel, but full integration into a secular academy with the belief that Judaism had something to contribute to the larger world. Neusner's contention was that "Judaism, viewed dispassionately and analytically, provides an interesting example of the continuing interactions between ideas and men, religion and society, history and culture" (1975, 18). He called this "the humanities of the Jewish heritage."

> What we want to know as humanities scholars is about Judaism as a cultural system, Judaism as a mode of interpreting history and Judaism as a means of binding Jewish society … That is, we want to know how Judaism constitutes a system for interpreting history and explain why that makes it paradigmatic. (1981, 143)

In other words, the subject is the Jews and their Judaism but the audience is the larger American academy.

Neusner opposed any confessional dimension to the academic study of Judaism and did not advocate that the scholar of Judaism set his or her sights on the Jewish community in their work:

> Judaism needs no special pleading, and in any case any effort at indoctrination would violate the canon of intellectual freedom and university discourse. The interest of most students of Judaism is not confessional. The criteria ought to be technical, including linguistic competence, sympathy and understanding. (1981, 24)

For Jewish Studies to succeed in the academy, according to Neusner, it must submit to the criteria and methods of the secular environment in which it operates. Neusner's assumption is that unlike the European academy of the nineteenth century, the American academy is not infused with a Christian supersessionist spirit such that Judaism must intervene to defend its integrity against Christian prejudice. It can, and should, do so if those assumptions arise. But in general its role is to present Judaism as an exemplar of a culture with a distinct history and perspective. For Neusner the role of the scholar of Judaism in the academy is not to focus, even indirectly, on making normative claims about Jewish belief or practice. Its audience is fellow scholars of other disciplines. Its place is the seminar room and not the synagogue. It is not an engine to generate Jewish culture per se but to pursue knowledge in a secular American context.

Like Scholem, Neusner focused critically on *Wissenschaft des Judentums'* aim of making normative claims about Judaism. However, unlike Scholem, his critique was not about the *right kind of heresy*, but the heretical goal itself – the notion of the academic study of Jewish Studies as intervening into the tradition, even if through border-crossing:

> Indeed the prevalent attitudes of the Jewish scholars employed by Jewish institutions do continue those of the founders of the Science of Judaism, who were in a similar social situation and who espoused similar ideas about their scholarly tasks. But those attitudes tend to be insular and pedantic rather than objective and 'scientific.' The continuities are close and the parallels intact. (1981, 50–51)

Neusner was not against engaging in critical analysis of contemporary Jewish life. In fact, one of his earliest works, *Fellowship in Judaism: The First Century and Today*, written in 1963, is a fascinating analysis of ancient Jewish sects and postwar American Judaism that served as an inspiration for the Havurah Movement close to a decade later.[30] And he wrote many books about American Jewish life and the future of Judaism that were informed by his scholarship, but that he would not consider scholarship. In effect, Neusner wanted to distinguish between scholarship and topical writing as directed at two different audiences – something he felt was not the case with old-style *Wissenschaft des Judentums* and its modern counterpart in Jewish seminaries.[31] Jewish Studies itself should not be a heretical enterprise in Neusner's estimation. When the Jewish Studies scholar chooses to turn their attention to the community and offer a critique of its normative beliefs and practices, that is another matter entirely.

Neusner felt that the contemporary context of the American academy no longer required a Jewish critical intervention. Although she never mentions Neusner in her essay, this is the claim that is contested by Susannah Heschel in "Jewish Studies as Counterhistory." Heschel notes that "the initial radical impulse

---

30 Neusner, *Fellowship in Judaism: The First Century and Today* (London: Valentine, 1963).
31 See Hughes (2016b, 80–97).

of Jewish history began to diminish by the turn of the century and was lost with the transfer of Jewish studies to the American university" (1998, 101). For her, the major thrust, and most significant intervention of *Wissenschaft des Judentums*, was its critique of Christian hegemony in the European academy (i.e., the second aim delineated above). While she argues that Geiger may have been its most forceful proponent, she maintains that this critique extended beyond Geiger into the world of other scholars as well.

Heschel disagrees with Neusner on two interrelated counts. First, she disagrees with the basic assumption upon which Neusner's theory is built, that the American academy has mostly cleansed itself from skewered views of Judaism. Second, she claims that even if that were so, the multicultural context of the academy raises new issues including gender bias and racial bias that plague Jewish Studies as an academic discipline. Thus, she wants to "revitalize the radicalism" of *Wissenschaft des Judentums* to address new perspectives that have arisen since multiculturalism. Jewish Studies should join with African American Studies and Gender Studies. It should seek to destabilize the Christian and Eurocentric assumptions of the Western academy rather than simply seeking to provide an illustration of Judaism as an exemplar within it – which is what we might call, by contrast, Neusner's conservative approach. For Heschel the goal of Jewish Studies "ought to be the establishment of a variety of gazes that will unsettle and throw into question the complacency of academic categories and analyses" (1998, 112).

What is novel about Heschel's approach from the perspective of heresy is that Heschel's desire to "radicalize" Jewish Studies is not exclusively limited to the academic arena but includes Jews and Jewish life as well. She ends her essay by stating: "These are the questions of multiculturalism, questions about identity and meaning, knowledge and power, experience and definition. They are the central questions asked by Jews, and of Jews" (1998, 113).

Thus for Heschel, Jewish Studies should function not solely as a critique of the academy but also as an intervention as to how Jews define, negotiate, and manage power and identity within their own communities. Neusner is not averse to that, at least in principle; he would only say that this is not the job of the Jewish Studies scholar, as scholar, but the job of those who read scholarship or rabbis who minister to Jewish communities. As a rabbi who transitioned into a scholar, Neusner was careful to keep those vocations separate.[32] The problem with Neusner's position is that it is based on a shaky assumption that these vocations can indeed be separated. It is founded on a more positivistic notion that questions

---

32 See Hughes (2016a, 39–72).

of meaning and identity can be bracketed such that one's scholarly work is not infused with the same kind of identarian assumptions as one's rabbinic work. Heschel, on the other hand, begins with a different epistemological assumption in regard to what it is to interrogate, to intervene with, any subject. The question is not "Does my scholarship implicate my identity?" but "In what ways does my scholarship construct a positionality that interrogates stable positions, including my own?" To criticize a position, as a scholar or a rabbi, is an act of destabilizing norms thereby making a claim of identity and its discontents.

For Heschel, the scholar, if she is doing her job, should also serve as a critic of the community (*with* her scholarship) even as she also serves as a critic of the academy. She would like to bring together the second and third goals of *Wissenschaft des Judentums*, to critique the community and the academy, as a joint venture. For Heschel then, the Jewish Studies scholar is indeed a heretic, or at least potentially so, and from the same Jewish positioning with which she serves as a critic of the secular academy. Some of the implications, with respect to identity and scholarship, become clearer in the contrast of two more recent essays on Jewish Studies with different perspectives on the vocation of the scholar of Judaism: Aaron Hughes' chapter "Imaging Judaism: Scholar, Community, Identity" in his 2013 *The Study of Judaism* and Martin Kavka's 2006 essay, "What Does it Mean to Receive Tradition? Jewish Studies in Higher Education," delivered as the Judah Goldin Memorial Lecture and subsequently published in expanded form in *CrossCurrents* (2006). In the former, Hughes decries what he considers the "apologetic" nature of Jewish Studies in the academy driven by various factors including donors, communal expectations, and the continued attachment of many Jewish Studies scholars to the Jewish communities where they live and worship. In the latter, Kavka speaks more about the students who take Jewish Studies courses, what they expect, what they want, and in what ways is the subject matter useful to them.

Apology takes various forms for Hughes. Constructing a Judaism that would make the case for Jewish emancipation would be one form – certainly one *Wissenschaft des Judentums* was guilty of (2013, 59). More problematic for Hughes is the integral relationship between academic Jewish Studies and the Jewish community in contemporary America, the way each feeds and depends on the other (2013, 68). Practically speaking, his concerns are well founded. The connection between universities and the communities outside the academy can be precarious, largely because when scholars feel bound or responsible to donors, or departments are financially dependent on them, this can hamper the pursuit of research and teaching for the sake of producing knowledge. Hughes cites numerous scholars who make quite open admissions of their sense of responsibility to the Jewish community, such as Jewish historian Joseph Blau, who stated that "for university professors to fail to inculcate in their students the notion of study as a mitzvah is to be unfaithful to their discipline" (as quoted in Levy 1974, 15). Such a stance assumes teaching Jewish Studies is an enterprise focused on Jewish students, which already subverts the notion of its place within a secular university (1974, 15).

For Blau, who was a professor of Jewish history at Columbia University until 1977, the aim of Jewish Studies is to create

> a place in American higher education for the studies in the life, thought, and culture of the Jews, past and present, not only as a means of stimulating the enrichment of educational content now, and as a factor in Jewish survival in time to come, but also because we are convinced that these studies have an intrinsic value that is like and yet unlike comparable studies of other ethnic groups. (as quoted in Levy, 1974, 69)

Hughes contests the notion that Jewish Studies is about Jewish survival and that it is both "like and unlike" comparable studies, suggesting some kind of unique nature or quality of Jews or Judaism. And he is right that "the need for scholarly legitimation, on the one hand, and the acknowledgment of the uniqueness of the Jewish tradition, on the other hand, is one of the tensions that runs throughout the academic study of Judaism" (Levy, 1974, 70).

But there is something that Hughes is not noticing. As I define heresy above, even the scholar who claims to be "defending" the tradition is, in effect, a heretic in that the very deployment of critical methods, even in the service of defending tradition, has already altered the tradition untouched by those methods. This is because academic scholarship, even in its myriad forms, requires an epistemology that underlies the entire enterprise. One can be somewhat selective in how one uses that epistemology, but a scholar cannot reject it outright without rejecting the academic endeavor entirely. Therefore, while a scholar may claim to be defending Judaism against *external* critique, oftentimes she is subverting Judaism through an *internal* critique, even if that critique is done under the guise of apologetics. Put otherwise, if he or she is not a border-crosser, they are not a scholar. And if they are border-crossers, then even if they return to defend the tradition, they return as smugglers, and unless they abandon the contraband at the border (if so, then why cross the border in the first place?), what they produce is already, to some extent, from the "outside." Their defensive posture may make them "apologetic" scholars, but the results of their research will invariably alter the tradition, or traditional interpretations, they are claiming to defend. From one traditional point of view, the Orthodox "scholar" is actually more dangerous than the secular one. The secular scholar poses no real danger to the believing community simply because he or she openly does not speak for them. But for the scholar who is also a believer, because he or she is taken seriously by the believing community, there is greater chance his or her research will have a deleterious impact.

One example from a different area to illustrate this point can be found in a small book written by the Hazon Ish mentioned above called *Emunah u Betahion*, published posthumously in 1953. The Hazon Ish argues against the importation of Musar into his yeshiva community. Musar, of course, is a form of Jewish piety of self-perfection expounded by highly traditional Jews. And yet, the Hazon Ish understood that the very premise of Musar, that the individual could work toward, and achieve, relative self-perfection through any means other than the study of Torah, introduces an idea of selfhood that, while not drawn from the realm of the secular, would eventually corrode the centrality of Torah study as the exclusive vehicle for self-perfection.[33] The analogy is not clean but the point can be made that the Hazon Ish knew that in some sense Musar has crossed a border into a realm of modern selfhood such that even if it remained in total fealty to the tradition, it would change the way the self was traditionally understood. Whether he was correct or not is immaterial, and he certainly did not think Musar leaders were heretics; in fact, one of the great Musar teachers in his generation, R. Eliyahu Dessler, taught in the yeshiva where the Hazon Ish was affiliated, and the Hazon Ish himself was trained in Musar as a young man in Europe before he rejected it.[34] My point is simply to suggest that those called "apologists" in Hughes' chapter are for me "heretics." They may not openly seek to undermine the tradition like other scholars who do make claims of normative deviance (who are *also* heretics). But when they cross back over the border to save and defend tradition, they do so in a matter that already changes it. In short, in most cases, the scholar who is an apologist and the heretic are mostly interchangeable. Each in their own way is a smuggler who redraws borders of their subject matter.

Martin Kavka offers a different view of the matter and thus presents a different assessment of Jewish Studies that creates a space between the scholar as heretic and Neusner's notion of the scholar as humanist. As I stated at the outset, heresy in this essay requires an act that makes claims on basic normative beliefs and practices and seeks to alter them through various means; claims of prophecy, critiques of tradition, and changing historical circumstances that would require radical rather than incremental change in thought, structure, or practice, etc. We can cite Sabbateanism as one kind of heresy, Zionism as another kind, and *Wissenschaft des Judentums* another (at least to the extent to which it makes normative claims).

---

[33] On this, see my "The Road from Religious Law (*halakha*) to the Secular: Constructing the Autonomous Self in the Musar Tradition and Its Discontents" (2019).
[34] In Chaim Grade's celebration book *The Yeshiva*, about the Musar yeshiva in Norordok in the early twentieth century, the Hazon Ish is a major character.

Unlike many scholars of Jewish Studies, Kavka *discovers* Judaism through Jewish Studies as an undergraduate at Princeton. This act of discovery may inform his focus on the student who receives tradition rather than one who comes to Jewish Studies to critique or transform it. Kavka is claiming that the role of Jewish Studies might not be about the tradition as the object of inquiry at all but rather about how the tradition becomes a tool for the identity formation of the student, how he or she receives it. "With this expansion [of Jewish Studies in the late 1960s] academia and scholarship became the vehicle of Jewish identity-formation in America" (2006, 185). Now one can argue that such an assessment would fall under Hughes' critique that Jewish Studies is only for Jews. But Kavka does not mean it that way:

> They [the Jewish students] gain this identity through exposure to other's [non-Jews] alienation and the group mentality that alienation can only strengthen. So both my Jewish and non-Jewish students come to see their secondhand experiences – of reading, watching, and listening – as first-hand experiences of their own acting and suffering.   (2006, 187)

What I think Kavka means here is that the Jewish students in part find themselves "as Jews" through exposure to how their non-Jewish classmates feel unable to find their way into the Jewish material being discussed. The tradition that many of the Jewish students felt at home with suddenly becomes foreign to them. He continues,

> Learning about the past saves us from the burdensome feeling of having to deal with the problems of existence from scratch. But at the same time, to use history as a coping mechanism in this manner is to a degree illegitimate, because we never leave past events as past events, we shape them from our own present position.   (2006, 189)

Kavka's claim here is that Jewish Studies, as it serves students, is not about an interrogation of the tradition through critical lenses to correct mistakes and make new normative claims *about* tradition. Rather, it is a means to present a tradition, or a history, for students to identify with it in some manner, not necessarily as members, in order to carve out their own identities in the process. Kavka does not want to erase anachronism, but to use it to enable students to find themselves in the alienation, and then reflection, of a past that is not theirs but can be "received" by them nonetheless. There is an existential component here that is reminiscent of Franz Rosenzweig's vision of the Lehrhaus in Frankfurt in the early twentieth century. But Rosenzweig's vision was of a center for adult *Jewish* education. He was thinking about and speaking mainly to *Jews*. Kavka is speaking to everyone who seeks some historical anchor upon which to find their place in the world, even if that place may be far from Judaism. In some way Kavka becomes

Rosenzweig in a pluralistic multicultural America. "The role of Jewish Studies in the university," Kavka concludes,

> is to allow students to perceive the ways in which 'to receive tradition' both inside and outside explicitly Jewish contexts, means nothing without an anachronistic process in which members of a community actually shape the past into something called 'tradition'.
> (2006, 195)

As I read Kavka, Jewish Studies is not heretical at all as Judaism is not the subject of the scholar per se, certainly not as teacher, but the subject through which the object – the student – comes to understand his or her own place in the world. The nature, fabric, and presentation of the tradition is less important than how it works on the one who "receives" it. There is nothing unique about Judaism in this regard, and here Kavka is not far from Neusner. Where he departs from Neusner is that for Neusner Judaism is the data that is critically assessed to contribute to American arts and letters – "Judaism as an example" – whereas for Kavka Judaism is one lens among many through which identity – Jewish and non-Jewish – is considered.

4 Conclusion

In this essay, I sought to interrogate whether the academic study of Judaism constitutes a heretical enterprise. In order to do that I used its progenitor *Wissenschaft des Judentums*, suggesting it originally had three distinct goals, only one of which might constitute heresy, defined as the deployment of scholarship as a critique of normative practices or beliefs for the sake of reform or reconstruction of the religious life of Jews. While I argued that today's Jewish Studies discipline still basically operates along the three goals of *Wissenschaft des Judentums*, there are differing views as to which should be primary and which auxiliary, or which should or should not exist at all. Perhaps the position that moves farthest away from the heretical imperative here is that of Jacob Neusner, who argued that Jewish Studies should produce what he called "the humanities of the Jewish heritage," unmoored from the Jewish community or critiquing the normative claims of Judaism. It would appear, though, that even in Neusner's lifetime he saw that project as difficult to implement as the ties connecting the academic study of Judaism and the Jewish community remained too entangled (here Hughes' critique is correct). In part as a result of this, Neusner resigned from the Association of Jewish Studies, the national organization for Jewish Studies in America, and joined the American Academy of Religion, where he spearheaded the section on

"The Study of Judaism," eventually serving as the president of that organization in 1969. It was only there, he believed, that Judaism could finally become a full member of the American humanities and social sciences.

It is certainly true that increasing numbers of non-Jews who have entered the Jewish Studies guild in the United States, and especially in Europe, have broadened the scope of Jewish Studies from the days when it was centered in a few seminaries and a group of select universities. And yet for all the reasons Hughes discusses in his study and the legitimate concerns Heschel articulates in her essay, severing Jewish Studies from the Jewish community, and thus moving Jewish Studies from a heretical enterprise (including what Hughes calls "apologetics") to a purely humanistic one, is far from complete. And for many, it is not even a goal. Kavka offers an intriguing alternative, an existentialist identarian program whereby Judaism as "tradition" becomes, following Neusner, "an example," but not of, as Neusner suggested, "the humanity of the Jewish heritage" but a lens to find one's own place in the world.

But as I write this, scholars of Judaism are still smuggling contraband back to Judaism, carrying it back to their offices and university classrooms, where they often serve in various roles as teachers, scholars, and mentors. And thus I suggest they are today's Jewish heretics, double border-crossers of a border that modernity has left largely unprotected. Perhaps then, at least to some degree, it is Jewish Studies scholars, as heretics and smugglers, who help insure Judaism's vibrancy, relevance, and survival.

Bibliography

Altmann, Alexander. "Jewish Studies: Their Scope and Meaning Today." *Go and Study: Essays in Honor of Alfred Jospe*. Hoboken: Ktav, 1980. 83–98.
Berger, Peter. *The Heretical Imperative*. Garden City: Anchor Press, 1979.
Biale, David. *Kabbalah and Counter History*. Cambridge, MA: Harvard University Press, 1979.
Blumenthal, David. "Where Does Jewish Studies belong?" *JAAR* 44.3 (1976): 535–546.
Boyarin, Daniel. *Border Lines: The Partition of Judaeo-Christianity*. Philadelphia: University of Pennsylvania Press, 2006.
Brenner, Michael. *The Renaissance of Jewish Culture in Weimar Germany*. New Haven: Yale University Press, 1998.
Breuer, Mordechai. *Modernity within Tradition: The Social History of Orthodox Jewry in Imperial Germany*. New York: Columbia University Press, 2004.
Bush, Andrew. *Jewish Studies: A Theoretical Introduction*. New Brunswick, NJ: Rutgers University Press, 2011.
Caplan, Kimmy. "'The Significance of a Jewish University': A Sermon on the Founding of the Hebrew University." *American Jewish Archives* 53.1–2 (2001): 65–82.

Dweck, Yaacob. "Editing Safed: The Career of Isaac Gerson." *Jewish Quarterly Review* 17 (2010): 44–55.
Dweck, Yaacob. *The Scandal of Kabbalah*. Princeton: Princeton University Press, 2011.
Farber, Zev. "Avraham Avinu Is My Father: Thoughts on Torah History and Judaism." TheTorah.com, n.d., at thetorah.com/torah-history-judaism-introduction.
Feiner, Shmuel. *Haskalah and History: The Emergence of Modern Jewish Consciousness*. London: Littman Library of Jewish Civilization, 2001.
Ferziger, Adam. *Exclusion and Hierarchy: Orthodoxy, Nonobservance, and the Emergence of Modern Jewish Identity*. Philadelphia: University of Pennsylvania Press, 2005.
Ferziger, Adam. *Beyond Sectarianism: The Realignment of American Orthodox Judaism*. Detroit: Wayne State University Press, 2015.
Goldish, Matt. *The Sabbatean Prophets*. Cambridge, MA: Harvard University Press, 2004.
Greenspahn, Frederick E. "The Beginnings of Judaic Studies in American Universities." *Modern Judaism* 20 (2000): 209–225.
Gurock, Jeffrey S., and Jacob J. Schacter. *A Modern Heretic and a Traditional Community: Mordecai M. Kaplan, Orthodoxy, and American Judaism*. New York: Columbia University Press, 1997.
Heschel, Susannah. "Jewish Studies as Counterhistory." *Insider/Outsider: American Jews and Multiculturalism*. Eds. D. Biale, M. Calchinsky, and S. Heschel. Los Angeles and Berkeley: University of California Press, 1998.
Heschel, Susannah. "Revolt of the Colonized: Abraham Geiger's *Wissenschaft des Judentums* as a Challenge to Christian Hegemony in the Academy." *New German Critique* 77 (Summer, 1999): 61–85.
Hughes, Aaron. *The Study of Judaism: Authenticity, Identity, Scholarship*. Albany: SUNY, 2013.
Hughes, Aaron. *Jacob Neusner: An American Jewish Iconoclast*. New York: NYU Press, 2016a.
Hughes, Aaron. *Jacob Neusner on Religion*. New York: Routledge, 2016b.
Kavka, Martin. "What Does it Mean to Receive Tradition? Jewish Studies in Higher Education." *CrossCurrents* (Summer, 2006): 180–197.
Kook, Avraham Yitzchak HaCohen. *Eder Ha-Yakar*. Jerusalem: Mosad ha-Rav Kook, 1906. [Hebrew].
Leiman, Sid. "Rabbi Abraham Isaac Ha-Kohen Kook: Invocation at the Inauguration of the Hebrew University." *Tradition* 29.1 (Fall 1994): 87–92.
Levy, Richard. "The American University and *Olam Ha-Bah*." *Religious Education* 69 (1974): 15.
Litvak, Olga. *Haskalah: The Romantic Movement in Judaism*. New Brunswick, NJ: Rutgers University Press, 2012.
Magid, Shaul. "Myth, History, and Mysticism: Gershom Scholem and the Contemporary Scene." *Jewish Quarterly Review* 101.4 (Fall, 2011): 511–525.
Magid, Shaul. "The Road from Religious Law (*halakha*) to the Secular: Constructing the Autonomous Self in the Musar Tradition and Its Discontents." *Jewish Spirituality and Social Transformation*. Ed. P. Wexler. Chestnut Ridge: Herder & Herder, 2019. 203–222.
Meyer, Michael. "The Emergence of Jewish Historiography: Motives and Motifs." *History and Theory* 27 (1988): 160–175.
Neusner, Jacob. *Fellowship in Judaism: The First Century and Today*. London: Valentine, 1963.
Neusner, Jacob. *The Academic Study of Judaism: Essays and Reflections*. New York: Ktav Publishing, 1975.
Neusner, Jacob. *Judaism in the American Humanities*. Chico: Scholars Press, 1981.

Nietzsche, Friedrich. *The Genealogy of Morals and Ecce Homo*. Ed. and Trans. Walter Kaufmann. New York: Vintage Books, 1967.

Ohana, David. *Nationalizing Judaism: Zionism as Theological Ideology*. Lanham: Lexington Books, 2017.

Pelican, Yarsilov. *The Vindication of Tradition*. New Haven: Yale University Press, 1984.

Ravitzky, Aviezer. *Messianism, Zionism, and Jewish Religious Radicalism*. Chicago: University of Chicago Press, 1996.

Raz-Krakotzkin, Amnon. *The Censor, the Editor, and the Text: The Catholic Church and the Shaping and the Jewish Canon in the Sixteenth Century*. Philadelphia: University of Pennsylvania Press, 2007.

Ritterband, Paul. *Jewish Learning in American Universities: The First Century*. Bloomington: Indiana University Press, 1994.

Ross, Tamar. "Orthodox and the Challenge of Biblical Criticism." *Journal of Modern Jewish Studies* 14.1 (2015): 6–26.

Sagi, Avi. "Models of Authority and the Duty of Obedience on Halakhic Literature." *AJS Review* 20.1 (1995): 1–24.

Scholem, Gershom. "The Science of Judaism: Then and Now." *The Messianic Idea in Judaism*. New York: Schocken Books, 1972.

Scholem, Gershom. *Sabbatai Zevi: The Mystical Messiah*. Princeton: Princeton University Press, 1973.

Scholem, Gershom. "Reflections on Modern Jewish Studies." *On the Possibility of Jewish Mysticism in Our Time*. Ed. Avraham Shapira. Philadelphia: Jewish Publication Society, 1997.

Schorsch, Ismar. *From Text to Context: The Turn to History in Modern Judaism*. Hanover and London: Brandeis University Press, 1994.

Schorsch, Ismar. *Leopold Zunz: Creativity in Diversity*. Philadelphia: University of Pennsylvania Press, 2016.

Shapiro, Marc B. *Changing the Immutable: How Orthodoxy Rewrites Its History*. London: Littman Library of Jewish Civilization, 2015.

Shaw, Steve. "Orthodox Reactions to the Challenge of Biblical Criticism." *Tradition* 10.3 (1969): 61–85.

Silver, Jeremy. *Maimonides Criticism and the Maimonidean Controversy 1180–1240*. Leiden: Brill, 1965.

Soloveichik, Haym. *Yeinam*. Jerusalem: Maggid Press, 2017. [Hebrew].

Sommer, Benjamin. *Revelation and Authority: Sinai in Jewish Scripture and Tradition*. New Haven: Yale University Press, 2015.

Stair, Rose. "Gershom Scholem's Critical Appropriation of *Wissenschaft des Judentums* and the Necessary Fiction of Historical Objectivity." *Pardes: Cultures of Wissenschaft des Judentums at 200*. Potsdam: Universitatsverlag Potsdam, 2018. 217–239.

Waxman, Mordechai. *Tradition and Change: The Development of Conservative Judaism*. New York: JTS, 1958.

Yedidya, Assaf. "Orthodox Reactions to *Wissenschaft des Judentums*." *Modern Judaism* (February, 2010): 69–94.

Yerushalmi, Yosef Hayim. *Zakhor*. New York: Schocken, 1989.

List of Contributors

Robert Alter, Class of 1937 Professor Emeritus of Hebrew and Comparative Literature, University of California, Berkeley.

Shraga Bar-On, Head of the David Hartman Center for Intellectual Leadership, Shalom Hartman Institute, and Lecturer for Talmud and Jewish Thought, Shalem College, Jerusalem.

Agata Bielik-Robson, Professor of Jewish Studies, University of Nottingham and the Institute of Philosophy and Sociology at the Polish Academy of Science in Warsaw.

Noam Gil, Lecturer, Department of English and American Studies, Tel Aviv University.

Willi Goetschel, Professor of German and Philosophy, University of Toronto.

Erich S. Gruen, Gladys Rehard Wood Professor Emeritus of History and Classics, University of California, Berkeley.

Moshe Idel, Max Cooper Professor Emeritus in Jewish Thought, Hebrew University.

Ruth Kara-Ivanov Kaniel, Senior Lecturer, Department of Jewish History / Jewish Thought, Haifa University.

Shaul Magid, Professor of Jewish Studies, Dartmouth College.

Eugene D. Matanky, PhD Candidate in Tel Aviv University and David Hartman Fellow in Shalom Hartman Institute.

Adiel Schremer, Professor, The Israel & Golda Koschitzky Department of Jewish History and Contemporary Jewry, Bar Ilan University.

Gilad Sharvit, Assistant Professor, Department of Philosophy and Religious Studies, Towson University.

David Suchoff, Professor of English, Colby College.

Index

Abraham 3, 4, 21, 50, 63, 96–98, 100, 103, 110, 112, 114–116
Abraham ibn Ezra 145
Abulafia, Abraham ben Samuel 9–10, 125–52
Adorno, Theodor W. 191, 204, 212
Afterman, Adam 100, 110
Aḥer/Akher see Ben Abuya, Elisha
Akhenaton 229
Akiva (Akiba), R. 9, 43, 51, 56–57, 66–70, 73, 75, 76, 177–78
Albotini, Yehuda 145
Alemanno, Yohanan 141
Alexander Polyhistor 22–23
Alkabetz, Shlomo Halevi 111–13
Alter, Robert 10
Amichai, Yehuda 164
Andreas-Salomé, Lou 236
Androgyny 94–95, 100, 104
Anti-Christ 222
Anti-Christian polemic 95, 118
Anti-Semitism V 195, 196, 230, 242, 271, 279
Antinomianism 12, 90, 93, 139, 247, 254–56, 259
Apostasy 51, 67, 209, 235, 241n15, 271, 275; Apostates 34, 36–38, 209–211, 233, 267
Aristotle 140, 277
Arnold, Matthew 17
Artapanos 8, 23–24
Ascension 52, 63, 66, 68, 69, 71, 73, 75
Asher ben David, R. 110
Atheists 42, 43
Auerbach, Berthold 214
Averroes 139
Avodah zarah (foreign worship) 54
Azriel of Gerona, R. 97, 100
Azulai, Ḥayyim Joseph David 140

Ba'al Shem Tov, Israel 143
Baeck, Leo 213, 239
Bauman, Zygmunt 195
Bahir, Book 96–98, 107, 110, 112
Bar Kokhba 73
Bar-On, Shraga 8–9
Bathsheba 104–105, 107–108

Bauer, Walter 5
Beckett, Samuel 176n3, 197–198, 204
Ben Abuya, Elisha (Acher, Akher) 8–9, 11, 13, 50–76, 177–185, 209, 228, 245
Ben Azzai, R. 66–69, 75, 112, 177, 228
Ben Zoma, R. 61–63, 65–69, 75, 177, 228
Benjamin, Walter 11–12, 175, 177, 183, 187–88, 225, 244–63
Bercovitch, Sacvan 175
Bernard of Clairvaux 119
Bible/Hebrew Bible 11, 19–22, 26–27, 51–54, 95, 119, 191n25, 134, 142, 146, 162, 164, 166, 174, 233, 241, 245, 275
Bielik-Robson, Agata 12
Biophilic Law 258, 261
Blau, Joseph 283–284
Boaz 109
Boyarin, Daniel 5, 40, 44, 130, 132, 266–67, 269
Breuer, Josef 92
Buber, Martin 9, 11, 213, 230–32, 239, 241–42
Butler, Judith 99, 195, 196n4

Canaan 168, 173; Canaanite 166, 171; Canaanite poets 10, 161
Canonization 7
Chajes, J H 92
Chariot 96; account of the Chariot 57–64, 68–69; fourth leg of the Chariot 94
Christianity 1, 5–6, 8, 17, 22, 31, 45–46, 52, 55, 88, 91–92, 95, 104, 118–19, 128, 132, 137, 139, 151, 202, 213, 218, 225, 239, 246, 248, 251–54, 257, 260, 266, 268, 271, 273–76, 279–82
Church Fathers 31–33, 46, 106
Clement of Alexandria 22
Cohen, David (Ha-Nazir) 147
Cohen, Hermann 2
Cohen, Shaye 32, 41, 45
Combination of letters 134, 137
Connell, Raewyn 93
Cordovero, Moshe R. 142
Covenant 33–34, 36–39

David, King 9, 94–119; Shield of David (Magen David) 115
Dead Sea Scrolls 21
Derrida, Jacques 11, 12, 195, 196n4, 228n2, 249–263
Deutscher, Isaac 209–10
Diaspora 7, 19, 22, 195, 199, 272, 274
Divine Name 128, 140, 259

Eleazar ben Arakh, R. 60–63
Eliezer, R. 41, 177–178
Elijah 55, 69, 71, 92
Eliot, T. S. 165
Elqayam, Avraham 91
Epiphanius 33
Epiurean, apikorez 1, 40, 43, 51–52, 139–40
Esther 25–27
Eupolemos 8, 22–23
Eusebius 22–23
Exagoge 24
Eve 107
Ezekiel 24–25, 57

Feminist revolution 88, 90
Feminity/Masculinity 9, 88, 90, 93–96, 99–100, 102–105, 108–110, 113–15, 117–19; Female 34, 87–96, 100–101, 104, 109, 113–114, 119, 194–195, 199–212
Fishbane, Eitan 110
Forces of evil 105, 109, 118 (see also kelipot and sitra aḥra)
Foreigner 38
Frances, Emanuel ben David 91
Frankists 7, 88–89, 91, 93, 231, 252
Freud, Sigmund 3, 11–12, 209, 213–215, 218, 228–42, 249; Return of the Repressed, the 235–238; Trauma, theory of 228, 233, 235–238, 240–242; *Moses and Monotheism* 3, 12, 228–242; *Totem and Taboo* 233–235, 237n10, 240

Geiger, Abraham 271, 273–274, 282
Gender 87–119, 287; equality 88; fluidity 100
Gentiles 34–35, 38–39, 41, 125, 130–33, 199

Gil, Noam 11
Gilgul, reincarnation, transmigration, impregnation 111; levirate marriage 113
Gnosticism 55, 72–73, 184–86
Goetschel, Willi 11
Goldstein, Rebecca 212
Goshen-Gottstein, Alon 68–70, 72n53, 184, 186
Graetz, Heinrich 4, 88, 213
Green, Art 95, 119
Gross, Amnon 146, 150
Grözinger, Karl 178
Gruen, Erich 8
Gymnasium 18–19

Haggadah/aggadah 2, 20, 61, 256
Ḥagigah, Tractate 56–60, 63, 66, 70–71, 180, 185, 228
Halacha/Halakha 2, 20, 87, 148, 180, 254, 256, 258, 268, 269
Halevi, Jehuda 110
Harshav, Benjamin 175, 178
Hasidism 92, 143, 146, 148, 268
Haskalah 7, 202, 269
Haven, Alexander van der 91
Ḥayyat, Yehuda 140
Heine, Heinrich 17, 176, 209, 213–215, 232
Hellenism 8, 17–18, 21, 25
Heresy/heretics 1–13, 25, 27, 30–33, 38, 39, 42, 44, 46, 50–54, 61, 62, 69, 71–72, 74–76, 87–90, 94, 105, 113–114, 118, 125, 131, 139, 140, 152, 158, 162, 173, 175, 177–178, 183–186, 188–191, 197, 209–212, 214–225, 228, 232–242, 244–246, 254, 263, 266–287
Heschel, Susannah 13, 269, 273–275, 280–283, 288
Hess, Moses 213–214
Heterodoxy 8, 18–20, 26–27
Ḥokhmat Yisrael 268, 277, 280
Holocaust 195–201, 203–204
Holy deceit 106–107
Hugo, Victor 257
Hughes, Aaron 269, 283–288
Huss, Boaz 117
Hutzpit, R. (Ha-Meturgeman) 182-3

Iconoclastic 53, 165,
Idel, Moshe 10, 107
Idolatry 36, 53–54
Immanuel of Rome 162
Irenaeus 31, 33, 46
Isaac 20, 96–98, 100, 103, 110, 112, 114–15
Isaac of Acre, R. 103–104, 128, 135
Isaac La Peyrere 253
Isaac the Blind, R. 97–98, 100, 104, 110

Jacob 20, 96–98, 100, 110, 112, 114–51
Jacob bar Sheshet, R. 97–98, 100, 104, 110–111, 117
Jewish Studies 11, 13, 267–269, 272–273, 277–283
Jerusalem 6, 17, 18, 19, 23, 104, 146, 150, 152, 253, 256
Jesse 106, 109, 117
Jesus 5, 119, 135, 161, 231, 241, 251–53, 257, 273, 276
Joachim da Fiore 253
Job 171
Josephus 1, 8, 20–21, 27, 43, 106
Joseph Gikatilla, R. 102–103, 141
Joseph ibn Tzayyaḥ 150
Joseph of Shushan, R. 102, 112–13
Joshua, R. 41, 61–63, 65
Judah ha-Nasi, R. 9, 51, 56, 60, 62, 64, 76
Jung, Carl Gustav 101, 239
Justin Martyr 44–45

Kabbalah, Kabbalists 1, 4, 9–10; 87–114, 117–19, 125–52; ecstatic Kabbalah 125–26, 140; intellectual Kabbalah 134; prophetic Kabbalah 138; theosophical-theurgical Kabala 101–105, 141, 144, 149; universal Kabbalah 130
Kadish, Rachel 212
Kafka, Franz 9, 11, 175–191, 204, 239n12, 241, 246, 248–250, 254, 256; "Before the Law" 181, 261n27; *Castle* 248; "Letter from the Emperor" 246; "The Hunter Gracchus" 188–189
Kaplan, Mordecai 268, 279
Kara-Ivanov Kaniel, Ruth 9
Kareitz, R. Abraham Yeshaya (Hazon Ish) 277–278, 285

Karo, Joseph 112–13
Katechon 254–255
Kavka, Martin 13, 269, 283–287
Karaites 7
Kelipot 105–106, 108, 118
Kitzutz 95, 118
Kook, Abraham R. 275
Kudszus, Winfried 190

Le Boulluec, Alain 6, 266
Lawrence, D. H. 161
Leibniz, Gottfried Wilhelm 211–12
Lemlein, Asher 141–42
Leon de Modena 268
Lessing, Gotthold Ephraim 217–18
Levirate marriage 112–113
Liebes, Yehuda 73, 104, 105, 107
Liquidation of Theology 244–245, 248, 262–263
Luria, Isaac 94, 105–109, 111, 114, 143–149, 253
Luther, Martin 219
Luxemburg, Rosa 209
Lyman, J. Rebecca 6

Maccabees, Book of 18–19
Magid, Shaul 13
Maimon, Salomon 213
Maimonides, Moses 51, 110, 125–26, 131–33, 138–39, 189, 268, 277
Marinetti, Filippo 171
Marranos 12, 211, 244–63
Marx, Karl 209, 231
Mary 95, 118–19
Mazo-Karras, Ruth 104
Matanky, Eugene D. 8–9
Me'ah She'arim 9–10, 145–48, 150–52
Memmi, Albert 225
Menahem Mendel of Shklov 147
Mendelssohn, Moses 213, 254
Merkavah: see Chariot
Messiah, Messianism 3, 9–10, 87–97, 99–100, 105–107, 110–111, 113–118, 125–26, 135–36, 138, 140, 142, 146, 191, 233, 238, 244–46, 248–56, 262, 270; feminized Messiah 113; meal of the Messiah (Melave Malka) 114; bread of

the poor (lechem oni) 115; transgenderization 119
Metatron 71–74, 131, 138, 184–87
minut/minim 2, 5–6, 31–33, 39, 42, 46, 51
Miron, Dan 199, 202n9
Mishnah 9, 31–33, 40–44, 56–65, 70–71, 75, 134, 137, 166
Modernism 165, 190, 198–199, 202
Monotheism 12, 50, 52–53, 162, 172–73, 228–29, 235–37
Montaigne, Michel de 223
Mordecai 25–27
Moses 2, 3, 12, 20, 22–25, 50, 112, 129, 146, 228–41, 246, 251–52, 254
Moses de Leon, R. 101–102
Mother of the Messiah 91
Multitude of Rabbis 133, 135–36, 139
Musar 268, 285
Mysticism 3, 7, 8–10, 50–52, 55–70, 73–76, 87–88, 92–93, 96, 98, 101, 104, 110, 113, 119, 125–27, 134, 139–52, 228, 259, 261–62

Nadler, Steve 212
Nahmanides, Moses 94, 100, 108, 112, 136–37
Nationalism 176, 185–186, 190, 274, 277–278
Nathan of Gaza 87, 90, 94, 109, 116, 119
Nathan ben Sa'adyah Har'ar 134–35
Neumann, Eric 101
Neusner, Jacob 13, 269, 278, 280–282, 285, 287–288
Nietzsche, Friedrich 231, 272

Oko, Adolf S. 213
Orchard (pardes) 52, 56, 60, 64–71, 74–75, 130–31, 177–78, 180, 228
Orthodoxy 5, 10, 18, 39, 42, 45–46, 144–47, 151–52, 161, 197, 229–31, 233, 244–46, 248, 250, 252, 254, 266–67, 270, 274–77, 284

Paganism 10–12, 53, 161–164, 166, 168, 173–4, 218, 248
Pappenheim, Bertha 92
Paul the Apostle 12, 248, 251–260,

Pedaya, Haviva 98, 100, 117, 278
Pardes see orchard
Polytheism 52–53, 168, 229
Postsecular see Secular
Priest 2, 18, 23, 65, 104, 129n13, 161, 167, 198, 23–235
Prophecy 10, 25, 50–51, 53–55, 62, 88, 92–94, 104, 125, 132–38, 140–43, 145, 147, 150–52, 167, 214, 216, 219–21, 223, 234, 253, 267, 270, 285; female prophecy 92
Ptolemy 19

Qumran 22, 25, 55, 58–59, 66

Ravikovitch, Dahlia 164
Rapoport-Albert, Ada 87–88, 93–94
Recanati, Menahem 112, 141
Redemption 90–91, 93, 95, 103, 105, 118, 127–28, 133, 249, 251, 270, 274
Renaissance 144n82, 162, 165, 211, 242,
Rosenzweig, Franz 251, 254–255, 286–287
Ruth 90, 113

Sabbath 74, 88, 114–117, 240
Sabbati Zevi 9, 87, 91–92, 94–95, 109, 113–18, 231, 233–34, 241
Sabbatianism 7, 9, 87–95, 100, 109, 111, 113–118
Sacrifice 34, 37n23, 216, 231, 259n23, 261
Safed 92, 105, 141
Sarah 91
Schäfer, Peter 95, 119
Scholem, Gershom 3–4, 12, 59, 87, 88, 92, 114, 115–17, 181, 191, 238–41, 245–50, 269, 271–76, 281
Schmitt, Carl 254
Schremer, Adiel 6, 8
Second Temple 5, 8, 19, 21, 27, 54–55, 59, 66, 74
Secularism 7, 11–12, 25, 93, 162, 210–212, 223–225, 231, 240–242, 245–246, 254, 263, 266, 266–277, 280–284; Postsecular 7, 11, 211, 224,
Sefirah of Malkhut 94–95, 98–99, 102, 104, 108, 118

Segal, Alan 5
Semites 161, 229,
Septuagint 19–20, 22, 72,
Sexuality 52, 56–57, 87–94, 100, 119, 170, 194, 196–97, 200–201, 234; promiscuity, transgressive deeds, deviant behavior 90–91; virginity 91, 93
Sharvit, Gilad 12
Shekhina 94–119
Shem Tov Ibn Falaquera 132
Shlomo ben Abraham ibn Adret 126, 136–37, 140–42, 145
Sifra 8, 33–39, 137
Simmel, Georg 210
Simon bar Yohai, R. 70, 98, 111
Singer, Isaac Bashevis 11, 194, 197, 199, 201, 203
Sitra aḥra (the other side) 118, 268
Solomon 23
Spiegler, Julius 213
Spinoza, Baruch de 11–12, 125, 209–225, 231–32, 252–54
Stewart, Matthew 211
Suchoff, David 11
Susman, Margarete 213

Talmud 1, 2, 9, 51–53, 56, 57, 63–64, 70–75, 89, 90. 97, 104, 111–12, 115, 119, 136–137, 146, 177, 180, 186, 228, 268, 278
Tamar 90, 113
Tannaites 32–36, 38, 39, 41–42, 45, 51, 55–56, 59, 60
Tchernikhovsky, Saul 10–11, 161–174; "To The Sun" 10, 163–166, 171–174
Tertullian 17, 33
Three Pilgrimage Festivals (shalosh regalim: Passover, Shavuot and Sukkot) 116
Tikla 109
Tikkun 91, 109
Togarmi, Barukh 144
Torgeman, Ohad 127, 147, 150
Torah 2, 3, 19, 23, 33, 36–38, 40, 43, 50, 52, 55, 59, 60, 66, 69–71, 74–76, 102, 116, 117, 130–33, 137, 142, 180, 183, 237, 245, 250, 269, 270, 274, 275, 277, 285
Tosefta 31, 33, 41–42, 56, 58–71
Transgression 1, 6–7, 9, 46, 63, 90, 93–94, 105, 112, 233–34, 236, 238, 266, 274
Trotsky, Leon 209

Ulysses 176, 190
Universal religion 130
Universal Torah 130

Vital, Haim 10, 92, 105–109, 111, 134, 142–43, 145, 147
Vitalism 165, 167–168, 248, 254

Weininger, Otto 194–197, 200–201
Wissenschaft des Judentums 270–282, 287
Wolf [i.e. Wohlwill], Immanuel 213, 271
Wolfson, Elliot 130, 132, 133, 149
Wolfson, Harry Austryn 279
Women's oppression 89
World to Come (Olam haba) 39–42, 51, 53, 66, 246

Yahadut 129, 130
Yehuda, Avraham Shalom 230
Yehuda Salmon, R. 136
Yiddish 161, 175–184, 189–190, 196, 198–202,
Yoḥanan ben Zakkai, R. 9, 51, 56, 60–63, 65, 76
Yosi, R. 63
Yovel, Yirmiyahu 211–12, 231n6, 246, 251–53
Yurovitz, Avraham 146

Zach, Natan 164
Zionism 76, 130, 171, 176, 196n4, 202, 214, 253n16, 270–274, 277–278, 285
Zohar 9, 93–95, 98–119, 141, 144, 149, 247, 268
Zunz, Leopold 57n21, 269
Zweig, Arnold 229
Zweig, Stefan 231–2

www.ingramcontent.com/pod-product-compliance
Lightning Source LLC
Chambersburg PA
CBHW030525230426
43665CB00010B/769